MERRILL'S GUIDE T

COMPUTER PERFORMANCE EVALUATION:
Analysis of SMF/RMF Data with SAS

by H.W. "BARRY" MERRILL, PH.D.

SAS Institute Inc.
SAS Circle
Box 8000
Cary, North Carolina 27511

The correct bibliographic citation for this manual is:

Merrill, H.W. *Merrill's Guide to Computer Performance Evaluation: Analysis of SMF/RMF Data with SAS.* Cary, NC: SAS Institute Inc., 1983. 340 pp.

Merrill's Guide to Computer Performance Evaluation: Analysis of SMF/RMF Data with SAS

by H.W. "Barry" Merrill, Ph.D.

For SHARE
and for sharing

Preface

This book is basically a cookbook, and cookbooks are generally rewrites of another's inventions. Most of the content herein is available in IBM's multiplicity of manuals on SMF, OS, VS, and other systems. I hope, however, that this cookbook will bring the needed information together in a more readily accessible reference.

While the analysis is clearly keyed to the capabilities of SAS, the descriptive content and analytic approach for managing computer performance should be usable with any language.

It is impossible for a book of this nature to be correct. Historically, SMF has undergone constant modification, both by IBM and by each installation. There is no reason to expect this fact to change. The currency of the content is based on VS1 Release 4, VS2 Release 1.7 (SVS), VS2 Release 3.8, VS2 System Extensions Release 2.0, and MVT Release 21.8. Within any operating system, however, PTFs and fixes as well as local modifications and purchased software can affect the data content of SMF. Thus, you must verify the validity of your SMF data before leaping to conclusions.

H.W. "BARRY" MERRILL

Note to the Third Printing:

While the cautions of the Preface still apply, the code distributed with this book has been continually updated. Version 1 of MVS migrated from Release 3.0 to System Extensions Releases 1 and 2; then to System Product Releases 1, 2, and 3 and finally to the MVS/370 Version 1, System Product Release 3.

Member CHANGES of the code library identifies the most recent change applied when your tape was created. When you apply updates yourself, update member CHANGES also to reflect the change status of your code.

The code listed in the TYPE appendices has not been reprinted with the changes; following the last appendix is the ADDENDUM that documents each of the SAS variables created by the changes to the code.

Future changes are available to you through the SAS DIAL-A-ZAP facility.

Contents

16
Installation of the SAS Machine-readable Tape   105
Description of the contents of SAS.SMF.SOURCE. Content of SAS.SMF.SOURCE partitioned data set. Installation-dependent considerations. Where to begin next.

Appendix 1
SAS Primer   113
Two logical states. SAS statements. SAS names. SAS data sets. DATA step. DATA statement. LENGTH statement. FORMAT statement. INFILE statement. STOPOVER.LENGTH.=LEN.COL=C. RECFM.=VBS LRECL=32756. INPUT statement. IF-THEN statement. Subsetting IF statement. LINK statement. OUTPUT statement. RETURN statement. GO TO statement. RETAIN statement. SUM function. MOD function. FLOOR function. Date, time, and date-time values and functions. SET statement. MERGE statement. Procedure step. PROC statement. BY statement. VAR(VARIABLES) statement. FORMAT statement. The PRINT procedure. The SORT procedure. The MEANS procedure. The FREQ procedure. The PLOT procedure.

Appendix 2
SAS Macros   125
_ACCTGET._DEVICE._EXCPGET._JOBCK._MACEND._MNTABLE._SMF. _TWOCHAN._TWOCHA._VSAMCAT.

Appendix of TYPE records   131

Addendum   327

Index   331

The Analysis of SMF/RMF Data
Chapters 1 through 16

The Purpose of
Computer Measurement
and Analysis

What this book is about.   This book introduces you to the vast array of information contained in SMF (System Management Facilities) and RMF (Resource Measurement Facility) records. The data in those records is described and decoded, and examples show how typical analyses can be accomplished with minimum effort and resource consumption.

SAS as a tool for SMF/RMF data analysis.   The tool we use to describe and analyze the SMF/RMF data is SAS, the Statistical Analysis System. Because SAS has proven a cost-effective and easily learned tool, the structure of this book leans on it heavily. However, understanding the information content does not require SAS. The book's real value is describing what information is found in which SMF/RMF record and how that information can be decoded and analyzed.

SAS is such a straightforward tool that you will be able to understand this book with a minimum knowledge of SAS syntax. If you are not a SAS user, appendix 1 provides a summary of the SAS language to help you follow the examples written in SAS.

Why measure computer performance?   SMF and RMF are excellent sources of data to analyze IBM 360/370 computer systems. This book is about using that data to measure those systems. Before we actually look at SMF and RMF data, however, we should discuss why measurement is important at all.

IBM and other manufacturers market combinations of hardware and software that provide general-purpose data processing. IBM's goal is to maximize its profit while providing sufficient hardware and software to meet the customer's needs. The customer, however, wants to minimize the cost of the hardware and software while meeting his users' requirements.

The generality of the hardware and software, which must provide flexibility for all potential users, can be "tuned" to provide maximum utility for a specific installation. Thus the primary purpose of computer performance measurement and evaluation is to optimize a general-purpose computing system for a specific installation's objectives.

Objectives and optimization.   In that statement of purpose, there are two concepts that are crucial to a measurement effort: **objectives** and **optimization.** Without objectives for the computing system, there can be no optimization. When objectives have been established, change can be measured, and optimization, even though it may be one small step at a time, can begin.

This book cannot set objectives for you, and it can only suggest some directions for optimization. It can, however, show you how to measure many objectives, and will suggest why some objectives may be more suited for you than others. Most of all, it will provide the tools by which descriptive data can be gathered and analyzed so that meaningful, relevant objectives can be defined.

Once this process is underway, ongoing measurements will reveal potential obstacles to meeting the objectives. At that point, optimization is simply the process of removing or circumventing those obstacles.

Objectives, then, are statements of what values certain variables should assume. Presumably, if the measured values are significantly different from the objectives, there will be an associated measure of discontent. Either the users are not happy with service, or the comptroller is not happy with the costs of the computing center.

The most basic objective is the recognition that there is a need for objectives. Objectives already exist in each installation, even if they are not written down. At some level of service, as measured by users, the computer is not providing "expected" service; at some value of investment, as measured by the comptroller, the computer service is too expensive.

The major role of the computer measurement effort is selecting appropriate criteria to be defined as objectives, proposing their acceptance, and measuring them against the objectives.

Basic objectives.   Computer systems service transactions: a transaction can be a job, an interactive response, a page printed, a message switched, or any other quantum that can be identified as belonging to a user and requiring resources. Transactions are introduced into the system at a given time, receive service (consume resources), and leave at another time. Thus the basic objectives can be described in terms of only two concepts:

1 the response time received
2 the resources consumed.

For different systems the methods of definition may change, and acceptable values for response and resources may differ. But at the bottom of every successful computer installation you will find objectives that are defined in terms of **response time** and **resource consumption.**

Examples of objectives.   Later chapters give explicit examples of objective measures that have been found useful. There is no one common set of objectives, because each installation (in fact, each computer within an installation) can and often should have diferent objectives. The response requirements of an on-line system may be so rigid that resource consumption is insignificant as a limiting criterion, while a batch system might have low response criteria with resource consumption as the more important objective.

The subjectivity of the owner of the computer resource is often needed to truly define the relevant objectives in management terms. The measurement analyst must translate these management goals ("This is an insurance company! We must pay our claims within 24 hours!") into measurable objectives ("All claims jobs will run at priority 15 and 95% must be turned around in 5 minutes.") Later chapters in the book address what measurable quantities exist in SMF and RMF and how they can best be measured and reported.

Why use SMF and RMF?   Given that objectives are important, why would we use SMF and RMF as our prime tools? What about hardware and software monitors?

The first argument for SMF analysis is that it is free. SMF is a software monitor that copies various control blocks when certain events occur. Since these control blocks are required for the operating system, the only overhead associated with SMF is the actual writing of the SMF records. Although a 3033 can easily produce 100,000 SMF records a day, these records are blocked so that less than 6000 physical records are written each day—not a significant overhead.

Considering the completeness of the data available from SMF, it is my philosophy that SMF is the only important tool absolutely required in IBM systems. Since SAS provides simple techniques for SMF analysis, it too is an important tool.

RMF, which exists only in MVS and MSE operating systems, similarly has little overhead (although it is not a free software package), since it too essentially copies the control blocks used by the System Resource Manager (SRM) in its scheduling algorithms. Because of the tremendous power the SRM gives an installation for tailoring the general-purpose MVS/MSE operating system to specific needs, and considering both the low cost and high usability of RMF data for performance management, especially capacity planning, I cannot envision a good MVS/MSE installation that does not have and use RMF.

SMF and RMF may not be the total answer for all measurement of all subsystems; there exist numerous software packages that monitor TSO, IMS, CICS and even the operating system, and these can be useful. However, until SMF and RMF have been milked to the fullest, I believe purchase of other software monitors is unwise. In fact, SMF and RMF can be used to identify those subsystems that are candidates for more intense monitoring before other software monitors are considered.

Hardware monitors once had a place in performance measurement, but their day is past, at least as far as measurement of the central processor and its peripherals are concerned. (They may be reincarnated to measure communications systems for a few years, but ultimately intelligent software/firmware in the communications controllers will measure those systems.) There is essentially no information about the processor complex that cannot be directly measured or substantially inferred from software within the operating system.

In the early 1970's, hardware monitors were a most important tool, because of the insufficiency of SMF data and the high overhead of the then-existing software monitors. As the industry moved from the third to the fourth generation, however, the operating system itself became a measuring system, on which dynamic measures drive scheduling decisions, with user-supplied parameters available for tuning. Thus the operating system-based monitors such as SMF and RMF have eliminated the need for hardware monitors.

The Basic Structure of SMF:
How It Works and
Some Performance Suggestions

What SMF is. SMF, System Management Facilities, is an integral part of the IBM operating systems. It was added to OS as a result of work started between members of SHARE and IBM in 1969 to provide data for accounting purposes.[1]

SMF is basically an event-driven software monitor that writes various records to its own data set when certain events occur. Although SMF's purpose is accounting, the records tend to be copies of various control blocks, many of which are rich in performance data. Decoding these control blocks and merging various records from the same task can lead to very successful performance improvements.

How the operating system writes SMF records. The SMF records are variable-length, and each contains a standard SMF header with the record identification and a time stamp indicating when that record was moved to the SMF buffer. When the buffer fills, it is written to a system disk data set, SYS1.MANX.

If SYS1.MANX should fill, SMF automatically notifies the operator that MANX is full, and begins writing subsequent records to SYS1.MANY. At this point, the operator starts the dump program, which copies the contents of SYS1.MANX and SYS1.MANY to tape, and resets SMF to write to MANX. If MANY also fills before MANX is dumped, SMF recording is suspended; however, a count of lost records is maintained and a Data Lost event record is written to MANX when it becomes available again.

Choosing the SMF buffer size. The installation specifies the parameters for SMF through the SYS1.PARMLIB member SMFPRMxx. The most critical parameter, BUF, should be set to 8192, giving SMF two 4096-byte buffers. The allocation of the SYS1.MANX and SYS1.MANY data sets should specify DCB attributes of DCB=(RECFM=VBS,LRECL=32756, BLKSIZE=4096) under MVS, or DCB=(RECFM=VBS,LRECL=6412, BLKSIZE=4096) under any other operating system.

SMF and spanned records. Although it would appear from the VBS record format that SMF produces a spanned file—that is, the records always fill up

---

1. The committee that worked with IBM is now the well-known Computer Measurement and Evaluation Project (CME) of SHARE.

the blocksize—this is not the case. When the next record is larger than the space remaining in the current (4096-byte) buffer, SMF puts the record at the start of the second buffer. The record is spanned only when its total length is larger than the actual buffer size. The probability that a spanned record will occur is greatly reduced when the SMF buffer is increased to 4096 bytes. The block size increases as well, reducing I/O.

Why SMF does not always use spanned records.   Although spanned records can be a good way to save disk space in variable-length files, they can cause problems with SMF analysis programs. If a system crash is followed by an IPL, the records that have been moved to the buffer are not written into MANX. Thus, the MANX data set might contain the first part of a spanned record, but the later part would never be written. With normal QSAM access, this causes an 002 abend. SAS will not abend, but it will report that an invalid segment was read so the user will know that data was lost. Increasing the SMF buffer size essentially eliminates this problem, and more importantly, greatly reduces the I/O overhead of SMF.

Overhead required by SMF.   Given a reasonable buffer size (typically 2000-4000 bytes), SMF requires little overhead. Most SMF data is contained in control blocks; the only overhead attributable to SMF is the movement of these control blocks into the SMF buffer and the I/O associated with the MANX data set.

A great deal of misconception exists about the volume of activity to SYS1.MANX. A fully loaded 168 will typically write about 32,000 SMF logical records in an eight-hour peak shift. However, the VBS logical records are blocked about 16.6 records per physical 4096-byte record; therefore, that fully loaded 168 would only cause 247 physical I/O's per hour to SYS1.MANX, or an I/O rate of one physical record every 15 seconds. This is minimal compared to the I/O rates of many other system volumes and should be kept in perspective.

figure 2-1
Zap to Eliminate Write/Verify
LIB = SYS1.LINKLIB

NAME	IEEMB820	IEEMB822
VER	03C4	E2D4C6D4C1D5E7
VER	03D0	80000001
VER	042C	80000001
REP	03D0	00
REP	042C	00

Eliminating the Write/Verify.   In addition to using a large buffer, another significant performance change is eliminating the write/verify, the default for the SMF writer. Write/verify causes the record to be written, then to be reread to ascertain that the record was written correctly. Perhaps this additional software verification was necessary in the early days of disks. Now, however, there is enough redundancy at the hardware level that this extra I/O per block, as well as the full revolution wait, can be eliminated. The elimination of write/verify can be accomplished by a simple zap to eliminate the OPCODE W from the SMF DCB, as shown in figure 2-1.

Locating SYS1.MANX for better performance.   Another performance suggestion is to locate SYS1.MANX next to the Volume Table of Contents (VTOC) on the disk volume. This is necessary because the SMF writer issues a TCLOSE after every physical block is processed, which causes an update of the last-block-written pointer in the VTOC. Unnecessary arm motion can be eliminated by locating SYS1.MANX next to the VTOC. For 3350 devices, a better suggestion is to locate the VTOC under a fixed head. In this case, the physical location of SYS1.MANX with respect to the VTOC is unimportant.

Sequence of MANX records.   It is not possible to guarantee that the records in MANX are in exact time sequence, even though they are time-stamped as they are moved to the buffer. This lack of sequence is caused by the various enqueue chains and the different dispatching priorities of tasks in the system. Incorrect sequencing can also be caused by the time stamp. In some records, the time stamp is the event time, while in others it is the SMF buffer enqueue time.

The Job Log.   Many records written to SMF are specifically job-related, that is, they correspond to specific events for specific tasks. All records relating to a certain execution of a particular task, whether a job or a TSO session, can be tied together by the Job Log, which consists of the job name, the job reader date, and the job reader time. In the SAS code in this book, the Job Log is defined by two variables, JOB and READTIME, where READTIME is the date-time stamp of the job-read-in event. Thus, even though the records relating to the job are written at different times, there is only one read-time for each job or task, and all records relating to a single execution can be clustered by job name and read-time. Since restarted jobs are not reprocessed by the reader, their records (including multiple type 5's) will contain the same read-time stamp. This may or may not cause analysis problems, but should always be considered when grouping job-related records together.

3
SAS Data Sets
Containing the SMF/RMF Data

The most difficult part of SMF and RMF analysis is learning what data exists where. Forty-six types of SMF records and ten types of RMF records contain relevant information; over 1400 fields are described in the appendices to this book. This chapter indexes different records written by SMF and RMF and guides you to the appropriate appendix (which maps to the corresponding SAS code).

Basic structure of the SMF/RMF data sets. The basic structure of this analysis of SMF and RMF data is the creation of SAS data sets directly from SMF/RMF data. In many instances, it will be necessary only to process the raw SMF data with SAS code from a single appendix and print the desired data, whereas other analyses will require that you build multiple SAS data sets in one pass of SMF data, then manipulate these SAS data sets to perform the desired analysis. In all examples in this book, the SAS code both for building the basic SAS data set and for the subsequent analyses is contained in the appendices and is also available in machine-readable form as a partitioned data set (PDS).

Each appendix corresponds to a member in the PDS containing the SAS code. The members can be grouped into three categories:

- Members whose names begin with the letters TYPE process the SMF data and create one (occasionally two) SAS data set from closely related SMF/RMF record types. For example, the TYPE434 member reads an SMF file, selects type 4 and type 34 records (written at step termination for batch and TSO jobs), and builds a SAS data set named TYPE434.
- Members whose names begin with the letters MAC are SAS macros that permit creation of several SAS data sets in one pass of the raw SMF/RMF data. Their use is discussed in chapter 12, "Building Multiple SAS Data Sets in One Pass of SMF/RMF Data."
- The remaining members perform analyses using SAS data sets built by TYPE or MAC members. They are discussed in subsequent chapters of the book.

The easiest way to catalog the SMF/RMF data is by the SMF/RMF record identification (ID), even though this approach requires the uninitiated user to learn a numeric mapping from record ID to information content.

Data set name = appendix name = member name. The first place to begin, then, is to associate each SMF/RMF record ID with the SAS data set that will be built by the SAS code in the corresponding member, and shown in the corresponding appendix. For all SMF records and for nearly all RMF records, the SAS data set name, the appendix name, and the member name are identical. Each contains the record identification number (albeit encoded in some instances). While making the association from record type to appendix, it is also possible to categorize the record's content, at least in broad terms.

Record contents. Some records contain the name of the task (i.e., job name or user identification) that caused or was involved in an event, while other records relate to systemwide events. Some events recorded by SMF/RMF can be associated with given resources such as CPU, peripheral devices, memory, etc. Still other classifications can be made in terms of the data content's usefulness in measuring performance objectives, or in determining exception conditions: for example, outages or excessive resource consumption. Thus table 3-1 (SMF) and table 3-2 (RMF) both map the record identifications to the data content, and tabulate the type of information that may be found therein.

The appendices. The contents of the SAS data sets corresponding to these SMF/RMF records are completely described in the appendices. To fully appreciate the breadth of information contained in SMF/RMF, you should read each one completely. Although the brief descriptions are accurate, many records contain very important data that is not obviously related to the rest of the record. Only by reading the descriptions of each variable in each appendix can you realize the totality of information available.

The SAS data sets. The following descriptions of the SAS data sets built by the appendices will guide you to the kinds of information that can be found in the various data sets.

SMF records: TYPE0 through TYPE69

TYPE0: IPLs (SMF record ID = 0)
The TYPE0 data set contains a description of each IPL. Hence, it is useful for determining system reliability and uptime.

TYPE112: Non-MVS CPU wait (SMF record ID = 1, 12)
Applies only to non-MVS. Difficult to interpret, but can be used to estimate how active a pre-MVS CPU was.

TYPE434: Job/TSO step termination (ID = 4,34)

One record for every batch step and TSO session, written at step termination. It contains the most valuable data with regard to resource consumption that can be attributed directly to a specific execution of a job. TYPE434 is also the basis for billing data, since almost all resources that can be billed are recorded here. Detailed profiling of programs, jobs, or users that consume high resources can be done from this data.

TYPE535: Job/TSO termination (ID = 5, 35)

A record for every batch job and TSO session. Has some resources summed from corresponding TYPE434 records, and some data not in TYPE434. TYPE535's primary value is as the source for the job/session account information.

TYPE6: Output (print/punch) writer (ID = 6)

One record for each SYSOUT data set that was punched or printed. The TYPE6 data set is the only source of data concerning printer utilization. Since it contains the remote address, even RJE stations' print volume can be analyzed. It is also useful in identification of forms usage and jobs with high-volume print requirements.

TYPE7: SMF lost data (ID = 7)

You're already in trouble if you find an observation here. Type 7 records are written when the SMF data sets (see chapter 2) are filled and SMF/RMF recording is terminated. You have thus lost data (and probably revenue). It's best to ensure that operations knows how to dump the SMF data sets. Ocasionally, a runaway job (e.g., a DO loop around OPEN/CLOSE) will fill SMF data sets. A crosstabulation of job name and record ID for the interval in question would identify the culprit.

TYPES8911: I/O configuration (ID = 8, 9, 11)

Describes **all** devices that were on-line at each IPL and any devices that were subsequently varied on or off-line. Very useful in tracking operator actions with respect to devices, especially in a multiple-CPU environment where occasionally the same device unexpectedly ends up on-line to multiple systems.

TYPE10: allocation recovery (ID = 10)

Information here could be a good indicator of insufficient mountable devices, especially tape drives. However, it depends on how your operators respond to allocation recoveries—no record is written unless the operator responds with an off-line device. Data in TYPE434 is generally better (see ALOCTM variable and discussions in chapter 10, "Workload Analysis.")

TYPE1415: Non-VSAM data set activity (ID = 14, 15)
The **only** source of data at the data set level. Unfortunately, it is not straightforward if EXCP counts are important, as they are accumulated across type 14 and 15 records. It is still very important, especially in audit trails and in data base analysis; it's important enough to have its own complete analysis section in this book (see chapter 6, "Data Base Analysis and Audit.")

TYPE1718: Non-VSAM scratch and rename (ID = 17, 18)
Essential to audit tracking of critical data sets in installations with inadequate security.

TYPE19: DASD volume information (ID = 19)
Written at IPL, and whenever a DASD volume is dismounted. Provides information on space available on each DASD volume. However, information provided by utility programs (such as MAPDISK, LISTVOL, etc.) run against the VTOC is generally cheaper and better.

TYPE20: Job/session initiation record (ID = 20)
Written at beginning of execution for each job/session (note that the same "job" can have multiple type 20 records if restarted by the operator or JES). Contains account number, which will be important if the system crashes before the job terminates, since the only other source of account number (the type 5 or 35) would be lost. Also provides RACF information about the user and the terminal ID. The latter may be useful in determining the line speed of TSO users, if you can map the terminal line to a port, but such a mapping would change with each TCAM/VTAM gen.

TYPE21: Tape error statistics (ID = 21)
One record each time a tape is dismounted, with counts of temporary and permanent errors and total I/O count. Incredibly, there is no information on which job used the tape! Still, it is very useful in identifying tape volumes that need cleaning and/or re-certification, and tape drives that need maintenance. See member ESV and chapter 7, "Tape Drive Analysis."

TYPE22: Hardware configuration (ID = 22)
A record after every IPL and every time a channel, CPU, memory, or mass storage system is varied on or off-line. Probably useful by someone, but only if operators don't tell you what they're up to.

TYPE23: SMF Statistics (ID = 23)
New with MVS/SE2, this record describes the performance of SMF itself, and provides feedback by which the proper number of SMF buffers can be set. It should also be useful as an audit check on the number of logical SMF records written.

TYPE25: JES3 device setup (ID=25)

If you're going to pay the price for JES3 instead of JES2, you might as well get something in return. For each job which requires JES3 devices, the fairly complete time-stamping of acquisition of those devices is contained here. Be careful, though; detailed analysis might show that you should replace JES3 with JES2.

TYPE26J2: JES2 job/session purge (ID=26)
TYPE26J3: JES3 job/session purge

One record written when all SYSOUT for a job or TSO session has been printed. Thus it may not be found until several days after the job/session ended. This is the most important data for tracking job scheduling, since it is the only source of JES priorities and classes, and it contains very comprehensive time-stamping of the events JES knew about. It is also the only source of data on JES spool usage. Two different members and data sets are needed because this is one of the few places where there are significant differences in JES2 and JES3 data.

TYPE30: Work Termination and Interval Reporting (ID=30)

New with MVS/SE2, this is a composite of information from the old type 20, 4/34, 5/35 and 40 records, eliminating the need for their merge. It furthermore can be written at intervals as well as at termination.

TYPE31: TSO initialization (ID=31)

A record each time TSO is started (i.e., made available to TSO users). Very useful in tracking the availability of TSO, except that there is no corresponding record when TSO is shut down. See chapter 9,"Availability Analysis," on subsystem availability.

TYPE32: TSO Command Record

New with MVS/SE2, this record contains resource statistics and counts of executions of each command issued by a TSO session. It also can be written at intervals. Unfortunately for CALL and TEST commands, there is no record of program called, and thus it is not a replacement for TSO/MON. It also doesn't contain any response measures.

Type 34 and 35 (ID=34, 35)

Just a reminder. Type 34 and 35 (TSO sessions) are treated as batch jobs and their data is included with type 4 and type 5 records in the TYPE434 an TYPE535 data sets.

TYPE40: dynamic allocations (ID=40)

One record whenever a dynamic allocation is concatenated, freed (unallocated), or deconcatenated. Remember that batch jobs and on-line systems other than TSO use dynamic allocation. TYPE40 is absolutely essential in tracking EXCP count: whenever a dynamic allocation is freed, all EXCPs to that allocation are contained in the type 40 record, and the type 4 or 34 will have zero EXCPs for that file. Even more critical, whenever any dynamic allocation is deconcatenated (quite common in TSO CLISTs), **all** EXCPs to **all** dynamic allocations are written out in a type 40, and the EXCP counters in the type 4 or 34 are reset to zero! Thus if you do not use type 40 records in accounting, the smart user can get all his I/O free by simply deconcatenating before termination. The type 40 for a deconcatenation is a copy of the UCB segments of the type 4 or 34.

TYPE4345: JES start or stop (ID=43, 45)

First note that VSPC also writes type 43 and 45 records: an internal flag identifies the subsystem (JES2, JES3, or VSPC) involved. TYPE4345 contains a record each time JES is started or stopped, and thus is useful in tracking subsystem availability. For starters, see how long it takes from IPL (TYPE0) to JES start, and you may discover an operator problem robbing you of 10-15 minutes availability at each outage.

TYPE43PC: VSPC start, stop or modify (ID=43)

A record is written each time the VSPC subsystem is started, stopped, or changed. Looks usable for tracking VSPC.

TYPE4789: JES RJE sessions (ID=47, 48, 49)

A record is written whenever an RJE station signs on or off. The availability of each remote site can be determined from TYPE4789. Additionally, the SIGNOFF record contains EXCP counts and line-error counts, which are very useful in tracking communication problems.

TYPE47PC: VSPC user LOGON (ID=47)

A record is written each time a VSPC user logs on. Status of the previous VSPC session by the user is maintained here. The VSPC ACCOUNT program also writes a type 47 record.

TYPE48PC: VSPC user LOGOFF (ID=48)

This is the accounting record for a VSPC session, and contains resource consumption by the session. Unfortunately, there is little descriptive data about resource consumption beyond total CPU and I/O counts, and some appears to be accumulated from session to session. Unlike most data in this book, VSPC data has not been extensively validated, so use with caution.

TYPE49PC: VSPC user security (ID=49)

A record is written whenever a VSPC user specifies an incorrect password during LOGON or file access.

TYPE5568: NJE session (ID=55, 56, 58)

These records are written at each node in a network when that node signs on, signs off, or uses an invalid password. This data could be useful in tracking network availability, but will be difficult to combine from the different SMF files since the records are written to the SMF data set at each node. Furthermore, since there is no way to guarantee that all clocks in all CPUs in a network have the same time, it may be difficult to determine the true sequence of events.

TYPE57: NJE SYSOUT transmission (ID=57)

There is one record written at each node in a network when a SYSOUT data set is transmitted between nodes. Thus this data is important in evaluating potential delays due to volume of data transmission in an NJE network.

TYPE62: VSAM component/cluster opened (ID=62)

A record is written each time a VSAM component or cluster is opened (but not for JOBCAT or STEPCAT DDs); thus the duration that VSAM data sets are open (as opposed to allocated) can be determined from TYPE62 and TYPE64.

TYPE64: VSAM component/cluster closed (ID=64)

A record is written each time a VSAM component or cluster is closed, the volume switches, or it runs out of space. This record contains extensive statistics concerning the amount of activity occurring in this use of this VSAM component or cluster, and also data concerning the data set itself. However, since both totals since creation and change due to this job are included, one must be concerned with other jobs' intervening type 64 records in order to correctly track VSAM usage.

TYPE6367: VSAM entry defined/deleted (ID=63, 67)

Whenever a VSAM catalog entry (i.e., a component, cluster, catalog, alternate index, path, or non-VSAM data set in a VSAM catalog) is defined or altered, it will be tracked here, along with information concerning the catalog entry before and after the event, and the job causing the change. Thus it is useful in audit tracking of VSAM data sets.

TYPE68: VSAM entry renamed (ID=68)

Whenever a VSAM catalog entry is renamed, it will be tracked here. Also useful in audit tracking of VSAM.

TYPE69: VSAM data space defined, extended, or deleted (ID=69)

Whenever a VSAM data space is defined, extended, or deleted a record will occur here. Unfortunately, there is no data describing whether the event was a define, extend, or delete—simply that one of three events occurred.

SMF RECORDS

Record ID	Brief Description	SAS Data Set Name	Job	System	Sub-system	CPU	I/O	Memory	Objectives	Exceptions
						Resources			**Uses**	
						CPU	I/O	Memory	Objectives	Exceptions
0	IPL	TYPE0		Y		Y	Y	Y	Y	Y
1	Non-MVS CPU wait	TYPE112		Y		Y	Y	Y	Y	Y
4	Job Step Termination	TYPE434	Y			Y	Y	Y	Y	Y
5	Job Termination	TYPE535	Y			Y	Y	Y	Y	Y
6	Output (Print/Punch) Writer	TYPE6	Y		Y		Y			Y
7	SMF Lost Data	TYPE7	Y	Y						Y
8	I/O Configuration	TYPE8911		Y	Y	Y	Y	Y		
9	Vary Devices On-line	TYPE8911		Y	Y	Y	Y	Y		
10	Allocation Recovery	TYPE10	Y				Y			Y
11	Vary Devices Off-line	TYPE8911		Y	Y	Y	Y	Y		
14	Non-VSAM Data Set Activity-Input	TYPE1415	Y				Y			Y
15	Non-VSAM Data Set Activity-Output	TYPE1415	Y				Y			Y
17	Non-VSAM Data Set Scratch	TYPE1718	Y				Y			Y
18	Non-VSAM Data Set Rename	TYPE1718	Y				Y			Y
19	DASD Volumes Status	TYPE19		Y			Y			
20	Job/TSO Initiation	TYPE20	Y						Y	
21	Tape Error Statistics	TYPE21			Y		Y			Y
22	Hardware Configuration	TYPE22		Y		Y	Y	Y		
25	JES3 Device Allocation	TYPE25	Y				Y		Y	
26	JES2 Job/TSO Purge	TYPE26J2	Y				Y		Y	Y
26	JES3 Job/TSO Purge	TYPE26J3	Y				Y		Y	Y
31	TSO Initialization	TYPE31		Y	Y					Y
34	TSO Step Termination	TYPE434	Y			Y	Y	Y	Y	Y
35	TSO Job Termination	TYPE535	Y			Y	Y	Y	Y	Y
40	Dynamic Allocation	TYPE40	Y				Y			Y
43-JES	JES Startup	TYPE4345			Y					Y
43-VSPC	VSPC Startup	TYPE43PC			Y					Y
44VSPC	VSPC Modify	TYPE43PC			Y					Y
45-JES	JES Stop	TYPE4345			Y					Y
45-VSPC	VSPC Stop	TYPE43PC			Y					Y

table 3-1

table 3-1, continued

Code	Description	TYPE						
45-VSPC	VSPC Stop	TYPE43PC		Y				Y
47-JES	JES RJE Session SIGNON	TYPE4789		Y				Y
47-VSPC	VSPC User LOGON	TYPE47PC	Y	Y	Y	Y		Y
48-JES	JES RJE Session SIGNOFF	TYPE4789		Y	Y	Y	Y	Y
48-VSPC	VSPC User LOGOFF	TYPE48PC	Y	Y				Y
49-JES	JES RJE Invalid Password	TYPE4789		Y				Y
49-VSPC	VSPC User Security Violation	TYPE49PC	Y	Y	Y			
55	NJE Start Networking	TYPE5568			Y			
56	NJE Invalid Password	TYPE5568			Y			
57	NJE SYSOUT Transmission	TYPE57	Y	Y	Y			
58	NJE Terminate Networking	TYPE5568	Y		Y			
62	VSAM Open	TYPE62	Y		Y			
63	VSAM Define/Alter	TYPE6367	Y		Y			
64	VSAM Close	TYPE64	Y		Y			
67	VSAM Delete	TYPE6367	Y		Y			
68	VSAM Rename	TYPE68	Y		Y			
68	VSAM Data Space Change	TYPE69	Y		Y			

RMF records: TYPE70 through TYPE77
(MVS and MVS/SE only)

TYPE70: Overall CPU activity and address space statistics (ID=70)

This SAS data set is built coincident with TYPE72 and its code is contained in member TYPE7072. This is **the** prime source of data on CPU activity. The data on CPU-busy time has been extensively validated with hardware monitors, and thus total CPU-busy time is easily acquired: simply print TYPE70. There are also valuable statistics concerning the number of address spaces that are IN, READY, etc., which can assist in tracking SRM parameters.

TYPE71: Paging and swapping activity (ID=71)

The prime source of data on memory management in MVS, and also an excellent source of overall performance of the system. Paging rates and swapping rates can be determined (note that different releases of MVS and MVS/SE use different paging and swapping parameters). The fixed memory and pagable memory usage statistics, along with paging data, are the best source of determining when real memory is needed.

TYPE72: Task workload activity (ID=72)

This SAS data set is built co-incident with TYPE70 (because the type 70 is the only source of CPU type, and the type 72 contains CPU service units which must be converted to CPU time by a CPU-type-dependent factor) and its source code is in TYPE7072. Data on CPU, I/O, and memory usage by each performance group (actually even more detailed, as the data is by period within each performance group) is collected. This data provides the best source of capacity planning data, since system tasks are included, whereas SMF data does not include their resources. By combining with TYPE70, which contains total CPU active time, the system CPU overhead can be calculated directly. By combining with TYPE73P, the system I/O overhead can be inferred (it can't be directly calculated because some sub-systems, notably IMS, do not record their I/O in type 72 I/O service units).

TYPE73P: Physical channel activity (ID=73)

This SAS data set is created co-incident with TYPE73L and its source code is contained in member TYPE73. Physical channel I/O counts are maintained, and sampling of channel-busy provides good measures of channel activity and channel balance. This is also the simplest source of data for total I/O counts.

TYPE73L: Logical channel activity (ID=73)

See TYPE73P. From the perspective of the logical channel, I/O counts and I/O queuing are collected. This is a much more accurate picture of channel activity as it relates to performance: good performance means no delays, and the amount of I/O delay can be determined from the deferred I/O counts and the depth of queues for the logical channels.

TYPE74: Device activity (ID=74)

This is the largest of the RMF SAS data sets since it contains one record per device per RMF interval. It is **the** best source of data for balancing I/O devices, since total I/O to each device is recorded. Average I/O time to each device can be calculated and used as a measure of those devices which should be investigated (perhaps with GTFSEEK, an IBM tool) for data set replacement on the volume.

TYPE75: Page/swap data sets (ID=75)

The activity of the page and swap data sets, as viewed by the Auxiliary Storage Manager (ASM), is reported here. Comparison of the ASM's view of data-set-busy with TYPE74's view of device-busy can reveal undesired usage of volumes containing page/swap data sets, and can suggest control unit/channel contentions which degrade the paging sub-system.

TYPE76: RMF trace record (ID=76)

When RMF trace is turned on, very detailed tracking of internal SRM/ASM/RSM control blocks can be collected here for subsequent analysis. This is a seldom-needed but very valuable tool in tracking the internals of MVS.

TYPE77: Enqueue conflict (ID=77)

Whenever the use of ENQ (enqueue to ensure serialization of non-sharable resources) causes a conflict or delay to a task, the description of that event is recorded here. Although not normally turned on (because most ENQ conflicts are necessary), it is good to review a day's data periodically to ensure that all conflicts are understood and irresolvable.

SMF record: TYPE90

TYPE90: Operator Commands Record (ID=90)

New with MVS/SE2, this long-needed record describes operator commands which can significantly alter the system, such as SET TIME, DATE, IPS, OPT, etc. Not only is the command's existence logged, but also before and after values of changed parameters are usually given.

RMF RECORDS

Record ID	Brief Description	Name of Source	SAS Data Set Name	Resources			Exceptions
				CPU	I/O	Memory	
70	Overall CPU Activity	TYPE7072	TYPE70	Y			Y
71	Paging/Swapping Activity	TYPE72	TYPE72		Y	Y	Y
72	Task Workload Activity	TYPE7072	TYPE72	Y	Y	Y	Y
73	Physical Channel Activity	TYPE	TYPE73P		Y		Y
73	Logical Channel Activity	TYPE73	TYPE73L		Y		Y
74	Device Activity	TYPE74	TYPE74		Y		Y
75	Page/Swap Data Sets	TYPE75	TYPE75				Y
76	RMF Trace	TYPE76	TYPE76				Y
77	Enqueue Conflict	TYPE77	TYPE77				Y
79	Monitor II Session	TYPE79	TYPE79				Y

table 3-2

4

Measurement and Analysis of Service Objectives: Did Your Batch Workload Meet Its Schedule?

SMF data analysis begins with a look at service objectives—whether your system meets its schedules for serving users. For batch work, SMF provides all the information required to determine if your installations's service objectives are being met.

Deriving service objectives.   An installations's primary service objectives are typically derived from the duration that jobs spend in various queues. In essence, you can regard the operating system and the job entry subsystem as a pair of queue managers operating in tandem. Since SMF data provides a nearly complete time-stamping of all the events in the life of a job, the time in queue for any job can be easily calculated by subtracting time stamps.

Before we begin to discuss the analysis of service objectives, it would be helpful to identify the many time stamps existing in SMF records, and relate them to the corresponding system events.

Time stamps in batch jobs.   Figure 4-1 maps the time stamps that exist in the SAS data sets from most of the job-related SMF records, and gives an excellent picture of the various checkpoints in the life of a job that can be identified from SMF.

Naming SAS variables.   In this book variables whose names end in TIME are time stamps—the date and time that an event occurred. They are stored as internal SAS date-time values, and their default format is DATATIME19.2; for example 07SEP78:10:15:13.64.

Variable names ending in TM are SAS time values that represent durations. They are stored as internal SAS time values and their format is TIME12.2; for example 27:16:58.87 means 27 hours, 16 minutes, and 58.87 seconds.

What figure 4-1 represents.   In figure 4-1, each name is a SAS variable containing a time stamp. The number in parentheses under each name identifies the SAS data set (see the appendices) that contains the variable.

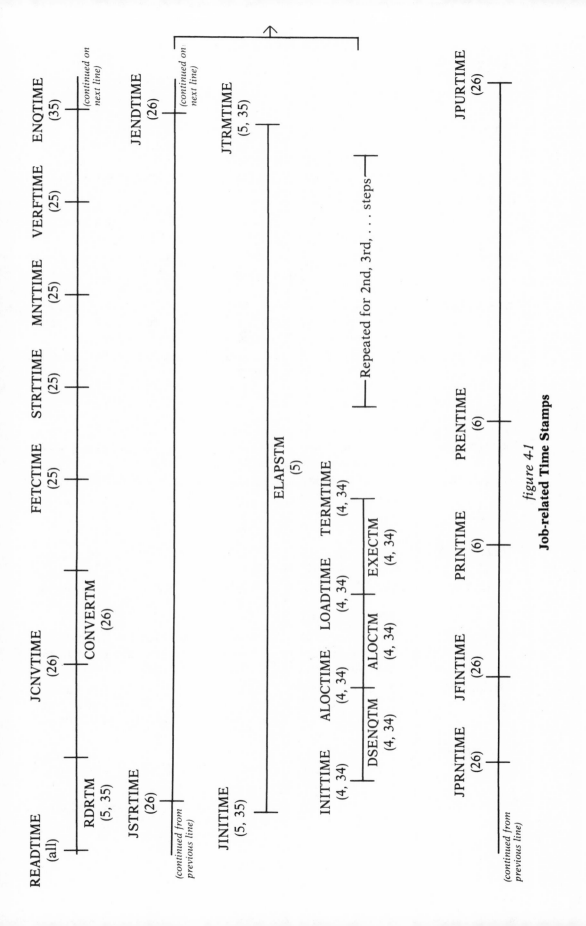

figure 4-1
Job-related Time Stamps

READTIME   The variable READTIME exists in all job-related records: the read-date and read-time are combined into the time stamp READTIME. As mentioned in the last chapter, READTIME and JOB constitute the Job Log number, a unique identifier that can be used to combine all records associated with a specific execution of a specific job.

  The READTIME value is the time the job was physically presented to the system.

RDRTM   The RDRTM value, from the type 5 and 35 records, gives the amount of time that the job was actually processed by the reader—generally, this time is very short.

JCNVTIME   The next time stamp, JCNVTIME, is the time the converter processed the physical card images, and in most cases, JCNVTIME immediately follows READTIME.

CONVERTM   CONVERTM shows the length of time required to convert the job control statements.

The next four time stamps exist only in the JES3 environment.

FETCTIME   The FETCTIME is the time that mountable volumes were fetched from the library.

STRTTIME   The STRTTIME represents the time that the start setup was issued in the JES3 environment.

MNTTIME   The MNTTIME is the time that the first mount was issued by JES3.

VERFTIME   The VERFTIME is the time at which the first mountable volume was verified.

ENQTIME   The ENQTIME time stamp exists only for TSO sessions and is the time at which the user was enqueued on the SYS1.UADS data set.

JSTRTIME   The JSTRTIME is the job-start time stamp—that is, the time when the job-entry subsystem passed the job to the operating system for execution of a job.

JINITIME   The JINITIME comes from the type 5 or 35 records and is the operating system's response to the job-entry subsystem passing the job. There should be no delay between JSTRTIME and JINITIME.

JTRMTIME   The end of execution, as perceived by the operating system, is reflected by JTRMTIME, which also comes from the type 5 and 35 SMF records.

ELAPSTM   The duration of initiation for batch jobs and session time for TSO is contained in the variable ELAPSTM.

Within execution, a job is comprised of one or more steps. Each step has four time stamps.

INITTIME   INITTIME is the beginning of initiation for this step.

ALOCTIME   ALOCTIME is the beginning of device allocation for this step.

LOADTIME   LOADTIME is the completion of allocation and the beginning of problem program execution for this step.

TERMTIME   The final time stamp is TERMTIME, the termination of step execution. The four time stamps above are repeated for subsequent steps until the last step is executed.

The durations between these step time stamps are also defined.

DSENQTM   DSENQTM is the interval from initiation to allocation; after the first step, this time should be short unless the processor is placed in a stop or a long delay occurs to the operating system.

However, for the first step in a HASP or JES2 environment, the DSENQTM represents the delay that results from a data set enqueue conflict. When a job enters execution, it actually enters the first step execution, and at that point, the enqueue is issued for all data set names to be used by the job/session. If a data set required for this job is held by another job, the operator is notified to reply WAIT or CANCEL. If the operator does not cancel the newly-arrived job, it waits until the data set is available. At that time, the job enqueue will be successful and the ALOCTIME will occur for the newly-arrived job.

Thus, DSENQTM represents the time that jobs wait for data set enqueue conflicts to be resolved.

ALOCTM   The second duration at the step level, ALOCTM, represents the length of time the job step waits for allocation. In most cases, ALOCTM is relatively short. However, if devices are not available and the job step enters allocation recovery, the time from the allocation recovery until the devices are made available is represented by ALOCTM.

EXECTM   The final duration in each step record is EXECTM, the maximum time the job step is actually capable of executing instructions. In fact, if the job step has to wait for tape mounts or is swapped out, it cannot execute instructions during these events, and thus EXECTM is the maximum time that a job step could have been in execution.

JENDTIME   At job termination time, all steps have completed and the job-entry subsystem is notified by the operating system.

JENDTIME is the off-execution-processor time stamp. There should be essentially no difference between JEND-TIME and JTRMTIME.

Time stamps for output.   Although the job has completed execution, the job-entry subsystem still must process the output.

JPRNTIME   JPRNTIME is the start time of the output processor.

JFINTIME   JFINTIME is the finish time of the output processor.

The output processor duration is normally short because the output processor simply manipulates the control blocks on the spool for output processing—it does not do the printing. The job then enters the print queue and waits for printers based on its priority, remote destination, and so on.

The next time stamps encountered are:

PRINTIME   PRINTIME signifies the start of printing.

PRENTIME   PRENTIME signifies the end of printing for each file.

Since a job may print many files, there may be many PRINTIME to PREN-TIME durations. These may be serial if only one printer is available, or parallel if the files can be printed in parallel on multiple printers. In an MVS environment, printing can start while the job is still in execution. For example, if FREE=CLOSE is specified on a SYSOUT data set, the printing will start when the file is closed, rather than waiting until after the execution processor and output processor have completed their work. Because of this variability between PRINTIME and PRENTIME time stamps, the duration of time in the print queue is the only value difficult to determine from SMF data.

JPURTIME   When the final SYSOUT has been printed, the last time stamp, JPURTIME (the job purge time), occurs. At this point, all control blocks associated with the job have been processed; all records dealing with the job have been written by the operating system to SMF; and the job is now purged from the system.

Confusion caused by time stamps.   The multiple CPU environment probably causes the most confusion. In a multiple-operating-system environment, it is possible for a job to be read in on one system, executed on the second, and printed on either the first or the second. Time stamps come from each system involved; if the clocks for the two systems are not exactly synchronized, it is possible to get a later JCNVTIME than JSTRTIME, or another "impossible" stamp. The only satisfactory solution, other than operational management, is to be sure that the operators in a multi-system environment understand the need for exact synchronization of CPU clocks.

Restarted jobs.   Accounting systems that contain code modifying some of the time stamps are a second source of confusion. For example, in a JES2 environment, jobs are often restarted after initiation. When a job enters data set enqueue conflict, a frequent operational procedure is to restart the job that went into data set enqueue and place it in hold until the job owning the data set finishes. At this time, the second job is manually released by the operator and enters execution.

To JES, that is all one job. The records written by SMF, however, show that the job had two executions. At a minimum, the first execution has type 4 and 5 records written because the job did enter execution; furthermore, that execution reflects an abend, a system 222, because the job was cancelled. Then there will be subsequent type 4 and 5 records written for the "real" execution. However, in the type 26 records, the time stamps corresponding to execution will pertain only to the last execution, and there will be only one type 26 record for that job.

Thus, restarted jobs can produce confusion unless steps are taken to identify them. The situation is further complicated in that some accounting packages, notably PACES/KOMAND, process restarted jobs so that the second restart has a different read-time than the first execution—PACES bumps the read-time by .01 seconds for each execution. This discrepancy can be confusing when you attempt to map specific jobs from PACES back to real SMF data.

Before you decide how to treat restarted jobs, you must investigate the kinds of accounting packages and modifications in the system. For exact mapping or duplication, an algorithm similar to the one used by PACES may have to be included. However, it is usually better to recognize a restart as one job and to construct a single observation containing all of the needed information. Keeping start and end times of the first executions, the start and end times of the last executions, and the number of intervening restarts is usually sufficient.

Missing values.   A final warning about time stamps concerns how they are built by the operating system. The images for some SMF records, especially type 26, are initialized with hexadecimal zeros and the time stamps are filled in as events occur.

If an event never occurs, the time stamp remains hexadecimal zeros in the written record. SAS, using the SMFSTAMP8. format for input in such cases, recognizes hexadecimal zeros as missing values. Subtracting a missing value from a nonmissing value leads to a missing value for the duration.

In calculating durations, test the variables to make sure they are non-missing. READTIME is the only variable guaranteed to be nonmissing. JCNVTIME can be missing for a job placed in hold that is cancelled before conversion. The JES3 time stamps, FETCTIME, STRTTIME, MNTTIME, and VERFTIME, are only nonmissing for jobs which go through JES3 device setup. ENQTIME is valid only for TSO sessions. JSTRTIME is missing for all JCL errors detected at converter time and for any job cancelled before execution. JENDTIME is missing for any job with a missing JSTRTIME; more importantly, JENDTIME is missing for any job active when the operating system crashes. JPRNTIME and JFINTIME can be missing for JCL errors. PRINTIME and PRENTIME are missing for any job that does not produce printed output.

Negative time differences can result not only from time stamp differences between systems as described above, but also from restarted jobs which are active during system crashes. JSTRTIME is correct for the execution, but JENDTIME still has the value from the restart.

Finally, when a system is IPLed, those records in the SMF buffer at the time of the IPL are lost unless the SMF buffers are written to the MANX/MANY data set before the IPL. There is no simple solution to this problem. The HALT EOD command purges those records from the SMF buffer if it is issued before the IPL. Unless the system is fully quiesced, however, there may be records written to the buffer after the HALT EOD and before the IPL.

As supplied by IBM, the HALT EOD command also switches SMF recording to the other MAN data set. Some installations have written HALT EOD to purge the SMF buffer and eliminate the switch by writing two large records. But in many cases, the system hangs up and the operator consoles are not functional; it is simply not possible to purge the records from the buffers into MANX. It might be possible to take a stand-alone dump, read the dump tape, and retrieve the SMF buffers, but these steps are so expensive that most installations choose to ignore these few lost records.

Time stamps in TSO sessions.   The preceding discussion dealt mostly with batch jobs, but most of the time stamps mentioned also exist for TSO sessions. The READTIME variable corresponds to the logon time and the JENDTIME corresponds to the logoff time. Of course, a TSO session will have only one step record, but TSO sessions which produce printed output will have PRINTIME and PRENTIME time stamps. Since all TSO sessions are handled by the job-entry subsystem, all time stamps from the type 26 records can exist for TSO sessions.

Using time stamps to analyze the delivery of service objectives.   Most installations schedule their batch workload by a combination of job class and job priority. The service objectives are usually stated as measures of turnaround time, initiation wait time, or queue time (the time from read-in until start-initiation). To analyze service objectives, translate the objectives into groupings and use the SMF data to analyze how well you are meeting those objectives.

For example, consider a JES2 installation which schedules its batch work by job class and measures its performance by turnaround time (read-in time to completion of all printing). Example 4-1 shows how the data from type 26 records can be used to produce a report of service delivered.

SAS data set TURNARND is created from TYPE26J2 by first selecting only batch jobs and then keeping only those jobs with a nonmissing value of JSTRTIME. Since a missing value of JSTRTIME indicates a JCL error, including such jobs in average turnaround statistics would unfairly bias the average to a lower-than-actual value.

TURNARND is calculated by subtracting READTIME from JPURTIME, and dividing by 3600 (because the internal storage of formattted SAS time stamps is in units of seconds). Thus, TURNARND will contain each job's turnaround time in hours.

Finally, the shift variable is constructed from the JSTRTIME variable. (The shift is defined as the shift on which the job started execution, and is determined by the hour of JSTRTIME.)

Sort this data set by shift and job class, and use the MEANS procedure by shift and job class to build a new output data set named STATS, which contains the number and average turnaround for all of the jobs by shift and job class. Finally, use PROC PRINT to print a report which shows the complete profile of service delivered in this installation.

```
DATA TURNARND;
  SET TYPE26J2;
  IF JOB_TSO='J';
  IF JSTRTIME NE .;
  TURNARND=(JPURTIME-READTIME)/3600;
  SHIFT='PRIME';
  IF HOUR(JSTRTIME)>16 THEN SHIFT='EVE';
  IF HOUR(JSTRTIME)<8 THEN SHIFT='NIGHT';
  KEEP SHIFT JOBCLASS TURNARND;
PROC SORT;
  BY SHIFT JOBCLASS;
PROC MEANS NOPRINT MAXDEC=2;
  BY SHIFT JOBCLASS;
  OUTPUT OUT=STATS N=NRJOBS MEAN=AVGTURN;
PROC PRINT;
  ID SHIFT;
  VAR JOBCLASS NRJOBS AVGTURN;
  TITLE INSTALLATION SERVICE OBJECTIVES;
  TITLE2 MEAN TURNAROUND REPORT;
```

INSTALLATION SERVICE OBJECTIVES
MEAN TURNAROUND REPORT

SHIFT	JOBCLASS	NRJOBS	AVGTURN
EVE	A	210	2.58
EVE	B	109	5.13
EVE	C	13	2.84
EVE	D	109	3.87
EVE	E	19	12.71
NIGHT	A	209	1.56
NIGHT	B	109	4.18
NIGHT	C	19	2.81
NIGHT	D	108	2.43
NIGHT	E	18	13.18
PRIME	A	208	1.71
PRIME	B	99	3.82
PRIME	C	13	0.47
PRIME	D	110	4.00
PRIME	E	19	14.69

example 4-1

The number of jobs started per shift and class provides a clear understanding of how the users of this installation submit their work. In only fourteen lines of SAS code, we can produce a complete report showing how well this installation meets its service objectives. If the installation has specific objectives for the value of average turnaround time for each class, it can report to its users the success of the service it has provided.

Weaknesses of job turnaround time and an alternative.   Although you can readily calculate average turnaround time, it is not a good measure of service objectives because it suffers from several weaknesses.

First, since turnaround time is measured from read-time to purge-time, users can unduly influence their own turnaround by "holding" the printing of their job. Because purge does not occur until all printing has been completed, the turnaround time of a job with held printing will reflect not the service delivered to that job, but the user's personal decision as to when the print the job.

Furthermore, the turnaround time is the sum of unrelated durations: the time the job waited for execution, the time the job actually executed, and the time the job waited for printing. The waits for execution and printing are measures of how well the supplier is delivering service. But the duration of execution is primarily under the control of the user, since he determines the number of steps and the amount of work accomplished by the job.

So a better measure of service delivered is how well the supplier scheduled the job, rather than how much work the user requested. It is true that job elongation during execution can result from a poorly configured installation, but this also directly affects total service delivered, since waits for execution of other jobs also increase. Therefore, for batch services, queue time for execution is a better indicator of service delivered.

Weaknesses of using the average value and an alternative.   Using a value such as average queue time for the primary measure of services is a mistake. The nature of queues in computer systems is such that this kind of measure tends to be misleading to the supplier and unsatisfying to the user. The user does not see average values, but counts: how many times last week was my system late?

A better choice, then, is to use distributions (percentiles). For example, one installation stated its service objective in terms of the 90th percentile queue time value—that is, the 90th percentile value for queue time was to be less than some number.

Calculating the 90th percentile value is very expensive, because the only existing algorithm sorts by the percentile value and counts to the 90th percentile to determine its value. Furthermore, wide variance in the magnitude of the 90th percentile value sometimes occurs, even though the service does not vary significantly according to other measures. These variances occur especially often for turnaround values, which are subject to many other perturbations.

A good alternative to the 90th percentile value is the percentage of the subclass's work meeting a specific value. This appears to be the most effective, accurate, and understandable measure of service objectives. The installation chooses the variable on which objectives are to be based and defines the acceptable values. The measurement process simply counts the number of times the stated objectives were met.

Calculating percent of jobs meeting objectives: example. Example 4-2 carries out such an analysis. At this installation, jobs are submitted at priorities 3, 4, and 5. Priority 3 jobs have an objective of twelve hours queue time; priority 4 jobs, four hours queue time; and priority 5 jobs, one hour queue time.

All of the needed information comes from the TYPE26J2 data set for the JES2 type 26 records. First, exclude non-batch jobs and JCL errors by testing for JSTRTIME not equal to missing. The queue time (QUETIME), converted to units of hours, is defined as the time from read-time to start of execution. Set NRJOBS=1 for each record and then set NRMET=1 if the job meets its objective. Then calculate the shift (defined as the shift on which the job started execution). In this installation, there are only two shifts defined, off-prime and on-prime. To reduce data handling, use the KEEP statement. Then sort data set QUETIME by shift and input priority before calling the MEANS procedure by shift and input priority. MEANS creates an output data set named SUMS, containing one observation for each shift and input priority. The number of jobs and the number of jobs which met their objectives for the shift and input priority appears in each observation.

Data set STATS takes the output of the MEANS procedure and calculates the percentage of jobs which met the objectives. Finally, these percentages are printed with **PROC PRINT**, which shows the distribution of work by shift and priority.

```
DATA QUETIME;
  SET TYPE26J2;
  IF JOB_TSO='J';
  IF JSTRTIME NE .;
  QUETIME=(JSTRTIME-READTIME)/3600;
  NRJOBS=1;
  IF INPRTY=3 AND QUETIME<12 THEN NRMET=1;
  IF INPRTY=4 AND QUETIME<4 THEN NRMET=1;
  IF INPRTY=5 AND QUETIME<1 THEN NRMET=1;
  SHIFT='OFF PRIME';
  IF 8<=HOUR(JSTRTIME)<=17 THEN SHIFT='PRIME';
  KEEP INPRTY QUETIME SHIFT NRJOBS NRMET;
PROC SORT;
  BY SHIFT INPRTY;
PROC MEANS NOPRINT;
  BY SHIFT INPRTY;
  OUTPUT OUT=SUMS SUM=NRJOBS NRMET;
  VAR NRJOBS NRMET;
DATA STATS;
  SET SUMS;
  PCTMET=100*NRMET/NRJOBS;
  FORMAT PCTMET 5.1;
PROC PRINT;
  ID SHIFT;
  VAR INPRTY NRJOBS NRMET PCTMET;
  TITLE INSTALLATION PERFORMANCE OBJECTIVES;
  TITLE2 PERCENT MEETING OBJECTIVE;
```

example 4-2

```
              INSTALLATION PERFORMANCE OBJECTIVES
                 PERCENT MEETING OBJECTIVE

      SHIFT        INPRTY      NRJOBS     NRMET     PCTMET

     OFF PRIME       3          155        149       96.1
     OFF PRIME       4           99         99      100.0
     OFF PRIME       5           83         83      100.0
     PRIME           3          198        197       99.5
     PRIME           4          281        281      100.0
     PRIME           5          496        446       89.9
```

example 4-2, continued

Management understands these kinds of statistics, and the user understands what the supplier means by advertising that 90% of the work submitted at priority 3 will be executed in less than twelve hours.

Variations.   Variations on analyses of services are endless. After defining and measuring objectives, you can subcategorize—look at account fields, perhaps, to define the logical groups of work. Or you might choose production and development as two categories and compute the percentages of each of those units of work that are getting service requested. If service delivered is poorer than anticipated, the supplier can often find the group within his installation that is abusing the job scheduling scheme and preventing others from receiving good service.

Although accounting information does not exist in type 26 records, job name information does. Since most installations encode their job names in a manner that identifies the submitter, it is a simple matter to identify who is submitting work at which priority by crosstabulating a portion of job name with input priority. Economic sanctions (charging more for higher priority) or management control can be applied to the abusive submitters of work to level the service provided for all users.

Example 4-3 provides a simple crosstabulation of the first letter of job name versus input priority. (Assume the first letter indicates the submitting department.) A profile of departments shows which departments submit most of the higher priority work (note Department C with 12% of the priority 5 work). A breakdown, by priority, of the percentage of work within each department (82% of Department C's work is at priority 5), and a breakdown of overall priority assignment (37% of all jobs were at priority 5), are also shown. This profile can be used as a lever to persuade out-of-line departments to stop abusing the service.

```
TITLE CROSSTABULATION OF FIRST LETTER OF JOB NAME WITH INPUT PRIORITY;
PROC FREQ DATA=TYPE26J2;
   TABLES JOB*INPRTY;
   FORMAT JOB $1.;
```

example 4-3

CROSSTABULATION OF FIRST LETTER OF JOB NAME WITH INPUT PRIORITY

TABLE OF JOB BY INPRTY

JOB   INPRTY

FREQUENCY PERCENT ROW PCT COL PCT	3	4	5	TOTAL
A	38 2.41 17.51 6.55	92 5.83 42.40 22.66	87 5.51 40.09 14.67	217 13.74
B	40 2.53 30.77 6.90	27 1.71 20.77 6.65	63 3.99 48.46 10.62	130 8.23
C	18 1.14 7.35 3.10	26 1.65 10.61 6.40	201 12.73 82.04 33.90	245 15.52
D	10 0.63 37.04 1.72	12 0.76 44.44 2.96	5 0.32 18.52 0.84	27 1.71
T	180 11.40 85.31 31.03	31 1.96 14.69 7.64	0 0.00 0.00 0.00	211 13.36
V	79 5.00 71.82 13.62	17 1.08 15.45 4.19	14 0.89 12.73 2.36	110 6.97
X	33 2.09 18.03 5.69	58 3.67 31.69 14.29	92 5.83 50.27 15.51	183 11.59
Y	10 0.63 15.38 1.72	42 2.66 64.62 10.34	13 0.82 20.00 2.19	65 4.12
Z	172 10.89 43.99 29.66	101 6.40 25.83 24.88	118 7.47 30.18 19.90	391 24.76
TOTAL	580 36.73	406 25.71	593 37.56	1579 100.00

example 4-3, continued

What the analyses of service objectives show.   If your service objectives relate to your users' perceptions of computing, and if the service objectives are met consistently, you will have satisfied users. If you are meeting the service objectives and your users are dissatisfied, either they are unreasonable, or, more likely, the service objectives are not relevant to their concerns. If you consistently meet service objectives and users are satisfied, it is possible that you have excess resources. They should be identified in order to reduce operation costs. If, however, realistic service objectives are not being met, resource consumption in the system should be examined.

5
Overall System Performance: Resource Usage

The importance of resource usage analysis. Analyzing overall system resource usage is as important as analyzing services delivered. Who uses what portion of the system's resources? Where are impediments to job transaction, and I/O scheduling located? Are the resources consumed—as measured in CPU time, EXCPs and so on—being distributed properly through the billing system? For example, if IMS uses 30% of prime shift, does it recover 30% of the prime shift revenue?

The revenue question is addressed by the installation's billing algorithm. In this chapter, we look at the view from the supplier of services, rather than from the user's view.

The advantages of RMF records. Some information needed for the analysis of the total system performance is available in SMF, but it is difficult to analyze an MVS installation without the use of the Resource Measurement Facility (RMF). RMF is a licensed program product for which an installation must pay a monthly fee to IBM. The information contained in the RMF/SMF records, however, more than justifies its additional cost.

RMF produces its own reports, but their value is far outweighed by the ability to use SAS for exception reporting, trend analysis, and combining RMF records. Before looking at the information in the RMF records, however, the system multiprogramming level should be evaluated.

Evaluation of system multiprogramming level. The job scheduling systems of most third-generation computer installations are, at best, second-generation. Frequently, the major impediment to throughput is a combination of the operation staff's inability to start and stop initiators and an archaic class scheduling scheme. Well-designed scheduling algorithms, which match class and number of initiators, often fail to produce their desired objectives because of manual, untrackable manipulation. SMF does not log initiators' starts and stops in any explicit fashion; therefore, changes in the class structure of the initiators dramatically affect job scheduling.

Calculating the average number of active initiators. The first analysis of system resource consumption determines the average multiprogramming ratio, that is, the average number of active initiators. That average can be found by looking at the data set TYPE535.

Example 5-1 shows an approximation of the average multiprogramming ratio. First, the data set TYPE535 is subsetted into data set JOBS, so that only batch jobs are included. Then, some simple statistics are acquired using PROC MEANS. The ELAPSTM is the number of total initiator seconds. The difference between the minimum and maximum values of the variable JTRMTIME is the duration of the interval in which the sum of elapsed time is accumulated.

Thus, the ratio of the sum of the elapsed time to the duration of the interval is a measure of the average multiprogramming level—that is the average number of active initiators, here equal to 6.1. If the supplier expects ten active initiators from the processor and the workload has not been exceptionally light, he might investigate why only 60% of the possible initiators were used.

Remember that the result is an approximation. The interval is defined by the minimum and the maximum termination times, whereas the elapsed time is defined by the total elapsed time of all batch jobs terminated in that interval. If a long job initiates before the interval begins and terminates during this interval, a significant portion of the job's elapsed time might occur outside the interval. Thus, the average multiprogramming level calculated by this ratio is only an approximation to the actual average MPL. Furthermore, long jobs which initiate in the interval, but do not terminate, contribute to the true MPL but are not reflected in the average calculated in this manner. If the interval spans a typical working day and these effects are balanced, this calculation can be used. It is an excellent indicator in this example, because typically only six batch initiators are active.

```
DATA JOBS;
  SET TYPE535;
  IF JOB_TSO='J';
PROC MEANS N MEAN MIN MAX SUM;
  VAR ELAPSTM JTRMTIME;
```

VARIABLE	N	MEAN	MINIMUM VALUE	MAXIMUM VALUE	SUM
ELAPSTM	549	544.968	0.15	35746.20	299187
JTRMTIME	549	586094511.846	586063131.47	586112201.36	321765887004

$$\text{AVG MPL} = \frac{\text{SUM(ELAPSTM)}}{\text{MAX(JTRMTIME)} - \text{MIN(JTRMTIME)}} = \frac{299187}{49069.89} = 6.1$$

example 5-1

Determining a good number of initiators. Is six a good number of initiators? That depends entirely on the size of the processor and the nature of the batch and non-batch workload. If the processor is a 370/168 with large IMS, TSO, and CICS systems, then 6.1 might be an excellent average multiprogramming level for batch work. However, if it is a 3033 processing batch jobs only, 6.1 is probably not an appropriate number of active initiators.

Plotting the multiprogramming level versus time-of-day. A more informative approach is to plot the multiprogramming level versus time-of-day. Example 5-2 takes data set TYPE535 and subsets it into data set MULTPROG so that only batch jobs are considered. Each batch job is subdivided into one observation for each ten-second interval that the job was active. (A job whose elapsed time was less than ten seconds is discarded.) Then, these observations are sorted by time and counted into data set INTERVAL, which contains the number of active initiators for each ten-second interval.

A ten-second data plot would look very busy, so the FORMAT statement is used to produce data set MINUTE, containing the average number of initiators (AVGINIT) for each minute. The interval in data set MULTPROG could have been set to sixty seconds initially, but jobs under sixty seconds would have been lost. This technique of sampling at ten-second intervals and then averaging adjacent samples appears to give a more accurate representation than taking the average of active initiators, and also results in a significant reduction of the data to be plotted.

```
DATA MULTPROG;
  SET TYPE535;
  IF JOB_TSO='J';
  IF JINITIME=. OR JTRMTIME=. THEN DELETE;
  * SPECIFY INTERVAL IN SECONDS;
  INTERVAL=10;
  IF (JTRMTIME-JINITIME)<INTERVAL THEN DELETE;
  TIME=JINITIME-MOD(JINITIME,INTERVAL);
  OUTPUT;
  LOOP: IF TIME>=JTRMTIME THEN RETURN;
  TIME=TIME+INTERVAL;
  OUTPUT;
  GOTO LOOP;
  FORMAT TIME DATETIME19.2;
  KEEP TIME SYSTEM;
PROC SORT;
  BY SYSTEM TIME;
PROC MEANS NOPRINT;
  BY SYSTEM TIME;
  OUTPUT OUT=INTERVAL N=NRACTIVE;
  VAR TIME;
PROC MEANS NOPRINT;
  BY SYSTEM TIME;
  FORMAT TIME DATETIME13.;
  OUTPUT OUT=MINUTE MEAN=AVGINIT;
  VAR NRACTIVE;
PROC PLOT;
  BY SYSTEM;
  FORMAT TIME DATETIME13.;
  PLOT TIME*AVGINIT/VREVERSE VPOS=144;
  TITLE MULTI-PROGRAMMING LEVEL (AVERAGE OF 10 SECOND SAMPLES);
PROC MEANS DATA=INTERVAL;
  BY SYSTEM;
  VAR NRACTIVE;
PROC FREQ DATA=INTERVAL;
  TABLES NRACTIVE;
  BY SYSTEM;
```

example 5-2

```
           MULTI-PROGRAMMING LEVEL (AVERAGE OF 10 SECOND SAMPLES)

          PLOT OF TIME*AVGINIT     LEGEND: A = 1 OBS, B = 2 OBS, ETC.

            TIME |
 28JUL78:02:26 +
               |      B
               |      K     A         E
               |            C   ABA   J
 28JUL78:03:33 +      GA   H
               |      Q
               |      H       AEA   B
               |              A   LC
 28JUL78:04:40 +              Q
               |              E           E     A       A    A A    BA
               |                      ANA
               |
               |            AP
 28JUL78:05:46 +             C    HKA A
               |            CA   DA AEA
               |          G   AG  B
               |          Q
 28JUL78:06:53 +          D    BDAA C A
               |              A  ACD   EB A
               |                     KA   AB       B
               |              EC BAA   C  A
 28JUL78:08:00 +               C   B        CAB AB     B A
               |                                A   AABDEC
               |          A AAB  D  A   A  AAB   A
               |              ABABBA B  A A  B A A
 28JUL78:09:06 +              CA  BBA A   A   AA A BA
               |        AA      BA  A  AB  AAABA A
               |      AAAA   ACAACB A  A
               |      A   AA BB AC A CAA
 28JUL78:10:13 +    A   C   BE BAA   A
               |      A   BBC AG    A
               |          CA H  AA B     CAAAAA
               |                  A   CC   BAABBA
 28JUL78:11:20 +           AA CAA BBAB       A  A
               |                   C   A   BC  AA  DAA
               |              GA AC   C A
               |                 A  ABAAA A BDAB
 28JUL78:12:26 +     A AB ADA  B   C     AA
               |   AA AA  AAA BABAB          A
               |     A       AA   B     A DA  CB A
               |                     ACGC   AAA
 28JUL78:13:33 +                     AHF A
               |                   B KA A AA
               |                     C   BJB
               |                     FFD
 28JUL78:14:40 +                     DEBAABAA
               |                     A BEFAB
               |                         IBBAB
               |                 FA BBBAAB
 28JUL78:15:46 +                    AIEAA
               |                  ABAFCAAA
               |                  DEBBABA
               |                 A CACGAA
 28JUL78:16:53 +    A    A  AA   A    A  CB
                +-------+-------+-------+-------+-------+-------+
                0       2       4       6       8      10      12

                                AVGINIT
```

example 5-2, continued

Plotting the average number of initiators versus time-of-day. Example 5-2 also plots AVGINIT versus time-of-day. In this installation, the system is reasonably inactive until a brief peak of work around 5 a.m. Then the systems lulls again until around 8 a.m. A buildup occurs until around 10 a.m., when a lull occurs, and a second drop-off occurs around 12:30. The afternoon remains fairly consistent until the 5 p.m. "go home" time. (The 10 a.m. drop-off was later discovered to result from an operator draining active initiators!)

Notice that SAS further compacts the data; the default number of lines produced vertical axis intervals of around 17 minutes.

Example 5-3 extends the analysis to provide statistics on the distribution of the actual number of initiators active during each ten-second interval. Although two intervals had as many as 13 initiators active, 55% of the intervals had six or fewer initiators active. In this case, the average MPL calculated from the elapsed time ratio (6.1) is very close to the true multiprogramming ratio.

In the example, all batch initiators were grouped together. In a more typical analysis, the data might be sorted by class to produce separate plots of the active initiator count by class. This type of information, especially the graph, is very useful in management communications—particularly to operations management, since the operations manager has the most direct control over the multiprogramming level. Shops that permit operators to modify initiators' classes, or to start and stop initiators at their discretion, are rarely able to sustain an actual MPL of more than 75% of the desired average multiprogramming level. Plotting actual multiprogramming level versus time-of-day is most effective in convincing operations management to keep the operators' hands off the initiators.

example 5-3

```
PROC FREQ DATA=INTERVAL;
  TABLES NRACTIVE;
```

MULTI-PROGRAMMING LEVEL (AVERAGE OF 10 SECOND SAMPLES)

NRACTIVE	FREQUENCY	CUM FREQ	PERCENT	CUM PERCENT
1	284	284	5.588	5.588
2	103	387	2.027	7.615
3	465	852	9.150	16.765
4	662	1514	13.026	29.791
5	646	2160	12.712	42.503
6	667	2827	13.125	55.628
7	527	3354	10.370	65.998
8	788	4142	15.506	81.503
9	518	4660	10.193	91.696
10	227	4887	4.467	96.163
11	168	5055	3.306	99.469
12	25	5080	0.492	99.961
13	2	5082	0.039	100.000

```
PROC MEANS DATA=INTERVAL;
```

		MULTI-PROGRAMMING LEVEL (AVERAGE OF 10 SECOND SAMPLES)			
VARIABLE	N	MEAN	STANDARD DEVIATION	MINIMUM VALUE	MAXIMUM VALUE
TIME	5082	586086805.000	14671.006657	586061400.00	586112210.00
NRACTIVE	5082	6.073	2.562763	1.00	13.00

example 5-3, continued

The value of RMF records.   RMF provides extremely accurate and detailed data with essentially no overhead to an MVS installation. Hardware monitor analysis has shown that even when RMF records are written every minute and all are selected that are written with a cycle (sample) time of 1000 milliseconds, RMF uses less than one CPU second per 100 elapsed seconds.

Therefore, given RMF's ability to track the utilization of an installation's computer system, the cost is quite worthwhile, especially since it is seldom necessary to write RMF records with that frequency. An interval of 60 minutes and a cycle time of 1000 milliseconds is adequate for almost every analysis. Writing records with higher frequency is necessary only in detailed benchmarks of hardware and software. Furthermore, it is advantageous to have the RMF records written every hour to permit day-to-day comparisons. Since this is not part of the current version of RMF, either a separate systems task can be written by the installation to start RMF and then restart it on the next hourly interval, or the operator can stop and restart the RMF on the first hour after each IPL.

Analysis of resource consumption.   RMF is without peer for the analysis of resource consumption. Although there are nine different record types written to RMF, only six, those in data sets type 70-75, pertain to the ongoing resource consumption analysis. Because of RMF's interval recording, it is feasible to combine these records and thus combine RMF's different perspective on the overall system performance. For example, the RMF type 70 and 72 records deal with CPU utilization while the RMF type 71 records deal with paging. With the SAS and SAS/RMF data sets described here, it is easy to merge these records into one that can be used to correlate I/O rates, CPU utilization, paging, and so on.

Before discussing the merging of various RMF data sets, however, we can examine the individual data sets from the perspective of overall system performance to gain some possible areas for analysis.

Type 70 RMF records. The TYPE70 data set primarily contains statistics on the total CPU activity. Actually, it contains statistics on the CPU wait state, which are then converted to CPU-active statistics. Numerous verifications conducted with hardware monitors of this wait time measurement have proven it accurate. Although not directly related to system performance, several other interesting facts are carried in the TYPE70 data set, including the CPU serial number, the CPU type, and a variable called SUPATERN, which is a bit map of all selectable units installed in the processor.

The final collection of information in the type 70 RMF record is a series of statistical distributions of the number of tasks in various conditions—the number of batch users, the number of users swapped in memory, the number of users logically ready (MVS/SE), the number of users logically waiting (MVS/SE), the number of users on the outqueue, the number of users who are ready, the number of started tasks active, the number of TSO users logged on, and the number of tasks in a wait state.

Some of these categories overlap and mean little. The number of in-users and ready-users are good indicators of the overall status of the system in terms of workload available. Because of the large volume of data for these distributions, they are not very useful in long-term analysis. They have, however, been useful in gaining additional perspective during peak intervals.

CPU wait time. In any case, the primary value of type 70 records is the CPU wait time (CPUWAITM), which gives the total time during which the processor is in the wait state for each RMF interval. The percentage of CPU activity (PCTCPUBY) is readily available from CPUWAITM and DURATM (duration of RMF interval).

For the first analysis, plot PCTCPUBY versus time-of-day. Any interval with less than 90% CPU warrants further investigation, since this repesents a significant waste of the most expensive resource. Either insufficient work was presented, or the system was under-initiated, or external effects to the operating system (such as high paging wait or reserves), prevented utilization of the processor. A daily plot of PCTCPUBY versus start-time is a good indicator of when problems may have occurred. However, knowing the percentage of CPU activity is only part of the story.

Type 72 RMF records. Of equal importance in analyzing the overall system is determining who uses the processor. Data set TYPE72 provides complete information on the utilization of the CPU by performance group. Under MVS, RMF provides only TCB CPU time, while MVS/SE provides both TCB and SRB CPU time in the type 72 records.

Since type 72 records are written for each period for each performance group for each interval, it is necessary to sum TYPE72 by STARTIME to get the total type 72 CPU time per RMF interval. The difference between the total CPU time recorded in the type 70 (DURTM − CPUWAITM) and the sum of the type 72 CPU times is the processor utilization by the operating system which was not directly attributable to an address space (ASID), plus SRB time if under MVS without SE.

Although it is not correct to attribute all of that difference to operating system overhead, because portions of that time resulted from users' actions, the difference does reflect the overhead operating system functions of the SRM, task dispatching, and so on. A better suggestion would be to sum the TYPE72 data set by performance group. If the installation defines performance groups in a meaningful fashion, an interpretation of the sum of the CPU time for each performance group will permit an accurate description of how much each performance group uses the processor.

It is especially valuable to assign each started task to a different performance group, since SMF does no accounting on started tasks. Using a PROC MEANS by performance group, it is easy to produce a distribution of the previous day's processor utilization when different performance groups are assigned to major subsystems (JES, CICS, IMS) and when TSO and batch users are in different performance groups.

Example 5-4 combines the type 70 and 72 records to produce such a report. Three other statistics carried in type 72 can eliminate the need for merging records in some cases: the number of swap sequences (SWAPSEQ), the number of transactions (TRANS), and the elapsed time of completed transactions (ELAPSTM). The number of swaps is accumulated per interval, per performance group, per period. When other indications point to a high swapping rate, investigation of type 72 points out which performance group is being swapped at a high rate (which may or may not be desirable).

The number of transactions ended in each period is a mild indicator of system performance, although it appears to be related more to the workload than to the system. If the installations's IPS is adequately designed, ELAPSTM can be divided by TRANS (TSO transactions which terminate in the first period, PERIOD=1) to get an average TSO response time for commands at each interval. Care must be taken here, because the SRM defines a transaction in a different manner from most other transaction definitions.

```
PROC SORT DATA=TYPE70 OUT=TYPE70S (KEEP=STARTIME CPUWAITM DURATM PCTCPUBY);
  BY STARTIME;
DATA TYPE72;
  SET TYPE72;
  IF 8<=HOUR(STARTIME)<=15;
  IF PERFGRP=2 OR PERFGRP=23 THEN PERFORM='TSO/TCAM';
  IF PERFGRP=5 THEN PERFORM='BATCH';
  IF PERFGRP=6 OR PERFGRP=8 THEN PERFORM='IMS/CICS';
  IF PERFGRP=20 THEN PERFORM='JES';
  IF PERFORM=' ' THEN PERFORM='MISCL';
PROC SORT DATA=TYPE72;
  BY STARTIME PERFORM;
PROC MEANS NOPRINT;
  BY STARTIME PERFORM;
  OUTPUT OUT=TYPE72S SUM=CPUTCBTM CPUSRBTM;
  VAR CPUTCBTM CPUSRBTM;
PROC MEANS NOPRINT;
  BY STARTIME;
```
                                                            example 5-4

```
  OUTPUT OUT=TYPE72T SUM=CPU72TTM CPU72STM;
  VAR CPUTCBTM CPUSRBTM;
DATA CPUUSAGE;
  MERGE TYPE70S TYPE72T TYPE72S (IN=INS);
  BY STARTIME;
  IF INS;
  CPUACTIV=DURATM-CPUWAITM;
  CPUIN72=SUM(CPU72TTM,CPU72STM);
  PCTOVHD=100*(CPUACTIV-CPUIN72)/DURATM;
  PCTGROUP=100*SUM(CPUCBTM,CPUSRBTM)/DURATM;
  TIME=STARTIME; DURAT=DURATM;
  IF FIRST.STARTIME THEN GOTO OUTPUT;
  CPUACTIV=.; PCTCPUBY=.; PCTOVHD=.; TIME=.; DURAT=.;
  OUTPUT: OUTPUT;
  KEEP PERFORM PCTGROUP CPUACTIV PCTCPUBY PCTOVHD TIME DURAT;
  FORMAT CPUACTIV HHMM5. PCTGROUP PCTCPUBY PCTOVHD 5.1
     TIME DATETIME13. DURAT HHMM5.;
PROC PRINT;
  ID TIME;
  VAR PERFORM PCTGROUP DURAT CPUACTIV PCTCPUBY PCTOVHD;
  TITLE DISTRIBUTION OF PRIME SHIFT CPU USAGE BY PERFORMANCE GROUP;
  TITLE2 PERCENTAGES ARE RELATIVE TO ELAPSED TIME;
```

```
            DISTRIBUTION OF PRIME SHIFT CPU USAGE BY PERFORMANCE GROUP
                   PERCENTAGES ARE RELATIVE TO ELAPSED TIME
```

TIME	PERFORM	PCTGROUP	DURAT	CPUACTIV	PCTCPUBY	PCTOVHD
04AUG78:08:00	BATCH	16.1	1:00	0:50	84.2	28.2
	IMS/CICS	6.1				
	JES	21.1				
	MISCL	2.1				
	TSO/TCAM	10.5				
04AUG78:09:00	BATCH	29.0	1:00	0:58	97.6	33.0
	IMS/CICS	7.8				
	JES	15.9				
	MISCL	1.6				
	TSO/TCAM	10.4				
04AUG78:10:00	BATCH	30.1	0:59	0:57	95.1	30.8
	IMS/CICS	8.8				
	JES	14.5				
	MISCL	1.3				
	TSO/TCAM	9.6				
04AUG78:11:00	BATCH	28.4	1:00	0:58	96.7	31.0
	IMS/CICS	8.8				
	JES	17.8				
	MISCL	1.8				
	TSO/TCAM	8.9				
04AUG78:12:00	BATCH	22.5	0:59	0:55	91.8	34.0
	IMS/CICS	7.2				
	JES	16.4				
	MISCL	2.3				
	TSO/TCAM	9.4				
04AUG78:13:00	BATCH	17.8	1:00	0:52	87.4	32.1
	IMS/CICS	6.5				
	JES	18.1				
	MISCL	1.0				
	TSO/TCAM	12.0				
04AUG78:14:00	BATCH	27.1	1:00	0:58	97.5	32.7
	IMS/CICS	6.6				
	JES	16.9				
	MISCL	1.2				
	TSO/TCAM	13.0				
04AUG78:15:00	BATCH	26.3	0:59	0:54	91.1	30.7
	IMC/CICS	5.0				
	JES	15.8				
	MISCL	3.1				
	TSO/TCAM	10.3				

example 5-4, continued

Example 5-5 shows how to calculate and report the average TSO response in this manner. (The details of an SRM transaction are contained in a footnote in the *MVS Tuning and Installation Guide,* but the main point is that whenever a TSO user goes into a wait state for output buffer, a new transaction is counted.)

Type 72 RMF records, which contain only the CPU service units, do not provide sufficient information to recover the CPU time for each performance group. The type 70 record, which contains the CPU identification, is also captured because it is necessary to know the processor type (168, 3033, etc.) to apply the correct conversion factor, so that CPU times can be calculated from CPU service units. The RMF record writing sequence always writes a type 70 as the first record in each interval.

```
DATA TSORESP;
  SET TYPE72;
  IF 8<= HOUR(STARTIME) <= 15;
  IF PERFGRP=2 AND PERIOD=1;
  AVGRESP=ELAPSTM/TRANS;
  KEEP AVGRESP TRANS STARTIME;
  FORMAT STARTIME DATETIME13. AVGRESP 5.2;
PROC PRINT;
  ID STARTIME;
  VAR AVGRESP TRANS;
  TITLE PRIME SHIFT TSO AVERAGE (RMF CALCULATED) RESPONSE TIME;
```

PRIME SHIFT TSO AVERAGE (RMF CALCULATED) RESPONSE TIME

STARTIME	AVGRESP	TRANS
04AUG78:08:00	1.52	1451
04AUG78:09:00	2.88	1660
04AUG78:10:00	1.51	1814
04AUG78:11:00	1.45	1132
04AUG78:12:00	1.38	973
04AUG78:13:00	1.54	1730
04AUG78:14:00	3.00	1823
04AUG78:15:00	1.69	1259

example 5-5

Type 71.   Type 71 is nearly as complex as the SRM itself. Most measurables about the SRM are contained or implied in type 71. An entire printing of the type 71 record is useful in identifying the sources of problems such as unmet service objectives, low multiprogramming level, or low CPU activity during certain intervals. If workload elongation is suspect, the number of swaps is a good place to start, as is paging rate if low CPU is the problem. Fixed frame counts often cause problems, and although frame counts cannot be directly related to the owning task through RMF here, an RMF Monitor II session could be invoked (having used type 71 to identify the time of day when the problem is most severe). The Monitor II output could supply the probable cause. This is only one path that could be followed in a simple comparison of two intervals—one with good service, the other with poor service.

Type 75. Type 75 records describe the page data sets and swap data sets in use. The most significant value of type 75 is that the type of page/swap data set and its physical address (UNITADR) are listed. The percentage that the data set is busy (DSBUSY) is a significant indicator and should be compared with device busy from type 74. The DSBUSY in type 75 is the auxiliary storage manager's view of the page data set's percent-busy, whereas the type 74 is the IOS's view of the device's percent-busy. A significant discrepancy between the type 74 and 75 records suggests either multi-system usage of the volume on which the page data set is used, or the possibility of incorrectly-set parameters (ASMQLO and ASMQHI) in the SRM, which causes the ASM to schedule I/O inefficiently.

MVS/SE now includes SIO counts and the number of pages transferred for each interval in its type 75 records. Both counts appear to be good indicators of page activity and permit calculations of the average number of pages per start I/O.

Using TYPE434 with type 71 and 75 records. Type 71 and 75 records deal with total system paging and swapping. Page rates and swap counts are provided for most paging from any area. However, no information in type 71 and 75 directly attributes paging to specific tasks. The TYPE434 data set must be used to determine the source of the paging. Whether the task being paged is a batch job or TSO session, its paging activity will be contained in the TYPE434 data set.

Type 73. Type 73 records, dealing with channel percent-busy, are not as clearly related to overall system performance, but are useful in evaluating whether or not the I/O itself is a source of performance problems. Although RMF writes a single type 73 record containing both physical and logical channel information, the record is split into two SAS data sets, TYPE73P (dealing with physical channels), and TYPE73L (dealing with logical channels). In TYPE73P, the most useful variables are the start I/O count (SIO-COUNT) and the percentage of the interval in which the physical channel is busy (PCHANBY). However, physical channel percent-busy indicates little. Utilization has historically been measured only because no better measure was available. At most, high utilizations imply delays to other requests.

TYPE73L, the logical channel statistics record in which the number of deferred I/O requests is available, provides a better measure. The percentage of deferred I/O requests (PCTDEFER) is a clear indicator of overloaded channels. Since utilization values can only imply deferred requests, and since actual deferred requests counts are available, use the actual indicator to balance I/O channels and devices.

Size of the queue. As valuable as deferred request counts is the size of the queue. Variables QUEUE0-QUEUE4 provide statistics on the percentage of the interval in which none, one, two, three, four, or more requests queued. The closer QUEUE0 is to 100%, the less conflict there is on the channel.

Low values of QUEUE0 and corresponding high values of QUEUE1-4 indicate the occurrence of I/O bottlenecks. Type 73 can isolate the bottlenecks to the logical channel.

Type 74.   Now, it is up to type 74 to identify the device(s) responsible. Type 74 identifies the logical channel to which each device is connected, and gives similar statistics concerning the percentage of requests deferred and the number of requests queued for each individual device. In general, it is an easy task to observe a period of high conflict in TYPE73L and to use type 74 to identify the device(s) primarily involved in delayed I/O.

It is difficult to provide any stable guidelines for the analysis of I/O because of the diverse applications, goals, and purposes of installations. However, the complete information in RMF 73 and 74 records permits a good analysis of which device is causing significant I/O delays. At that point, data set usage can be identified through SAS data set TYPE1415 and the data base analysis described in the next chapter, or, less optimally, GTF analysis (perhaps using the IBM GTF seek analysis program) may be used to determine data set placement on the volumes causing delays.

Data Base Analysis and Audit

Combining information with __DBANAL. SMF provides comprehensive information on data set placement, usage, and audit trails. The SAS TYPE1415 data set contains most of the information of interest. However, to properly analyze the usage of data sets, it is necessary to combine the information in TYPE1415 and TYPE535 data sets. The macro __DBANAL contains the necessary SAS code to join these records and build a SAS data set named DATABASE. This combination shows which job used which program in TYPE434, and which account number in TYPE535 used the data set described in TYPE1415.

Three structural designs make the combination difficult. First, multiple type 14 or 15 records can be written for the same data set in the same step, because a 14 or 15 record is written each time a file is closed. Second, there is no step number in type 14 or 15 records. Thus, the use of the same file and data set names in two different steps cannot be differentiated from the same file in one step. Finally, the EXCP count in each individual type 14 or 15 record cannot be trusted, because the EXCP count to a file occurs only in the last close for that file for that step.

How __DBANAL solves combination problems. These problems are resolved in __DBANAL, which first sorts each of the three input data sets, TYPE1415, TYPE434, and TYPE535. All records for a job are sorted together by the time of the event. Data set ADDPROG is built by interleaving these data sets by the SMF time, permitting a step number (STEP) to be constructed for each of the observations in TYPE1415. During this interleave, several variables from the step records—PROGRAM, ABEND, CONCODE, and STEPNAME—are added to the type 14 or 15 information, while at the same time, the first two account fields are acquired from the job records.

Data set ADDPROG is then re-sorted within the job by STEP, the DDname (DDN), the unit address (UNITADR), and the SMF time. The logic then "unaccumulates" the accumulated EXCPs to produce entries in data set SUBEXCP, which has correct EXCPs for each individual OPEN of each file. After SUBEXCP has been sorted, the data set DATABASE is built; variables EXCP and BLKCNTS are accumulated to produce one observation with the total EXCPs for each type of OPEN for each file, and the data set and volume serial used in each job. This data set, DATABASE, can now be helpful in the analysis of data set usage.

Identifying users of I/O resources. An unlimited number of analyses may be performed against DATABASE. DATABASE is useful for identifying exceptionally light and heavy users of I/O resources. The output, resulting from a **PROC MEANS** of **DATABASE**, is shown in example 6-1. By scanning the minimum or maximum values of selected variables, you can obtain a profile of I/O usage at your installation and then decide if the values are reasonable or unreasonable.

For example, notice that the maximum value of NROPENs (the number of times a file was opened in the same step) is 572. Although multiple OPENs are sometimes necessary, 572 OPENs in the same step indicate poor programming. By selecting records with NROPENs greater than 500 from **DATABASE**, programs using I/O inefficiently could be identified.

```
PROC MEANS N MEAN MIN MAX SUM;
```

OVERALL STATISTICS ON DATABASE ANALYSIS

VARIABLE	N	MEAN	MINIMUM VALUE	MAXIMUM VALUE	SUM
RECIND	11299	37.19055	0.00000000	112.00	420216.0
NUCB	11299	1.21860	1.00000000	11.00	13769.0
TIOESTTA	11299	1.68103	1.00000000	17.00	18994.0
TIOEWTCT	11299	1.00690	1.00000000	3.00	11377.0
TIOELINK	11299	30.64342	0.00000000	128.00	346240.0
TIOESTTC	11299	0.00000	0.00000000	0.00	0.0
BUFNO	11299	0.00000	0.00000000	0.00	0.0
MSSCVOLI	11299	0.00000	0.00000000	0.00	0.0
VOLSEQ	11299	0.00292	0.00000000	4.00	33.0
JFCBUFNO	11299	0.49553	0.00000000	32.00	5599.0
BUFTEK	11299	9.23480	0.00000000	98.00	104344.0
BUFFLEN	11299	361.43402	0.00000000	12960.00	4083843.0
JFCBOPCD	11299	13.81069	0.00000000	219.00	156047.0
BLKSIZE	11299	5265.12497	0.00000000	32760.00	59490647.0
LRECL	11299	841.05301	0.00000000	32768.00	9503058.0
NRVOLS	11299	1.01097	1.00000000	5.00	11423.0
JFCFLGSI	11299	126.53297	0.00000000	160.00	1429696.0
AVGBLK	11299	495.51748	0.00000000	19069.00	5598852.0
DCBOFLGS	11299	55.03151	19.00000000	159.00	621801.0
DCBOPTCD	11299	3.47482	0.00000000	219.00	39262.0
DEBOFLGS	11299	131.34038	0.00000000	255.00	1484015.0
DEBOPATB	11299	10.65953	0.00000000	255.00	120442.0
DEBVLSEQ	11299	1282.17639	0.00000000	65416.00	14487311.0
FILESEQ	802	1.38653	1.00000000	10.00	1112.0
TRTCH	802	0.00000	0.00000000	0.00	0.0
DEN	802	5993.51621	200.00000000	6250.00	4806800.0
KEYLEN	10497	0.66114	0.00000000	58.00	6940.0
PRIALOC	10497	61.16519	0.00000000	6000.00	642051.0
JFCBCTRI	10497	130.37744	0.00000000	201.00	1368572.0
SECALOC	10497	1192.83748	0.00000000	25688.00	12521215.0
TTRN	10497	2788074.85567	0.00000000	3777429504.00	29266421760.0
TRKREL	10497	2.01943	0.00000000	1470.00	21198.0
EXTREL	10497	0.00171	0.00000000	15.00	18.0
CRDATE	11299	74837.06178	0.00000000	78203.00	845583961.0
EXPDT	11299	3344.67298	0.00000000	99366.00	37791460.0
LIMCT	983	100.49339	0.00000000	19254.00	98785.0
UCBSTAB	11299	13.40933	8.00000000	80.00	151512.0
NEXTENT	11299	1.92619	0.00000000	16.00	21764.0
UNITADR	11299	744.49075	512.00000000	1663.00	8412001.0
DSSEQCNT	802	1.38529	0.00000000	10.00	1111.0
DSSEQNR	802	1.38529	0.00000000	10.00	1111.0
TRKSALOC	10497	364.81433	0.00000000	16650.00	3829456.0
NRLEVELS	598	0.90301	0.00000000	1.00	540.0
EXCPOFLO	598	12.09030	0.00000000	447.00	7230.0
RECPRIME	598	62519.76087	2.00000000	2784179.00	37386817.0
TRKSLEFT	598	33.59197	0.00000000	298.00	20088.0

example 6-1

RECOFLOW	598	88.85452	0.00000000	2093.00	53135.0
CYLOFULL	598	0.08027	0.00000000	2.00	48.0
EXTINDEX	598	0.35284	0.00000000	1.00	211.0
EXTPRIME	598	1.33445	1.00000000	2.00	798.0
EXTOFLO	598	0.19732	0.00000000	1.00	118.0
CYLINDEX	598	0.42809	0.00000000	10.00	256.0
CYLPRIME	598	20.09365	1.00000000	420.00	12016.0
CYLOFLO	598	0.61538	0.00000000	10.00	368.0
STEP	9910	4.73986	1.00000000	60.00	46972.0
CONDCODE	9910	57.32886	0.00000000	8264.00	568129.0
NROPENS	11299	1.96557	1.00000000	572.00	22209.0
EXCPS	11299	399.43075	0.00000000	155330.00	4513168.0
BLKCNTS	11299	102.85485	0.00000000	44253.00	1162157.0

example 6-1, continued

Increasing the block size.   In any installation, the most significant performance improvements will be achieved by increasing the block size to reduce the I/O. This reduces the elapsed time, the number of passes through IOS, the EXCP count, and the CPU time of a task. You can use DATABASE to identify those data sets and programs using unblocked I/O.

Example 6-2 shows how to trace unblocked I/O through a simple crosstabulation of record format (RECFM) and data set organization (DSORG) weighted by the number of EXCPs. The output shows not only the breakdown of the unblocked files, but also the kind of data sets and record formats in use at this installation.

PROC FREQ with weighting is helpful in initial data surveys. Column percentages show that 61.6% of this installation's I/O is physical sequential. Over 20% of all EXCPs—921,648—are counted by fixed record format against physical sequential data sets (which, in most cases, should be fixed-blocked). One crosstabulation has identified 20% of the EXCPs needing improvement!

```
PROC FREQ;
  TABLES RECFM*DSORG;
  WEIGHT EXCPS;
```

example 6-2

```
                         TABLE OF RECFM BY DSORG

     RECFM              DSORG

     FREQUENCY |
     PERCENT   |
     ROW PCT   |
     COL PCT  |DA       |IS       |PO       |PS       |    TOTAL
     ---------+---------+---------+---------+---------+
     F        | 158214  | 111610  |  13467  | 921648  |1204939
              |   3.51  |   2.47  |   0.30  |  20.42  |  26.70
              |  13.13  |   9.26  |   1.12  |  76.49  |
              |  38.17  |  11.98  |   3.51  |  33.11  |
     ---------+---------+---------+---------+---------+ --------+
     FB       |     32  | 819758  |  32267  |1025870  |1877927
              |   0.00  |  18.16  |   0.71  |  22.73  |  41.61
              |   0.00  |  43.65  |   1.72  |  54.63  |
              |   0.01  |  88.02  |   8.42  |  36.85  |
     ---------+---------+---------+---------+---------+
     U        |  99048  |      0  | 336540  | 480850  | 916438
              |   2.19  |   0.00  |   7.46  |  10.65  |  20.31
              |  10.81  |   0.00  |  36.72  |  52.47  |
              |  23.89  |   0.00  |  87.81  |  17.27  |
     ---------+---------+---------+---------+---------+
     V        |      0  |      0  |      0  |  10816  |  10816
              |   0.00  |   0.00  |   0.00  |   0.24  |   0.24
              |   0.00  |   0.00  |   0.00  | 100.00  |
              |   0.00  |   0.00  |   0.00  |   0.39  |
     ---------+---------+---------+---------+---------+
     VB       | 157235  |      0  |    996  | 157004  | 315235
              |   3.48  |   0.00  |   0.02  |   3.48  |   6.98
              |  49.88  |   0.00  |   0.32  |  49.81  |
              |  37.93  |   0.00  |   0.26  |   5.64  |
     ---------+---------+---------+---------+---------+
     VBS      |      0  |      0  |      0  | 176097  | 176097
              |   0.00  |   0.00  |   0.00  |   3.90  |   3.90
              |   0.00  |   0.00  |   0.00  | 100.00  |
              |   0.00  |   0.00  |   0.00  |   6.33  |
     ---------+---------+---------+---------+---------+
     VS       |      0  |      0  |      0  |  11716  |  11716
              |   0.00  |   0.00  |   0.00  |   0.26  |   0.26
              |   0.00  |   0.00  |   0.00  | 100.00  |
              |   0.00  |   0.00  |   0.00  |   0.42  |
     ---------+---------+---------+---------+---------+
     TOTAL      414529    931368    383270   2784001  4513168
                  9.18     20.64      8.49     61.69   100.00
```

example 6-2, continued

Why is so much I/O done with RECFM=F at physical sequential? Although other record types could be used, example 6-3 follows the fixed physical sequential data usage to find the answer. Here, DATABASE is subsetted for only those observations which are physical sequential files with RECFM=F. Perhaps a program specifying fixed-record format is poorly written, so a frequency tabulation of program names that could be causing the problem is produced. (The 5405 EXCPs with no program names are from TYPE1415 observations which did not match up with TYPE434, because the step was still active when SMF was dumped.) The program EASYTREV stands out because it produced over 33% of the total I/O.

```
DATA;
  SET DATABASE;
  IF DSORG='PS' AND RECFM='F';
PROC FREQ;
  TABLES PROGRAM;
  WEIGHT EXCPS;
```

example 6-3

PROGRAM	FREQUENCY	CUM FREQ	PERCENT	CUM PERCENT
	5405	.	.	.
CLEARS2K	366	366	0.040	0.040
CPXUPTSM	68	434	0.007	0.047
CSCBDB01	7	441	0.001	0.048
DFSRRC00	212	653	0.023	0.071
DGFP2C02	2	655	0.000	0.071
DGIS2C03	10	665	0.001	0.073
DGIS2C07	9600	10265	1.048	1.120
DGIS2C17	9000	19265	0.982	2.103
EARCSC75	1368	20633	0.149	2.252
EASYTREV	308342	328975	33.653	35.905
FSPSCOMP	893	329868	0.097	36.002
FSPSREPL	8	329876	0.001	36.003
FSSM3100	16	329892	0.002	36.005
HEWL	5735	335627	0.626	36.631
HMPGA112	754	336381	0.082	36.713
HSPGA112	259	336640	0.028	36.741
HWFA0C10	12900	465640	14.079	50.821
IBISCON	3	465643	0.000	50.821
IEBGENER	6114	471757	0.667	51.488
IEHLIST	22364	494121	2.441	53.929
IEV90	158	494279	0.017	53.946
IEWL	3325	497604	0.363	54.309
IKFCBL00	9608	507212	1.049	55.358
IKJEFT01	46647	553859	5.091	60.449
INIT3350	34501	588360	3.765	64.214
MFEDIT1	430	588790	0.047	64.261
NITAWL	500	589290	0.055	64.316
OPSSMF	5	589295	0.001	64.316
PCOMPMP	304	589599	0.033	64.350
PRCOMC	15208	604807	1.660	66.009
RAIL1390	1507	606314	0.164	66.174
SIMIFSS	40417	646731	4.411	70.585
SYS2K	31	646762	0.003	70.588
S2000	183	646945	0.020	70.608
TCRCREAT	372	647317	0.041	70.649
TMSDATA	150505	797822	16.426	87.075
TP2000	2884	800706	0.315	87.390
UPDTWR	13	800719	0.001	87.392
VMSEDIT	115524	916243	12.608	100.000

example 6-3, continued

Example 6-4 shows three different tabulations, weighted by EXCPs, of those DATABASE observations which executed EASYTREV. The file name (DDname) tabulation shows that all are user-specified file names rather than files created internally by EASYTREV. From the examination of data set names, it is found that most of the unblocked I/O by EASYTREV went to temporary data sets.

From a look at the jobs using EASYTREV, the problem finally becomes clear. One job, DRUGNOL, accounts for 71% of the fixed EXCPs. This data, combined with the preceding information, shows that one user of EASYTREV is creating user-specified temporary files, which are physical sequential and RECFM=F. The user probably is not aware of the impact of such a specification.

```
DATA;
  SET DATABASE;
  IF PROGRAM='EASYTREV';
PROC FREQ;
  TABLES DDN DSNAME JOB;
  WEIGHT EXCPS;
```

example 6-4

DDN	FREQUENCY	CUM FREQ	PERCENT	CUM PERCENT
FILEA	95226	95226	30.883	30.883
FILEB	213083	308309	69.106	99.989
FILE2	33	308342	0.011	100.000

DSNAME	FREQUENCY	CUM FREQ	PERCENT	CUM PERCENT
CPM.A3E500.SUNMA	88508	88508	28.704	28.704
SYS78203.T063055	177015	265523	57.409	86.113
SYS78203.T084554	19755	285278	6.407	92.520
SYS78203.T093251	19329	304607	6.269	98.789
SYS78203.T100637	3150	307757	1.022	99.810
SYS78203.T122239	206	307963	0.067	99.877
MVTVY03.T124809	206	308169	0.067	99.944
SYS78203.T131639	2	308171	0.001	99.945
CPM.SORT.UPDATE	42	308213	0.014	99.958
CPM.SORTED.ADDS	129	308342	0.042	100.000

JOB	FREQUENCY	CUM FREQ	PERCENT	CUM PERCENT
VECXA71	171	171	0.055	0.055
DRUGNOL	221269	221440	71.761	71.816
C35CA20	86488	307928	28.049	99.866
WKD601F	414	308342	0.134	100.000

example 6-4, continued

Problems with DATABASE analyses.   Except for several SMF anomalies, the preceding discussion and analysis of DATABASE is generally complete. Not all type 14 and 15 records reflect the number of EXCPs issued: EXCP accounting does not occur for many cases when the access method is EXCP (for example, most SORTWORK I/O); EXCPs done by program FETCH from STEPLIBs are not counted; and concatenated partitioned data sets reflect only the name of the first data set in the concatenation list and create only one type 14 or 15 record per open, even though many different data sets may be involved. Although the information received from DATABASE would be correct if non-zero EXCPs occur, there are many occurrences where DATABASE contains an EXCP count of zero when the data set is actually used.

Using type 74 RMF records.   For these reasons, it is sometimes necessary to turn to other sources of data base information. As previously discussed, the type 74 record contains the number of start I/Os issued to each unit address during each RMF interval. Thus, the total I/O counts, even those not recorded in SMF, are available through RMF.

Type 4, 34, and 40 SMF records.   In some cases, it may be necessary to find all tasks which use a specific unit address—for example, in a conversion from 3330 to 3350 disks. DATABASE can provide all tasks which open a data set on the device, but to determine all allocations, you must turn to SMF data for the type 4, 34, and 40 records.

The code which builds TYPE434 and TYPE40 can be easily modified to output an observation for all allocations to a specific device. The OUTPUT statements in the TYPE434 and TYPE40 members must be deleted (fourth line from the bottom of the TYPE434 code; third line from the bottom of the TYPE40 code), and a new line, testing for the desired primary unit address (in this example, address hex 284) must be inserted after line 18500 in the macro __EXCPGET:

IF CHAN=2 AND UADR=8*16+4 THEN OUTPUT;

Printing the resulting TYPE434 and TYPE40 data sets gives all recorded allocations to device 284. If the desired device happens to be a 3330, it is simpler to modify the __MNTABLE macro, which normally identifies mountable 3330 devices, so that the desired device address is treated as the only mountable 3330. Then, TYPE434 and TYPE40 data sets can be built and scanned for any observations with a non-zero value for D3330DRV.

It may not be necessary to look at DATABASE to analyze I/O, since TYPE434 does contain total EXCPs to each device class. In many cases, simply identifying where the I/O comes from, in terms of which job and to which class of device, is sufficient. For example, to get rid of 2314 devices, it is not necessary to know the allocations of 2314 devices, or to build a DATABASE data set. From TYPE434, EXCP2314, and D2314DRV, users who have allocated 2314 devices can be identified.

If possible, the use of __DBANAL should be minimized because of its high expense. It takes approximately four minutes of 168 CPU time to build DATABASE for an eight-hour period on a 168; it is cost-effective to run only once or twice a year against a week's SMF data.

A final example of the value of DATABASE is given in example 6-5, a series of frequency distributions on significant variables, which thoroughly describe the use of the I/O resource in an installation.

```
TITLE OVERALL STATISTICS ON DATABASE ANALYSIS;
PROC FREQ DATA=DATABASE;
   TABLES ALOC;
PROC FREQ DATA=DATABASE;
   TABLES ACCESS DSORG RECFM TEMP OPEN;
   WEIGHT EXCPS;
PROC FREQ DATA=DATABASE;
   TABLES DISP*TEMP  TEMP*OPEN;
   WEIGHT EXCPS;
```

OVERALL STATISTICS ON DATABASE ANALYSIS

ALOC	FREQUENCY	CUM FREQ	PERCENT	CUM PERCENT
	3269	.	.	.
ABSTR	819	819	10.199	10.199
BLOCK	2634	3453	32.802	43.001
CYL	4577	8030	56.999	100.000

example 6-5

```
              OVERALL STATISTICS ON DATABASE ANALYSIS

   ACCESS    FREQUENCY   CUM FREQ    PERCENT   CUM PERCENT

   BDAM        143240      143240      3.174       3.174
   BDSAM        14634      157874      0.324       3.498
   BISAM       181765      339639      4.027       7.526
   BPSAM        89850      429489      1.991       9.516
   BSAM        666994     1096483     14.779      24.295
   EXCP       1009853     2106336     22.376      46.671
   QISAM       749603     2855939     16.609      63.280
   QSAM       1657229     4513168     36.720     100.000
```

```
              OVERALL STATISTICS ON DATABASE ANALYSIS

   DSORG     FREQUENCY   CUM FREQ    PERCENT   CUM PERCENT

   DA         414529      414529      9.185       9.185
   IS         931368     1345897     20.637      29.822
   PO         383270     1729167      8.492      38.314
   PS        2784001     4513168     61.686     100.000
```

```
              OVERALL STATISTICS ON DATABASE ANALYSIS

   RECFM     FREQUENCY   CUM FREQ    PERCENT   CUM PERCENT

   F         1204939     1204939     26.698      26.698
   FB        1877927     3082866     41.610      68.308
   U          916438     3999304     20.306      88.614
   V           10816     4010120      0.240      88.854
   VB         315235     4325355      6.985      95.839
   VBS        176097     4501452      3.902      99.740
   VS          11716     4513168      0.260     100.000

   TEMP      FREQUENCY   CUM FREQ    PERCENT   CUM PERCENT

   PERM      3392791     3392791     75.175      75.175
   TEMP      1120377     4513168     24.825     100.000

   OPEN      FREQUENCY   CUM FREQ    PERCENT   CUM PERCENT

   INOUT      159148      159148      3.526       3.526
   INPUT     2643042     2802190     58.563      62.089
   OTHER      152790     2954980      3.385      65.475
   OUTIN      107990     3062970      2.393      67.867
   OUTPUT    1259718     4322688     27.912      95.779
   UPDATE     190480     4513168      4.221     100.000
```

example 6-5, continued

```
OVERALL STATISTICS ON DATABASE ANALYSIS

           TABLE OF DISP BY TEMP

   DISP           TEMP

   FREQUENCY|
    PERCENT |
    ROW PCT |
    COL PCT |PERM     |TEMP     |  TOTAL
   ---------+---------+---------+
   MOD      |  750681 |  903300 |1653981
            |   16.63 |   20.01 |  36.65
            |   45.39 |   54.61 |
            |   22.13 |   80.62 |
   ---------+---------+---------+
   OLD      |1092240  |  212122 |1304362
            |   24.20 |    4.70 |  28.90
            |   83.74 |   16.26 |
            |   32.19 |   18.93 |
   ---------+---------+---------+
   SHR      |1549870  |    4955 |1554825
            |   34.34 |    0.11 |  34.45
            |   99.68 |    0.32 |
            |   45.68 |    0.44 |
   ---------+---------+---------+
   TOTAL     3392791   1120377  4513168
               75.18     24.82   100.00
```

```
           OVERALL STATISTICS ON DATABASE ANALYSIS

                 TABLE OF TEMP BY OPEN

TEMP          OPEN

FREQUENCY|
 PERCENT |
 ROW PCT |
 COL PCT |INOUT   |INPUT   |OTHER   |OUTIN   |OUTPUT  |UPDATE  |  TOTAL
---------+--------+--------+--------+--------+--------+--------+
PERM     | 144083 |2289135 | 152665 |  35420 | 661247 | 110241 |3392791
         |   3.19 |  50.72 |   3.38 |   0.78 |  14.65 |   2.44 |  75.18
         |   4.25 |  67.47 |   4.50 |   1.04 |  19.49 |   3.25 |
         |  90.53 |  86.61 |  99.92 |  32.80 |  52.49 |  57.88 |
---------+--------+--------+--------+--------+--------+--------+
TEMP     |  15065 | 353907 |    125 |  72570 | 598471 |  80239 |1120377
         |   0.33 |   7.84 |   0.00 |   1.61 |  13.26 |   1.78 |  24.82
         |   1.34 |  31.59 |   0.01 |   6.48 |  53.42 |   7.16 |
         |   9.47 |  13.39 |   0.08 |  67.20 |  47.51 |  42.12 |
---------+--------+--------+--------+--------+--------+--------+
TOTAL      159148  2643042   152790   107990  1259718   190480  4513168
             3.53    58.56     3.39     2.39    27.91     4.22   100.00
```

example 6-5, continued

7
Tape Drive Analysis

Using TYPE21 records to control tape problems. SMF data provides several sources of information concerning tape drives, tape errors, and tape-related job delays. Data set TYPE21, the error-statistics-by-volume (ESV) record, is probably the most valuable information source.

Each time a tape is dismounted, a type 21 record is written. This record describes the volume serial number and the unit address on which the tape was mounted, and provides statistics for different kinds of errors. Since this type 21 record is written for each dismount, it is not obvious whether errors are the result of the tape or the tape drive.

Example 7-1 performs a tabulation of the TYPE21 records, using the code in the member ESV. For each unit address, you can see the statistics for all tapes dismounted. This tabulation (especially PCTMNT, the percentage of mounts with errors) shows which tape drives may need cleaning, although a high error count on a particular drive could result from a defective tape volume.

The second report also provides a detailed listing of each drive and gives the volumes with errors. The third report tabulates those volume serial numbers with permanent I/O errors.

Again, the fact that a volume mounted had a permanent error does not mean that the volume is defective—the permanent error could have been hardware-related. Nevertheless, volumes with high error frequencies or permanent errors should be candidates for physical cleaning, or perhaps certification.

By monitoring the error-statistics-by-volume on a daily basis, the problem of tape errors can be brought under control. Often, most of the volumes involved in tape errors are in a particular series, perhaps a series that is five or six years old, and it may be appropriate to replace those volumes.

On the other hand, installations with poor tape-head cleaning practices have a significant number of errors on all tape drives. Showing management the ESV report, by shift, usually leads to cleaner tape drives and fewer problems.

DATA FOR THIS RUN WAS COLLECTED BETWEEN FOLLOWING DATE/TIMES

SYSTEM	MINTIME	MAXTIME
C168	29JUL78:03:43:05.42	29JUL78:08:31:55.22

TAPE READ/WRITE ERRORS BY CHANNEL, CONTROLLER, AND DRIVE ADDRESS

------------------------------ SYSTEM=C168 ------------------------------

UNIT ADR	NR USER	NS ERR	PCT MNT	SIO COUNT	ERRORS	PCT ERR	TEMP READ	TEMP WRIT	PERM READ	PERM WRIT	NOISE	ERASE CLEAN	SIO HARD
470	5	1	20.0	7108	1	0.0	0	1	0	0	0	1	0
471	8	2	25.0	10329	8	0.1	1	7	0	0	0	7	0
472	3	0	0.0	5766	0	0.0	0	0	0	0	0	0	0
473	7	1	14.3	11776	1	0.0	0	1	0	0	0	1	0
474	8	3	37.5	26850	11	0.0	0	11	0	0	0	11	0
475	4	0	0.0	3342	0	0.0	0	0	0	0	0	0	0
476	5	0	0.0	9084	0	0.0	0	0	0	0	0	0	0
478	4	3	75.0	7466	5	0.1	2	3	0	0	0	3	0
479	6	0	0.0	2211	0	0.0	0	0	0	0	0	0	0
47B	2	0	0.0	230	0	0.0	0	0	0	0	0	0	0
47C	2	0	0.0	622	0	0.0	0	0	0	0	0	0	0
47D	1	0	0.0	284	0	0.0	0	0	0	0	0	0	0
47E	1	0	0.0	214	0	0.0	0	0	0	0	0	0	0
47F	1	0	0.0	30	0	0.0	0	0	0	0	0	0	0
490	1	0	0.0	2	0	0.0	0	0	0	0	0	0	0
491	22	2	9.1	38627	3	0.0	0	2	0	0	0	2	1
492	5	1	20.0	21471	452	2.1	0	255	0	0	0	452	0
493	5	0	0.0	5884	0	0.0	0	0	0	0	0	0	0
494	15	1	6.7	83788	1	0.0	0	1	0	0	0	1	0
495	11	2	18.2	15448	4	0.0	0	4	0	0	0	4	0
496	12	3	25.0	43516	51	0.1	0	4	0	0	0	4	47
497	16	3	18.8	19626	11	0.1	0	7	0	0	0	11	0
498	5	0	0.0	6551	0	0.0	0	0	0	0	0	0	0
49B	5	0	0.0	21332	0	0.0	0	0	0	0	0	0	0
49C	5	0	0.0	21165	0	0.0	0	0	0	0	0	0	0
49D	4	1	25.0	319	1	0.3	0	1	0	0	0	1	0
49E	1	0	0.0	2	0	0.0	0	0	0	0	0	0	0
49F	3	0	0.0	16649	0	0.0	0	0	0	0	0	0	0
670	2	0	0.0	533	0	0.0	0	0	0	0	0	0	0
671	13	3	23.1	9390	14	0.1	3	1	0	0	0	1	11
672	4	0	0.0	1320	0	0.0	0	0	0	0	0	0	0
673	3	0	0.0	2823	0	0.0	0	0	0	0	0	0	0
674	7	3	42.9	47928	5	0.0	0	5	0	0	0	5	0
675	5	2	40.0	14610	8	0.1	6	2	0	0	0	2	0
676	6	0	0.0	5746	0	0.0	0	0	0	0	0	0	0
678	1	0	0.0	21	0	0.0	0	0	0	0	0	0	0
679	1	0	0.0	5368	0	0.0	0	0	0	0	0	0	0
67A	2	1	50.0	342	1	0.3	0	1	0	0	0	1	0
67C	4	1	25.0	2071	2	0.1	0	2	0	0	0	2	0

example 7-1

UNIT ADDRESS STATISTICS WITH ALL ERROR VOLUMES LISTED BY VOLSER

---------------------- SYSTEM=C168   UNITADR=492 ----------------------

VOLSER	NRUSE	NRUSER	PCTMNT	SIOCOUNT	ERRORS	PCTERR	TEMPREAD	TEMPWRIT	PERMREAD	PERMWRIT	NOISE	ERASE	CLEAN	SIOHARD
234928	1	1	100.0	359	2	0.3	0	0	2	0	0	0	2	0
238578	1	1	100.0	3306	452	0.0	0	0	255	0	0	0	452	0

UNIT ADDRESS STATISTICS WITH ALL ERROR VOLUMES LISTED BY VOLSER

---------------------- SYSTEM=C168   UNITADR=494 ----------------------

VOLSER	NRUSE	NRUSER	PCTMNT	SIOCOUNT	ERRORS	PCTERR	TEMPREAD	TEMPWRIT	PERMREAD	PERMWRIT	NOISE	ERASE	CLEAN	SIOHARD
238598	1	1	100.0	1727	1	0.1	0	0	1	0	0	0	1	0

UNIT ADDRESS STATISTICS WITH ALL ERROR VOLUMES LISTED BY VOLSER

---------------------- SYSTEM=C168   UNITADR=495 ----------------------

VOLSER	NRUSE	NRUSER	PCTMNT	SIOCOUNT	ERRORS	PCTERR	TEMPREAD	TEMPWRIT	PERMREAD	PERMWRIT	NOISE	ERASE	CLEAN	SIOHARD
197553	1	1	100.0	5368	1	0.0	0	0	1	0	0	0	1	0
214091	1	1	100.0	1541	3	0.1	0	0	3	0	0	0	3	0
218586	1	1	100.0	2529	1	0.0	1	1	0	0	0	0	0	0
240824	1	1	100.0	168	1	0.6	0	0	1	0	0	0	1	0

example 7-1, continued

```
VOLSERS WITH HIGH NUMBER OF USES WITH ERRORS OR HIGH ERRORS

------------------------------ SYSTEM=C168 ------------------------------

              N            S              T    T  P  P               S
              R            I              E    E  E  E               I
      V       U      P     O       E   P  M    E  E  E               O
      O   N   S      C     C       R   C  R    M  R  R         E  C  H
      L   R   E      T     O       R   T  P    P  M  M  N      R  L  A
      S   U   E      M     U       O   E  R    W  E  R  O      R  E  R
      E   S   R      N     N       R   R  E    R  E  I  I      O  A  D
      R   E   R      T     T       S   R  A    I  A  S  S      R  N
                                       D  T    T  D  T  E      R

   208211  3  3  100.0  3692   65   1.8  1    7  0  0  0    7  58
   238578  1  1  100.0  3306  452  13.7  0  255  0  0  0  452   0
   239176  2  1   50.0   525    8   1.5  0    4  0  0  0    8   0
```

example 7-1, continued

Tape drive utilization.   How many tape drives are needed? What impact do tape drives have on work scheduling? The following discussion deals specifically with tape drive utilization in a JES2 environment. (In JES3 with pre-execution volume fetch, the analysis is slightly more difficult, but the data in the type 25 records is adequate to permit a similar approach.)

Since tape drives are allocated at the step basis in JES2, the step records provide most of the information concerning tape drive utilizaton.

Using type 10 records to measure delays.   As previously discussed, utilization is only part of the story; also interesting are delays resulting from nonavailability of tape drives. The type 10 allocation recovery record is a good measure of delays, as well as a good indicator of how often a job step is delayed for a tape drive allocation.

Unfortunately, the type 10 allocation recovery record is not always written. When an allocation recovery event occurs, the operator can make three possible responses:

1   the job raising the allocation recovery can be canceled

2   the job can be placed in WAIT (with or without holding other devices already allocated

3   the operator can respond with a unit address that is currently off-line, and thus satisfy the allocation by giving the job step that currently off-line device.

A type 10 SMF record is written only in situation 3. Thus, in many installations where all tape drives are currently on-line, the strategy for any allocation recovery is to reply WAIT with NOHOLD. In that case, the job step does wait until sufficient devices become available as a result of other step terminations, but no type 10 allocation recovery record is written. Thus, the usefulness of the allocation recovery message for the analysis of recoveries depends on the operator's response to the allocation recovery event.

Using ALOCTM to analyze delays.   All is not lost, however, because the job step that does enter allocation recovery does so at the time stamp ALOC-TIME. All allocations for that step are completed at LOADTIME. By looking at ALOCTM in data set TYPE434, which is the difference between LOAD-TIME and ALOCTIME, those job steps which had an allocation recovery can be detected.

It is sometimes possible for ALOCTM to be significant and yet not be the result of an allocation recovery. If the processor is placed in STOP while the step is in allocation, or if a RESERVE conflict prevents the operating system from responding to the allocation, the allocation can imply an allocation recovery when one did not actually occur. Knowing the nature of delays in an installation should permit an intelligent analysis of ALOCTM.

Using TYPE434 records to analyze delays.   Assuming the preceding types of system-wide delays are few in number, ALOCTM can be used as a good indicator of probable allocation delays.

An allocation time greater than five seconds per DD is excessive. (The mean allocation time is about 500 milliseconds per DD with a standard deviation of 1000 milliseconds.) Since NUMDD exists in TYPE434, it is easy to flag each step with an ALOCTM greater than five seconds per DD, and to calculate a variable, delay time (DELAYTM, equal to ALOCTM for those delayed steps.

Example 7-2 shows how simply delays caused by tape drive allocation can be observed. By selecting TYPE434 records for jobs that allocated tape drives, and by calculating DELAYTM for those steps that were delayed, the PROC MEANS output shows that for all steps which used tape drives, the total step elapsed time was 3,219,724 seconds; the total delay time for the 262 delayed steps (ALOCTM greater than five seconds per DD) was only 85,432 seconds. Thus, less than three percent of the total initiated time of all steps using tape drives was spent awaiting tape drive allocation. That is a reasonably small percentage for most cases.

```
DATA DELAYS;
   SET TYPE434;
   IF TAPEDRVS > 0;
   IF ALOCTM > 5*NUMDD THEN GOTO DELAY;
   RETURN;
   DELAY:
      DELAYTM=ALOCTM;
   KEEP NUMDD EXECTM SELAPTM TAPEDRVS ALOCTIME ALOCTM DELAYTM;
PROC MEANS;
   TITLE STATISTICS ON ALLOCATION DELAYS;
PROC PLOT;
   PLOT DELAYTM*ALOCTIME;
```

example 7-2

STATISTICS ON ALLOCATION DELAYS

VARIABLE	N	MEAN	MINIMUM VALUE	MAXIMUM VALUE	SUM
NUMDD	8231	12.537	0.00	179.00	1.031940E+05
EXECUTM	8231	374.177	0.05	58577.02	3.079852E+06
SELAPSTM	8231	391.170	0.09	58657.60	3.219724E+06
TAPEDRVS	8231	0.459	0.00	9.00	3.778000E+03
ALOCTIME	8231	586087818.733	584983231.58	586147534.23	4.824089E+12
ALOCTM	8231	15.932	0.01	3823.55	1.311327E+05
DELAYTM	262	326.078	0.01	3823.55	8.543236E+04

example 7-2, continued

The graph in example 7-3 may be even more informative. The plot of the delay time versus time-of-day shows that somewhere around midday on July 28, an event occurred which caused a series of job steps to be delayed much longer than at any other time during the day. Investigating SYSLOG showed that an operator had varied a bank of ten tape drives off-line, which was not discovered for nearly an hour!

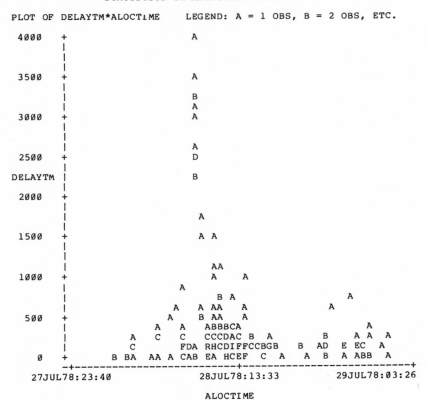

example 7-3

The percentage of initiator time acceptable as delayed time is very much a condition of the nature of the installation's service objectives and of the workload. For example, had this long delay occurred during non-prime hours, it probably would not have been a real concern, provided that the delayed jobs met their service objectives. But a significant number of delays lasting over an hour during prime shift could indicate that the installation needs more tape drives.

Scheduling conflicts.   On the other hand, the total number of tape drives might be adequate; it may be the work scheduling which causes peak drive usage. In those cases, it is still easy to use TYPE434 data to identify the job steps that were delayed; the job steps that were active during the time of day when jobs were delayed; and the number of tape drives in use by which tasks. A listing of the active jobs and the delayed jobs might well suggest that certain jobs could be moved to a different time of day to reduce conflicts for tape drives.

The tape drive resource is an uncommonly visible one to operations management because many people are involved in mounting tape volumes. It is thus easy to lose perspective and create a major issue concerning the correct number of tape drives. Instead, the preceding approaches provide data by which rational decisions can be made.

Just as operations management often sees tape drives as a limiting resource, printer utilization is of concern because printed output is the final feedback to the user. It is not uncommon to find a $6,000,000 computer not meeting objectives because of insufficient $50,000 printers.

Fallacies of TYPE26 time stamps.   There are several sources of information with regard to printing, some of which can be very deceptive. As described before, the TYPE26J2 and TYPE26J3 data sets (referred to hereafter as TYPE26) contain time stamps for the time that the output processor finished making all output for the job available for printing (JFINTIME), and for the time all printing was completed (JPURTIME). Unfortunately, between JFINTIME and JPURTIME many things occur, including printing. The duration should represent the time in the print queue plus the time to print. However, output may be held (especially output to be viewed by TSO users) at the user's request, causing a very long duration. Thus, it is not correct to take the duration from JFINTIME to JPURTIME as the print queue plus printer elapsed time.

Using TYPES 6 and 26 records to analyze printer delays.   The best approximation for analyzing printer delays requires merging the TYPE6 and TYPE26 data sets as shown in example 8-1. PRINTIME is the time in TYPE6 at which each file actually begins to print. The selection must eliminate TSO sessions for two reasons:

- much of the TSO SYSOUT printing is done while the session is still in execution (prior to JFINTIME)
- the print queue time is not measurable (at least not without significant labor and gross assumptions), because it would require matching the time of the TYPE40 record, which freed the file, with the TYPE6 record, which indicates that the file was actually printed.

```
PROC SORT DATA=TYPE6;
  BY READTIME JOB;
PROC SORT DATA=TYPE26J2;
  BY READTIME JOB;
PROC MEANS DATA=TYPE6 NOPRINT;
  BY READTIME JOB;
  OUTPUT OUT=PRINTGOT SUM=NRLINES MIN=PRINTIME;
  VAR NRLINES PRINTIME;
DATA PRINTER;
  MERGE TYPE26J2(IN=INJES) TYPE6(IN=INWTR);
  BY READTIME JOB;
  IF INJES AND INWTR;
  IF JOB_TSO='J';
  QUEPRNT=(PRINTIME-JFINTIME)/60;
  TMEPRNT=(JPURTIME-PRINTIME)/60;
  KEEP NRLINES TMEPRNT QUEPRNT;
PROC CHART;
  HBAR NRLINES QUEPRNT TMEPRNT;
  TITLE DISTRIBUTION OF CALCULATED PRINT QUEUE AND PRINT EXECUTION TIMES;
```

example 8-1

The estimated time in the printer queue (QUEPRNT) and the estimated time to print (TMEPRNT) are easily calculated, and **PROC CHART** is then used to produce the three frequency distributions, as shown in example 8-2. Even though there are still potential errors in both the queue time and the printing time, these three charts show that the vast majority (75%) of printing is started within two hours (midpoint=60 minutes implies interval lengths of 120 minutes) and that, in this installation, 97% of printing took less than 80 minutes. The third chart shows that 96% of all jobs printed less than 30,000 lines, although at least one job printed over 225,000 lines. The durations here are affected by mounting forms, stopping the printer to replace paper, and so on. It is possible to do a more detailed analysis of the TYPE6 record, but accuracy seldom requires it.

```
         DISTRIBUTION OF CALCULATED PRINT QUEUE AND PRINT EXECUTION TIMES


                                  FREQUENCY BAR CHART
         MIDPOINT

         NRLINES                                    FREQ  CUM.   PERCENT    CUM.
                                                          FREQ              PERCENT


            15000  |***************************  277   277    96.85     96.85
                   |
            45000  |                               1   278     0.35     97.20
                   |
            75000  |                               2   280     0.70     97.90
                   |
           105000  |                               3   283     1.05     98.95
                   |
           135000  |                               2   285     0.70     99.65
                   |
           225000  |                               1   286     0.35    100.00
                   |
                   ----+----+---+----+----+---
                      50   100  150  200  250

                   FREQUENCY
```

example 8-2

```
       DISTRIBUTION OF CALCULATED PRINT QUEUE AND PRINT EXECUTION TIMES

                            FREQUENCY BAR CHART
    MIDPOINT

    QUEPRNT                                 FREQ   CUM.    PERCENT     CUM.
                                                   FREQ                PERCENT
               |
         60    |***************************** 216    216    75.52      75.52
               |
        180    |**                            18    234     6.29      81.82
               |
        300    |*                              7    241     2.45      84.27
               |
        420    |**                            13    254     4.55      88.81
               |
        540    |***                           21    275     7.34      96.15
               |
        660    |                               3    278     1.05      97.20
               |
        780    |                               2    280     0.70      97.90
               |
       1020    |*                              6    286     2.10     100.00
               |
               ----+---+---+---+---+---+---+-
                  30  60  90  120  150 180 210

                            FREQUENCY
```

```
       DISTRIBUTION OF CALCULATED PRINT QUEUE AND PRINT EXECUTION TIMES
                            FREQUENCY BAR CHART
    MIDPOINT

    TMEPRNT                                 FREQ   CUM.    PERCENT     CUM.
                                                   FREQ                PERCENT
               |
         40    |**************************** 278    278    97.20      97.20
               |
        120    |                               4    282     1.40      98.60
               |
        200    |                               3    285     1.05      99.65
               |
        600    |                               1    286     0.35     100.00
               |
               -----+----+----+----+----+---
                   50   100  150  200  250

                            FREQUENCY
```

example 8-2, continued

By taking the preceding data for QUEPRNT and excluding those jobs that exceeded two hours, a more meaningful distribution of queue time is pictured. Seventy-seven percent of this sample waited less than 16 minutes in the print queue. This type of analysis, which selects and individually evaluates exceptions and then presents the remaining, more typical data, provides management with a realistic evaluation of the delays for printing devices.

```
PROC SORT DATA=TYPE6;
  BY READTIME JOB;
PROC SORT DATA=TYPE26J2;
  BY READTIME JOB;
PROC MEANS DATA=TYPE6 NOPRINT;
  BY READTIME JOB;
  OUTPUT OUT=PRINTGOT SUM=NRLINES MIN=PRINTIME;
  VAR NRLINES PRINTIME;
DATA PRINTER;
  MERGE TYPE26J2(IN=INJES) TYPE6(IN=INWTR);
  BY READTIME JOB;
  IF INJES AND INWTR;
  IF JOB_TSO='J';
  QUEPRNT=(PRINTIME-JFINTIME)/60;
  TMEPRNT=(JPURTIME-PRINTIME)/60;
  IF QUEPRNT<120;
  KEEP NRLINES TMEPRNT QUEPRNT;
PROC CHART;
  HBAR QUEPRNT;
  TITLE DISTRIBUTION OF PRINT QUEUE TIME FOR JOBS WAITING LESS THAN 120 MIN;
```

```
        DISTRIBUTION OF PRINT QUEUE TIME FOR JOBS WAITING LESS THAN 120 MIN

                          FREQUENCY BAR CHART
      MIDPOINT

      QUEPRNT                                FREQ  CUM.   PERCENT    CUM.
                                                   FREQ              PERCENT

            |
         8  |********************* 167        167   77.31    77.31
            |
        24  |**                     15        182    6.94    84.26
            |
        40  |*                      10        192    4.63    88.89
            |
        56  |*                       7        199    3.24    92.13
            |
        72  |*                       6        205    2.78    94.91
            |
        88  |*                       5        210    2.31    97.22
            |
       104  |                        3        213    1.39    98.61
            |
       120  |                        3        216    1.39   100.00
            L---+---+---+---+---+--
               30  60  90  120  150

               FREQUENCY
```

example 8-3

Using TYPE4789 to analyze RJE line usage. The final area in which the printing information records are valuable is the area of RJE line usage. There are two sources of information dealing with RJE line usage. The data set TYPE4789 contains information from SMF records TYPE47 (sign-on), TYPE48 (sign-off), and TYPE49 (invalid password). The data from type 47 and 48 records can be combined, producing a record with total EXCP count and duration of the RJE session. Since the remote ID is contained in type 47 and 48 records, a SORT and MEANS by remote ID provides meaningful descriptions of which remotes use the lines efficiently and which remotes have low traffic volumes. This type of information can be used by the teleprocessing group to recommend more economical and appropriate changes in line speeds.

Since the TYPE6 record for printing at remotes contains the remote ID,[1] a SORT and MEANS of TYPE6 by remote will identify total lines printed by each remote. This might also be useful in determining the number of printers wanted, especially if the data is further subdivided by shift. These are but a few examples of the uses of the printing information contained in TYPE6, 26, and 48 SMF records.

---

[1]The remote ID is not explicitly contained, but is decoded from the output device name.

9
Availability Analysis

SMF provides relatively poor information about system availability. However, several records in SMF are useful in tracking incidents which affect availability, although they may not provide precise numeric values of the availability.

IPLS: the TYPE0 data set. The first and most obvious record for tracking availability is the type 0 record, the IPL record. Simply by printing the TYPE0 data set each day, one can learn several things. First, the existence of a type 0 indicates that the operating system was IPLed. An IPL may or may not be desirable. Some installations schedule IPLs daily; thus the existence of an IPL is expected. Unexpected IPLs should be confirmable on the shift supervisor's log of system incidents. Further examination of the list of IPLs might show that at a given time of day several IPLs occurred in very short order. This could result from the operator hitting the LOAD key several times, usually indicative of an operator attempting to recover; the recovery failing; the operator attempting recovery a second time; a third time; and so on. Thus multiple IPLs at very close intervals suggest a need for operator education in proper recovery.

How long was the system down? There is no completely accurate method to determine how long the operating system was down prior to an IPL. One can infer, however, periods of probable downtime by determining the time between the previously written SMF record and the IPL record time stamp.

Example 9-1 shows how you might determine downtimes. Data set DOWNTIME is built by passing SMF records and retaining the time stamp, as variable OLDTIME, of the previous record's time stamp. When an IPL record is encountered, the downtime is calculated. A PROC PRINT shows that, in this example, the system was down at about 2 p.m., for 47 minutes. There were two IPLs very close to 2 p.m., and it appears that the system finally recovered at 14:22. Later that same evening the system was down at 9 p.m. for about 21 minutes.

Two cautions about this technique are necessary. Some locally written SMF records may have time stamps that do not relate to the time they were written to the SMF buffer; thus it may be necessary to exclude certain record types. Secondly, the fact that no SMF records are written does not necessarily mean the system is down. Certainly a system with RMF should have RMF records written at every RMF interval, but unless files are being closed, dynamic allocations are occurring, or job steps are terminating, SMF records are not written. On-line started tasks could be executing; since they may not write SMF records, you might infer a larger than actual downtime. Depending on the nature of the work load, however, in most installations this measure is an excellent approximation of total system downtime.

```
DATA DOWNTIME;
  INFILE SMF LRECL=32756 RECFM=VBS MISSOVER;
  INPUT @2 ID PIB1. @3 SMFTIME SMFSTAMP8.;
  IF ID=0 THEN GOTO IPL;
  OLDTIME=SMFTIME;
  RETAIN OLDTIME;
  RETURN;
  IPL: DOWNTIME=SMFTIME-DOWNTIME;
       OUTPUT;
       OLDTIME=SMFTIME;
       RETURN;
  KEEP DOWNTIME SMFTIME;
  FORMAT DOWNTIME TIME12.2 SMFTIME DATETIME19.2;
PROC PRINT;
  TITLE ESTIMATED SYSTEM DOWN TIME;
```

```
            ESTIMATED SYSTEM DOWN TIME

              SMFTIME              DOWNTIME

        07AUG78:14:21:03.6      00:47:14:17.2
        07AUG78:14:21:33.6      00:00:00:30.0
        07AUG78:14:22:30.2      00:00:00:56.6
        07AUG78:21:14:16.3      00:00:21:14.6
```

example 9-1

Subsystem availability.   As important as total system availability is subsystem availability. The operating system may be up but TSO may be down. Some subsystems, such as JES, provide start and stop records: determination of JES uptime is thus a matter of analyzing the TYPE4345 data set, since it produces a record for each start and stop of the job entry subsytem. The TSO subsystem, however, only provides a start record.

An example: determining TSO availability.   Example 9-2 shows an approach, similar to the one in example 9-1, for the determination of TSO availability. A type 31 record is written when TSO is started, and one expects to find frequent dynamic allocations in a normal TSO environment. Thus you can use the time interval between the last type 40 dynamic allocation record and the next type 31 record to determine periods during which TSO was presumably not available. Additionally, in example 9-2 IPL records are selected and kept so that in viewing the occurrences of TSO nonavailability, you can determine whether the outage was systemwide or simply a loss of the TSO subsystem.

The type 40 record does not indicate whether it is from a batch job or TSO user. Since batch jobs as well as TSO users issue dynamic allocations, and you want to count only those dynamic allocation records from TSO you must use logic on your installation's USERID to select the TSO type 40s. Note that in example 9-2 the logic for detecting type 40 dynamic allocation records also tests to see the type 40 is from a TSO user. Here, TSO users have six-character user IDs, and the first letter of the user ID is restricted to the several letters of the alphabet shown.

```
DATA UPTIME;
   INFILE SMF RECFM=VBS LRECL=32756 MISSOVER;
   INPUT @2 ID PIB1. SMFTIME SMFSTAMP8. SYSTEM $4. @;
   IF ID=31 OR ID=40 OR ID=0;
   IF ID=0 THEN GOTO IPL;
   IF ID=40 THEN GOTO DYNAM;
   IF ID=31 THEN GO TO CALC;
   RETURN;
CALC: DOWNTIME=SMFTIME-OLDTIME;
      OUTPUT;
      OLDTIME=SMFTIME;
      IPLFLG=0;
      RETURN;
IPL: IPLFLG=1;
      OUTPUT;
      RETURN;
DYNAM: IF NOT IPLFLG;
      INPUT @15 TSOCHAR $1. @21 BLANKS $2. ;
      IF BLANKS=' ';
      IF 'V'<= TSOCHAR <='Z' OR TSOCHAR=:'T';
      OLDTIME=SMFTIME;
      RETURN;
   DROP IPLFLG BLANKS TSOCHAR;
   RETAIN  OLDTIME IPLFLG;
   FORMAT SMFTIME OLDTIME DATETIME19.2;
PROC PRINT;
PROC MEANS SUM;
   VARIABLE DOWNTIME;
   TITLE TOTAL DOWN TIME;
```

example 9-2

Determining RJE availability. Another area for which subsystem availability can be inferred is from RJE records. A type 47 SMF record is written at RJE signon, and a type 48 SMF record is written at RJE signoff. These records are contained in data set TYPE4789, and you can summarize these records by remote ID and line number to produce RJE session statistics. When reporting to a user who expects his RJE station to be connected all day, these figures are useful for showing him the total time that his RJE station was active and connected.

Note, however, that no RJE signoff record is written when JES is stopped, and thus it is necessary to interleave the information in TYPE4345 (JES start and stop) with TYPE4789 and effectively fabricate a signoff record corresponding to the JES event, if actual connect time of the RJE station is of concern.

SMF availability.   One record directly relating to availability is the type 7 SMF record, which indicates that both SYS1.MANX and SYS1.MANY have been filled with SMF data, with SMF no longer recording. A type 7 record should never occur. Its impact can be disastrous on a billing system as well as on a performance system based on SMF. It usually means that the operators have missed several messages and have failed to properly dump MANX, although it can occur when a runaway job is creating SMF records at an extremely high rate. For example, if a file is opened and closed repeatedly in a tight loop, it is possible to fill up MANX and MANY with type 14 or 15 SMF records and thus cause the lost data event.

Other subsystems.   There are no other subsystems explicitly reported by SMF data. However, many subsystems of interest can and should be run as batch jobs. IMS, CICS, and WYLBUR are all systems that should be tracked with SMF reporting.

Extensive evaluation of IMS as a started task versus a batch job has shown, for example, that under MVS when the IMS program libraries are all authorized libraries, there is no degradation to IMS when running the control region as a batch job rather than a started task. (Furthermore, one gains measures of CPU and I/O from the control region.) Thus by tracking the job names of the message regions and the control region, you can get a measure of system uptime for an IMS system and its message regions.

Example: subsystem availability.   Similarly, any other on-line system run as a batch job can be reported, and its uptime can be plotted. An example of plotting availability for several on-line systems is shown in example 9-3, actually a modification to the multiprogramming analysis described in a previous chapter. In this example, the three systems of interest are IMS, CICS, and System 2000. Knowing these systems' job names, the logic is straightforward: set up a variable named SYS and a variable named ONLINE, and print the plot, which shows that System 2000 was up from early morning until midday; CICS was up from about 9:30 until 3:00; and IMS was up all day except for one period a little after 9:30. Thus the reporting mechanism for on-line system availability can be easily handled through SMF provided that the on-line systems are executing as batch jobs.

```
DATA ONLINE;
  SET TYPE535;
  IF JOB_TSO='J';
  IF JINITIME=. OR JTRMTIME=. THEN DELETE;
  IF JOB='IMS' THEN GOTO IMS;
  IF JOB='CICS' THEN GOTO CICS;
  IF JOB='SYS2000' THEN GOTO S2K;
  DELETE;
  IMS: SYS='I';
       ONLINE=1;
       GOTO REST;
  CICS:  SYS='C';
         ONLINE=2;
          GOTO REST;
  S2K: SYS='S';
       ONLINE=3;
       GOTO REST;
  REST:
        *SPECIFY INTERVAL IN SECONDS;
        INTERVAL=60;
        IF (JTRMTIME-JINITIME)<INTERVAL THEN DELETE;
        TIME=JINITIME-MOD(JINITIME,INTERVAL);
        OUTPUT;
  LOOP: IF TIME>=JTRMTIME THEN RETURN;
  TIME=TIME+INTERVAL;
  OUTPUT;
  GOTO LOOP;
  KEEP TIME SYS ONLINE;
PROC PLOT;
  PLOT ONLINE*TIME=SYS;
  FORMAT TIME TOD8.;
  TITLE ONLINE SYSTEM UP TIME PLOT;
  TITLE2  I=IMS      C=CICS          S=SYSTEM 2000;
```

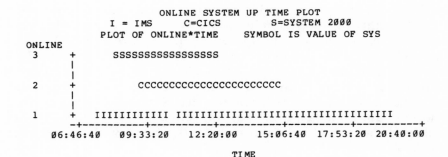

example 9-3

Much of SMF data analysis revolves around the step records—type 4 for batch and type 34 for TSO. Especially before RMF, these records were the only source of resource consumption. Even with RMF, they are still essential for associating resource consumption with individual tasks. RMF can identify consumption of resources at the performance group level; howevever, within the same performance group it is often necessary to analyze the type 4 and 34 records to determine the utilization by individual tasks.

Any performance improvement based on improving application programs will ultimately require information from TYPE434. Almost all benchmarks of operating systems, configuration, memory and so on will eventually need the detailed data from the step executions. Therefore, this chapter deals with the TYPE434 data set.

Time stamps, durations, and accumulations. First we will look at the time stamps, time durations, and time accumulations that exist in TYPE434. Recall the naming conventions for time values: those variable names ending in TIME are time-of-day values; those ending in TM represent time durations. Time stamps, which are printed using the SAS format DATETIME19.2, represent the date and time of day at which an event occurred. From these time stamps, several durations can be calculated by subtraction. SMF also accumulates several other durations contained in the TYPE434 data set.

Time stamps and durations for a typical job step. Figure 10-1 details time-related variables for a typical job step. The time stamp INITTIME represents the initiation time for this step.

The next event in the life of the step is ALOCTIME, the beginning of device allocation. The duration from INITIME to ALOCTIME is called DSENQTM, because global data set enqueues are issued during this interval in the first step for all data sets to be used by the job. Additionally, during the DSENQTM interval the control blocks built by the converter are scanned for the final time; thus some data-set-related terminations (JCL errors such as "data set not found") can occur here.

At ALOCTIME the system begins to acquire the devices required by the job. If the devices are mountable, the mounts are not necessarily issued here, but the ownership of the devices commences at this point. Thus the duration from ALOCTIME to LOADTIME is called ALOCTM, and represents the elapsed time required by the system to allocate all devices.

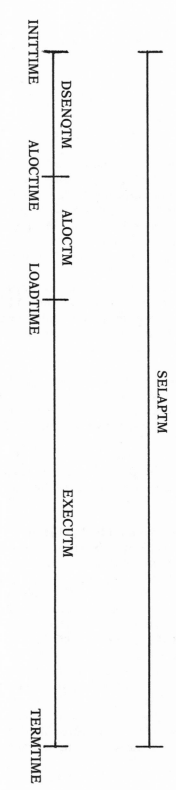

figure 10-1
**Time Stamps and Elapsed Durations
in TYPE434**

The third time stamp in the life of a job step is the step LOADTIME. A holdover from MVT days when the program was loaded into real memory, the LOADTIME is now more correctly called the problem program start time. It represents the point when all allocations have been satisfied (but not necessarily mounted) and the job step begins execution.

Initial mounts required for the job are generally issued between ALOC-TIME and LOADTIME. MVT and SVS required mountable disks to be physically ready before program execution; MVS passes control to the problem program, which executes until the first open requiring one of the mountable devices.

The duration from LOADTIME to TERMTIME, called EXECUTM, is the maximum possible execution time of the step; that is, the program had access to the processor for, at most, the EXECUTM duration.

The sum of DSENQTM, ALOCTM, and EXECUTM is called SELAPTM, the step elapsed time. SELAPTM represents the duration that the step was in initiation, and is the same as TERMTIME minus INITTIME.

Relationships between duration values in TYPE434. The preceding discussion maps actual time stamps with the duration labels. Figure 10-2 compares several accumulated durations with the calculated EXECUTM duration.

The accumulated counter ACTIVETM is maintained by the system resource manager (SRM) and will always be less than or equal to EX-ECUTM, since ACTIVETM is the time the SRM recognized this step as active (i.e., eligible to execute). Active time can be subdivided into the time the task was active in memory, or resident, and the time the task was marked active but had not yet been swapped in.

The portion of active time during which the task was resident is accumulated in the variable INMEMTM, which is the duration the step was in real storage.

For some portion of this residency time, the step was executing instructions. The accumulated CPU time while under the task's TCB is accumulated by SMF in the variable CPUTCBTM, while the accumulated processor time under the tasks service request blocks (SRB) is accumulated in CPUSRBTM.

Questions of validity. The sum of CPUTCBTM and CPUSRBTM is CPUTM, which represents the total CPU time used by this step. It is the CPUTM value that has caused greatest concern for the validity of SMF data, yet the accuracy in absolute terms of the CPUTM measurement by SMF is irrelevant to most concerns. Most of the value of CPU analysis (even in MVT days) was the identification of the portion used. Even if the absolute numbers has not been correct, the indication provided the analyst by comparing CPUTM values was quite worthwhile. In fact, the CPUTM measurements under MVT and MFT in total were reasonably accurate. The major error of MVT was to misdistribute the accumulated CPUTM at the time of an interupt: the

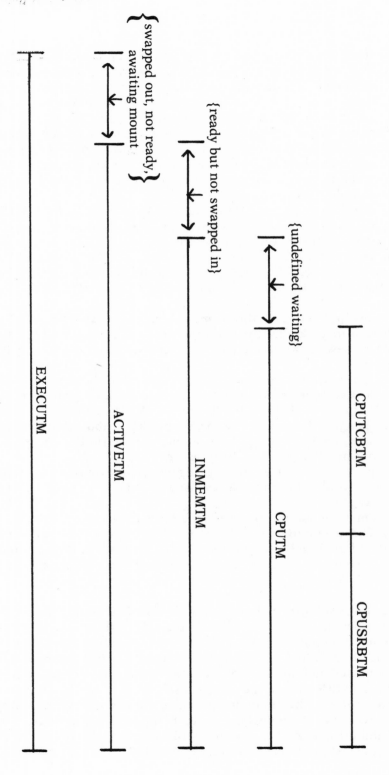

figure 10-2
Accumulated Durations in TYPE434

task causing the interrupt generally was charged for CPU time rather than the task that had control of the processor just before the interrupt. This action led to CPU measurement variation of up to 40% in some anomalous situations.

In SVS, the attempt was made to produce repeatable CPU measures. As a result, the charge for interrupt time was totally eliminated. The repeatability of SVS data improved, but the total TCB time measured in an SVS batch environment rarely amounted to more than 40% of total true active time, whereas under MVT it was not uncommon to recover 65% to 75% of total CPU active time in a batch environment in TCB time.

MVS has come a long way in improving the measurement of CPU time and properly attributing it to tasks. With MVS/SE, the SRB time is reported not only at the task level in the type 4 and 34 records but also is finally reported by RMF. Comparisons show excellent agreement between hardware monitor active time and the percentage of CPU recovered in type 4 and type 34 data, as well as the total of the RMF type 72 records. Chapter 11, "Recovery of Batch CPU Time," shows such comparisons.

To learn more about CPU variability, read the appendices to the MVS SMF manual for a good discussion of what is and is not accumulated in CPU time. Additionally, two excellent papers have been presented at GUIDE and SHARE by Tom Giblin concerning variability not only of CPU accounting but also of EXCP accounting across MVT, SVS, and MVS. My point here is that my experience has been very positive in the utilization of the CPU measurements in the type 4 and 34 records in both absolute and relative terms.

Other resource consumption variables in TYPE434.   The CPU is not the only resource in a computer system: additional resource consumption variables are contained in data set TYPE434. The EXCPs accumulated by the step are grouped by device type (EXCP2314, EXCP3330, etc.). The number of tape drive allocated by each step is there, as well as the number of mountable disk devices.

The range of possible analyses is limited only by the problem at hand. Typically, one is concerned with finding consumers of excessive resources. This approach can be extended by looking at combinations of resource consumption: for example, high I/O counts and high CPU time.

The SAS procedure FREQ and its associated WEIGHT statement provide powerful tools for gaining a perspective of resource consumption. Some areas to analyze can be determined by a PROC MEANS of TYPE434, since that report will provide not only averages but also minimum and maximum values for all numeric variables.

For example, looking at a variable like tape drives and seeing a maximum value of twelve suggests that some job steps may be abusing the tape drive resource. A system that requires twelve concurrently open tape files bears investigation. Generally, a large number of tape drives per step suggests a user who is unfamiliar with job control language and does not use unit affinity (UNIT=AFF) so that sequentially read data sets (often concatenated) are mounted on the same physical tape drive.

After MEANS, crosstabulation (PROC FREQ with a TABLES statement) is probably the next most useful tool in analyzing the step data. TYPE434 data is primarily useful in identifying which program or programs are involved in a problem situation. For example, when RMF data suggests a consistently high paging rate during a period of the day, selecting step records active during that period and tabulating their page rates is useful in finding conflicts between two programs. See example 10-3 for a typical case.

```
DATA PGMPAGES;
  SET TYPE434;
  DATE=MDY(9,6,79);
  IF INITTIME>DHMS(DATE,13,20,00) &
     INITTIME>DHMS(DATE,13,40,00);
  KEEP PROGRAM PAGEINS;
PROC FREQ;
  TABLES PROGRAM;
  WEIGHT PAGEINS;
```

example 10-3

An example. The FREQ procedure is very useful for analysis, but in regular reporting the frequency distribution of CPU time for each program would have as many entries as there are unique programs executed. For that reason, example 10-4 uses a series of MEANS procedures to identify the top twenty-five programs in four categories of resource consumption.

The code sorts by program name (PROGRAM) and the four resources CPUTCBTM, EXCPDASD, EXCPTAPE, and PAGEINS by each program. Then four descending sorts are used and the first twenty-five observations are selected to produce four new data sets: HICPU, HIDASD, HITAPE, and HIPAGES. By printing each of these data sets, you see in descending order programs with high resource usage; example 10-4 includes the PROC PRINT output for HICPU.

The other three resource sums for each program are also listed, and you can expand this report by using PROC RANK so that rank position is given as well.

This is just one example of how easily you can identify who is using which resource from the type 4 and type 34 records.

```
PROC SORT DATA=TYPE434 OUT=BYPROG
  (KEEP=PROGRAM CPUTCBTM EXCPDASD EXCPTAPE PAGEINS);
PROC MEANS NOPRINT;
  BY PROGRAM;
  OUTPUT OUT=SUMS SUM=CPUTCBTM EXCPDASD EXCPTAPE PAGEINS;
  VAR CPUTCBTM EXCPDASD EXCPTAPE PAGEINS;
PROC SORT DATA=SUMS;
  BY DESCENDING CPUTCBTM;
OPTIONS OBS=25;
DATA HICPU;
  SET;
  OPTIONS OBS=MAX;
PROC SORT DATA=SUMS;
  BY DESCENDING EXCPDASD;
OPTIONS OBS=25;
DATA HIDASD;
  SET;
  OPTIONS OBS=MAX;
PROC SORT DATA=SUMS;
  BY DESCENDING EXCPTAPE;
OPTIONS OBS=25;
DATA HITAPE;
  SET;
  OPTIONS OBS=MAX;
PROC SORT DATA=SUMS;
  BY DESCENDING PAGEINS;
OPTIONS OBS=25;
DATA HIPAGES;
  SET;
  OPTIONS OBS=MAX;
PROC PRINT DATA=HICPU;
  TITLE TOP 25 USERS OF CPU;
PROC PRINT DATA=HIDASD;
  TITLE TOP 25 USERS OF DASD;
PROC PRINT DATA=HITAPE;
  TITLE TOP 25 USERS OF TAPE;
PROC PRINT DATA=HIPAGES;
  TITLE TOP 25 USERS OF PAGING;
```

TOP 25 USERS OF CPU

OBS	PROGRAM	CPUTCBTM	EXCPDASD	EXCPTAPE	PAGEINS
1	IKJEFT01	14:13:31.46	2401151	0	1690725
2	DFSRRC00	10:28:47.62	4701788	1188946	130513
3	EASYTREV	8:07:34.87	4302660	7622893	93991
4	SAS	6:02:35.61	724178	282059	48508
5	DFSMGRC0	4:56:32.02	509082	712934	258262
6	FDR	4:18:57.73	1558023	1367326	2674
7	IKFCBL00	3:37:03.00	950042	0	65264
8	PEXECMP	2:43:35.78	1058122	259597	29497
9	DFHSIP	2:37:56.36	1500836	0	191811
10	IEBGENER	2:25:15.93	968643	2960899	42143
11	SORT	2:21:43.78	850718	659094	30794
12	SHARDUMP	1:47:56.72	1016647	226991	3661
13	HDEC1F21	1:37:34.81	285267	7425	1369
14	PRSLEDIT	1:24:45.62	3929	453405	11672
15	EARCSC19	1:24:37.43	595957	85660	1590
16	IERRCO00	1:24:02.04	345735	380490	17230
17	HQJ18C01	1:23:45.64	207	70847	2161
18	PGM=*.DD	1:15:53.22	342164	322487	9066
19	HMEX2C10	1:15:12.87	262	138429	302
20	IEBCOPY	1:14:39.95	1903684	234127	15940
21	MATCHUP	1:07:30.70	672469	30754	42489
22	IEWL	0:59:29.62	1385743	2115	38388
23	SAVEDUMP	0:56:07.24	1282950	231936	2068
24	SHHDLOAD	0:53:51.39	429763	95364	1044
25	EASY72	0:50:44.49	315640	242922	8819

example 10-4

11
Recovery of Batch CPU Time
in an MVS Environment

Determining the amount of CPU time used by batch tasks is important not only for billing but also for capacity planning. The process of determining where CPU time went is **recovery.** This chapter describes a real-world investigation of CPU time recovery in a non-SE MVS environment.

Sources of information. At this installation, the sources of CPU usage data are RMF, SMF, and the Display Active TSO command. Figure 11-1 shows these sources graphically.

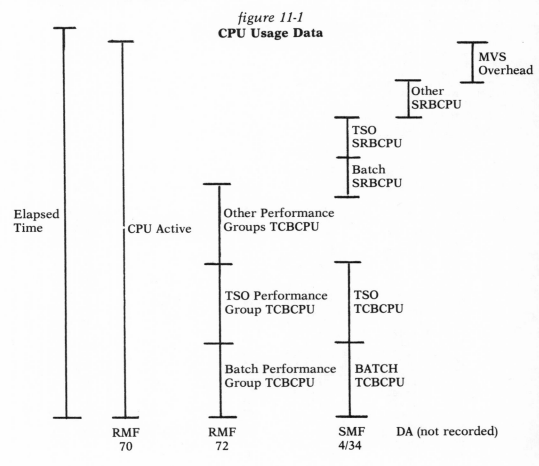

figure 11-1
CPU Usage Data

From the type 70 RMF record we get the total CPU active time (in the TYPE70 data set, this is PCTCPBY1—percent of CPU busy). The TYPE72 RMF data set breaks down the TCB portion of CPU active for each performance group (variable CPUTCBTM in TYPE72). The SMF type 4 and type 34 records contain both TCB and SRB CPU times (variables CPUTCBTM and CPUSRBTM). Finally, the Display Active TSO command displays (but does not record) the SRB time not recorded in SMF. By summing the appropriate data from the TYPE72, TYPE434, and DA sources, we can subtract to determine MVS overhead.

Linearizing SMF CPU times. The major problem in acquiring this sum is the need to linearize, or prorate, the SMF CPU times. While RMF is accumulating the CPU busy statistic across its interval—60 minutes at this installation, the SMF CPU time is written only at step termination. If the step started before the interval began or ended after the interval, the SMF CPU time must be partitioned. The only feasible way to distribute the CPU time is to fraction it according to the elapsed time of the step.

Figure 11-2 takes four separate RMF intervals and the corresponding SMF data; then compares the RMF TCB time for batch with the linearized SMF time. Significant discrepancies can be seen, with the percent error ranging from –21% to 12% of the RMF TCB time for the interval. Nevertheless, only by thus prorating or linearizing the SMF SRB time can we evaluate the CPU recovery for batch.

figure 11-2

Comparison of RMF and Linearized SMF Time for Batch

SYSTEM	UP				MP			
Time of interval	77299:19:40		77301:20:24		77299:00:30		77301:02:20	
BATCH DATA (minutes)	**TCB**	**SRB**	**TCB**	**SRB**	**TCB**	**SRB**	**TCB**	**SRB**
Start and end in interval	1.23	.33	.44	.05	39.81	8.08	33.03	7.28
Ended in interval	2.07	.53	1.18	.73	40.66	8.67	6.35	1.98
Started before, ended after	29.83	.09	33.50	.10	.52	.19	16.30	3.80
Started in interval	.80	.27	1.64	.55	5.67	2.37	2.65	1.10
Total linearized SMF time	**33.93**	1.23	**36.77**	1.43	**86.64**	19.31	**58.33**	14.17
RMF TCB	**43.00**		**42.40**		**77.30**		**60.40**	
SMF time linearized for non-batch in SMF	0.75	.07	.83	.08	1.64	.29	0	0
Total interval SRB		1.30		1.51		19.60		14.17
Percent error linearized SMF versus RMF		–21%		–13%		+12%		–3%

Tabulating the CPU recovery. Figure 11-3 shows the tabulation of the detailed CPU times for four separate intervals in which only batch was significant. Where possible, RMF times are used since they are collected during the interval, but linearized SMF times are used when necessary.

In first column, you can see that the CPU was active 59.1 minutes, but 7.7 CPU minutes were consumed by non-batch TCB (mostly JES) and .1 minutes by non-batch SRB. Thus a total of 51.3 CPU minutes are attributable to MVS and batch.

The batch TCB time was 43.0 minutes (the 33.9 minutes from linearized SMF is given only for comparison) and the batch SRB is estimated at 1.2 minutes. Thus the measurable batch CPU time is 44.2 minutes. Subtracting this from the 51.3 minutes leaves an MVS overhead of 7.1 minutes not attributable to a specific job or user.

Thus of the 51.3 CPU minutes used by MVS plus batch, 86.2% is measurable and attributable to batch jobs. Note, however, that we threw out the non-batch work, which in the batch environment is JES and other non-chargable systems. So we can see that only 74.8% of the total CPU active (44.2-59.1) is actually chargable to batch work.

figure 11-3
Batch CPU Recovery

SYSTEM	UP		MP	
Time of interval	77299:19:40	77301:20:24	77299:00:30	77301:02:20
Percent CPU active	98.4	99.0	98.1	77.3
CPU active minutes (RMF70)	59.1	59.4	118.0	92.7
Non-batch TCB (RMF72)	7.7	8.5	2.2	1.3
Non-batch SRB (Type 4)	.1	.1	.3	0
Resultant batch +MVS	**51.3**	**50.8**	**115.5**	**91.4**
Batch TCB (RMF72)	43.0	42.4	77.3	60.4
Batch TCB (linearized SMF)	(33.9)	(36.8)	(86.6)	(58.3)
Batch SRB (linearized SMF)	1.2	1.4	19.3	14.2
Measurable batch (RMF72+SRB)	**44.2**	**43.8**	**96.6**	**74.6**
MVS overhead	7.1	7.0	18.9	16.8
Percent of MVS + batch which is measurable	86.2%	86.2%	83.6%	81.6%
Percent of CPU active which is chargable	74.8%	73.7%	83.6%	81.6%

Conclusions.   This evaluation demonstrates the very high recovery of CPU time under MVS (compared with only 30-45% recovery under SVS) and reflects the relatively low overhead of MVS in terms of non-chargable CPU usage. The evaluation is not globally extendable, as on-line systems tend to require significantly more MVS resources than batch. Thus recovery percentages in a more on-line system can be expected to be less than for this strictly batch environment.

12
Building Multiple SAS Data Sets
in One Pass of SMF/RMF Data

The SAS code in the members that begin with the letters TYPE is used to build one SAS data set in a pass of the SMF/RMF data. Although this approach is helpful for understanding the record structure, using it to build a data base would be inefficient indeed.

For that reason, the SAS code to build each data set is also available in a second form: as two macros that can be used as building blocks with other macros to create multiple SAS data sets in a single pass of the SMF/RMF data.

For example, the SAS code to build the TYPE434 data set is found in member TYPE434. This code is also found, in slightly different form, as two macros in member MAC434. These two macros in member MAC434 are called __VAR434 and __CDE434. __VAR434 contains the SAS code to define the variables contained in the TYPE434 data set; __CDE434 contains the SAS code to read the type 4 and 34 records and to build the TYPE434 data set.

To put these macros together with others also requires two general-purpose macros, __SMF and __MACEND.

A typical DATA step. A typical DATA step to build multiple SAS data sets in one pass begins with the DATA keyword, **not** followed by a semicolon. Then give the __VAR macro name corresponding to each data set that you want, and end the list with the __SMF macro name. Next come IF statements, one for each data set you are creating, indicating which records are to be selected for processing. These are followed by __CDE macro names, one for each data set. Finally, the __MACEND macro wraps up the step.

An example. Example 12-1 shows the structure and statements necessary to build the three SMF SAS data sets TYPE434, TYPE535, and TYPE26J2 in one pass of the SMF data.

```
//  EXEC SAS                                              1
//SMF  DD   SMF data set                                  2
//SYSIN DD   DSN=SAS.SMF.SOURCE(MACROS),DISP=SHR          3
//  DD   DSN=SAS.SMF.SOURCE(MAC434),DISP=SHR              4
//  DD   DSN=SAS.SMF.SOURCE(MAC535),DISP=SHR              5
//  DD   DSN=SAS.SMF.SOURCE(MAC26J2),DISP=SHR             6
//  DD   *                                                7
DATA                                                      8
__VAR434                                                  9
__VAR535                                                  10
```

example 12-1

```
__VAR26J2                                               11
__SMF                                                   12
IF   ID=4 OR ID=34 THEN LINK TYPE434;                   13
IF   ID=5 OR ID=35 THEN LINK TYPE535;                   14
IF   ID=26 THEN LINK TYPE26J2;                          15
__CDE434                                                16
__CDE535                                                17
__CDE26J2                                               18
__MACEND                                                19
```

example 12-1, continued

Using an underscore as the first character of macro names makes SAS code quite readable, and thus all macros follow that convention. Lines 3 through 6 define the macros to be used in this execution.

Line 8 provides the DATA keyword, and lines 9-11 invoke the three __VAR macros that name the data sets and variables to be kept. Line 12 invokes the __SMF macro to define the input file and input the ID variable, which is then tested in lines 13-15. Lines 16-18 invoke the __CDE macros which actually build the SAS data sets, and __MACEND invokes the general system macros that may be necessary.

The naming conventions are as consistent as possible with table 2-1. All suffixes are keyed to the TYPE name listed in the SAS source column of that table. Thus the SAS source name TYPE0 has a corresponding macro member named MAC0, which contains macros __VAR0 and __CDE0; the label to be linked to is named TYPE0. The names of the SAS data sets that are built in this manner are also consistently named with the TYPE convention, with only the following exceptions for performance considerations:

name and label	builds SAS data sets
TYPE7072	TYPE70 and TYPE72
TYPE73	TYPE73P and TYPE73L

It is feasible to have the JCL set up to process all macros; then, the __VAR, __CDE, and IF statements required for a specific run can be edited. The entire compile-time processing of all MAC members requires 400 EXCPs and 2 CPU seconds on a 3033.

13
Building A Performance Data Base

The information presented thus far is useful in all respects except one: it can be expensive to acquire. This is because the structure that has been presented would essentially require a pass of the SMF/RMF data each time you want an analysis. Further expense would have be expended because all fields of all selected records would be decoded, even though only a small number of variables were actually required. Thus it is fair to say that the preceding information (and the appendices) are of value in one-time investigations, but would be expensive as part of on-going performance analysis.

Performance Data Base. In fact, that is true. Ongoing performance analysis with SAS is much better accomplished by building a Performance Data Base, which can then contain the most significant variables from the most significant SMF/RMF records. Not only does a PDB eliminate multiple passes of the SMF/RMF data, but a good selection of variables and data sets can provide a source of data which is compact and readily usable interactively under TSO, as well as being a source for regular reporting.

As with performance objectives, the contents of a PDB will vary significantly from installation to installation, depending on the purposes of computing and the type of scheduling, subsystems, etc. Furthermore, the choices of variables to be kept is very much a function of the tradeoff between resources consumed (especially DASD space) in building a PDB and the completeness of data available. I have found a reasonable compromise in every installation I have investigated, but the exact content is a matter of your choice.

What variables for the PDB? The first step toward building a PDB is to determine the information desired. The minimum PDB should contain data at the job level (for batch objectives measurement and workload analysis); at the step level (for program performance measurements); and RMF data (for overall performance, utilization, and capacity planning). As you gain experience, other candidates for inclusion will become obvious as you expand your horizons of investigation.

The second step is to tailor the code so that only the needed variables are kept. The code in the appendices is comprehensive, and thus it is expensive. To become truly cost-effective, only those variables which are really useful should be kept. Unfortunately, what is useful to my installation is often insignificant to yours. Therefore, a good plan of attack, after having determined which SAS data sets are potential candidates for inclusion, is to build each SAS data set with a day's (or week's) SMF/RMF data and then investigate each data set to see which variables are important in terms of your installation's purpose.

One technique is to use the SAS procedures MEANS and FREQ to determine if any variables are invariant; i.e., their values don't change. A variable that seldom or never changes is not of much value in analysis and should be excluded. Another technique is to eliminate variables that cannot occur; for example, EXCP counts to 3340 devices are useless for installations without 3340 devices.

Using PROC CONTENTS to list the variables that are kept can also assist you in reducing the number of variables. Initially, the reduction can be done simply by eliminating the variable name in the KEEP= list for each data set. Longer range, one should also remove the unnecessary variables from INPUT, LENGTH, and FORMAT statements, as well as any unnecessary decoding or calculating. This will speed execution and reduce resources spent in building a PDB.

The member BUILDPDB provides a fully functional example of a minimal Performance Data Base containing most of the variables repeatedly found to be useful in analysis. Most of the examples in this book could be executed against the data sets built by BUILDPDB.

The code is somewhat commented, and a pattern JCL for its execution is JCLPDB. BUILDPDB will not be as fast in execution as it could be, since it was created essentially by taking the constituent TYPExxxx members and eliminating the undesired variables only from the KEEP list; thus there are significant expenditures of CPU and I/O if BUILDPDB is executed as is.

The best choice is to become more familiar with the nature of your installation's data by "playing with" the mainline members TYPE434, TYPE535, and the TYPE70 through TYPE75 data sets, as well as IPLS, and then using BUILDPDB as a model of an approach, including only the data sets and variables of importance to your installation. Keep only the needed variables, and clean up the code so that no unnecessary INPUT or assignment statements are executed. You can then achieve the efficiency and speed of Performance Data Base as described in the next chapter.

14
An Earlier PDB
and Some Examples of Its Use

The following paper has been presented several times on an earlier design of a PDB. Because it uses user-written SMF records, and describes an earlier implementation, the logic flow description is abbreviated. The real value is as an example of the analyses that can be performed by using a SAS-based Performance Data Base.

The major problem in computer system measurement and performance evaluation is the data collection system. SMF and RMF are replete with valid and needed data; the absence of structure in the data pieces within SMF requires that comprehension be added by the data collection system.

This chapter describes the building of the Performance Data Base using SMF/RMF data and SAS, and its use in a comprehensive Performance Reporting System. Figure 14-1 summarizes the magnitude of the problem: a system with three 370/168s, running MVS, which creates 120,000 SMF records daily. The Performance Reporting System described here permits seven weeks' data to be stored on a single 3330-11 for on-line recall.

1 Built daily

120,000	Input SMF records
25 Min	Job elapsed time
6 Min	Job CPU Time (168)
$200	Daily cost

2 Resulting SAS data set
   20 cylinders of 3330 per day

3 Typical daily contents and size

SAS member	Number of records	Number of tracks
Jobs	2500	10
Steps	6500	160
Tape errors/mounts	2800	10
RJE sessions	230	5
RMF device activity	3300	15
All other RMF records	1500	18

4 Merged weekly SAS data set from dailies
   No sort required
   Uses 100 cylinders of 3330

5 Six daily plus six weekly PDB's fit on a 3330-11

figure 14-1
The Performance Data Base

Records that are written to the SMF file can be roughly divided into two functional divisions: job-related records and system-related records. The Performance Data Base contains a series of data sets derived from the SMF records. Figure 14-2 briefly describes the data sets in the Performance Data Base.

STEPS	One record per SMF step (4, 34) record combined with mount and dynamic allocation information.
JOBS	One record per job/session combining all job-related information from JES, MVS, and system records.
CONNECT	One record for each RJE session.
MOUNTS	One record for each tape dismount, with error statistics on each tape used.
RECOVERY	One record for each allocation recovery.
IPLS	One record for each time the operator depressed LOAD.
LOSTDATA	One record for each time SMF data logging ceased.
RMF70 thru RMF76	Complete information on all RMF records written to the SMF file.

figure 14-2
The Performance Data Base Contents

Figure 14-3 is a listing of the SMF records that might occur for a normal job. Three user-written records are used: the 129 and 128 records are holdovers from a KOMAND system; the 129 is an enhanced type 20 record, and the 128 traps the dismount message, which is then written to SMF. The type 225 record is locally written to record operator commands (CANCEL, HOLD, RELEASE, PRIORITY CHANGE, etc.) Note that information from all records except the 14-18 records is carried into the Performance Data Base.

47	RJE sign on
129	Job readin/submitted
225	Priority changed, released
-	Job selected for initiation (time in 5)
10	Allocation recovery
-	Step initiated (time in 4)
40	Dynamic allocations
14/15	Data set records
17/18	Scratch/rename
21	Tape volumes dismounted
128	Dismount message
4	Step terminated
5	Job terminated
6	Sysout printed
26	Job purged
48	RJE stations sign off

figure 14-3
SMF Records from a Job

Phase 1: passing the SMF data.   The raw SMF data is passed daily by SAS once, building nineteen SAS data sets in one 25-cylinder OS data set. Figure 14-4 describes the temporary SAS data sets built in this phase. Note that only 900 lines of SAS are needed and less than 3 CPU minutes of 168 time are required to process the 120,000 SMF records daily in this phase.

The power, flexibility, and simplicity of SAS in this application is clear: the entire SAS code to extract all the information from the type 4 and 34 SMF records is only 131 lines. All of the resource information from those records is extracted, condition codes are decoded into descriptive character strings, time stamps are consistently created and this data is stored as a SAS data set named STEPS.

SAS data sets appear to the user as an OS partitioned data set (although they are actually direct access, using SAS's own access method), and thus we can think of the nineteen SAS data sets built in Phase 1 as members of a temporary PDS.

Extraction of the data from the SMF records is thus relatively easy; however, it is far from the logical data set desired. In the case of the STEPS data set, note that the MOUNT information and DYNAMIC allocation information are in separate records that must be merged together. Furthermore, since the raw SMF data is copied while other jobs are running, we may have received only some of the SMF records for a job or step. Thus Phase 2 will handle the combining of associated records and the decision logic to resolve the possibilities.

SMF record type	SAS data set description	SAS name
0	IPLS	IPLS
4/34	STEP/TSO/WYLBUR	STEPS
5/35	Job/session	JOBS
6	Output writer	WRITER
7	SMF data lost	LOSTDATA
10	Allocation recovery	RECOVERY
21	Tape error statistics	ESV
26	JES purge	PURGE
40	Dynamic deallocation	DYNAM
47/48	RJE sign on/off	RJE
128	Tape dismount message	MOUNTS
129	Job initiation	JOBINIT
225	Operator changes	CHANGE
70-75	RMF records	RMF70-75

900 SAS Statements
3 CPU Minutes

figure 14-4
SAS Data Sets Built in Phase One

Phase 2: combining records   Figure 14-5 loosely follows the first portion of this phase. Two OS data sets, OLDSPIN and TEMP, contain the input SAS data sets. OLDSPIN contains the steps, mounts and dynamics from yesterday (from jobs active while SMF was being dumped). TEMP0 contains the nineteen SAS data sets built in Phase 1; here, we are interested in JOBS, STEPS, DYNS, and MNTS, which are first sorted by READTIME and JOB into TEMP1 to cluster all records from the same job together.

These records and the OLDSPIN records are then brought together and compared to determine if each job has ended (i.e., is there a record in JOBS?) If so, the records are passed into TEMP2 data sets. Otherwise, the records are probably from a job which is still active, and they are passed into TEMPSPIN0 data sets.

It is also possible that a system crash has occurred that would cause the missing JOBS record. Thus TEMPSPIN0 is re-sorted by SYSTEM and SMFTIME into TEMPSPIN1. Today's IPL records (if any) in TEMP0 are sorted into TEMP4 and compared with the possible spin records. If an IPL has occurred, the records are flagged with an ABEND value of 'CRSH' and passed into the CRSHTEMP data set. Otherwise, these records are passed to the NEWSPIN data set, which will replace OLDSPIN tomorrow.

At this point, then, all data on completed (or crashed) jobs is contained in the SAS data sets TEMP2 and CRSHTEMP.

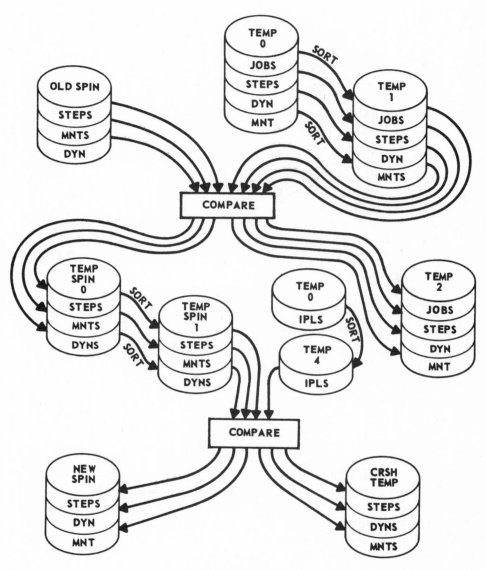

figure 14-5

In figure 14-6, the second half of this phase, we see the re-sort of CRSHTEMP and TEMP2 so that the pairs of STEPS, DYNS, and MNTS can be merged into TEMP6; JOBS is separately passed to TEMP7.

The DYN and MNT data sets, however, still contain one record per event whereas we want one summary record per step containing the total EXCPs to dynamic allocation and total mounts. Thus these two are sorted into TEMP8, and the SAS procedure MEANS is invoked to create the summary statistics in TEMP9.

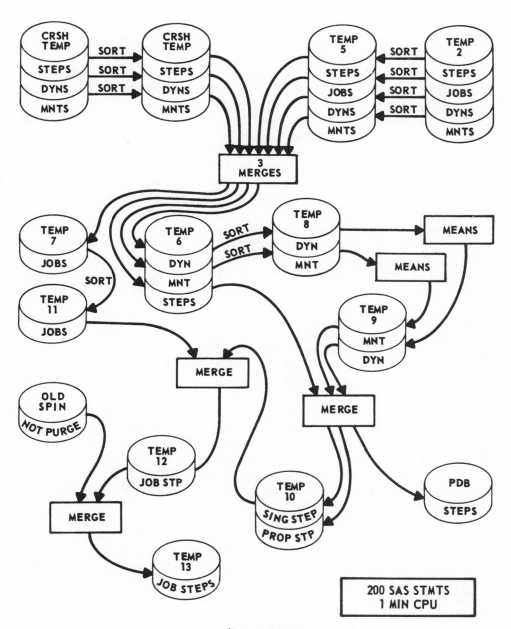

figure 14-6

The STEPS data from TEMP6 is then merged with the MNT and DYN data to produce a single record per STEP in the Performance Data Base data set STEPS, which contains all the desired resource information and time stamps. At the same time, the step information is collapsed and summarized into SINGLSTP in TEMP10, which contains all the resource usage summarized, one record per job. SINGLSTP is then merged with the JOBS data set to create JOBSTP in TEMP12, which is now a record of both resource consumption and account information, one consolidated record per job.

Finally, the OLDSPIN data set and NOTPURGE (which contains data for yesterday's jobs which had ended but had not been purged) are combined to create JOBSTEPS, which contains all of the execution information (resources, time stamps, accounts, etc.) at the job level.

The complexity of the flow just described suggests the difficulty of combining data from different SMF records to create usable data sets. The real power and ease of SAS can be seen when you realize that the entire second phase just described in figures 14-5 and 14-6 needs only 100 SAS statements, and executes in less than one minute of CPU time for each daily run!

Phase 3. The remaining phase will not be described in detail; the structure is similiar to the foregoing, but now the JOBSTEPS data set must be matched with operator change records, writer records, and purge records to build the remaining members of the Performance Data Base. This final phase requires less than one CPU minute and also is on the order of 200 SAS statements.

RMF records. The structure just described, then, handles the normal SMF records to build the entries in the Performance Data Base. The RMF records do not require this degree of matching; their problem is the mapping from the description in the RMF manual to the understanding of their meaning. Basically, the RMF records are described and simply added to the seven SAS data sets RMF70 through RMF76 in the PDB.

Using the information. Not only is the building of the PDB by SAS efficient, but the speed with which the information can be retrieved and analyzed is of great value. Since the data is stored in internal format on the SAS data set, no overhead for conversion is encountered.

The analysis is typically invoked through SAS procedures, which are load modules with simple option specifications to select the desired statistics. Figure 14-7 presents two simple analyses of the JOBS data set. First, a frequency distribution of ABEND (a constructed variable for CRaSH, JCL Errors, NOEXecution, NOTPurged, ReTuRN code, SYSTem or USER abend) shows the distribution of job terminations. A distribution by development area, for example, can be useful to identify areas which need education in JCL.

Second, some univariate statistics from the MEANS procedure are shown. These simple operations against the PDB provide significant insight into the resource consumption of the users of the computer system. The IWTREQ and IWTREC are the Initiation Wait Time Requested and Received, in hours, and thus we not only see average resource consumption (e.g., CPU TCB and SRB hours, but also batch response time delivered).

```
PROC FREQ DATA=PDB.JOBS;
   TABLES ABEND;
```

ABEND	FREQUENCY	CUM	PERCENT	CUM PCT
	1728	.	.	.
CRSH	1	1	.139	.139
JCL	129	130	17.292	18.031
NOEX	7	137	.971	19.001
NOTP	2	139	.277	19.279
RTRN	386	525	53.537	72.816
SYST	166	691	23.024	95.839
USER	30	721	4.161	100.000

```
PROC MEANS DATA=PDB.JOBS;
```

VARIABLE	N	MEAN	MIN	MAX	SUM
IWTREQ	1959	3.84	.25	168.0	
IWTREC	1943	.40	.00	18.7	
CPUTCBHR	2312	.0098	.00	2.007	22.7
CPUSRBHR	2309	.0021	.00	0.159	5.1
NTAPEDD	2309	1.521	0	66	3512
NUMDD	2309	29.19	0	600	67411
TAPEMNTS	866	2.67	1	33	2312
ELAPSHRS	2311	.29	.00	10.28	672.8

figure 14-7

While average IWT is of interest, average values of response variables are seldom as useful as distribution statistics. Thus the reporting of batch service (response) is based on the concept of IWT scheduling. Figure 14-8 outlines the scheduling approach in this system. It is a classless system. with no resource constraints and clearly stated objectives known to the user and supplier. The user specifies (through a locally designed JES2 control card) the desired response time of his job. Several concepts are important in making this scheduling work:

• The objectives are known and measurable by both supplier and the user.

- Actual dollars are charged: more for faster service, discounts for slower service.
- The user specifies desired response in his terms (hours and minutes) rather than in the supplier's terms (priority and class).
- Daily reporting of service delivered is supplied the user.

IWT Start Time is Maximum of:
  a Read in time, or
  b Last release from hold, or
  c Last change to IWT requested

IWT is initiation time minus IWT start time.

Valid IWT requests are:

15 min	1 hr	overnight
30 min	2 hr	weekend
	4 hr	

No Job Classes

No Resource Constraints

Aging is used so that after 2 hours in the system, a 4 hr job will be equal to a newly arrived 2 hr job.

Age up to 30 min only

Operators neither schedule work nor change IWT requested; that is the user's responsibility.

figure 14-8

Initiation Wait Time (IWT)

Figures 14-9 and 14-10 are the two primary reports on service delivered. Both are structured similarly; columns are headed by the response time requested, while rows represent the time period (shift) being reported. Within each major column heading are two columns, representing service delivered (% MET) and workload proportion (% JOBS or % CWU).

In Figure 14-9, the number of jobs that met the desired response time and the percentage of total jobs submitted for the response time are shown. An interesting problem was the definition of shift; should read-in-time or initiation time be used? Since users specify their response time to the supplier, and since users control read-in, release, etc., the expected initiation time was calculated as the IWT start time plus IWT requested, and thus the shift definition is the shift on which the user expected the job to run.

	15 MIN		30 MIN		1 HR	
	% MET	% JOBS	% MET	% JOBS	% MET	% JOBS
7AM-4PM	92.2	48.3	63.6	4.8	68.6	33.1
4PM-12PM	99.5	38.4	100.0	1.6	92.9	31.8
12PM-7AM	97.7	29.9	100.0	2.7	100.0	12.9
ALL SHIFTS	94.2	42.5	70.1	3.7	76.5	30.0

	2 HR		4 HR		TOTAL	
	% MET	% JOBS	% MET	% JOBS	% MET	% JOBS
7AM-4PM	68.6	4.5	82.9	9.3	81.1	1135
4PM-12PM	100.0	2.5	98.4	25.8	97.1	285
12PM-7AM	100.0	8.2	100.0	46.3	99.3	147
ALL SHIFTS	78.7	4.1	93.3	16.3	87.4	1830

figure 14-9
% Jobs Meeting Objectives

Figure 14-10 attempts to answer objections to using job counts as the service variable. In it, the Computer Work Unit (a linear composite of CPU, EXCP, device hours, mounts, etc.) is shown, first as the percentage of CWU which met objectives, and second, within the same IWT and shift, the percentage of total CWU in each category and shift.

These two reports, produced daily and also weekly, have received high acceptance from users and suppliers.

	15 MIN		30 MIN		1 HR	
	% MET	% CWU	% MET	% CWU	% MET	% CWU
7AM-4PM	94.4	46.9	35.3	4.2	67.8	34.1
4PM-12PM	99.9	38.9	100.0	4.8	91.1	10.7
12PM-7AM	83.0	29.9	100.0	3.5	100.0	9.4
ALL SHIFTS	94.7	38.3	74.2	4.1	75.9	18.9

	2 HR		4 HR		TOTAL	
	% MET	% CWU	% MET	% CWU	% MET	% CWU
7AM-4PM	75.0	4.2	58.4	10.6	78.2	
4PM-12PM	100.0	3.2	99.8	42.3	98.9	
12PM-7AM	100.0	18.7	100.0	38.5	94.9	
ALL SHIFTS	93.8	6.5	93.7	27.3	90.2	

figure 14-10
% CWU Meeting Objectives

RMF analysis. The preceding reports generally dealt with job-related or service-oriented reporting. Capacity planning and overall resource consumption can be evaluated from the STEPS data set in the PDB, but with the advent of MF1 and now RMF, the RMF records are a far superior source. Figure 14-11 simply plots the data from the RMF type 73 record with two SAS statements:

```
PROC PLOT DATA=PDB.RMF73;
  PLOT PCTBUSY*STARTIME=CHAN;
```

and graphically displays the channel activity on each channel versus time-of-day.

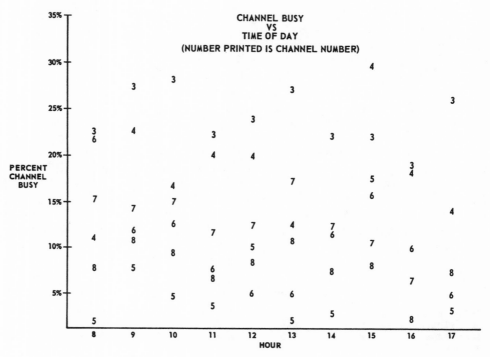

figure 14-11

The RMF72 record contains service units delivered, broken down by CPU, I/O, and Memory. Figure 14-12 shows a plot from the weekly PDB for prime shift, plotting service delivered (T=Total, C=CPU, I=IO, M=Memory) versus time of day. This type of weekly trend is a visual aid to the identification of system downs and delays.

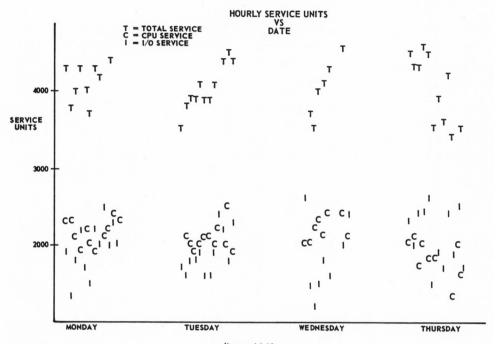

figure 14-12

Since all RMF records cover the same interval, it is very easy to merge the wait time, CPU service, and paging information from the RMF70, 71, and 72 records and produce composite resource statistics. Figure 14-13 shows how simply composite variables are defined from these three records.

CPUTCB = CPUUNITS/(SU__SEC*60*CPUCOEFF);
SYSAVAIL = DURAT; (= 2*DURAT for MP or AP)
PAGEFALT = PAGDAT1 + PAGDAT3;
PFRATE = (PAGDAT1 + PAGDAT2 + PAGDAT5 + PAGDAT6)/(60*DURAT);
CPU__FPLT = CPUTCB*60000/PAGEFALT;
CPUACT = SYSAVAIL − CPUWAIT;
CPULOST = CPUACT − CPUTCB;
PCTRECOV = 100*CPUTCB/CPUACT;
PCTCPUBY = 100*CPUACT/SYSAVAIL;
CPUSUSEC = CPUUNITS/(CPUCOEFF*60*DURAT);
CPUPAGIN = (100*.38*PAGDAT1*CPUCOEFF)/CPUUNITS;
EXCP__SEC = IOUNITS/(IOCOEFF*60*DURAT);

NOTE: SU__SEC = 151 for 168
                125 for 165
                51.2 for 158
                42 for 155
                24 for 145

figure 14-13

Almost always, the first question raised about SMF/RMF deals with the CPU time recovered. With the composite record, CPU Active can be calculated from the wait time in the RMF70 and the TCB time is calculated from the RMF72 CPU service units. Then the percent of CPU recovered can be evaluated. Figure 14-14 plots PCTTCBBY (Percent Total CPU Busy) to demonstrate that the CPU time recoverable generally correlates well with active CPU time.

These same composite variables can be used for not only routine reporting and trending, but also for specific evaluations. Recently, two megs of additional memory were added and the PDB was the data used in the evaluation. Figure 14-15 tabulates the hourly averages for two hours under three different configurations (6 MEG with 2 drums, 7 and 8 MEG with no drums). The numbers show the impact of additional memory, but the message is the simplicity of the evaluation with the Performance Data Base in place.

In summary, the comprehensive selection and combining of SMF and RMF data into a SAS-generated Performance Data Base has proven to be a valuable, cost-effective approach to performance measurement and tuning of MVS.

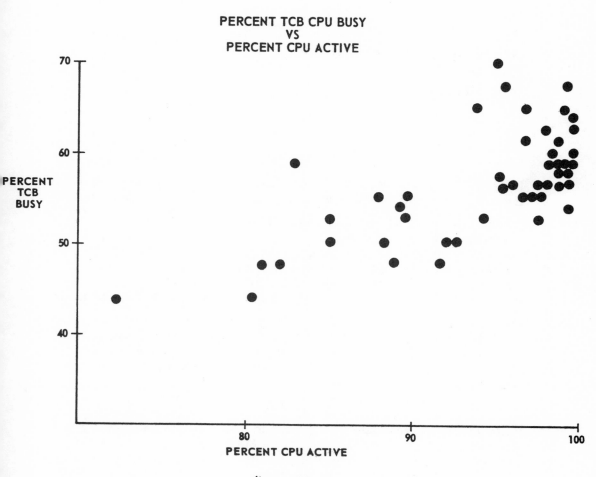

figure 14-14

	PCTCPUBY	CPUSU_SEC	PCTTCBBY	CPUPAGIN	PFRATE	CPU_PFLT
6/2	95.7	168	55.8	5.3	26	43
	96.8	175	58.1	5.6	29	40
7/0	98.8	186	61.6	2.7	15	81
	98.5	172	57.0	3.2	16	68
8/0	99.7	178	58.9	1.8	10	116
	99.9	180	59.7	1.7	9	123

	EXCP_SEC	AVQCOUNT	FIXEDAVG	UNILATERAL	EXCHANGE
6/2	171	27	543	366	36
	142	52	551	543	55
7/0	134	145	515	581	49
	159	34	561	862	114
8/0	193	110	542	803	79
	184	91	596	706	78

figure 14-15

15
MVS System Extensions,
Release 2.0:
The "New SMF"

In April 1979 IBM announced Release R2.0 of Version 1 of the MVS/System
Extension Program Product, which contains several notable new features:

- more stable TSO response under light loads
- memory isolation by task
- load balancing based on memory usage
- an interface for subsystem transaction reporting
- moving of the SRM constants into PARMLIB
- central control of performance group by a single PARMLIB member.

More important, however, was the announcement of a substantial rewrite
of SMF. The announcement was universally greeted with positive acceptance (especially in the eyes of the Computer Measurement and Evaluation
Project of SHARE, which had thirteen of its outstanding Requirements to
IBM "Announced and Accepted").

The changes to SMF can be grouped into four areas:

Performance improvements.   MANX and MANY are replaced by up to 36
(26 letters + 10 numbers) data sets MANA-MAN9, which are now VSAM, and
the SMF writer has been completely rewritten. It now uses an SMF lock (approximately 25 instructions) versus the old ENQ/DEQ on the SMF buffer
(approximately 1600 instructions); thus the SMF buffer should no longer be
a cause of contention. Furthermore, the SMF writer now has a number of
4K buffers (the number is installation-specified) and the number in use is
variable, dependent on need. Branch entry into the SMF writer and fast-
path VSAM significantly increase the rate at which SMF records can be
handled.

Flexibility enhancements.   Records to be written by SMF can now be
selected at the record ID level, but even further selection is possible. The
new SMF divides the world into subsystems (jobs, TSO, system tasks), and
records by record type can be specified separately for each subsystem.

Interval accounting is finally supported. For each of the three subsystems
above, an interval can be specified, in elapsed time, and certain SMF
records will be written out at that interval for all long-running tasks. A
MAXDORM value can be specified so that data in the SMF buffers will be
written at least that often.

System task accounting now permits data for all work in the system (including system tasks and problem programs started from the console) to be collected in record types 4, 5, 14, 15, 20, and 40. CPU times (TCB and SRB) for tasks in privileged state (i.e., the initiators) are now collected and associated with the task owning the initiator.

New records created. Four new SMF records have been created, and minor changes to existing SMF and RMF records have been made to support the new SRM changes.

Type 14 and 15: Data set close record (changed)
Open time of the data set is now provided (but not the open date).

Type 23: SMF statistics (new)
Comprehensive counts of buffer usage, physical I/O, and logical record counts processed by the SMF writer are reported, finally permitting performance monitoring of SMF itself.

Type 30: Work termination and interval recording (new)
This blockbuster combines much (but unfortunately not all) of the data currently spread across the type 4, 5, 20, 34, 35, and 40 SMF records, which are unchanged and are still written in SE2. A record is written at the beginning and end of each TSO session, batch step, batch job or started task, and additionally at the end of every interval. The records written at end of interval (and a special interval record written at end of step) contain the "delta" resources, i.e., the resources used just within that interval; the other type 30 records contain the total resources across the step or job.

Type 32: TSO command record (new)
Requiring the TSO Command Package for its data, this record accounts for TSO usage by command. Interval records (and total session records) contain a segment for each command executed, with a count of executions of each command and the CPU and I/O resources consumed by those executions. Unfortunately, no measure of response time (not even command elapsed time) is provided, but the information is still valuable since it will finally permit TSO usage to be profiled by command.

Type 90: Operator command record (new)
This long overdue record provides an audit check on most operator actions that affect SMF or the SRM. Commands logged in a type 90 (usually containing the time of command and new values of the changed parameters) are:

SET TIME	SET DATE	SET DMN	SET IPS
SWITCH SMF	HALT EOD	IPL PROMPT	IPL SMF
SET OPT	SET ICS	SET SMF	IPL SRM

Other features: Since the actual MANa data sets are VSAM (and a non-standard VSAM at that), IBM has provided an excellent dump program which transforms the VSAM SMF data into a standard BSAM sequential file. In addition to dumping the MAN data sets (and providing statistics on records dumped), the program can be invoked to read MAN without clearing. Thus SMF/RMF data can still be read "on the fly." Consequently none of the current programs that read SMF data need be changed, even though the records are initially written in VSAM.

New internal structure of records: the future way.   The four new SMF records no longer are described by fields located in fixed positions. Instead, all data is contained in relocatable segments in the BSAM records, pointed to by offsets (which themselves sometimes are in relocatable segments). This means that when future enhancements are made, existing analysis code will not become invalid (providing, of course, that future enhancements are made at the end of a relocatable segment). Thus it should be easier for IBM's SMF designers to make changes, since transparency of change has always been a limiting factor in SMF improvements. These relocatable segments will undoubtedly cause many languages and packages problems. Fortunately for us, the pointer form of input in SAS handles these relocatable segments without difficulty.

New record contents are valuable.   The new records in MVS/SE2 are certainly of significant value to the measurement analyst. Three of the records provide new information that simply wasn't available: SMF Statistics (type 23), TSO Command Usage (type 32), and Operator Commands (type 90). These additions alone are very important, because they recognize the importance of performance evaluation based on SMF data.
    The type 30 record is certainly welcome because it puts into one place data which was formerly scattered across three or four records, but it is far more important to users who have never heard of SAS. With the exception of data loss conditions (due to records in the buffer), the new type 30 provides users with nothing which was not available to a SAS user who used the MERGE statement. Had the new SMF only provided interval accounting for the type 4/34, 4/35, 40 and 20 records, the SAS user would have no need for the type 30 at all. This should be in no way construed as criticism of the new SMF, but rather a compliment to the power and ease with which SAS can combine a multiplicity of records. Certainly future PDBs will use the type 30. We may see a decline in the utility of the records which it might replace, but that is primarily because of the interval accounting feature rather than the data content of the type 30.

The machine-readable tape that is available with this book contains two files.

- The first file, DSN=SAS.SMF.SOURCE, contains the source library of SAS code. It is an unloaded partitioned data set containing approximately 100 members, with about 8000 SAS statements. It requires 41 tracks of 3350 disk space (BLKSIZE=3360) and 6 directory blocks. This file was created by SAS's PROC SOURCE, and is thus an IEBUPDTE-compatible sequential file that, when reloaded, will create the partitioned data set.
- The second file contains a small sample of SMF data from which some of the examples in the book were drawn. There are 486 logical records in this file, which will require 8 tracks of 3350 disk space.

The job shown in example 16-1 (contained in member JCLCOPY of SAS.SMF.SOURCE) allocates the required space and builds the SAS.SMF.SOURCE library. You will have to provide appropriate accounting information on the JOB card, and change the volume serial number XXXXXX to that of the 3350 device on which the data sets are to reside.

The first step not only builds the PDS, but also prints each member, producing approximately 200 pages of output. If the PDS is to be stored on a 3330 device, the UNIT= must be changed in each step, and the primary space allocation for the PDS needs to be 64; for the second data set, the primary space allocation needs to be 12.

```
//jobname JOB account,name
// EXEC PGM=IEBUPDTE,PARM=NEW
//SYSPRINT DD SYSOUT=A
//SYSIN    DD DSN=SAS.SMF.SOURCE,DISP=SHR,UNIT=TAPE,VOL=SER=SASSMF,
//            DCB=(RECFM=FB,LRECL=80,BLKSIZE=6160)
//SYSUT2   DD DSN=SAS.SMF.SOURCE,DISP=(,CATLG),VOL=SER=XXXXXX,
//            DCB=(RECFM=FB,LRECL=80,BLKSIZE=3360),UNIT=3350,
//            SPACE=(TRK,(45,3,8))
//S2 EXEC SAS
//IN      DD DSN=SAS.SMF.TESTDATA,DISP=SHR,UNIT=TAPE,VOL=SER=SASSMF,
//            DCB=(RECFM=VBS,LRECL=32756,BLKSIZE=4096),LABEL=(2,SL)
//OUT     DD DSN=SAS.SMF.TESTDATA,DISP=(,CATLG),VOL=SER=XXXXXX,
//            DCB=(RECFM=VBS,LRECL=32756,BLKSIZE=4096),UNIT=3350,
//            SPACE=(TRK,8)
//SYSIN   DD *
DATA _NULL_;
  INFILE IN;
  FILE OUT;
  INPUT;
  PUT _INFILE_;
```
example 16-1

Description of the contents of SAS.SMF.SOURCE. The members of SAS.SMF.SOURCE can be classified into four categories, identifiable from the member names:

JCLxxxx
Contains JCL of one form or another, either to copy the library or to use the source library for analysis.

MACxxxx
Contains the SAS macros used to build multiple SAS data sets in one pass of the SMF data.

TYPExxxx
Contains the SAS code to process the SMF data into one (in rare cases, two) SAS data sets per record type.

other
Examples of analysis using the SAS data sets built by MACxxxx or TYPExxxx code from SMF. Some general utility functions are also in these members.

Content of SAS.SMF.SOURCE partitioned data set

Member	Records	Description	Reference in Text
BUILDPDB	452	Build a performance data base.	chapter 13
CHANGES	16	Documentation of changes to contents of tape since previous version.	self-documenting
DBANAL	88	Data base analysis example.	chapter 6
DEBLOCK	32	SAS utility for deblocking VBS records. Used to detect bad VBS records.	self-documenting
ESV	94	Tape error statistics example.	chapter 7
HIUSEAGE	21	High resource usage programs example.	chapter 10
JCLCOPY	14	JCL to unload the tape.	example 16-1
JCLDBANL	530	JCL and code to perform DBANAL (data base analysis) with each phase of the analysis saved on separate tapes. This permits breaking up a very long and expensive job into pieces.	chapter 6
JCLMAC	60	JCL to use all the MAC members of the SAS.SMF.SOURCE PDS against SMF data.	example
JCLPDB	22	JCL to build a performance data base.	example
JCLPRALL	30	JCL and code to print (actually, to use any SAS procedure with) all SAS data sets in a single OS data set.	self-documenting

JCLTEST	210	JCL to test the SMF data at your installation. This two-step job should be run upon installation. It takes your SMF data as input, subsets two records of each ID, and then passes that subsetted SMF data through almost all of the members of the SAS.SMF.SOURCE data set.	example
JCLTYPE	63	JCL to use all of the TYPE members of the SAS.SMF.SOURCE PDS against SMF data.	example
LISTSMF	19	SAS utility to produce a hex and character listing of SMF records, and a cross reference of record type and location within the SMF data.	self-documenting
MACROS	385	The master MACRO file. All of the installation-dependent SAS code for SAS.SMF.SOURCE is contained in this member. See following discussion for installation-dependent values.	appendix 1
MACTEST	117	Example of building several SAS data sets from one pass of SMF using MACxxxx members.	chapter 12
MAC0	27	Macros for TYPE0.	TYPE0 appendix
MAC10	28	Macros for TYPE10.	TYPE10 appendix
MAC112	13	Macros for TYPE112.	TYPE112 appendix
MAC1415	377	Macros for TYPE1415.	TYPE1415 appendix
MAC1718	32	Macros for TYPE1718.	TYPE1718 appendix
MAC19	22	Macros for TYPE19.	TYPE19 appendix
MAC20	21	Macros for TYPE20.	TYPE20 appendix
MAC21	25	Macros for TYPE21.	TYPE21 appendix
MAC22	67	Macros for TYPE22.	TYPE22 appendix
MAC25	28	Macros for TYPE25.	TYPE25 appendix
MAC26J2	94	Macros for TYPE26J2 (JES2).	TYPE26J2 appendix
MAC26J3	64	Macros for TYPE26J3 (JES3).	TYPE26J3 appendix
MAC31	19	Macros for TYPE31.	TYPE31 appendix
MAC40	27	Macros for TYPE40.	TYPE40 appendix
MAC43PC	42	Macros for TYPE43PC.	TYPE43PC appendix
MAC434	116	Macros for TYPE434.	TYPE434 appendix
MAC4345	75	Macros for TYPE4345.	TYPE4345 appendix
MAC47PC	25	Macros for TYPE47PC.	TYPE47PC appendix
MAC4789	60	Macros for TYPE4789.	TYPE4789 appendix
MAC48PC	38	Macros for TYPE48PC.	TYPE48PC appendix
MAC49PC	18	Macros for TYPE49PC.	TYPE49PC appendix
MAC535	78	Macros for TYPE535.	TYPE535 appendix
MAC5568	26	Macros for TYPE5568.	TYPE5568 appendix
MAC57	22	Macros for TYPE57.	TYPE57 appendix
MAC6	86	Macros for TYPE6.	TYPE6 appendix

MAC62	31	Macros for TYPE62.	TYPE62 appendix
MAC6367	48	Macros for TYPE6367.	TYPE6367 appendix
MAC64	69	Macros for TYPE64.	TYPE64 appendix
MAC68	18	Macros for TYPE68.	TYPE68 appendix
MAC69	22	Macros for TYPE69.	TYPE69 appendix
MAC7	14	Macros for TYPE7.	TYPE7 appendix
MAC7072	318	Macros for TYPE7072.	TYPE7072 appendix
MAC71	111	Macros for TYPE71.	TYPE71 appendix
MAC73	92	Macros for TYPE73.	TYPE73 appendix
MAC74	66	Macros for TYPE74.	TYPE74 appendix
MAC75	43	Macros for TYPE75.	TYPE75 appendix
MAC76	45	Macros for TYPE76.	TYPE76 appendix
MAC77	35	Macros for TYPE77.	TYPE77 appendix
MAC8911	23	Macros for TYPE8911.	TYPE8911 appendix
MULTPROG	27	Multi-programming analysis.	chapter 10
MVT	196	Analysis of MVT SMF data. This code builds data sets from MVT data which are structurally identical to MVS data sets, but which have fewer variables due to less data in MVT SMF.	self-documenting
ONLINEUP	26	Analysis of on-line systems uptime.	chapter 9
PRINTERS	15	Analysis of printer requirements.	chapter 8
PRINTING	269	Print all SAS data sets built by TYPE or MAC members.	self-documenting
TAPEDRVS	27	Analysis of tape drive requirements.	chapter 7
TSORESP	12	Analysis of TSO response from RMF.	chapter 9
TSOUPTME	21	Analysis of TSO sub-system uptime.	chapter 9
TURNARND	16	Analysis of turnaround objectives.	chapter 4
TYPE0	28	Type 0 SMF records.	TYPE0 appendix
TYPE112	14	Type 1 and 12 SMF records.	TYPE112 appendix
TYPE1415	379	Type 14 and 15 SMF records.	TYPE1415 appendix
TYPE1718	34	Type 17 and 18SMF records.	TYPE1718 appendix
TYPE19	24	Type 19 SMF records.	TYPE19 appendix
TYPE20	23	Type 20 SMF records.	TYPE20 appendix
TYPE21	26	Type 21 SMF records.	TYPE21 appendix
TYPE22	68	Type 22 SMF records.	TYPE22 appendix
TYPE23	32	Type 23 SMF records (MVS SE2).	TYPE23 appendix
TYPE25	29	Type 25 SMF records.	TYPE25 appendix
TYPE26J2	95	Type 26 SMF records (JES2).	TYPE26JES2 appendix
TYPE26J3	86	Type 26 SMF records (JES3).	TYPE26J3 appendix
TYPE30	144	Type 30 SMF records (MVS SE2).	TYPE30 appendix
TYPE31	20	Type 31 SMF records.	TYPE31 appendix
TYPE32	51	Type 32 SMF records (MVS SE2).	TYPE32 appendix
TYPE40	29	Type 40 SMF records.	TYPE40 appendix
TYPE43PC	43	Type 43 VSPC records.	TYPE43PC appendix

TYPE434	119	Type 4 and 34 SMF records.	TYPE434 appendix
TYPE4345	78	Type 43 and 45 SMF records.	TYPE4345 appendix
TYPE47PC	27	Type 47 VSPC records.	TYPE47PC appendix
TYPE4789	61	Type 47, 48, and 49 SMF records.	TYPE4789 appendix
TYPE48PC	35	Type 48 VSPC records.	TYPE48PC appendix
TYPE49PC	19	Tyep 49 VSPC records.	TYPE49PC appendix
TYPE535	80	Type 5 and 35 SMF records..	TYPE535 appendix
TYPE5568	27	Type 55, 56, and 58 NJE SMF records.	TYPE5568 appendix
TYPE57	23	Type 57 NJE SMF records.	TYPE57 appendix
TYPE6	87	Type 6 SMF records.	TYPE6 appendix
TYPE62	33	Type 62 SMF records.	TYPE62 appendix
TYPE6367	49	Type 63 and 67 SMF records.	TYPE6367 appendix
TYPE64	71	Type 64 SMF records.	TYPE64 appendix
TYPE68	19	Type 68 SMF records.	TYPE68 appendix
TYPE69	22	Type 69 SMF records.	TYPE69 appendix
TYPE7	15	Type 7 SMF records.	TYPE7 appendix
TYPE7072	319	Type 70 and 72 RMF records.	TYPE7072 appendix
TYPE71	112	Type 71 RMF records.	TYPE71 appendix
TYPE73	93	Type 73 RMF records.	TYPE73 appendix
TYPE74	74	Type 74 RMF records.	TYPE74 appendix
TYPE75	45	Type 75 RMF records.	TYPE75 appendix
TYPE76	46	Type 76 RMF records.	TYPE76 appendix
TYPE77	36	Type 77 RMF records.	TYPE77 appendix
TYPE8911	25	Type 8, 9 and 11 SMF records.	TYPE8911 appendix
TYPE90	113	Type 90 SMF records (MVS SE2).	TYPE90 appendix
USEAGE	38	CPU usage analysis by performance group.	chapter 5

Installation-dependent considerations. All of the installation-dependent values are in single member MACROS of SAS.SMF.SOURCE. Appendix 2 should be read carefully to understand the possible impact those macros might have on your analysis.

However, in terms of data accuracy, the only area of installation dependency deals with mountable device counts. In the processing of step records and related records (i.e., 4, 30, 34, and 40), the number of tape drives and 2314 drives allocated for each step is stored in the variables TAPEDRVS and D2314DRV. Also counted is D3330DRV, the number of 3330 drives that were allocated and that by address are identified as mountable devices. For the latter, a table of addresses is needed (_MNTABLE macro in member MACROS).

For all three values (TAPEDRVS, D2314DRV, and D3330DRV), it is necessary to know which devices are addressable from two channels, because the first device segment may contain address X580 and the second may contain address X380; if channels 3 and 5 are two-channel-switched, that device is actually the same. With the correct two-channel description, the code will count that as one device allocated rather than two.

Thus if you have two-channel switching anywhere in your system, you must correctly describe that logic in the __TWOCHAN and __TWOCHA macros. If you have mountable 3330 devices, if not all 2314 devices are considered mountable, or if you have any other mountable devices, you will need to modify macro __MNTABLE and possibly its reference in macro __EXCPGET. Read completely the discussion of the MACROS member in appendix 2.

If you do not have two-channel switching, it is still very necessary that you read and understand the description and the assumptions that are made in that code.

If you encounter I/O errors upon attempting to read the SMF file, you should read the discussion of the __SMF macro, also in appendix 1.

Where to begin next.   By this time you have probably read the chapters of the book, if not all of the appendices. If you have not, edit and submit the JCLTEST member of SAS.SMF.SOURCE.

JCLTEST is a good place to start, as it will select a couple of records of each record type, process them with the basic code, and print them out. This should help you to adapt to the variable names, and you will begin to see how they relate to the data from your own system.

Before you leap into a performance data base, appreciate the magnitude of information contained in only one record type (or in only one SAS data set, such as TYPE535 or TYPE434). This book is quite comprehensive; it is a complete mapping of all the data available in all the SMF records. It is extremely inefficient use of your computer resources if you start storing all of the SAS data sets that could be built with this code and your SMF records. You must adapt the information content available in SMF with the objectives of your installation, and save only the relevant. It is better to start small and build up, in terms of the number of SAS data sets built into a performance data base, and the number of variables placed in each data set. If your present performance reporting system meets present needs, it may be not only unwise but also counterproductive to try and sell an entire new reporting scheme based on SAS. In such a case, use SAS to fill in where information doesn't exist, rather than compete.

It is not even clear that the objective of an installation with this book should be to build a performance data base. While many have found that a worthwhile effort, it can only be of value if enough talent is available to analyze the data, and only if management can be persuaded to make decisions based on data. Fight battles that you can win, and avoid the conflict when you think you can't win.

SAS Primer
SAS Macros
Appendices 1 and 2

Appendix 1
SAS Primer

This primer's purpose is to explain the SAS code in this book. Statements of the language are not exhaustively described; for more information about the SAS language, consult the *SAS User's Guide*, available from SAS Institute.

Two logical states.   While SAS is executing, it is in one of two states. Either it is building a SAS data set, or it is analyzing a SAS data set with a SAS procedure (which could also build a new SAS data set).

The DATA statement signals the beginning of building a data set; the PROC statement signals the beginning of analyzing a data set.

A logical piece of work to SAS consists of all SAS statements between a DATA or PROC statement and the next DATA or PROC statement. SAS interprets those statements when it encounters the second DATA or PROC statement and performs the requested functions at that time. SAS then continues to scan the statements for the next DATA or PROC statement, and the process continues until all the DATA and PROC steps in the job have been completed.

SAS statements.   All SAS statements are free-form. Columns 1 through 80 are scanned (columns 1-72 of line-numbered records), and a semicolon delimits each statement. There is no continuation symbol; the absence of a semicolon indicates a continued statement. SAS permits multiple statements on a single line, and blank lines can be inserted with no effect. Blanks must separate keywords and names, but are not required between special characters and keywords or names. Where a single blank is permitted, any number of blanks may occur.

SAS names.   Names of data sets, files, variables, and so on are limited to 8 characters and must begin with an alphabetic character or underscore. Unlike languages such as PL/I, the same name may be used repeatedly in a SAS program for different purposes (e.g., the name can be the same for a SAS data set, a SAS variable within that data set, and a label in the program).

SAS data sets.   SAS stores its data in direct-access BDAM OS data sets on disk, or in BSAM OS data sets on tape. A single OS data set used by SAS can contain a number of SAS data sets. Each SAS data set is a collection of **observations,** which may be regarded as rows of a matrix. Each observation of a data set is a collection of **variables,** whose name is assigned by the user, and each variable can be regarded as a column of a matrix. The number of variables is constant for all observations, although some observations may have missing values for some variables.

```
DATA TYPE434(KEEP=JOB READTIME CPUTM);
  LENGTH DEFAULT=4 READTIME 8;
  FORMAT READTIME DATETIME19.2 CONDCODE HEX3.;
  INFILE SMF STOPOVER LENGTH=LENGTH COL=C    RECFM=VBS
        LRECL=32756;
INPUT @2 ID PIB1. @3 SMFTIME SMFSTAMP8.
      @23 READDATE PD4. @16 JOB $8. @;
  IF ID=4 THEN GO TO TYPE4;
  IF ID=4;
  BEGIN=105;
  LINK EXCPGET;
  OUTPUT TYPE434;
  X=.;
  EXCPTOT=SUM(EXCP2314,EXCP3330,EXCP3350);
  RIGHTBIT=MOD(BYTE,2);
  LEFTBIT=FLOOR(BYTE/128);
  . . .
```

DATA step.   A SAS DATA step takes input data (which could be an OS data set on tape or disk, a previously built SAS data set, or any combination of any number of OS or SAS data sets) and builds one or more new data sets. During this phase, the complete repertoire of the SAS language is available to the user. The following sequence of statements, which reads an SMF data set and builds a single SAS data set, is typical of the code in this book.

DATA TYPE434(KEEP = JOB READTIME CPUTM);

DATA statement.   The DATA statement tells SAS to invoke the SAS compiler, and names the SAS data set to be built (TYPE434). Additionally, options can be stated through the parenthetical expression. In this example, the KEEP= option is used, which causes only the variables JOB, READTIME, and CPUTM to be kept in data set TYPE434.

LENGTH DEFAULT = 4 READTIME 8;

LENGTH statement.   SAS numeric variables are stored as floating-point numbers. The default length is 8 bytes (double precision); however, in SMF applications, there is seldom a need for that accuracy, and significant disk space can be saved through the use of the LENGTH statement. Here, the default for all numeric variables being built in this phase is changed to 4. At the same time, however, the READTIME variable is kept at a length of 8, because the date and time (to hundredths of a second) do require a full eight bytes.

FORMAT READTIME DATETIME19.2 CONDCODE HEX3. ;

FORMAT statement.   You can associate formats for output from SAS variables at the time the data set is built, and these formats are then used unless overridden by another FORMAT statement. SAS has an extensive collection of date, time, and date-time formats, and a series of functions for constructing dates, times, etc. In this FORMAT statement, the DATETIME19.2 format converts the value of READTIME, which is the number of seconds since January 1, 1960, to print out as

04JUL79:12:23:02.34

INFILE SMF STOPOVER LENGTH=LENGTH COL=C
 RECFM=VBS LRECL=32756;

INFILE statement. The INFILE statement names the DD (input file name or Data Definition) containing the data to be read. In addition, several options can be specified:

STOPOVER. SAS permits a user to read more than one logical record with one INPUT statement. This is not desired in handling SMF data, but can occur if an incomplete record is written to SMF. The STOPOVER option causes SAS to stop processing if it is directed to read beyond the present logical record, and causes the bad record to be printed on the SAS log.

LENGTH=LEN. The LENGTH= keyword allows the user to specify a variable name (here, LEN), which contains the actual length of the logical record being processed. LENGTH is needed in processing some SMF records, since only by knowing the length can the user identify which release of the operating system wrote the record; there are often field relocations between releases.

COL=C. The COL= keyword allows the user to specify a variable name (here, C), which will contain the current position of the pointer to the input record (i.e., the current column). This feature is needed in SMF processing, not only to take care of different releases, but also to prevent STOPOVER errors from occurring.

RECFM=VBS LRECL=32756. The DCB attributes of the input file can be specified on the INFILE statement, on the DD card, or in the data set label on the tape or disk SMF file. However, since the attributes may not be correct on the actual data set, the correct attributes are also specified here. See appendix 2.

INPUT @2 ID PIB1. @3 SMFTIME SMFSTAMP8.
 @23 READDATE PD4. @16 JOB $8. @;

INPUT statement. The INPUT statement extracts data from the OS records based on the input format specified for each variable, and stores it into SAS variables which are "created" by the INPUT statement. The @ symbol locates the pointer to the desired column. The variable (ID) is then named, and its format on the OS record is given (PIB1., for positive integer binary of length one byte). Similarly, the variable SMFTIME is found starting in the 3rd column or byte of the OS record, and a special format SMFSTAMP8. converts the four-byte date and four-byte time into a SAS date-time value. At column 23, the read date, with an OS packed decimal format of length 4, is stored into the READDATE variable. The JOB variable, a character string of length 8, is picked up starting in column 16 of the OS record. The last item in the INPUT statement, a trailing @ sign, causes SAS to remain on the same input record for the next INPUT statement.

IF ID=4 THEN GO TO TYPE4;

IF-THEN statement.   This IF-THEN statement controls the logic flow of a SAS DATA step. With Boolean connectives (AND, OR, NOT), the expression tested can be highly complex and yet compact. In the example above, the result of a true expression (ID=4) is the execution of the GO TO statement. The expression can be any SAS expression, and the statement can be any executable statement. SAS permits both the spelled-out Boolean connectives AND, OR, NOT, as well as their symbols from the 64-character set (&, |, ⌐), and the symbols and characters can be intermixed. Furthermore, SAS supports "bounded" expressions such as

   IF 70 <= ID <= 79 THEN LABEL='RMF';

More complex logic can be handled with the 1979 version of SAS which contains structured programming capabilities including IF-THEN/ELSE, and DO statements. However, very little of this syntax is used here.

IF ID=4;

Subsetting IF-statement.   The IF statement is a shorthand form of the IF-THEN statement. If the expression is true, the next statement is executed. If the expression is not true, the current record is not added to the data set being built, and the SAS program returns to get the next input record.

BEGIN=105;
LINK EXCPGET;

LINK statement.   The LINK statement is a branch-and-return subroutine call. The label EXCPGET is branched to, and when a RETURN statement is encountered, SAS returns to the statement following the LINK statement. Arguments for the subroutine are assigned (BEGIN=105) before the LINK is issued.

OUTPUT TYPE434;

OUTPUT statement.   The OUTPUT statement permits the user to tell SAS explicitly when to add the current observation to the SAS data set being built. In the case of multiple output data sets, the OUTPUT statement names the SAS data set to which the observation is added. If a SAS program contains no OUTPUT statement, each observation is automatically added to the SAS data set when the last statement is executed, or when a RETURN statement is encountered.

RETURN statement.   The RETURN statement has two distinct uses in SAS. When a LINK statement has been executed, and a RETURN statement is encountered, SAS returns to the statement following the LINK statement. When no LINK statement has been executed, the RETURN statement causes SAS to return to get the next record. In addition, when no OUTPUT statements appear in the SAS program, the RETURN statement causes SAS to add the current observation to the SAS data set being built. Internally, a RETURN statement is automatically added as the last statement of each SAS program.

GO TO statement.   The GO TO (or GOTO) statement causes SAS to begin execution at the label named. Labels are simply SAS names followed by a colon. They may appear on the same line as the statement, or on a preceding line.

   X = .;

Missing values.   The concept of a missing value of a variable is quite important in SAS and especially important in SMF analysis, where missing values are frequent. The missing value concept differentiates between a zero value and a non-existent value. For example, an initiation time of 0 would mean 0 seconds, or midnight, whereas a job that did not initiate at all would have a missing value. (Internally, numeric missing values have the value of the smallest negative value in the universe).

To prevent incorrect statistics, SAS also ensures integrity in arithmetic operations.

Arithmetic operations on missing values produce a result of a missing value. Thus you must be aware of the possibility of missing values. If a numeric value can be missing and it appears in an arithmetic statement, you must take other steps; for example, use the SUM function.

The symbol for setting or testing of missing variables is the period:

   IF X = . THEN MISS = 'YES';

Note that the period is not enclosed in quotes; to do so would be to make the test a character test for period rather than a numeric test for a missing value. For character variables, the missing value is a blank character string.

RETAIN statement.   At the beginning of each SAS program, SAS sets all variables to missing values, and then begins to input or assign values. Thus a value read in will not be inadvertently retained from one observation to the next. If, however, you desire to retain the value of a variable from one observation to the next, naming that variable in a RETAIN statement will cause SAS to preserve the value from one observation to the next.

   EXCPTOT = SUM(EXCP2314,EXCP3330,EXCP3350);

SUM function.   The SUM function is used with variables that might have missing values. For example, if the number of EXCPs to 2314s could be missing, the statement

   EXCPTOT = EXCP2314 + EXCP3330 + EXCP3350;

would cause EXCPTOT to have a missing value any time one of the three values were missing. Note that if all three EXCP counts were missing, the EXCPTOT would be missing. If the SUM function were used instead, the value of EXCPTOT would be the sum of the non-missing values. If it were written

EXCPTOT = SUM(EXCP2314, EXCP3330, EXCP3350, 0);

even if all three EXCPs were missing, the EXCPTOT would be zero rather than missing.

RIGHTBIT = MOD(BYTE,2);

MOD function.   The MOD function returns the modulo (remainder) of the first argument when the first argument is divided by the second argument. The example above would cause RIGHTBIT to have the value 1 if BYTE were odd, and the value of 0 if BYTE were even.

LEFTBIT = FLOOR(BYTE/128);

FLOOR function.   The FLOOR function returns the largest integer that is less than or equal to the argument. In the example above, LEFTBIT would have the value 1 if BYTE were greater than 127 and less than 256 (assuming BYTE was read in with a format of PIB1.) and the value 0 if BYTE were less than or equal to 127. The FLOOR function is also used to truncate the fraction portion of a numeric value. It also sees use (because of the absence of a BIT function in the 1976 release of SAS and earlier releases) in combination with the MOD function to set pseudo-bit variables. For example, the third bit from the left of a one-byte field can be tested:

IF FLOOR(MOD(BYTE,64)/32) = 1 THEN THIRD = 'ON';

Date, time, and date-time values and functions.   SAS provides extensive facilities for reading and manipulating dates, times, and date-time values. Dates are stored as the number of days since January 1, 1960; through formats, the date can be printed. For date comparisons and tests, the desired test values must be converted into SAS dates via SAS functions (since we normally don't carry around in our head the number of days since January 1, 1960). In addition, in SMF, most of the dates are contained as Julian dates in a packed decimal field, requiring a conversion into SAS internal dates. Thus two alternatives may be found in this book:

INPUT DATE PD4.;
IF DATE = 79034;

or

INPUT DATE PD4.;
SASDATE = DATEJUL(DATE);
IF SASDATE = MDY(02,03,1979);

In general, the second choice is preferred, as most people are more comfortable with real dates rather than with Julian dates.

SAS time values are stored internally as seconds and a number of formats to print them are also provided. There are also functions for conversion:

```
INPUT TIME HHMM5.;            (input would contain 10:15)
IF TIME = HMS(10,15,0);
```

SAS date-time values are stored as the number of seconds since January 1, 1960. Since many of the time functions or formats operate on a modulo 24-hour basis, many are applicable to date-time values as well. However, the date functions are not constructed to handle directly the date portion of a SAS date-time value, so two special functions exist for partitioning date-time values:

```
DATE = DATEPART(DATETIME);
TIME = TIMEPART(DATETIME);
```

Finally, there is a generating function that allows the user to create a SAS date-time value:

```
DATETIME = DHMS(MDY(02,03,1979),10,15,0);
```

to create a date-time value, which, when printed with the DATETIME13. format, would be

02FEB79:10:15

Since the date and time formats truncate from the right (rather than round) when the format underspecifies the field, storing the SMF time and date combinations as SAS date-time values, and then using SAS formats to control BY grouping has been found very useful. Specifically, if a date-time value is formatted DATETIME7., the data can be clustered by date, without any loss of the full date-time value.

SAS created the SMFSTAMP8. input format for SMF data. The SMFSTAMP8. format reads the Julian date from four packed decimal bytes, then reads the time of day from the next four bytes and converts the eight bytes directly into a SAS date-time value. You must associate the format DATETIME19.2 with the variable to print out its complete value.

A final observation on dates, times, and date-times: in handling SMF data, the dates and times can be stored in variables with a length (using the LENGTH statement) of 4 bytes. For a date-time value, however, the value will be truncated unless a length of 8 bytes is specified. Thus all of the LENGTH statements use DEFAULT=4 and then enumerate the date-time values that are to have length 8.

SET statement.   The SET statement is like the INPUT statement, except that its input is from a previously built SAS data set rather than raw OS records. In addition, multiple SAS data sets can be brought together throught the SET statement. There are two different ways in which multiple data sets can be combined, depending on whether a BY statement is present:

```
DATA ALL;
   SET DAILY WEEKLY MONTHLY;
```

Data set ALL would contain all of the observations of DAILY, followed by all the observations of WEEKLY, and finally by all the observations of MONTHLY. Thus, without a BY statement, the SET statement concatenates the SAS data sets from left to right.

```
DATA ALLJOBS;
  SET LASTWEEK THISWEEK;
  BY READTIME;
```

The new data set ALLJOBS would be the interleaved combination of LASTWEEK and THISWEEK and would be sorted by READTIME (both LASTWEEK and THISWEEK must already be sorted by READTIME).

Following the SET (or BY statement, if any), other SAS statements can be used to subset the data.

The real power of the SET statement (and also the MERGE statement, below) lies in the special variables that can be established by the user. Consider this example:

```
DATA OK535S   OK434S;
  SET TYPE535 (IN=IN535)   TYPE434 (IN=IN434);
  BY READTIME JOB;
  IF IN535 AND IN434 THEN DO;
    IF IN535 THEN OUTPUT OK535S;
    IF IN434 THEN OUTPUT OK434S;
    RETURN;
    END;
  IF NOT FIRST.JOB THEN RETURN;
  IF IN535 THEN PUT 'MISSING STEP RECORD FOR '
    JOB= READTIME= ;
  IF IN434 THEN PUT 'MISSING JOB RECORD FOR '
    JOB= READTIME=;
  RETURN;
```

Two new data sets (OK535S and OK434S) are built, taking the two previous data sets TYPE535 and TYPE434 as input. The IN= keyword is used on the SET statement to create two new variables (IN535 and IN434) that are associated with the two data sets: The variable is set to 1 (true) if the current values of the BY variable are contained in its associated data set, and is set to 0 (false) otherwise. Thus the DO group is executed only for input data where both a TYPE535 observation and a TYPE434 observation have the same READTIME and JOB.

The statement following the DO group exposes another class of special variables, the FIRST. and LAST. variables. By linking FIRST. or LAST. with any variable in the BY statement, not only can existence of values be tested with IN= variables, but also the first or last occurence of the value can be determined. In this example, the error message is wanted only once per JOB. (Note that FIRST.JOB is logically true if the READTIME variable changes, so that only the last variable needs to be FIRST. tested).

MERGE statement.   Depending on your computer background, you will consider the MERGE statement perfectly named, or you will revolt at the mis-use of the word MERGE. The MERGE statement is syntactically quite like the SET statement, and is used to combine multiple SAS data sets into one or more new data sets. However, it does not function like the merge in Sort/Merge—that facility of interleaving records is done with the SET statement and a BY statement in SAS.

The MERGE statement in SAS takes the observations from several input SAS data sets that have common values of BY variables and creates one observation containing all of the variables in the input SAS data sets. Thus the function of the MERGE statement is to merge variables from several data sets into one data set. The IN= keyword and the FIRST. and LAST. variables can be used just as with the SET statement. The following example demonstrates the results with the MERGE statement in a typical application:

SAS data set JOBS

JOB	ACCOUNT
a	123456789
b	234567890
d	456789012
e	467890123

SAS data set STEPS

JOB	PROGRAM	CPUTCBTM
a	SAS	10:30.02
a	IEDCAMS	:20.01
b	IEBGENER	:15.03
c	TESTPGM	:02.00
d	ANDI	:01.00

```
DATA PGMACCTS;
   MERGE JOBS (IN=INJ) STEPS (IN=INS);
   BY JOB;
   IF INJ AND INS THEN OUTPUT;
```

SAS data set PGMACCTS

JOB	ACCOUNT	PROGRAM	CPUTCBTM
a	123456789	SAS	10:30.02
a	123456789	IEDCAMS	:20.01
b	234567890	IEBGENER	:13.03
d	456789012	ANDI	:01.00

SAS data set PGMACCTS (no IF statement)

JOB	ACCOUNT	PROGRAM	CPUTCBTM
a	123456789	SAS	10:30.02
a	123456789	IEDCAMS	:20.01
b	234567890	IEBGENER	:13.03
c		TESTPGM	02.00
d	456789012	ANDI	:02.00
e	467890123		

Procedure step.   The PROC step of SAS (as differentiated from the DATA step) is signified by the presence of a PROC statement, requesting SAS to execute a particular load module. The procedure step is the statistical power of SAS, just as the DATA step is the data-handling power. However, there are several statistical procedures that are used heavily in handling SMF. Discussion of the statistical routines is beyond the scope of this primer, but the commonly used procedures are described below to assist in reading the code in this book.

PROC statement.   The PROC statement varies slightly between procedures but generally has the folowing features:

PROC *procname* DATA=*input* OUT=*output options;*

The procname is the load module that is linked to (a true link is issued, and thus non-SAS modules can be accessed via a PROC statement). The DATA= keyword, if supplied, specifies the SAS data set to be processed by the procedure (if the DATA= specification is not present, the most recently built SAS data set is used). The OUT= keyword applies to some procedures that build output data sets, and permits you to name the new data set.

For each procedure there are options that may be specified. A common option for many procedures is NOPRINT, which suppresses printed output of the procedure, and usually accompanies an OUT= keyword when a procedure is used to build a new data set.

BY statement.   The BY statement may be used with all procedures, and is a very powerful tool for clustering observations together. It causes the procedure to be invoked for each group of BY variables that have common values. For example, the statements

PROC PLOT;
  BY DATE;

produce a separate plot (graph) for each value of DATE encountered.

VAR (VARIABLES) statement.   You can restrict SAS to certain variables in the data set being processed by the VAR statement.

FORMAT statement. The same FORMAT statement described under the DATA step can be associated with a procedure execution. The essential difference is that when a format is associated with a variable in the PROC step, the format association exists only for the life of the procedure, and does not permanently alter the variable's format. FORMAT statements find heavy use with the FREQ procedure and the PRINT procedure.

The PRINT procedure. The PRINT procedure is the most frequently used SAS procedure in SMF analysis. It simply prints all of the variables in a SAS data set (or only those variables desired, if a VAR statement is used). The only commonly used option is the PAGE option, which, when a BY statement is used, will cause each new BY-group to start on a new page:

```
PROC PRINT PAGE DATA=TYPE535;
  BY ACCOUNT;
  VAR CPUTCBTM CPUSRBTM JOB READTIME;
```

The PRINT procedure formats the page based on the device you are using (i.e., if you print to a 3270-type TSO terminal with only 80 positions, SAS knows the line width and formats the output appropriately and attempts to make the printed page as readable as possible. In fact, if the variable names are all long but the data values are short, SAS will print the variable names vertically so that all the data will fit on a single line. The majority of the printed reports are produced with simple PROC PRINTs.

The SORT procedure. Since it is our nature to want to cluster similar things, the SORT procedure is heavily used.

```
PROC SORT DATA=IN OUT=OUT;
  BY JOB DESCENDING DATE;
```

In the absence of the OUT= keyword, SAS sorts and restores the data in the input data set. The BY statement describes the sort fields, and the keyword DESCENDING (since it is 9 characters long, there can be no ambiguity with a variable name) describes those variables that are to be sorted in descending order, as opposed to the default of ascending value.

The MEANS procedure. The MEANS procedure provides univariate statistics, but is more frequently used to build an output data set. (Its usage can be expected to drop dramatically with the new PROC SUMMARY in the 1979 version of SAS.) The statements

```
PROC MEANS DATA=IN NOPRINT;
  VAR CPU EXCPS ELAPSED;
  OUTPUT OUT=STATS
  SUM=SUMCPU SUMEXCPS SUMELAP
  MAX=MAXCPU MAXEXCPS MAXELAP;
```

produce a new data set named STATS, containing a single observation (since there is no BY statement) of six variables. The choice of statistics output by the MEANS procedure is determined by the keywords used in the OUTPUT statement. The SUM= keyword gives, in left-to-right order, the new variable names containing the sum of the values of the variables in the VAR statement. Thus the position of the variables in the VAR statement and the OUTPUT statement must match exactly. Similarly, the three variables MAXCPU, MAXEXCPS and MAXELAP contain the maximum value of the three corresponding variables.

The FREQ procedure.   The FREQ procedure is used to produce frequency distributions and crosstabulations. It sees its heaviest use in early scanning of data to determine anomalies, but is also used to produce tabulations. Since it uses the format of the variable to cluster its observations, it is a very flexible too. The statements

```
PROC FREQ;
   TABLES READTIME;
   FORMAT READTIME DATETIME7.;
```

produce a tabulation of the date on which jobs were read in. The count of jobs read in one each day is given, as well as the percentages and cumulative frequencies of job counts. With the WEIGHT statement however, the FREQ proc weights each observation by the value of the WEIGHT variable, and thus the statements

```
PROC FREQ;
   TABLES READTIME;
   FORMAT READTIME DATETIME7.;
   WEIGHT CPUTM;
```

provide the distribution of CPU time used for each date on which jobs were read in.

Crosstabulation is very useful in determining who is doing what, since it displays the occurrences of each value of the crosstabulated variables. Crosstabulation is invoked by connecting the variables with an asterisk in the TABLES statement: for example, the statements

```
PROC FREQ;
   TABLES JOBCLASS*ACCOUNT;
```

provide a table showing which accounts used which job classes.

The PLOT procedure.   The PLOT procedure provides a simple tool for producing graphs and plots of data:

```
PROC PLOT;
   PLOT CPUTCBTM*SELAPSTM;
```

Other procedures are also useful in the analysis of SMF data; for more information about them, refer to the *SAS User's Guide.*

Several SAS macros are used in building the SAS SMF data sets. By convention, all macro names begin with an underscore _ to improve readability of the SAS code.

The macros serve to reduce repetition of the same code; they also contain installation-dependent code, and code which would be changed if new devices were announced.

Macro _EXCPGET defines the mountable 3330 devices by unit address, and requires that two-channel switches (if installed) be described to properly count mountable devices. Ensure that these macros are closely examined and modified for your installation before using this code.

The macros described below are contained in member MACROS of the SAS source.

_ACCTGET

The _ACCTGET macro is used to decode the multiple account fields that can occur in the type 4, 5, 20, 35, and JES3 type 26 SMF records. These records contain a variable number of account fields: _ACCTGET decodes the first nine account fields, then assigns the contents and the length of each of the nine fields to variables named ACCOUNT1-ACCOUNT9 and LEN1-LEN9. The actual number of fields decoded is contained in the variable NRFLDS in those SAS data sets.

You can optimize this macro by determining the maximum number of account fields your installation permits and the maximum length of each account field. Build a TYPE535 SAS data set (see appendix TYPE535) for a week's data. Then use PROC FREQ to tabulate the data:

    PROC FREQ DATA=TYPE535;
      TABLES NRFLDS LEN1-LEN9 ACCOUNT1-ACCOUNT9;

Reduce the number of blanks in the initialization of each of the ACCOUNTn variables (lines 800 through 1600 in _ACCTGET) to the maximum for each ACCOUNTn. For example, if the maximum value of NRFLDS is less than 9 (e.g., 5) change the line which now reads

    IF NRFLDS=5 THEN RETURN;   (line 4200)

to read

    RETURN;

This change will eliminate unnecessary tests while preserving the original structure of the code; also, it will reduce the size of the SAS data sets built with this code.

__DEVICE

The __DEVICE macro is used to decode the UCB type field which occurs in SMF type 8, 9, 10, 11, 14, 15, 19, 62, 64, 74, and 75 records. The UCB type is decoded into a variable named DEVICE containing the common name of the device, (e.g., 3330, 3330-11, TAPE, etc.). There should be no need to change this macro, as it maps all current device types (2311 is excluded as "current"). If new devices are announced or if you want to expand some of the classifications (for example, all communications devices are lumped together), you can change the definitions here. It will also be necessary for you to check the references to __DEVICE to ensure that your modifications do not affect any logic that may use the resulting value of the DEVICE variable.

__EXCPGET

The __EXCPGET macro handles the multiple DD segments that are recorded in the type 4, 34, and 40 SMF records. It uses two other macros to define two-channel switching (__TWOCHAN and __TWOCHA), and uses __MNTABLE to define 3330 mountable device addresses. It assumes all 2314 devices are mountable, and puts out a series of error messages when unexpected values are encountered.

   __EXCPGET takes the multiple DD segments of the step (and associated) records and groups the EXCP counts in a logical clustering based on device type. At the same time, it counts the number of unique devices of certain types (TAPEDRVS, D333ODRV, etc.). This macro is the source of data for the variables listed below in these data sets that are created from the 4, 30, 34 and 40 records. Thus you should thoroughly understand __EXCPGET before you accept the validity of these variables:

   NUMDD NDASDDD NTAPEDD TAPEDRVS D2314DRV D333ODRV
   EXCP2305 EXCP2314 EXCP3330 EXCP3340 EXCP3350 EXCPCOMM
   EXCPGRAF EXCPMSS EXCPTAPE EXCPUREC EXCPTOT EXCPVIO

Provided you understand the assumptions above, and that the three dependent macros __TWOCHAN, __TWOCHA, and __MNTABLE are correct, __EXCPGET provides accurate and meaningful data.

__JOBCK

This is a convenience macro. As provided, it has no effect except to suppress job-related records with invalid job names. Its purpose is to permit easy selection of specific occurences of SMF records. It occurs in the code for every record which should contain a job name: types 4, 5, 6, 10, 14, 15, 17, 18, 20, 25, 26, 30, 32, 34, 35, 40, 62, 63, 64, 67, 68, and 69.

   In those SMF records that have job-related information and contain the job name, __JOBCK is located immediately after the INPUT statement that reads the job name, read time, and local information fields. The __JOBCK macro permits testing for specific jobs, so that if you want to select only

SMF records for a specific job, you code the desired job name in the test in
__JOBCK.

Additionally, since read time and local information as well as SMF time
and system are defined at the point at which __JOBCK is logically located,
you can add additional tests to __JOBCK to select only specific executions
of specific jobs.

__MACEND

A "dummy" macro used in BUILDPDB.

__MNTABLE

The __MNTABLE macro defines the specific unit addresses of mountable
3330 devices, since there is no information in the UCB that a device is mountable or permanently resident. It is **installation-dependent.** In this implementation, all 2314 drives are counted as mountable, and this macro is
implemented to identify the 3330 devices (by address) which are mountable.
__MNTABLE is referenced only in the __EXCPGET macro in processing
type 4, 30, 34 and 40 records. Should your installation have mountable
3340s, or if only some of your 2314s are mountable, you can follow the pattern here and modify as necessary. Notice that the variable UADR contains
(and is tested against) a decimal value; the test provided defines devices 201,
701, 281 and 781 as mountable 3330s.

__SMF

The __SMF macro defines the SMF file attributes and certain key variables.
It is referenced every time that raw SMF data is processed, and establishes
the LENGTH and COL variables sometimes needed to determine the version
of the operating system. It also defines the ID variable, which contains
record identification number (record type).

__SMF forces the LRECL of the input SMF data to be 32756, since MVS
SMF records can be that long, and forces the RECFM to be VBS. Even if the
SMF data is being re-processed into VB records, this statement will cause
correct reading of the SMF file, provided that the blocksize of the records is
correct on the SMF data set.

There is one potential problem, and that is in reading the SMF data
directly from SYS1. MANx (which is not recommend until you have high
confidence in yourself, and until the SYS1.MANx data sets are protected so
that you can never write to them). If you do read SYS1.MANx directly, you
may find that the DCB attributes in the DSCB are not correct. The DCB attributes were determined when the data set was allocated, but are never
used by the SMF writer. As a result, you may have to add an explicit
BLKSIZE= operand to the INFILE statement in this macro.

To determine the actual blocksize of any data set, the following SAS code
gives you the actual size of each block of data. (OBS=10 here limits the scan
to the first ten physical blocks):

```
OPTIONS OBS = 10;
DATA   __NULL__;
  INFILE SMF RECFM = U BLKSIZE = 19069 LENGTH = LENGTH;
  INPUT;
  PUT LENGTH = ;
```

__TWOCHAN

The __TWOCHAN macro defines the pairs of physical channels that are connected to two-channel switches, if any are installed. __TWOCHAN is necessary to properly count the number of mountable drives used and is **installation-dependent.**

__TWOCHA

The __TWOCHA macro is identical to __TWOCHAN, but uses the variable CH rather than CHAN. It is needed as a part of the __EXCPGET macro. It too is **installation-dependent.**

If you are lucky, your installation will have two-channel logic that is the same for all CPUs. The code to handle this situation is simple, as the example shows. However, it may be necessary to significantly increase the complexity of the logic to include tests for system identification (variable SYSTEM, which is defined to these two macros), and possibly to include tests down to the device level (variable UA for __TWOCHA and variable UADR for __TWOCHAN, which will contain the decimal value corresponding to the HEX unit address being tested).

That is the bad news about these two macros. The good news is that their impact is limited to the three variables counting mountable drives, TAPEDRVS, D3330DRV and D2314DRV, although errors in these two macros can either raise or lower the values from their correct value.

__VSAMCAT

This macro exists simply to reduce the size of the VSAM record-handling code. Unlike the other macros in MACROS, this is not a global macro, and it should not have any installation dependencies nor should it need to be changed or updated. It simply is a use of the SAS macro facility to avoid repetition of code.

The SAS Data Sets
TYPE0 through TYPE90

The TYPE0 Data Set: IPL

Data set TYPE0 contains one observation for each type 0 SMF record, written when the operator pushes the LOAD key on the master console. The TYPE0 data set is useful in tracking system uptime, since an IPL signifies a complete start-up of the system, usually because the system crashed.

IBM CE diagnostics executed during Preventive Maintenance often write over the clock area, and occasionally IPL's during these PM periods contain incorrect dates and times, usually dates with years 97-99.

Contents

DSV   SMF gen parameter: data set and DASD volume records.

value	generate SMF records:	suppress SMF records:
0	none	14-19, 62-69
1	19, 69	14-18, 62-68
2	14-18, 62-68	19, 69
3	14-19, 62-69	none

EXT   SMF gen parameter: are SMF exits permitted? 'YES' or 'NO'.

OPT   SMF gen parameter: job step records.

value	suppress SMF records:
1	4, 34
2	none

REALSIZE   Real memory size, in 1024 (1K) bytes. Not necessarily correct in MP environment.

REC   SMF gen parameter: scratch records for temporary data sets.

value	suppress SMF records:
0	17 (temporary only)
2	none

SMCAJWTM   JWT parameter: time that a task can wait before a system ABEND 522 occurs.

SMFBUFF   SMF buffer size, in bytes. Blocksize of records written to SYS1.MANX or SYS1.MANY will be half this value.

SMFTIME Time stamp of IPL: the time the operator pushed the LOAD key on the master console.

SYSTEM System identification that was IPL'ed.

VIRTSIZE Virtual memory size, in 1024 (1K) bytes.

variable	type	length	format
DSV	numeric	4	
EXT	character	3	
OPT	numeric	4	
REALSIZE	numeric	4	
REC	numeric	4	
SMCAJWTM	numeric	4	TIME12.0
SMFBUFF	numeric	4	
SMFTIME	numeric	8	TIME19.2
SYSTEM	character	4	
VIRTSIZE	numeric	4	

```
*********MEMBER=TYPE0********************************************;
DATA TYPE0
            (KEEP=DSV EXT OPT REALSIZE REC SMCAJWTM
                 SMFBUFF SMFTIME SYSTEM VIRTSIZE);
LENGTH DEFAULT=4 SMFTIME 8 ;
FORMAT  SMCAJWTM TIME12.0 SMFTIME DATETIME19.2 ;
  INFILE SMF STOPOVER LENGTH=LENGTH COL=COL RECFM=VBS LRECL=32756;
  INPUT @2 ID PIB1. @;
 IF ID=0;
GOTO TYPE0;
TYPE0:
  INPUT @2 ID PIB1. @3 SMFTIME SMFSTAMP8. @11 SYSTEM $4.
        @15 SMCAJWTM PIB4. @19 SMFBUFF PIB4. @23 VIRTSIZE PIB4.
        @27 SMCAOPT PIB1. @28 REALSIZE PIB4.;
    REC=0;
    DSV=0;
    EXT='NO ';
 IF SMCAOPT>128 THEN OPT=1;
 IF MOD(SMCAOPT,128)>=64 THEN OPT=2;
 IF MOD(SMCAOPT,64)>=32 THEN EXT='YES';
 IF MOD(SMCAOPT,32)>=16 AND MOD(SMCAOPT,16)>=8 THEN DSV=3;
 IF MOD(SMCAOPT,32)>=16 AND NOT MOD(SMCAOPT,16)>=8 THEN DSV=2;
 IF NOT MOD(SMCAOPT,32)>=16 AND MOD(SMCAOPT,16)>=8 THEN DSV=1;
 IF MOD(SMCAOPT,4)>=2 THEN REC=2;
   SMCAJWTM=60*SMCAJWTM;
  OUTPUT TYPE0;
  RETURN;
```

The TYPE112 Data Set: Non-MVS Wait Time

Data set TYPE112 contains one observation for each type 1 or type 12 SMF record. These records are written only in SVS, MVT, and MFT systems. The type 1 record contains the accumulated wait time—the time that the CPU was in the wait state and not executing instructions—since the previous type 0, 1, or 12 record was written.

The type 12 record also contains the accumulated wait time since the previous type 1 record, and is written when the operator issues the HALT or SWITCH command.

Type 1 records are written after the first step termination that occurs more than ten minutes after the previous type 0, 1, or 12 record was written. Thus the timing of type 1 records is not precisely every ten minutes.

You can determine the amount of time that the CPU was busy by subtracting the wait time from the elapsed duration. A good discussion of the wait time records can be found in the SVS SMF manual *OS/VS System Management Facilities*, GC35-0004-4, IBM Corporation, 1973.

Contents

CPUWAITM Duration that system was in the wait state—not executing instructions—since the previous type 0, 1, or 12 SMF record.

SMFTIME Time stamp when the record was written

SYSTEM System identification of the system.

variable	type	length	format
CPUWAITM	numeric	4	TIME12.2
SMFTIME	numeric	8	DATETIME19.2
SYSTEM	character	4	

```
*********MEMBER=TYPE112********************************;
DATA TYPE112
           (KEEP=CPUWAITM SMFTIME SYSTEM);
LENGTH DEFAULT=4 SMFTIME 8;
FORMAT SMFTIME DATETIME19.2 CPUWAITM TIME12.2 ;
   INFILE SMF STOPOVER LENGTH=LENGTH COL=COL RECFM=VBS LRECL=32756;
   INPUT @2 ID PIB1. @;
  IF ID=1 OR ID=12;
GOTO TYPE112;
TYPE112:
   INPUT @3 SMFTIME SMFSTAMP8. @11 SYSTEM $4. @15 CPUWAITM PIB4.2;
   OUTPUT TYPE112;
   RETURN;
```

The TYPE434 Data Set: TSO/JOB Step Termination

From the workload viewpoint, the TYPE434 data set is the backbone of SMF analysis. It permits resource consumption to be classified according to users, jobs, programs, time of day, and so on. (See the section on workload analysis for more discussion of these abilities.)

Data set TYPE434 contains one observation for each type 4 (batch step) or type 34 (TSO step) record. Because there are so few differences between batch steps and TSO steps (some variables differ; TSO sessions are made up of only one step, while batch jobs might be made up of many steps), type 4 and type 34 records are grouped together.

Type 4 and 34 records are written for each step that terminated or was flushed, except steps terminating after an operator CANCEL command.

The basic SMF record consists of:
- a fixed portion, containing job and step identification information; step event time stamps; and step resources
- a variable portion, containing device information: one entry per DD statement that includes the unit address and unit type allocated to the DD, plus the EXCP count for the DD
- another variable portion, containing step accounting information; this information is rarely used since most installations do accounting at the job level rather than the step level
- a fixed portion with paging statistics.

The handling of the variable-length device portion is a matter of choice. To maximize the useful information and minimize the size of the TYPE434 data set, device information is consolidated by device type. Thus the TYPE434 data set contains the total EXCP count for each device type (e.g., TAPE, 3330, 3350, VIO, etc.) for the step. Additionally, the number of tape and 2314 drives that were allocated are counted, and 3330 device addresses used for "mountable" 3330's are also counted. The device portion is handled in the MACRO named _EXCPGET, which is installation-dependent. (See chapter 16.)

Contents

ABEND Step completion indicator.

value	meaning
blank	normal completion
CANCEXIT	step was cancelled by an SMF exit; see CONDCODE
FLUSH	step was flushed (previous step had failed)
OTHER	step ABENDed for unknown reason; see CONDCODE
RESTART	step was restarted; subsequent restart will have program name of IEFRSTRT
RETURN	step completed with non-zero condition code; see CONDCODE
SYSTEM	step completed with system ABEND; see CONDCODE
USER	step completed with user ABEND; see CONDCODE

ACCOUNT1-ACCOUNT9 Nine variables containing the account field on the EXEC statement; rarely used. See LEN1-LEN9 and NRFLDS.

ACTIVETM Step active time. Duration that the SRM (system resource manager) viewed the task as active.

ALOCTIME Allocation time stamp.

ALOCTM Step allocation time. Duration required for the step to allocate all devices.

AVGWKSET Average working set size, in pages (one page is 4096 bytes).

COMPAGIN Common area page-ins.

COMRECLM Common area page-reclaims.

CONDCODE Condition code. See ABEND.

ABEND value	contents of CONDCODE	
	value	cancelled by
	4	IEFUJI (job initiation)
CANCEXIT	2	IEFUSI (step initiation)
	1	IEFACTRT (step termination)
OTHER	completion code value	
RETURN	return code value	

SYSTEM	system ABEND code
USER	user ABEND code

CPUSRBTM Duration that processor was executing instructions under all SRBs (service request) for this task.

CPUTCBTM Duration that processor was executing instructions under all TCBs (task control blocks) for this task.

CPUTM Duration that processor was executing instructions for this task. Sum of CPUSRBTM and CPUTCBTM.

CPUUNITS MVS/SE only. The TCB CPU service units received.

DPRTY Dispatching priority at step termination.

DSENQTM Duration step waited between initiation and beginning of allocation.

D2314DRV The number of different 2314 disk drives that were allocated to this step.

D3330DRV The number of different 3330 "mountable" disk drives that were allocated to this step, where "mountable" is defined by an explicit list of unit addresses in the __EXCPGET macro.

EXCP2305 EXCPs to 2305 devices.

EXCP2314 EXCPs to 2314 devices.

EXCP3330 EXCPs to 3330 devices.

EXCP3340 EXCPs to 3340 devices.

EXCP3350 EXCPs to 3350 devices.

EXCPCOMM EXCPs to communications devices.

EXCPDASD Sum of EXCPs to 2305, 2314, 3330, 3340, and 3350 devices.

EXCPGRAF EXCPs to graphics devices.

EXCPMSS EXCPs to mass storage volume.

EXCPTAPE EXCPs to tape volumes.

EXCPTOT   Total step EXCPs.

EXCPUREC   EXCPs to unit record devices that were allocated directly to the step. For MVS, this does not include EXCPs to the JES spool devices.

EXCPVIO   EXCPs to virtual I/O.

EXECTM   Duration that step was in execution.

ID   Record identification.

value	meaning
4	batch step
34	TSO step

INITTIME   Initiation time stamp.

IOUNITS   MVS/SE only. I/O service units used by this step.

JOB   Job name (batch); user ID (TSO).

JOB_TSO   JOB or TSO flag.

value	meaning
J	batch step
T	TSO step

LEN1-LEN9   Lengths of the nine account fields on the EXEC statement; rarely used. See ACCOUNT1-ACCOUNT9 and NRFLDS.

LOADTIME   Load (problem program start) time stamp.

LOCLINFO   Locally defined field; filled in by the installation's SMF exit routines.

LPAGINS   MVS/SE only. Link pack area page-ins.

LPARECLM   MVS/SE only. Link pack area reclaims.

MAXADRSP   Address space (memory if VIRTREAL='R') used. Sum of PVTTOP and PVTBOT.

MSOUNITS   MVS/SE only. Memory service units received.

NDASDDD   Number of DD statement that allocated DASD devices.

NRFLDS   Number of accounting fields on the step EXEC statement (normally zero, since most installations do accounting at the job rather than the step level).

NTAPEDD   Number of DD statements that allocated TAPE devices.

NUMDD   Total number of DD statements in this step. Note that
              NUMDD – (NDASDD + NTAPEDD)
              equals the number of DDs for JES, VIO, MSS, COMM, UREC, and graphics allocations.

PAGEINS   Number of page-ins.

PAGEOUTS Number of page-outs.

PAGESECS Page-seconds used by this step. Divide this variable by CPUTCBTM (seconds) to get the AVGWKSET value.

PERFGRP   Performance group in which this step executed.

PKEY   Storage-protect key.

PROGRAM   Program name (PGM=) from EXEC statement. If backward reference was used, the PROGRAM value is '*.DD'. If the current step is a restarted step, its PROGRAM value and that of all subsequent steps will be 'IEFRSTRT'.

PVTAREA   If VIRTREAL='V' (virtual storage), the PVTAREA value is the size of the private area in 1024 (1K) bytes, which is constant and is the maximum region size (address space) that can be requested. If VIRTREAL='R' (real storage), the PVTAREA value is the REGION requested in K.

PVTBOT   If VIRTREAL='V' (virtual storage), the PVTBOT value is the address space used (in K) from the bottom of the private area—subpools 0-127, 251, and 252. If VIRTREAL='R', the PVTBOT value is the amount of contiguous real storage used, in K.

PVTTOP   If VIRTREAL='V' (virtual storage), the PVTTOP value is the address space used, in K, from the top of the private area—subpools 229, 239, 236-237, 253-255, and also including LSQA and SWA. If VIRTREAL='R', the PVTTOP value is the amount of storage used that was not from the contiguous storage reserved for the program.

READTIME   Job read-in (TSO logon) time stamp.

RECLAIMS   Pages reclaimed.

RESIDTM   Duration that the step was resident in real storage.

SELAPTM   Duration that the step was initiated.

SERVUNIT   Total step service units received.

SORTIME   A time stamp used when matching types 4 and 34 records with types 14 and 15 records to force proper order. Set equal to INITTIME.

SRBUNITS   MVS/SE only. The CPU (SRB only) service units received.

STEPNAME   The step name that appeared on the EXEC PGM= statement. Note that this is **not** the stepname that is used on an EXEC statement for a procedure.

STEPNR   The step number. This number is reset to 1 when a job is cancelled and restarted, so that it is possible for the same job to have steps with duplicate values. Additionally, this field starts back at 1 after the 256th step. This value is thus of limited usefulness.

STOLPAG   Pages stolen from this step.

SWAPS   Number of times this step was swapped out.

SWPAGIN   Number of pages swapped in.

SWPAGOUT   Number of pages swapped out.

SYSINCNT   Number of card-image records in DD DATA and DD * data sets read by the reader for this step.

SYSTEM   Identification of the system on which the step executed.

TAPEDRVS   The number of different tape drives that were allocated to this step.

TERMTIME   Step termination time stamp.

TGETS   TSO only. The number of terminals GETS satisfied—the number of times that the TSO user pushed the ENTER key.

TPUTS   TSO only. The number of terminal PUTS issued—the number of times that one or more lines were sent to the terminal.

VIOPAGIN   Virtual I/O page-ins.

VIOPAGOU   Virtual I/O page-outs.

VIORECLM   Virtual I/O page reclaims.

VIRTREAL   Type of address space requested.

value	requested
R	real storage (ADDRSPC=R specified)
V	virtual storage

variable	type	length	format
ABEND	character	8	
ACCOUNT1-ACCOUNT9	character	40	
ACTIVETM	numeric	4	TIME12.2
ALOCTIME	numeric	8	DATETIME19.2
ALOCTM	numeric	4	TIME12.2
AVGWKSET	numeric	4	5.
COMPAGIN	numeric	4	
COMRECLM	numeric	4	
CONDCODE	numeric	3	HEX4.
CPUSRBTM	numeric	4	TIME12.2
CPUTCBTM	numeric	4	TIME12.2
CPUTM	numeric	4	TIME12.2
CPUUNITS	numeric	4	
DPRTY	numeric	2	HEX2.
DSENQTM	numeric	4	TIME12.2
D2314DRV	numeric	4	
D3330DRV	numeric	4	
EXCP2305	numeric	4	
EXCP2314	numeric	4	
EXCP3330	numeric	4	
EXCP3340	numeric	4	
EXCP3350	numeric	4	
EXCPCOMM	numeric	4	
EXCPDASD	numeric	4	
EXCPGRAF	numeric	4	
EXCPMSS	numeric	4	
EXCPTAPE	numeric	4	
EXCPTOT	numeric	4	
EXCPUREC	numeric	4	
EXCPVIO	numeric	4	
EXECTM	numeric	4	TIME12.2
ID	numeric	2	
INITTIME	numeric	8	DATETIME19.2
IOUNITS	numeric	4	
JOB	character	8	

JOB__TSO	character	1	
LEN1-LEN9	numeric	4	
LOADTIME	numeric	8	DATETIME19.2
LOCLINFO	character	8	
LPAGINS	numeric	4	
LPARECLM	numeric	4	
MAXADRSP	numeric	4	
MSOUNITS	numeric	4	
NDASDDD	numeric	4	
NRFLDS	numeric	4	
NTAPEDD	numeric	4	
NUMDD	numeric	4	
PAGEINS	numeric	4	
PAGEOUTS	numeric	4	
PAGESECS	numeric	4	
PERFGRP	numeric	4	
PKEY	numeric	2	HEX2.
PROGRAM	character	8	
PVTAREA	numeric	4	
PVTBOT	numeric	4	
PVTTOP	numeric	4	
READTIME	numeric	8	DATETIME19.2
RECLAIMS	numeric	4	
RESIDTM	numeric	4	TIME12.2
SELAPTM	numeric	4	TIME12.2
SERVUNIT	numeric	4	
SORTIME	numeric	8	DATETIME19.2
SRBUNITS	numeric	4	
STEPNAME	character	8	
STEPNR	numeric	4	
STOLPAG	numeric	4	
SWAPS	numeric	4	
SWPAGIN	numeric	4	
SWPAGOUT	numeric	4	
SYSINCNT	numeric	4	
SYSTEM	character	4	
TAPEDRVS	numeric	4	
TERMTIME	numeric	8	DATETIME19.2
TGETS	numeric	4	
TPUTS	numeric	4	
VIOPAGIN	numeric	4	
VIOPAGOU	numeric	4	
VIORECLM	numeric	4	
VIRTREAL	character	1	

```
**********MEMBER=TYPE434**********************************;
DATA TYPE434
              (KEEP=ABEND ACCOUNT1-ACCOUNT9 ACTIVETM ALOCTIME
               ALOCTM AVGWKSET COMPAGIN COMRECLM CONDCODE
               CPUSRBTM CPUTCBTM CPUTM CPUUNITS DPRTY DSENQTM
               D2314DRV D3330DRV EXCP2305 EXCP2314 EXCP3330
               EXCP3340 EXCP3350 EXCPCOMM EXCPDASD EXCPGRAF
               EXCPMSS  EXCPTAPE  EXCPTOT  EXCPUREC
               EXCPVIO EXECTM ID INITTIME IOUNITS JOB
               JOB_TSO LEN1-LEN9 LOADTIME LOCLINFO LPAGINS LPARECLM
               MAXADRSP MSOUNITS NDASDDD NRFLDS NTAPEDD NUMDD
               PAGEINS PAGEOUTS PAGESECS PERFGRP PKEY
               PROGRAM PVTAREA PVTBOT PVTTOP READTIME
               RECLAIMS RESIDTM SELAPTM SERVUNIT SORTIME
               SRBUNITS STEPNAME STEPNR STOLPAG SWAPS SWPAGIN
               SWPAGOUT SYSINCNT SYSTEM TAPEDRVS TERMTIME
               TGETS TPUTS VIOPAGIN VIOPAGOU VIORECLM
               VIRTREAL );
LENGTH DEFAULT=4
   ALOCTIME INITTIME LOADTIME READTIME SORTIME TERMTIME 8
   DPRTY ID PKEY 2
   CONDCODE RECIND 3;
FORMAT
   ALOCTIME INITTIME LOADTIME READTIME SORTIME TERMTIME DATETIME19.2
   ALOCTM DSENQTM EXECTM SELAPTM RESIDTM ACTIVETM
   CPUTCBTM CPUSRBTM CPUTM TIME12.2
   DPRTY PKEY HEX2.
   CONDCODE RECIND HEX4.
   AVGWKSET 5.;
  INFILE SMF STOPOVER LENGTH=LENGTH COL=COL RECFM=VBS LRECL=32756;
  INPUT @2 ID PIB1. @;
 IF ID=4 OR ID=34;
GOTO TYPE434;
TYPE434:
  INPUT @3 TERMTIME SMFSTAMP8. @11 SYSTEM $4.
        @15 JOB $8. @23 READTIME SMFSTAMP8. @;
_JOBCK
  INPUT @31 LOCLINFO $8. @39 STEPNR PIB1. @40 INITTIME PIB4.2 @;
 IF ID=34 THEN INPUT @44 TPUTS PIB4. @48 TGETS PIB4. @;
 IF ID=4  THEN INPUT @44 INITDATE PD4. @48 SYSINCNT PIB4. @;
  INPUT @52 COMPCODE PIB2. @54 DPRTY PIB1. @55 PROGRAM $8.
        @63 STEPNAME $8. @71 PVTAREA PIB2. @73 PVTTOP PIB2.
        @75 PVTBOT PIB2. @83 PKEY PIB1. @84 STRMIND PIB1.
        @87 ALOCTIME PIB4.2 @91 LOADTIME PIB4.2
        @96 CPUSRBTM PIB3.2 @99 RECIND PIB1.
        @101 OFFSET PIB2. @103 NUMDD PIB2. @;
 IF ID=4 THEN JOB_TSO='J';
 IF ID=34 THEN JOB_TSO='T';
 IF MOD(STRMIND,4)>=2 THEN AB=1;
 IF MOD(STRMIND,8)>=4 THEN RE=1;
   EX=FLOOR(STRMIND/8);
 IF MOD(STRMIND,2)=1 THEN FL=1;
 IF AB=1 AND COMPCODE>=32768 THEN ABEND='USER    ';
 IF AB=1 AND COMPCODE<16384 THEN ABEND='SYSTEM';
 IF AB=1 AND ABEND=' ' THEN ABEND='OTHER ';
 IF ABEND='OTHER' THEN CONDCODE=COMPCODE;
 IF AB NE 1 AND COMPCODE >= 16384 THEN COMPCODE=COMPCODE-16384;
 IF ABEND='USER' THEN CONDCODE=COMPCODE-32768;
 IF ABEND NE 'USER' THEN CONDCODE=COMPCODE;
 IF ABEND = ' ' AND CONDCODE NE 0 THEN ABEND='RETURN';
 IF EX>=1 THEN ABEND='CANCEXIT';
 IF RE=1 THEN ABEND='RESTART';
 IF EX LT 1 AND FL =1 THEN ABEND='FLUSH';
 IF EX >0 THEN CONDCODE=EX;
 IF ABEND NE 'USER' AND ABEND NE 'RETURN' THEN GOTO GETCORE;
```

```
      DGT1=FLOOR(CONDCODE/1000);CONDCODE=CONDCODE-1000*DGT1;
      DGT2=FLOOR(CONDCODE/100);CONDCODE=CONDCODE-100*DGT2;
      DGT3=FLOOR(CONDCODE/10);DGT4=CONDCODE-10*DGT3;
      CONDCODE=DGT4+16*DGT3+256*DGT2+4096*DGT1;
GETCORE:
     MAXADRSP=PVTTOP+PVTBOT;
     VIRTREAL='V';
  IF MOD(RECIND,2)=1 THEN VIRTREAL='R';
  IF ALOCTIME=0 AND LOADTIME=0 AND MAXADRSP=0 THEN ALOCTIME=.;
  IF LOADTIME=0 AND MAXADRSP=0 THEN LOADTIME=.;
  IF ID=34 THEN INITDATE=DATEPART(READTIME);
  IF ID=4 THEN INITDATE=DATEJUL(INITDATE);
     INITTIME=DHMS(INITDATE,0,0,INITTIME);
  IF ID=34 AND INITTIME<READTIME THEN INITTIME=INITTIME+DHMS(1,0,0,0);;
     SORTIME=INITTIME;
     ALOCDATE=DATEPART(INITTIME);
     IF ALOCTIME NE . THEN ALOCTIME=DHMS(ALOCDATE,0,0,ALOCTIME);
  IF ALOCTIME<INITTIME THEN ALOCTIME=ALOCTIME+DHMS(1,0,0,0);;
     IF ALOCTIME NE . THEN LOADDATE=DATEPART(ALOCTIME);
     IF ALOCTIME NE . THEN LOADTIME=DHMS(LOADDATE,0,0,LOADTIME);
  IF . < LOADTIME<ALOCTIME THEN LOADTIME=LOADTIME+DHMS(1,0,0,0);;
     IF ALOCTIME NE . THEN DSENQTM=ALOCTIME-INITTIME;
     IF ALOCTIME NE . AND LOADTIME NE . THEN ALOCTM=LOADTIME-ALOCTIME;
     IF LOADTIME NE . THEN EXECTM=TERMTIME-LOADTIME;
     SELAPTM=TERMTIME-INITTIME;
     BEGIN=105;
LINK EXCPGET;
     LOCCPU=106+8*NUMDD;
     INPUT @LOCCPU CPUTCBTM PIB3.2 NRFLDS PIB1. @;
LINK ACCTGET;
     OFFSET+1;
     INPUT @OFFSET PAGEINS PIB4.
           @OFFSET+4 PAGEOUTS PIB4.   @OFFSET+8 SWAPS PIB4.
           @OFFSET+12 SWPAGIN PIB4.   @OFFSET+16 SWPAGOUT PIB4.
           @OFFSET+20 VIOPAGIN PIB4.  @OFFSET+24 VIOPAGOU PIB4.
           @OFFSET+28 SERVUNIT PIB4.  @OFFSET+32 ACTIVETM PIB4.
           @OFFSET+36 PERFGRP PIB2.   @OFFSET+38 RESIDTM PIB4.
           @OFFSET+42 RECLAIMS PIB4.  @OFFSET+46 VIORECLM PIB4.
           @OFFSET+50 COMPAGIN PIB4.  @OFFSET+54 COMRECLM PIB4.
           @OFFSET+58 STOLPAG PIB4.   @OFFSET+62 PAGESECS PIB8.3 @;
  * TEST FOR MVS/SE LENGTH RECORD;
  IF LENGTH >= OFFSET+93 THEN
     INPUT @OFFSET+70 LPAGINS PIB4.   @OFFSET+74 LPARECLM PIB4.
           @OFFSET+78 CPUUNITS PIB4.  @OFFSET+82 IOUNITS PIB4.
           @OFFSET+86 MSOUNITS PIB4.  @OFFSET+90 SRBUNITS PIB4. @;
  IF CPUTCBTM>0 THEN AVGWKSET=PAGESECS/CPUTCBTM;
     RESIDTM=HMS(RESIDTM*1.024/3.6E6,0,0);
     ACTIVETM=HMS(ACTIVETM*1.024/3.6E6,0,0);
     CPUTM=CPUTCBTM+CPUSRBTM;
  OUTPUT TYPE434;
  RETURN;
_EXCPGET
_ACCTGET
_
```

The TYPE535 Data Set: Job Termination/Session LOGOFF

Data set TYPE535 contains one observation for each type 5 record (batch job termination) or type 35 record (TSO session termination). As with the TYPE434 data set, the high degree of similarity between batch jobs and TSO sessions permits this grouping.

Type 5 and 35 records are written at job termination. Note, however, that a restarted job has more than one execution and hence more than one type 5 record: each type 5 record corresponds to a single execution of the job.

The basic type 5 or type 35 record contains a fixed portion followed by a variable accounting portion. Since the design and usage of the account field on the JOB statement is installation-dependent, the first nine account fields and their lengths are extracted from the job record to permit analysis of the accounting fields. (For TSO users, only one account field is allowed.) Extraction of these nine account fields is done in the __ACCTGET macro.

Contents

ABEND   Step completion indicator.

value	meaning
blank	normal completion
CANCEXIT	job was cancelled by an SMF exit
OTHER	job ABENDed for unknown reasons
RETURN	job completed with non-zero condition code
SYSTEM	job completed with system ABEND
USER	job completed with user ABEND

ACCOUNT1-   Nine account fields on the JOB statement.
ACCOUNT9   See LEN1-LEN9 and NRFLDS.

CONDCODE   Condition code. See ABEND.

ABEND value	contents of CONDCODE	
	value	cancelled by
	1	IEFUSI (step initiation)
CANCEXIT	2	IEFUJI (job initiation)
	4	IEFUJV (job validation)
OTHER	completion code value	

	RETURN	return code value
	SYSTEM	system ABEND code
	USER	user ABEND code

CPUSRBTM   Duration that processor was executing instructions under all SRBs (service request blocks) for this task.

CPUTCBTM   Duration that processor was executing instructions under all TCBs (task control blocks) for this task.

CPUTM   Duration that processor was executing instructions this task. Sum of CPUSRBTM and CPUTCBTM.

ELAPSTM   Duration that the job was initiated for this execution.

ENQTIME   TSO only. LOGON enqueue time stamp.

JACTIVTM   Sum of step ACTIVETMs for this execution.

JCPUNITS   MVS/SE only. Sum of step CPUUNITS for this execution.

JINITIME   Job initiation time stamp for this execution.

JIOUNITS   MVS/SE only. Sum of step IOUNITS for this execution.

JMSOUNIT   MVS/SE only. Sum of step MSOUNITS for this execution.

JOB   Job name (batch); user ID (TSO).

JOB_TSO   JOB or TSO flag.

value	meaning
J	batch job
T	TSO session

JOBCLASS   Job class.

JOBPRTY   Job priority after job was passed from JES to MVS. Does not relate to job scheduling priority in the type 26 record.

JOBSERV   Sum of step SERVUNITs for this execution.

JPERFGRP   Performance group at job termination.

JPKEY   Storage-protect key.

JRESIDTM   Sum of step RESIDTM for this execution.

JSRBUNIT   MVS/SE only. Sum of step SRBUNITS for this execution.

JTRMTIME   Termination time stamp of this execution.

LEN1-LEN9   Lengths of the nine account fields on the JOB statement. See NRFLDS and ACCOUNT1-ACCOUNT9.

LOCLINFO   Locally defined field; filled in by an installation-written SMF exit routine.

NRFLDS   Number of accounting fields on the JOB statement.

NRTRANS   TSO only. Number of transactions as counted by the SRM.

NSTEPS   Number of steps in this execution. This value is modulo 256.

PGMRNAME   Programmer name field from JOB statement.

RDRCLASS   Reader class

RDRTM   Duration the MVS reader was active while reading this job.

RDRTYPE   Reader type.

READER   'INTERNAL' if this job was processed by the internal reader; blank otherwise.

READTIME   Job read-in (TSO LOGON) time stamp.

SORTIME   A time stamp used when matching type 5/type 35 records with type 14/type 15 records to force proper order. Set equal to JINITIME for jobs, READTIME for TSO sessions.

SYSINCNT   Batch only. Number of card-image records in DD DATA and DD * data sets read by the reader for this execution.

SYSTEM   Identification of the system on which this job executed.

TGETS   TSO only. The number of terminal GETs satisfied this session.

TPUTS   TSO only. The number of terminals PUTs issued this session.

variable	type	length	format
ABEND	character	6	
ACCOUNT1-ACCOUNT9	character	40	
CONDCODE	numeric	4	HEX4.
CPUSRBTM	numeric	4	TIME12.2
CPUTCBTM	numeric	4	TIME12.2
CPUTM	numeric	4	TIME12.2
ELAPSTM	numeric	4	TIME12.2
ENQTIME	numeric	8	DATETIME19.2
JACTIVTM	numeric	4	TIME12.2
JCPUNITS	numeric	4	
JINITIME	numeric	8	DATETIME19.2
JIOUNITS	numeric	4	
JMSOUNIT	numeric	4	
JOB	character	8	
JOB_TSO	character	1	
JOBCLASS	character	1	
JOBPRTY	numeric	4	
JOBSERV	numeric	4	
JPERFGRP	numeric	4	
JPKEY	numeric	4	HEX2.
JRESIDTM	numeric	4	TIME12.2
JSRBUNIT	numeric	4	
JTRMTIME	numeric	8	DATETIME19.2
LEN1-LEN9	numeric	4	
LOCLINFO	character	8	
NRFLDS	numeric	4	
NRTRANS	numeric	4	
NSTEPS	numeric	4	
PGMRNAME	character	20	
RDRCLASS	numeric	4	HEX2.
RDRTM	numeric	4	TIME12.2
RDRTYPE	numeric	4	HEX2.
READER	numeric	8	
READTIME	numeric	8	DATETIME19.2
SORTIME	numeric	8	DATETIME19.2
SYSINCNT	numeric	4	
SYSTEM	character	4	
TGETS	numeric	4	
TPUTS	numeric	4	

```
*********MEMBER=TYPE535*********************************;
DATA TYPE535
                (KEEP=ABEND ACCOUNT1-ACCOUNT9 CONDCODE CPUSRBTM
                CPUTCBTM CPUTM ELAPSTM ENQTIME JACTIVTM
                JCPUNITS JINITIME JIOUNITS JMSOUNIT JOB JOB_TSO
                JOBCLASS JOBPRTY JOBSERV JPERFGRP
                JPKEY JRESIDTM JSRBUNIT JTRMTIME LEN1-LEN9
                LOCLINFO NRFLDS NRTRANS NSTEPS PGMRNAME
                RDRCLASS RDRTM RDRTYPE READER READTIME
                SORTIME SYSINCNT SYSTEM TGETS TPUTS);
LENGTH DEFAULT=4 ENQTIME JINITIME JTRMTIME READTIME SORTIME 8;
FORMAT
    ENQTIME JINITIME JTRMTIME READTIME SORTIME DATETIME19.2
    CPUTM CPUTCBTM CPUSRBTM ELAPSTM JRESIDTM RDRTM JACTIVTM TIME12.2
        JPKEY JTRMIND RDRCLASS RDRTYPE HEX2. CONDCODE HEX4.;
    INFILE SMF STOPOVER LENGTH=LENGTH COL=COL RECFM=VBS LRECL=32756;
    INPUT @2 ID PIB1. @;
 IF ID=5 OR ID=35;
GOTO TYPE535;
TYPE535:
 IF ID=5 THEN JOB_TSO='J';
 IF ID=35 THEN JOB_TSO='T';
    INPUT @3 JTRMTIME SMFSTAMP8. @11 SYSTEM $4.
        @15 JOB $8. @23 READTIME SMFSTAMP8. @;
_JOBCK
   INPUT @31 LOCLINFO $8. @39 NSTEPS PIB1. @;
 IF ID=5 THEN INPUT @40 JINITIME SMFSTAMP8.
                    @48 SYSINCNT PIB4. @;
 IF ID=5 THEN SORTIME=JINITIME;
 IF ID=35 THEN SORTIME=READTIME;
 IF ID=35 THEN INPUT @44 TPUTS PIB4. @48 TGETS PIB4. @;
  INPUT @52 COMPCODE PIB2. @63 JTRMIND PIB1. @;
 IF MOD(JTRMIND,4)>=2 THEN AB=1;
   EX=FLOOR(JTRMIND/8);
 IF AB=1 AND COMPCODE>=32768 THEN ABEND='USER  ';
 IF AB=1 AND COMPCODE<16384 THEN ABEND='SYSTEM';
 IF AB=1 AND ABEND=' ' THEN ABEND='OTHER';
 IF AB NE 1 AND COMPCODE >= 16384 THEN COMPCODE=COMPCODE-16384;
 IF ABEND='USER' THEN CONDCODE=COMPCODE-32768;
 IF ABEND NE 'USER' THEN CONDCODE=COMPCODE;
 IF ABEND = ' ' AND CONDCODE NE 0 THEN ABEND='RETURN';
 IF EX >=1 THEN ABEND='CANCEXIT';
 IF EX >0 THEN CONDCODE=EX;
 IF ABEND NE 'USER' AND ABEND NE 'RETURN' THEN GOTO GETREST;
   DGT1=FLOOR(CONDCODE/1000);CONDCODE=CONDCODE-1000*DGT1;
   DGT2=FLOOR(CONDCODE/100);CONDCODE=CONDCODE-100*DGT2;
   DGT3=FLOOR(CONDCODE/10);DGT4=CONDCODE-10*DGT3;
   CONDCODE=DGT4+16*DGT3+256*DGT2+4096*DGT1;
GETREST:
  INPUT @54 JOBPRTY PIB1. @;
 IF ID=5 THEN INPUT @55 RDRENTM SMFSTAMP8. @;
 IF ID=35 THEN INPUT @55 ENQTIME SMFSTAMP8. @;
  INPUT @65 JRESIDTM PIB4. @;
   JRESIDTM=HMS(JRESIDTM*1.024/3.6E6,0,0);
 IF ID=5 THEN INPUT @70 RDRCLASS PIB1. @71 RDRTYPE PIB1.
                @72 JOBCLASS $1. @;
 IF RDRCLASS=0 AND RDRTYPE=0 THEN READER='INTERNAL';
  INPUT @73 JPKEY PIB1. @74 CPUSRBTM PIB3.2 @77 JOBSERV PIB4.
        @81 JACTIVTM PIB4. @;
   JACTIVTM=HMS(JACTIVTM*1.024/3.6E6,0,0);
 IF ID=35 THEN INPUT @85 NRTRANS PIB4. @;
  INPUT @89 JPERFGRP PIB2. @;
 IF ID=5 THEN INPUT @94 PGMRNAME $20. @;
  INPUT @114 CPUTCBTM PIB3.2 @117 NRFLDS PIB1. @;
   CPUTM=CPUTCBTM+CPUSRBTM;
```

```
LINK ACCTGET;
*    TEST FOR MVS/SE RECORD;
 IF LENGTH >= COL +15 THEN INPUT
    JCPUNITS PIB4. JIOUNITS PIB4. JMSOUNIT PIB4. JSRBUNIT PIB4. @;
 IF ID=5 THEN GOTO JOB5;
    ELAPSTM=JTRMTIME-READTIME;
   GOTO OUTJOB;
JOB5:
    ELAPSTM=JTRMTIME-JINITIME;
    RDRTM=RDRENTM-READTIME;
OUTJOB:
  OUTPUT TYPE535;
  RETURN;
_ACCTGET
```

The TYPE6 Data Set: Output Writer

The TYPE6 data set contains one observation for each type 6 SMF record. JES2 or JES3 writes a type 6 SMF record for each SYSOUT data set printed or punched, as well as for output produced by external or installation-supplied writers that process SYSOUT data.

The type 6 record is written at the completion of each printing event, which normally occurs after job completion. However, if FREE=CLOSE is specified in the SYSOUT DD statement, the printing/punching occurs when the file is closed, and thus type 6 records may exist with time stamps prior to the job termination time.

The TYPE6 data set contains information about SYSOUT class and records processed. It does not explicitly contain the device type to which the SYSOUT was directed; by decoding the device name (OUTDEVCE), a SAS variable is created that identifies the SYSOUT as print or punch. This decoding assumes that your installation follows the normal conventions for naming JES remote devices.

The actual number of lines printed/punched is contained in the TYPE6 data set; the primary value of this data is in the analysis of printers and punches. If multiple copies are printed (as opposed to multi-part forms that are printed only once), the total lines actually printed is available. If printing is cancelled, only the actual number of lines printed is counted. Thus actual printer utilizations can be estimated.

Contents

BURST   3800 only.

value	meaning
YES	output was burst into sheets by burster

CONTRIND   Control indicators. The value may be blank or may have one of these values:

for JES2 or JES3: SPIN DATA SETS; OPR TERMINATED; OPR RESTARTED; INTERPRETED

JES2 only: OPR INTERRUPTED; CONTINUATION; OPR OVERRODE

JES3 only: RESTART WITH DEST; RECVD OPR RESTART; OPR STRT SINGLE SPACE

COPIES   3800 only. Total number of copies printed.

COPYMODF   3800 only. Names of the copy modification module used to modify the data.

DATAERRS   JES3 only. Possible error conditions when data set was complete or restarted. The DATAERRS value may be blank or may have one of these values: CNTRL, CHAR, ERR, REC LEN, ERR.

DCTCHAR1-   3800 only. Names of the character arrangement tables that
DCTCHAR4   define the characters used in printing.

FCB   FCB image identification.

FLASH   3800 only. Name of the forms overlay printed (flashed) on the copies.

FLASHCPY   3800 only. Number of copies on which the forms overlay was printed.

FORM   Form number.

JESNR   Job number assigned by JES.

JOB   Job name (batch) or user ID (TSO).

LOCLINFO   Locally defined field, filled in by an installation-written SMF exit routine.

NODE   JES2 only. Local or remote routing.

NRDSETS   Number of data sets processed (if multiple copies are produced, each copy is counted).

NRLINES   Number of logical records actually written, including JOBLOG and also including multiple copies printed.

OPTCD   3800 printer.

value	meaning
J	OPTCD=J was specified

OUTCLASS   SYSOUT class; blank for non-SYSOUT data sets.

OUTDEVCE   Output device name.

OUTPRTY   JES3 only. Output priority.

PAGECNT   For printer, approximate page count; for JES3 punch, number of cards punched.

PRENTIME   Print/punch ended time stamp.

PRINTIME   Print/punch started time stamp. (SMFTIME time stamp)

READTIME   Job read-in (TSO LOGON) time stamp.

RMOTID   JES2 only. Remote ID number.

STATUS   I/O status indicator: the STATUS value may be blank or may have one of these values: DATABUFF, ERROR, CNTLBUFF, ERROR.

SUBSYS   Subsystem: value may be either JES2 or JES3.

SUPGROUP   JES3 only. Logical output device group name.

SYSTEM   Identification of the system on which this job executed.

TYPE   JES2. Type of device:

value	device
PRINT	printer
PUNCH	punch
EXWTR	external writer

UCS   UCS image identification.

variable	type	length	format
BURST	character	3	
CONTRIND	character	21	
COPIES	numeric	4	
COPYMODF	character	4	
DATAERRS	character	14	
DCTCHAR1-DCTCHAR4	character	4	
FCB	character	4	
FLASH	character	4	
FLASHCPY	numeric	4	
FORM	character	4	
JESNR	numeric	4	
JOB	character	8	
LOCLINFO	character	8	
NODE	numeric	4	
NRDSETS	numeric	4	
NRLINES	numeric	4	
OPTCD	character	1	

OUTCLASS	character	1	
OUTDEVCE	character	8	
OUTPRTY	numeric	4	
PAGECNT	numeric	4	
PRENTIME	numeric	8	DATETIME19.2
PRINTIME	numeric	8	DATETIME19.2
READTIME	numeric	8	DATETIME19.2
RMOTID	numeric	4	
STATUS	character	14	
SUBSYS	character	4	
SUPGROUP	character	8	
SYSTEM	character	4	
TYPE	character	5	
UCS	character	4	

```
**********MEMBER=TYPE6**********************************;
DATA TYPE6
          (KEEP=BURST CONTRIND COPIES COPYMODF DATAERRS
                DCTCHAR1-DCTCHAR4 FCB FLASH FLASHCPY FORM JESNR JOB
                LOCLINFO NODE NRDSETS NRLINES OPTCD OUTCLASS OUTDEVCE
                OUTPRTY PAGECNT PRENTIME PRINTIME READTIME
                RMOTID STATUS SUBSYS SUPGROUP SYSTEM TYPE UCS);
LENGTH DEFAULT=4 PRENTIME PRINTIME READTIME 8;
FORMAT PRENTIME PRINTIME READTIME DATETIME19.2;
  INFILE SMF STOPOVER LENGTH=LENGTH COL=COL RECFM=VBS LRECL=32756;
  INPUT @2 ID PIB1. @;
 IF ID=6;
  GOTO TYPE6;
TYPE6:
  INPUT @3 PRENTIME SMFSTAMP8. @11 SYSTEM $4.
        @15 JOB $8. @;
 IF LENGTH NE 84 THEN INPUT @23 READTIME SMFSTAMP8. @;
_JOBCK
  INPUT @31 LOCLINFO $8. @39 OUTCLASS $1. @40 PRINTIME SMFSTAMP8.
        @48 NRLINES PIB4. @52 IOSTAT PIB1.
        @53 NRDSETS PIB1. @54 FORM $4. @58 P3800 PIB1.
        @59 SUBS PIB2. @63 DCI PIB2. @65 JESNR PIB4. @;
 IF MOD(IOSTAT,8)>=4 THEN STATUS='DATABUFF ERROR';
 IF MOD(IOSTAT,2)>=1 THEN STATUS='CNTLBUFF ERROR';
 IF MOD(DCI,128)>=64 THEN CONTRIND='SPIN DATA SETS
 IF MOD(DCI,64)>=32 THEN CONTRIND='OPR TERMINATED';
 IF MOD(DCI,16)>=8 THEN CONTRIND='OPR RESTARTED';
 IF MOD(DCI,2)>=1 THEN CONTRIND='INTREPRETED';
 IF SUBS=2 THEN SUBSYS='JES2';
 IF SUBS=5 THEN SUBSYS='JES3';
 IF SUBSYS='JES2' OR SUBSYS='JES3';
 IF SUBSYS='JES3' THEN GOTO JES3IND;
 IF MOD(DCI,32)>=16 THEN CONTRIND='OPR INTERRUPTED';
 IF MOD(DCI,8)>=4 THEN CONTRIND='CONTINUATION';
 IF MOD(DCI,4)>=2 THEN CONTRIND='OPR OVERRODE';
  GOTO REST6;
JES3IND:
 IF MOD(DCI,32)>=16 THEN CONTRIND='RESTART WITH DEST';
 IF MOD(DCI,8)>=4 THEN CONTRIND='RECVD OPR RESTART';
 IF MOD(DCI,4)>=2 THEN CONTRIND='OPR STRT SINGLE SPACE';
REST6:
 IF JESNR NE 0 THEN INPUT @65 JESNR 4. @;
  INPUT @69 OUTDEVCE $8. @77 FCB $4. @81 UCS $4. @;
 IF LENGTH=84 THEN GOTO EXTWRTR;
  INPUT @85 PAGECNT PIB4. @;
```

```
 IF SUBSYS='JES2' THEN INPUT @89 NODE PIB1. @90 RMOTID PIB1. +2 @;
 IF SUBSYS='JES3' THEN INPUT @89 DATAERR PIB1. @91 OUTPRTY PIB2.
      @93 SUPGROUP $8. +14 @;
 IF SUBSYS='JES2' THEN GOTO DEV;
 IF MOD(DATAERR,4)>=2 THEN DATAERRS='CNTRL CHAR ERR';
 IF MOD(DATAERR,2)>=1 THEN DATAERRS='REC LEN ERR';
DEV:
 IF 'PRINT'<=OUTDEVCE<='PRINT9' THEN GOTO LINES;
 IF 'PUNCH' <= OUTDEVCE<='PUNCH9' THEN GOTO PUNCH;
   LOC=69;
LOOP6:
   LOC+1;
 IF LOC=76 THEN GOTO EXTWRTR;
 INPUT @LOC CHAR $2. @;
 IF CHAR='.P' THEN GOTO HITIT;
 GOTO LOOP6;
HITIT:
   LOC+2;
 INPUT @LOC PR $1. ;
 IF PR='R' THEN GOTO LINES;
 IF PR='U' THEN GOTO PUNCH;
LINES:
   TYPE='PRINT';
 GOTO TEST3800;
PUNCH:
   TYPE='PUNCH';
 GOTO TEST3800;
EXTWRTR:
   TYPE='EXWTR';
 OUTPUT TYPE6;
 RETURN;
TEST3800:
 IF P3800<128 THEN GOTO OUT6;
   INPUT (C1-C8) (PIB1.) (DCTCHAR1-DCTCHAR4) ($4.) COPYMODF $4.
       FLASH $4. FLASHCPY PIB1. OPTBIT PIB1. @;
   COPIES=SUM(OF C1-C8);
 IF OPTBIT>128 THEN BURST='YES';
 IF MOD(OPTBIT,128)>=64 THEN OPTCD='J';
OUT6:
 OUTPUT TYPE6;
 RETURN;
```

The TYPE7 Data Set: Lost SMF Data

The TYPE7 data set contains one observation for each type 7 SMF record. The type 7 SMF record is written whenever both SYS1.MANX and SYS1.MANY have filled with SMF records, and thus the type 7 record signifies that SMF records will be counted but lost.

The type 7 record should never occur. By properly sizing the MANX/MANY data sets and by providing operators with adequate instruction on how and when to dump SMF, space should always be available in either MANX or MANY for records. MANX should be sized to hold all the SMF records that could be expected before the dump of SMF is run, and MANY should be sized so that it can hold all the records that could be written while the dump of SMF is run. Thus the only purpose served by the existence of observations in the TYPE7 data set is to point out some deficiency in operations or in sizing the MANX/MANY data sets.

The type 7 record is written whenever an SMF data set (MANX or MANY) becomes available for writing again. Other than a console message at the time MANX and MANY were both filled, you get no SMF information until after the problem has been fixed.

Contents

LOSTBEGN   Beginning-of-data-loss time stamp.

LOSTRECS   Number of records lost.

SMFTIME   End-of-data-loss time stamp.

SYSTEM   System identification.

variable	type	length	format
LOSTBEGN	numeric	8	DATETIME19.2
LOSTRECS	numeric	4	
SMFTIME	numeric	8	DATETIME19.2
SYSTEM	character	4	

```
*********MEMBER=TYPE7********************************;
DATA TYPE7
            (KEEP=LOSTBEGN LOSTRECS SMFTIME SYSTEM);
LENGTH DEFAULT=4 SMFTIME LOSTBEGN 8;
FORMAT SMFTIME LOSTBEGN DATETIME19.2;
  INFILE SMF STOPOVER LENGTH=LENGTH COL=COL RECFM=VBS LRECL=32756;
  INPUT @2 ID PIB1. @;
 IF ID=7;
  GOTO TYPE7;
TYPE7:
  INPUT @3 SMFTIME SMFSTAMP8. @11 SYSTEM $4.
        @15 LOSTRECS PIB2. @17 LOSTBEGN SMFSTAMP8.;
  OUTPUT TYPE7;
  RETURN;
```

The TYPE8911 Data Set: I/O Configuration

The TYPE8911 data set contains one observation for each device that was either on-line at IPL, or was varied on- or off-line by an operator VARY command.

SMF type 8, 9, and 11 records contain the information for the TYPE8911 data set. A type 8 SMF record is written at the completion of each IPL, and contains all of the devices on-line at that time. A type 9 SMF record is written for each VARY ONLINE command, and contains all devices affected by that command, while a type 11 SMF record is similarly written for VARY OFFLINE commands.

The TYPE8911 data set is thus useful for tracking changes in the I/O configuration. (Note that a device varied on-line in response to an allocation recovery will be contained in data set TYPE10.) Unfortunately, the volume on the device is not included in the SMF record, so that tracking of DASD mountable volumes is not possible.

Contents

DEVICE   Type of device (e.g., 3330, 3350, etc.). From __DEVICE macro.

REASON   Reason that record was written:

value	meaning
IPL	device was on-line at IPL
ONLINE	VARY ONLINE command was issued
OFFLINE	VARY OFFLINE command was issued

SMFTIME   Event time stamp.

SYSTEM   System identification.

UNITADR   Unit address of device.

variable	type	length	format
DEVICE	character	7	
REASON	character	7	
SMFTIME	numeric	8	DATETIME19.2
SYSTEM	character	4	
UNITADR	numeric	4	HEX3.

```
**********MEMBER=TYPE8911*********************************;
DATA TYPE8911
              (KEEP=DEVICE REASON SMFTIME SYSTEM UNITADR);
LENGTH DEFAULT=4 SMFTIME 8;
FORMAT SMFTIME DATETIME19.2 UNITADR HEX3.;
  INFILE SMF STOPOVER LENGTH=LENGTH COL=COL RECFM=VBS LRECL=32756;
  INPUT @2 ID PIB1. @;
 IF ID=8 OR ID=9 OR ID=11;
  GOTO TYPE8911;
TYPE8911:
  INPUT @3 SMFTIME SMFSTAMP8. @11 SYSTEM $4. @;
 IF ID=8   THEN REASON='IPL     ';
 IF ID=9   THEN REASON='ONLINE';
 IF ID=11 THEN REASON='OFFLINE';
  INPUT @15 NUM PIB2. @;
   NUM=(NUM-2)/4;
LOOP8911:
 IF NUM LE Ø THEN RETURN;
  INPUT DEVCLASS PIB1. DEVTYPE PIB1. UNITADR PIB2. @;
  LINK UCBTYP;
  OUTPUT TYPE8911;
   NUM=NUM-1;
  GOTO LOOP8911;
_DEVICE
```

The TYPE10 Data Set: Allocation Recovery

The TYPE10 data set contains one observation for each type 10 SMF record, written after any allocation recovery event that was successful because the operator replied with a unit address to be brought on-line. The type 10 record is not written if the operator replies WAIT or CANCEL. Thus the utility of the TYPE10 data set depends on the operator's instructions in dealing with allocation recoveries.

A better approach for determining the impact of allocation recoveries is to analyze the allocation delay time (ALOCTM) in TYPE434. (See chapter 7.)

Contents

DEVICE   Type of device (e.g., 3330, 3350, etc). From __DEVICE macro.

JOB   Job name (batch), user ID (TSO).

LOCLINFO   Locally defined field, filled in by an installation-written SMF exit.

READTIME   Job-read-in (TSO LOGON) time stamp.

SMFTIME   Allocation-recovery-completed time stamp.

SYSTEM   System identification.

UNITADR   Unit address supplied by operator.

variable	type	length	format
DEVICE	character	7	
JOB	character	8	
LOCLINFO	character	8	
READTIME	numeric	8	DATETIME19.2
SMFTIME	numeric	8	DATETIME19.2
SYSTEM	numeric	4	
UNITADR	numeric	4	HEX3.

```
*********MEMBER=TYPE1Ø***********************************;
DATA TYPE1Ø
              (KEEP=DEVICE JOB LOCLINFO READTIME SMFTIME SYSTEM UNITADR);
LENGTH DEFAULT=4 SMFTIME READTIME 8;
FORMAT SMFTIME READTIME DATETIME19.2 UNITADR HEX3.;
  INFILE SMF STOPOVER LENGTH=LENGTH COL=COL RECFM=VBS LRECL=32756;
  INPUT @2 ID PIB1. @;
 IF ID=1Ø;
  GOTO TYPE1Ø;
TYPE1Ø:
  INPUT @3 SMFTIME SMFSTAMP8. @11 SYSTEM $4. @15 JOB $8. @;
_JOBCK
 IF JOB EQ ' ' THEN GOTO SETNAME;
  INPUT @23 READTIME SMFSTAMP8. @;
  GOTO GETLEN;
SETNAME:
    JOB='SYS_TASK';
    READTIME=SMFTIME;
GETLEN:
  INPUT @31 LOCLINFO $8. @39 LEN PIB2. @;
    NUM=(LEN-2)/4;
LOOP1Ø:
 IF NUM LE Ø THEN RETURN;
  INPUT DEVCLASS PIB1. DEVTYPE PIB1. UNITADR PIB2. @;
  LINK UCBTYP;
  OUTPUT TYPE1Ø;
    NUM=NUM-1;
    GOTO LOOP1Ø;
_DEVICE
```

The TYPE1415 Data Set:
Non-VSAM Data Set Activity

The TYPE1415 data set contains almost everything you want to know about how your data sets are being used and by whom. It is the basis for analyses of data set placement, data set usage, media selection for data sets, program usage of data, and so on.[1]

The TYPE1415 data set contains one observation for each type 14 or type 15 SMF record. These type 14 and 15 records are written for all non-VSAM DASD or TAPE data sets defined by DD statements (excluding DD *, DD DATA, and SYSOUT) that are opened by a problem program. The records are written when the file is closed, either by an explicit close, or by end-of-volume processing for multiple volume and/or concatenated sequential files. The type 14 record is written for files opened for INPUT or RDBACK, while the type 15 is written for files opened for OUTPUT, UPDAT, INOUT, or OUTIN.

Type 14 and 15 records are written at each close, so that several records are written for files opened several times in the same step. Furthermore, EXCPs are accumulated across these multiple opens, so that you cannot simply sum the EXCPs in TYPE1415 to get true EXCPs.

There are other difficulties. Concatenated sequential files have blank DDnames in the record, so that if a step has multiple concatenations, it is impossible to correctly associate the concatenations. Probably the most serious omission affects concatenated BPAM data sets: a single record is written for the entire concatenation, giving only the first data set's name; however, the record does contain the UCBs for each of the concatenations.

In spite of these problems, the information in the TYPE1415 data set is of significant value in performance measurement.

---

1. The analysis macro __DBANAL uses TYPE1415 and other SAS data sets to perform data set analyses; see the discussion of __DBANAL in chapter 6 for more information.

Contents

ACCESS   Access method.

value	meaning
BDAM	Basic Direct Access Method
BDSAM	either BDAM or BSAM (cannot distinguish)
BISAM	Basic Indexed Sequential Access Method
BPSAM	either BPAM or BSAM (cannot distinguish)
BSAM	Basic Sequential Access Method
EXCP	Execute (self-written) Channel Program
QISAM	Queued Indexed Sequential Access Method
QSAM	Queued Sequential Access Method
blank	unknown

ALOC   DASD only. SPACE allocation units (see PRIALOC and SECALOC).

value	meaning
ABSTR	absolute track address
BLOCK	blocks
CYL	cylinders
MSSGP	mass storage allocation
TRK	tracks

AVGBLK   Average data block length (JFCBDRLH, +171).

BLKCNT   Tape only. Block count for this volume.

BLKSIZE   Blocksize. Can be incorrect if data set was opened more than once or if EXCP or open type J.

BUFFLEN   Buffer length.

BUFNO   Number of data buffers.

BUFTEK   JFCBFTEK control byte (buffering technique). Offset 89 (decimal) in JFCB. See Debugging Handbook.

CRDATE   Data set creation date (yyddd).

CYLINDEX   ISAM only. Number of cylinders in the independent index area.

CYLOFLO   ISAM only. Number of cylinders in the independent overflow area.

CYLOFULL   ISAM only. Number of cylinder areas that are full.

CYLPRIME   ISAM only. Number of cylinders in the prime data area.

DCBOFLGS   Flags used by open routine; these vary depending on the access method. See Debugging Handbook. DCB offset 48 (decimal).

DCBOPTCD   DCB option codes. These vary with access method; see Debugging Handbook, DCB offset decimal 52.

bit	BPAM/BSAM/ QSAM/EXCP	BISAM/QISAM	BDAM
1	W (write verify check)	N (write verify check)	W (write verify check)
2	U (allow data ck(1403))	M (full track index write)	M (track overflow)
3	C (chained scheduling)	M (master indexes)	E (extended search)
4	(1288/DOS options)	I (independent overflow)	F (feedback)
5	(ASCII translation)	Y (CYL overflow)	A (actual addressing)
6	Z (use reduced error recovery (TAPE)) Z (use search direct (DISK))		(dynamic buffering) (read exclusive)
7	(user totaling)	L (delete option)	
8	J (3800 printer)	R (reorg criteria)	R (relative block addr)

DDN   DDname. Blank for concatenated files.

DEBOFLGS   Data set status flags (offset 8 in DEB). Bits 1-2 are DISP.

bit	meaning
3	EOF encountered
4	DASD: RLSE specified tape: short blocks permitted
5	DCB modification
6	DASD: split cylinder tape: emulator 7-track
7	Non-standard labels
8	DASD: concatenated PO processed with BPAM tape: use reduced error recovery

DEBOPATB   DEB flags indicating method of I/O processing and disposition when EOV occurs:

bit	meaning
1	ABEND SYSABEND/SYSUDUMP data set
3-4	Positioning flags: 01 reread 11 leave

5-8	I/O accessing being done:
	0000 INPUT
	1111 OUTPUT
	0011 INOUT
	0111 OUTIN
	0001 RDBACK
	0100 UPDAT

DEBVLSEQ Volume sequence number. For DASD, relative to first volume in data set. For tape, relative to first volume processed.

DEN Tape only. Density: 200, 556, 800, 1600, or 6250 bytes per inch.

DEVICE Device type (e.g., 3330, 3350, etc.). From __DEVICE macro.

DISP Disposition of data set: MOD, NEW, OLD, OTHR, SHR.

DSNAME Data set name.

DSORG Data set organization:

value	meaning
blank	unknown
DA	direct access
IS	indexed sequential
PO	partitioned organization
PS	physical sequential (includes use of member of PDS if member name was included in JCL)
VI	virtual I/O

DSSEQCNT Tape only. Data set sequence count.

DSSEQNR Tape only. Data set sequence number.

EROPT Action to be taken (due to EROPT option) if I/O error occurs:

value	action
ABE	ABEND
ACC	accept the error and continue
SKP	skip this record and continue

EXCPOFLO ISAM only. EXCPs to overflow records which are not first in a chain of overflow records.

EXCPS EXCP count.

EXPDT   Expiration date of data set (0 if not date-protected).

EXTINDEX   ISAM only. Number of extents in the independent index area.

EXTOFLO   ISAM only. Number of extents in the independent overflow area.

EXTPRIME   ISAM only. Number of extents in the prime data area.

EXTREL   DASD only. Number of extents released (RLSE).

FILESEQ   Tape only. File sequence number (i.e., position on tape volume if more than one data set is on the same volume. Same as first position of LABEL parameter).

ID   Record ID.

value	meaning
14	opened for INPUT or RDBACK
15	opened for OUTPUT, UPDAT, INOUT, or OUTIN

JFCBCTRI   SPACE parameters (DASD only).

bits	meaning
1-2	space requested
	00 ABSTR
	01 AVG BLOCK LENGTH
	10 TRK request
	11 CYL request
3	request is for Mass Storage Volume Group (MSVGP)
5	CONTIG request
6	MXIG request
7	ALX request
8	ROUND request

JFCBOPCD   JFCB option codes.

bit	BPAM/BSAM/ QSAM/EXCP	BISAM/QISAM	BDAM
1	W (write verify check)	W (write verify check)	W (write verify check)
2	U (allow data ck)		(track overflow)
3	C (chained scheduling)	M (master indexes)	E (extended search)
4	(bypass DOS checkpoint)	I (independent overflow)	F (feedback)
5		Y (cylinder overflow)	A (actual addressing)

6	Z (reduced error recovery (TAPE))		
	Z (search direct (DASD))		
7		L (delete option)	
8	J (3800 printer)	R (reorg criteria)	R (relative block addr)

JFCBUFNO   Number of buffers.

JFCFLGS1   Flag byte (offset 159 decimal in JFCB).

bit	meaning
1	VS: delete when extending JOBQUEUE or SPOOL
2	tape data set has been opened
3	automatic data set protection indicator
5	CHKPT=EOV specified
6	VIO data set
8	UNIT=AFF specified

JOB   Jobname (batch). User ID (TSO).

KEEP   Data set catalog status.

value	action
blank	not cataloged
CATLG	data set is a cataloged data set

KEYLEN   DASD only. Key length if data set has keys.

LABEL   Data set label (second position of label):

value	meaning
blank	unknown label
AL	American National Standard
AUL	American User National Standard
BLP	Bypass Label Processing
LTM	Leading Tape Mark (DOS-created unlabeled)
NL	Non-Labeled
NSL	Non-Standard Label
SL	IBM Standard Label
SUL	Standard User Label

LIMCT   DASD direct access only. BDAM search limit.

LOCATION   Data set movability: blank or UNMOV if unmovable.

LOCLINFO   Locally defined field, filled in by an installation-written SMF exit.

LRECL	Logical record length.
MEMBER	PDS only. Member name (if specified on JCL).
MSSCVOLI	Mass Storage System Communicator (MSSC) volume selection index.
NEXTENT	Number of extents in the data set.
NRLEVELS	ISAM only. Number of index levels.
NRVOLS	Number of volume serial numbers. (JFCBNVOL + 118)
NUCB	Number of UCB segments. Always 1, except:

condition	value
concatenated BPAM	1 per data set
ISAM	1 for index 1 for overflow extent (if any)) 1 per volume for primary

OPEN	Type of OPEN: INOUT, INPUT, OTHER, OUTIN, OUTPUT, RDBACK, UPDATE.
OPENTIME	Data set open time stamp.
OPTCODE	Search direct (OPTCD=Z) specified. (See DCBOPTCD and JFCBOPCD).

value	meaning
blank	no
Z	OPTCD=Z

PRIALOC	DASD only. Size of primary allocation (see ALOC).
READTIME	Job-read-in (TSO LOGON) time stamp.
RECFM	Record format.

value	meaning
OTHR	unknown
[F] [B] [T]	{Fixed} {Blocked} {Track overflow}
[V] [B] [S] [T]	{Variable} {Blocked} {Spanned} {Track overflow}

RECIND   Record and data set indicator.

bit	meaning
1	record written by EOV
2	DASD device
3	temporary data set (doesn't include all temporary data sets)
4	DCBDSORG=DA (data set organization is direct access
5	DCBDSORG=IS and DCBMACRF not EXCP
6	JFCDSORG=IS (data set org is indexed sequential
7	VIO data set

RECOFLOW   ISAM only. Number of logical records in the overflow area.

RECPRIME   ISAM only. Number of logical records in the prime area.

RELGDG   Generation Data Group only. Relative generation number (when referenced in JCL through relative number).

RLSE   DASD only. Space was released: blank or RLSE.

SECALOC   DASD only. Size of secondary allocation (see ALOC).

SMFTIME   Close time stamp.

SORTIME   A time stamp used when matching 4/34, 14/15, and 5/35 records. Set equal to SMFTIME.

SYSTEM   Identification of system on which job executed.

TEMP   Temporary data set: PERM or TEMP.

TIOELINK   TIOT flag byte (offset 27 decimal in TIOT):

bit	meaning
1	this is a SYSOUT data set containing data
3	device is a terminal
4	DYNAM coded on DD statement
6	VS/1: entry for spooled SYSIN data set
7	VS/1: entry for spooled SYSOUT data set
	VS/2. Entry for a subsystem data set
8	entry for a remote device

TIOESTTA   TIOT status byte A (offset 25 decimal in TIOT):

bit	meaning
1	non-standard label (see LABEL)
2	no unallocation necessary (at termination)
3	rewind but no unloading (at termination)
4	JOBLIB indicator
5	DADSM allocation necessary
6	labeled tape (see LABEL)
7	tape: REWIND/UNLOAD the tape volume
	DASD: private volume
8	TAPE: rewind the tape volume
	DASD: public volume

TIOESTTC   TIOT status byte C (offset 39.). Unfortunately, used only at allocation, and reset to zero. Hence, always zero.

TIOEWTCT   Number of devices requested for this data set.

TRKREL   DASD only. Tracks released at close.

TRKSALOC   DASD only. Number of tracks allocated to this data set on this device.

TRKSLEFT   ISAM only. Number of tracks (whole or partial) remaining in the overflow area.

TRTCH   Tape recording technique.

TTRN   Physical and partitioned only. Track (TT), Record (R) number (and concatenation number (N) for concatenated BPAM) of the last record processed.

TYPE   Type of data set.

value	meaning
blank	normal
JESIO	data set is a SYSIN/SYSOUT data set.

UCBSTAB   Volume status (UCB offset 34 decimal):

bit	meaning
1	DASD: volume is demountable by data management routine.
	tape: device is not sharable among several CPUs
2	UCB is open and being used as a page file

3	DASD:	used during volume attribute processing
	tape:	additional volume label processing
4		private volume use status
5		public volume use status
6	DASD:	storage volume use status
	tape:	American National Standard Label
7		Volume sharable among job steps
8		DASD: control volume (a catalog is on this volume)

UNITADR   Unit address of this UCB segment.

VOLSEQ   Volume sequence number (JFCBVLSQ +70).

VOLSER   Volume serial number of this volume.

VOLSER1-   First five volume serial numbers for multi-volume data set.
VOLSER5

variable	type	length	format
ACCESS	character	5	
ALOC	character	5	
AVGBLK	numeric	4	
BLKCNT	numeric	4	
BLKSIZE	numeric	4	
BUFFLEN	numeric	4	
BUFNO	numeric	4	
BUFTEK	numeric	4	HEX2.
CRDATE	numeric	4	
CYLINDEX	numeric	4	
CYLOFLO	numeric	4	
CYLOFULL	numeric	4	
CYLPRIME	numeric	4	
DCBOFLGS	numeric	4	HEX2.
DCBOPTCD	numeric	4	HEX2.
DDN	character	8	
DEBOFLGS	numeric	4	HEX2.
DEBOPATB	numeric	4	HEX2.
DEBVLSEQ	numeric	4	
DEN	numeric	4	
DEVICE	character	7	
DISP	character	4	
DSNAME	character	44	
DSORG	character	2	
DSSEQCNT	numeric	4	
DSSEQNR	numeric	4	
EROPT	character	3	
EXCPOFLO	numeric	4	
EXCPS	numeric	4	
EXPDT	numeric	4	

EXTINDEX	numeric	4	
EXTOFLO	numeric	4	
EXTPRIME	numeric	4	
EXTREL	numeric	4	
FILESEQ	numeric	4	
ID	numeric	4	
JFCBCTRI	numeric	4	HEX2.
JFCBOPCD	numeric	4	HEX2.
JFCBUFNO	numeric	4	
JFCFLGS1	numeric	4	HEX2.
JOB	character	8	
KEEP	character	5	
KEYLEN	numeric	4	
LABEL	character	3	
LIMCT	numeric	4	
LOCATION	character	5	
LOCLINFO	character	8	
LRECL	numeric	4	
MEMBER	character	8	
MSSCVOLI	numeric	4	
NEXTENT	numeric	4	
NRLEVELS	numeric	4	
NRVOLS	numeric	4	
NUCB	numeric	4	
OPEN	character	7	
OPENTIME	numeric	8	DATETIME19.2
OPTCODE	character	1	
PRIALOC	numeric	4	
READTIME	numeric	8	DATETIME19.2
RECFM	character	4	
RECIND	numeric	4	HEX2.
RECOFLOW	numeric	4	
RECPRIME	numeric	4	
RELGDG	character	8	
RLSE	character	4	
SECALOC	numeric	4	
SMFTIME	numeric	8	DATETIME19.2
SORTIME	numeric	8	DATETIME19.2
SYSTEM	character	4	
TEMP	character	4	
TIOELINK	numeric	4	HEX2.
TIOESTTA	numeric	4	HEX2.
TIOESTTC	numeric	4	HEX2.
TIOEWTCT	numeric	4	HEX2.
TRKREL	numeric	4	
TRKSALOC	numeric	4	
TRKSLEFT	numeric	4	
TRTCH	numeric	4	HEX2.
TTRN	numeric	4	HEX8.
TYPE	character	5	
UCBSTAB	numeric	4	HEX2.
UNITADR	numeric	4	HEX3.
VOLSEQ	numeric	4	
VOLSER	character	6	
VOLSER1	character	6	
VOLSER2	character	6	
VOLSER3	character	6	
VOLSER4	character	6	
VOLSER5	character	6	

```
**********MEMBER=TYPE1415*********************************;
 DATA TYPE1415
                (KEEP=ACCESS ALOC AVGBLK BLKCNT BLKSIZE BUFFLEN
               BUFNO BUFTEK CRDATE CYLINDEX CYLOFLO CYLOFULL
               CYLPRIME DCBOFLGS DCBOPTCD DDN DEBOFLGS DEBOPATB
               DEBVLSEQ DEN DEVICE DISP DSNAME DSORG DSSEQCNT
               DSSEQNR EROPT EXCPOFLO EXCPS EXPDT EXTINDEX
               EXTOFLO EXTPRIME EXTREL FILESEQ ID JFCBCTRI
               JFCBOPCD JFCBUFNO JFCFLGS1 JOB KEEP KEYLEN
               LABEL LIMCT LOCATION LOCLINFO LRECL MEMBER
               MSSCVOLI NEXTENT NRLEVELS NRVOLS NUCB OPEN OPENTIME
               OPTCODE PRIALOC READTIME RECFM RECIND RECOFLOW
               RECPRIME RELGDG RLSE SECALOC SMFTIME SORTIME
               SYSTEM TEMP TIOELINK TIOESTTA TIOESTTC TIOEWTCT
               TRKREL TRKSALOC TRKSLEFT TRTCH TTRN TYPE UCBSTAB
               UNITADR VOLSEQ VOLSER VOLSER1-VOLSER5);
 LENGTH DEFAULT=4 OPENTIME READTIME SMFTIME SORTIME 8;
 FORMAT OPENTIME READTIME SMFTIME SORTIME              DATETIME19.2
        BUFTEK DCBOFLGS DEBOPATB ERROPT DCBOPTCD
        DEBOFLGS JFCBIND1 JFCBFLG2 JFCBTSDM JFCBCTRI
        JFCBOPCD JFCFLGS1 RECIND TAPEDEN TIOESTTA
        TIOEWTCT TIOELINK TIOESTTC TRTCH UCBSTAB                HEX2.
        UNITADR                                                 HEX3.
        TTRN                                                    HEX8.;
   INFILE SMF STOPOVER LENGTH=LENGTH COL=COL RECFM=VBS LRECL=32756;
   INPUT @2 ID PIB1. @;
 IF ID=14 OR ID=15 ;
   GOTO TYPE1415;
 TYPE1415:
   INPUT @3 SMFTIME SMFSTAMP8. @11 SYSTEM $4.
         @15 JOB $8. @23 READTIME SMFSTAMP8. @;
 _JOBCK
     SORTIME=SMFTIME;
   INPUT @31 LOCLINFO $8. @39 RECIND PIB1.    @42 NUCB PIB1.
         @42 NUCB PIB1. @45 OPENTIME PIB4.2
         @50 TIOESTTA PIB1. @51 TIOEWTCT PIB1.
         @52 TIOELINK PIB1. @53 DDN $8.
         @64 TIOESTTC PIB1. @65 DSNAME $44.
         @65 DSNTEMP $8.    @73 PER1 $2.         @75 PER2 $6.
         @117 JFCBTSDM PIB1. @125 BUFNO PIB2.
         @129 MSSCVOLI PIB2. @131 TAPELBL PIB1.
         @135 VOLSEQ PIB2.   @143 JFCBFLG2 PIB1.
         @145 CRDYY PIB1.    @146 CRDDD PIB2.
         @148 EXDYY PIB1.    @149 EXDDD PIB2.     @151 JFCBIND1 PIB1.
         @152 DISP1 PIB1.    @153 JFCBUFNO PIB1. @154 BUFTEK PIB1.
         @155 BUFFLEN PIB2.  @157 ERROPT PIB1.
         @159 TAPEDEN PIB1.  @163 JFCBORG1 PIB1.
         @164 JFCBORG2 PIB1. @165 JFCBRCFM PIB1. @166 JFCBOPCD PIB1.
         @167 BLKSIZE PIB2.  @169 LRECL PIB2.     @171 NCP PIB1.
         @182 NRVOLS PIB1.   @183 (VOLSER1-VOLSER5) ($6.)
         @224 JFCFLGS1 PIB1. @236 AVGBLK PIB3.    @239 VOLCT PIB1.
         @241 ORG PIB1.      @243 RECFMT PIB1.
         @244 MACRF1 PIB1.   @245 MACRF2 PIB1.
         @246 DCBOFLGS PIB1. @247 DCBOPTCD PIB1. @249 DEBOFLGS PIB1.
         @250 DEBOPATB PIB1. @251 DEBVLSEQ PIB2. @;
 * OPENTIME EXISTS ONLY IN MSV/SE REL 1.2.0;
   IF OPENTIME=0 THEN GOTO NOTSE2;
   IF OPENTIME>TIMEPART(SMFTIME) THEN ODATE=1;
   IF OPENTIME<=TIMEPART(SMFTIME) THEN ODATE=0;
     OPENTIME=DHMS(DATEPART(SMFTIME)-ODATE,0,0,OPENTIME);
     GO TO SE2OPEN;
 NOTSE2:
     OPENTIME=.;
 SE2OPEN:
   IF MOD(RECIND,64)<32 THEN GOTO INTAPES;
   IF MOD(RECIND,64)>=32 THEN GOTO INDISK;
```

```
INTAPES:
  INPUT @133 FILESEQ PIB2. @158 TRTCH PIB1. @253 BLKCNT PIB4. @;
    DEN0=FLOOR(TAPEDEN/128);
    DEN1=FLOOR(MOD(TAPEDEN,128)/64);
    DEN3=FLOOR(MOD(TAPEDEN,32)/16);
  IF NOT DEN0 AND NOT DEN1 AND NOT DEN3 THEN DEN=200;
  IF NOT DEN0 AND     DEN1 AND NOT DEN3 THEN DEN=556;
  IF     DEN0 AND NOT DEN1 AND NOT DEN3 THEN DEN=800;
  IF     DEN0 AND     DEN1 AND NOT DEN3 THEN DEN=1600;
  IF     DEN0 AND     DEN1 AND     DEN3 THEN DEN=6250;
    GOTO MISC;
INDISK:
  INPUT @158 KEYLEN PIB1.    @217 PRIALOC PIB3.
        @220 JFCBCTRI PIB1. @221 SECALOC PIB3.
        @253 TTRN PIB4.      @257 TRKREL PIB4. @261 EXTREL PIB1. @;
  IF JFCBCTRI=0 THEN ALOC='ABSTR';
  IF JFCBCTRI>127 AND NOT MOD(JFCBCTRI,128)>63 THEN ALOC='TRK ';
  IF JFCBCTRI>127 AND MOD(JFCBCTRI,128)>63 THEN ALOC='CYL';
  IF JFCBCTRI<128 AND MOD(JFCBCTRI,128)>63 THEN ALOC='BLOCK';
  IF MOD(JFCBCTRI,64)>31 THEN ALOC='MSSGP';
MISC:
  IF JFCBTSDM>127 THEN KEEP='CATLG';
  IF MOD(JFCBTSDM,64)>31 THEN TYPE='JESIO';
  IF MOD(JFCBFLG2,16)>7 THEN OPTCODE='Z';
  IF MOD(JFCBIND1,128)>63 OR JFCBIND1>127 THEN RLSE='RLSE';
  IF ERROPT >127 THEN EROPT='ACC';
  IF MOD(ERROPT,128)>63 THEN EROPT='SKP';
  IF MOD(ERROPT,64)>31 THEN EROPT='ABE';
    CRDATE=CRDYY*1000+CRDDD;
    EXPDT=EXDYY*1000+EXDDD;
  IF MOD(ORG,2)>=1 THEN LOCATION='UNMOV';
  IF MOD(RECIND,2)>=1 THEN GOTO VIODS;
  IF ORG>127 OR JFCBORG1>127 THEN GOTO IS;
  IF MOD(ORG,64)>=32 OR MOD(JFCBORG1,64)>=32 THEN GOTO DA;
  IF MOD(ORG,4)>=2 OR MOD(JFCBORG1,4)>=2 THEN GOTO PO;
  IF MOD(ORG,128)>=64 OR MOD(JFCBORG1,128)>=64 THEN GOTO PS;
    DSORG=' ';
  GOTO AFTORG;
DA:
    DSORG='DA';
  INPUT @160 LIMCT PIB3. @;
  IF MACRF1>=128 THEN GOTO ACCEXCP;
  IF 40<= MACRF1 <= 63 OR 40 <= MACRF2 <= 63 THEN GOTO ACCBDAM;
  IF MACRF1=36 AND MACRF2=36 THEN GOTO ACCBSAM;
  IF MACRF1=32 OR MACRF1=36 OR MACRF2=32 OR MACRF2=36
    THEN GOTO ACCBDSAM;
  IF MACRF1>63 OR MACRF2>63 THEN GOTO ACCQSAM;
    GOTO AFTORG;
IS:
    DSORG='IS';
  IF MACRF1>=128 THEN GOTO ACCEXCP;
  IF MACRF1 EQ 72 OR MACRF2 EQ 72 OR MACRF1 EQ 80 OR MACRF2 EQ 80
      OR MACRF2>=64 THEN GOTO ACCQISAM;
  IF MACRF1 = 32 OR MACRF1 = 34 OR MACRF1 = 36 OR MACRF1=38
  OR MACRF2 = 32 OR MACRF2 = 34 OR MACRF2 = 36 OR MACRF2=38
  OR MACRF1=40 OR MACRF1=41 OR MACRF2=40 OR MACRF2=41
      THEN GOTO ACCBISAM;
    GOTO AFTORG;
PO:
    DSORG='PO';
  INPUT @109 MEMBER $8. @;
  IF MACRF1>=128 THEN GOTO ACCEXCP;
  IF MACRF1=72 OR MACRF1=80 OR MACRF2=72 OR MACRF2=80 THEN GOTO ACCQSAM;
  IF MACRF1=34 OR MACRF1=38 THEN GOTO ACCBSAM;
  IF MACRF1=32 OR MACRF1=36 OR MACRF2 =32 OR MACRF2=36
      THEN GOTO ACCBPSAM;
```

```
      GOTO AFTORG;
  PS:
      DSORG='PS';
  ACCPS:
   IF MACRF1>=128 THEN GOTO ACCEXCP;
   IF MACRF1=72 OR MACRF1=80 OR MACRF2=72 OR MACRF2=80 THEN GOTO ACCQSAM;
   IF MACRF1=32 OR MACRF1=34 OR MACRF1=36 OR MACRF1=38 OR
      MACRF2=32 OR MACRF2=34 OR MACRF2=36 OR MACRF2=38 OR MACRF2=40
      THEN GOTO ACCBSAM;
      GOTO AFTORG;
  VIODS:
      DSORG='VI';
    GOTO ACCPS;
  *
  *     THE FOLLOWING DECODES APPEAR TO BE VALID BY WHICH THE ACCESS
  *     METHOD CAN BE DEDUCED FROM THE MACRF1 AND MACRF2 BYTES OF
  *     DATA.  IN A FEW INSTANCES, BPAM/BSAM AND BDAM/BSAM CANNOT BE
  *     UNIQUELY IDENTIFIED, SO THE ACCESS CODES BPSAM AND BDSAM
  *     ARE GENERATED IN THESE CASES.
  *     THE TWO BYTES AND THEIR BIT MEANINGS ARE AS FOLLOWS:
  *
  *     (HERE A WORD MEANS THE BIT IS ON FOR THAT TYPE USE, A
  *      LETTER R SIGNIFIES RESERVED, A 0 SIGNIFIES ALWAYS ZERO)
  *
  * MACRF1       EXCP      BSAM   QSAM    BPAM   BISAM   QISAM   BDAM
  *    1          1         0      0       0      0       0       0
  *    2                    0     GET      0      0      GET      0
  *    3                   READ    0      READ   READ    READ    READ
  *    4                    R     MOVE     R      0      MOVE    KEY
  *    5                    R    LOCATE    R      0     LOCATE    ID
  *    6                  POINT   SUBST   POINT  DYN      0      DYN
  *    7                  CNTRL   CNTRL    R     CHECK    R      EXCL
  *    8                    R     DATA     R      R       R      CHECK
  *
  *   MACRF2
  *
  *    1                    0      0       0      0      SETL     0
  *    2                    0     PUT      0      0      PUT/X    0
  *    3                  WRITE    0      WRITE  WRITE    0      WRITE
  *    4                    R     MOVE     R      0      MOVE    KEY
  *    5                  LOAD   LOCATE    R      0     LOCATE    ID
  *    6                  POINT   SUBST   POINT   0      PUTX     R
  *    7                  CNTRL  CNTRL     R      0      SETL    ADD
  *    8                  POOL    DATA     R      0      SETL    POOL
  *;
  ACCBDAM:
     ACCESS='BDAM ';
    GOTO AFTORG;
  ACCBDSAM:
     ACCESS='BDSAM';
    GOTO AFTORG;
  ACCBISAM:
     ACCESS='BISAM';
    GOTO AFTORG;
  ACCBPSAM:
     ACCESS='BPSAM';
    GOTO AFTORG;
  ACCBSAM:
     ACCESS='BSAM';
    GOTO AFTORG;
  ACCEXCP:
     ACCESS='EXCP';
    GOTO AFTORG;
  ACCQISAM:
     ACCESS='QISAM';
```

```
    GOTO AFTORG;
ACCQSAM:
   ACCESS='QSAM';
AFTORG:
 IF DSORG NE 'PO' THEN INPUT @109 RELGDG $8. @;
   LABEL='    ';
 IF TAPELBL=02 THEN GOTO SL;
 IF TAPELBL=01 THEN GO TO NL;
 IF TAPELBL=16 THEN GOTO BLP;
 IF TAPELBL=10 THEN GO TO SUL;
 IF TAPELBL=04 THEN GOTO NSL;
 IF TAPELBL=33 THEN GOTO LTM;
 IF TAPELBL=64 THEN GO TO AL;
 IF TAPELBL=72 THEN GO TO AUL;
   GOTO ENDL;
AL:
   LABEL='AL ';
   GO TO ENDL;
BLP:
   LABEL='BLP';
   GOTO ENDL;
SUL:
   LABEL='SUL';
   GOTO ENDL;
LTM:
   LABEL='LTM';
   GOTO ENDL;
NL:
   LABEL='NL';
   GOTO ENDL;
SL:
   LABEL='SL';
   GOTO ENDL;
NSL:
   LABEL='NSL';
   GOTO ENDL;
AUL:
   LABEL='AUL';
ENDL:
   TEMP='PERM';
 IF ( 'SYS70000'<=DSNTEMP<='SYS99999' AND PER1='.T'
     AND '000000'<=PER2<='999999' )
   OR (MOD(RECIND,32)>=16 ) OR (MOD(DISP1,2)>0) THEN TEMP='TEMP';
 IF MOD(DISP1,128)>63 AND DISP1>127 THEN GOTO NEW;
 IF DISP1>127 THEN GOTO MOD;
 IF MOD(DISP1,128)>63 THEN GOTO OLD;
   DISP='OTHR';
   GOTO RECFM;
NEW:
   DISP='NEW';
   GOTO RECFM;
OLD:
   DISP='OLD';
   DISP1=DISP1-64;
 IF DISP1>31 THEN DISP1=DISP1-32;
 IF DISP1>15 THEN DISP1=DISP1-16;
 IF DISP1<8 THEN GO TO RECFM;
   DISP='SHR';
   GO TO RECFM;
MOD:
   DISP='MOD';
   GOTO RECFM;
RECFM:
 IF RECFMT>191 THEN GOTO U;
 IF RECFMT>127 THEN GOTO F;
```

```
   IF RECFMT>063 THEN GOTO V;
   IF RECFMT=JFCBRCFM THEN GO TO OTHRR;
     RECFMT=JFCBRCFM;
    GOTO RECFM;
OTHRR:
    RECFM='OTHR';
    GO TO DEB;
U:
    RECFM='U   ';
    GOTO DEB;
F:
    RECFMT=RECFMT-128;
  IF RECFMT>31 THEN GO TO FT;
  IF RECFMT>15 THEN GOTO FB;
    RECFM='F   ';
    GO TO DEB;
FT:
    RECFMT=RECFMT-32;
  IF RECFMT>15 THEN GO TO FBT;
    RECFM='F T';GOTO DEB;
    GOTO DEB;
FBT:
    RECFM='FB T';
    GOTO DEB;
FB:
    RECFM='FB ';
    GOTO DEB;
V:
    RECFMT=RECFMT-64;
  IF RECFMT>31 THEN GOTO VT;
  IF RECFMT>15 THEN GOTO VB;
  IF RECFMT>7 THEN GO TO VS;
    RECFM='V   ';
    GO TO DEB;
VT:
    RECFMT=RECFMT-32;
  IF RECFMT>16 THEN GO TO VTB;
  IF RECFMT>7 THEN GOTO VTS;
    RECFM='V T';
    GOTO DEB;
VTS:
    RECFM='V ST';
    GOTO DEB;
VTB:
    RECFMT=RECFMT-16;
  IF RECFMT>8 THEN GOTO VTBS;
    RECFM='VB T';
    GO TO DEB;
VTBS:
    RECFM='VBST';
    GOTO DEB;
VB:
    RECFMT=RECFMT-16;
  IF RECFMT>7 THEN GOTO VBS;
    RECFM='VB  ';
    GOTO DEB;
VBS:
    RECFM='VBS ';
    GOTO DEB;
VS:
    RECFM='VS';
DEB:
    DEBOPAT=MOD(DEBOPATB,16);
  IF DEBOPAT=0 THEN GO TO INPUT;
  IF DEBOPAT=15 THEN GOTO OUTPUT;
```

```
 IF DEBOPAT=4 THEN GO TO UPDAT;
 IF DEBOPAT=3 THEN GOTO INOUT;
 IF DEBOPAT=7 THEN GO TO OUTIN;
 IF DEBOPAT=1 THEN GOTO RDBACK;
   OPEN='OTHER  ';
 GOTO GETUCB;
OUTPUT:
   OPEN='OUTPUT';
 GOTO GETUCB;
INPUT:
   OPEN='INPUT  ';
 GOTO GETUCB;
UPDAT:
   OPEN='UPDATE ';
 GOTO GETUCB;
INOUT:
   OPEN='INOUT  ';
 GOTO GETUCB;
OUTIN:
   OPEN='OUTIN';
 GOTO GETUCB;
RDBACK:
   OPEN='RDBACK ';
 GOTO GETUCB;
GETUCB:
   NX=NUCB;
   LOC=265;
LOOP1415:
 INPUT @44 ISAMEXT PIB1. @;
 IF NX<=0 THEN RETURN;
   INPUT @LOC CHAN PIB1. ADR PIB1. VOLSER $6. +2 DEVCLASS PIB1.
         DEVTYPE PIB1. UCBSTAB PIB1. NEXTENT PIB1. +2 EXCPS PIB4. @;
 IF CHAN=7 THEN CHAN=2;
 IF CHAN=5 THEN CHAN=4;
 IF CHAN=8 THEN CHAN=3;
   UNITADR=CHAN*256+ADR;
 IF MOD(RECIND,64)<32 THEN INPUT DSSEQCNT PIB2. DSSEQNR PIB2. @;
 IF MOD(RECIND,64)>=32 THEN INPUT TRKSALOC PIB4. @;
 LINK UCBTYP;
 IF MOD(RECIND,2)=1 THEN DEVICE='VIO     ';
   NX=NX-1;
   LOC=LOC+24;
 IF NX=0 AND ISAMEXT=28 THEN GOTO ISAMEXT;
   OUTPUT TYPE1415;
   GOTO LOOP1415;
ISAMEXT:
   INPUT +3 NRLEVELS PIB1. EXCPOFLO PIB4. RECPRIME PIB4.
         TRKSLEFT PIB2. RECOFLOW PIB2. CYLOFULL PIB2.
         +1 EXTINDEX PIB1. EXTPRIME PIB1. EXTOFLO PIB1.
         CYLINDEX PIB2. CYLPRIME PIB2. CYLOFLO PIB2. @;
   OUTPUT TYPE1415;
   RETURN;
_DEVICE
```

The TYPE1718 Data Set:
Non-VSAM Data Set Scratch or Rename

The TYPE1718 data set contains one observation for every type 17 or type 18 SMF record. A type 17 SMF record is written whenever a non-VSAM data set is scratched. (Note that the SMF option REC=2 must be specified if scratch records are to be written for temporary data sets. The usefulness of scratch records for temporary data sets is limited and thus REC=0 should be specified so that scratch records are produced only for non-temporary data sets.) A type 18 record is written whenever a non-VSAM data set is renamed.

The primary utility of TYPE1718 is thus in the tracking of the lost data sets.

Contents

DSNAME Data set name (old name for rename).

ID Record identification.

value	meaning
17	scratch
18	rename

JOB Job name (batch), user ID (TSO).

LOCLINFO Locally defined field, filled in by installation-written SMF exit.

NEWNAME New data set name (blank for scratch).

NRVOLS Number of volumes in the data set.

OPEN Type of action, SCRATCH or RENAME.

READTIME Job-read-in (TSO LOGON) time stamp.

SMFTIME Scratch/rename time stamp

SYSTEM Identification of system on which data set was scratched/renamed.

TEMP   Temporary or permanent data set: TEMP or PERM.

VOLSER   Volume serial number on which this data set is located.

variable	type	length	format
DSNAME	character	44	
ID	numeric	4	
JOB	character	8	
LOCLINFO	character	8	
NEWNAME	character	44	
NRVOLS	numeric	4	
OPEN	character	7	
READTIME	numeric	8	DATETIME19.2
SMFTIME	numeric	8	DATETIME19.2
SYSTEM	character	4	
TEMP	character	4	
VOLSER	character	6	

```
*********MEMBER=TYPE1718********************************;
DATA TYPE1718
            (KEEP=DSNAME ID JOB LOCLINFO NEWNAME NRVOLS OPEN
                  READTIME SMFTIME SYSTEM TEMP VOLSER);
LENGTH DEFAULT=4 READTIME SMFTIME 8;
FORMAT READTIME SMFTIME DATETIME19.2;
  INFILE SMF STOPOVER LENGTH=LENGTH COL=COL RECFM=VBS LRECL=32756;
  INPUT @2 ID PIB1. @;
 IF   ID=17 OR ID=18;
  GOTO TYPE1718;
TYPE1718:
  INPUT @3 SMFTIME SMFSTAMP8. @11 SYSTEM $4.
        @15 JOB $8. @23 READTIME SMFSTAMP8. @;
_JOBCK
  INPUT @31 LOCLINFO $8. @;
 IF ID=17 THEN GOTO TYPE17;
 IF ID=18 THEN GOTO TYPE18;
TYPE17:
  INPUT @41 DSNAME $44. @91 VOLSER $6. @88 NRVOLS PIB1.
        @41 DSNTEMP $8. @49 PER1 $2. PER2 $6. ;
   OPEN='SCRATCH';
  GOTO REC1718;
TYPE18:
  INPUT @132 NRVOLS PIB1. @135 VOLSER $6. @85 NEWNAME : $44.
        @41 DSNAME $44. @41 DSNTEMP $8. @49 PER1 $2. PER2 $6. ;
   OPEN='RENAME';
REC1718:
    TEMP='PERM';
 IF 'SYS70000'<=DSNTEMP<='SYS99999' AND PER1='.T'
    AND '000000'<=PER2<='999999' THEN TEMP='TEMP';
  OUTPUT TYPE1718;
  RETURN;
```

The TYPE19 Data Set: DASD Volumes

The TYPE19 data set contains one observation for each type 19 SMF record, written for every DASD volume that is on-line at IPL, HALT EOD, or SWITCH SMF; or when a batch job causes a DASD volume to be dismounted.

TYPE19 information includes space usage on the DASD volume and a flag that possible VTOC errors exist on the volume. The usefulness of TYPE19 information is limited.

Contents

CYLAVAIL   Number of unallocated cylinders.

DEVICE   Device type (3330, 3350, etc). From __DEVICE macro.

MAXCYLS   Number of contiguous cylinders in the largest unallocated extent.

MAXTRKS   Number of contiguous tracks in the largest unallocated extent.

MODULID   Module identification (drive number). Taken from bits 2-7 of sense byte 4 for the device.

NRALTRKS   Number of unused alternate tracks.

NRDSCB0   Number of available DSCBs (i.e., count of DSCB0s).

NRDSCBS   Total number of DSCBs.

NRUNEXTS   Number of unallocated extents.

SMFTIME   Event time stamp.

SYSTEM   Identification of system on which this device is available.

TRKAVAIL   Number of unallocated tracks.

UCBTYP   Unit control block type (all four bytes).

UNITADR   Unit address of this device.

VOLOWNER   Volume owner identification, normally filled in when volume was initially labeled.

VOLSER   Volume serial number.

VTOCADDR   Address on the volume of the volume table of contents.

VTOCIND   VTOC indicator.

value	meaning
2	VTOC error has been fixed
4	possible VTOC error

variable	type	length	format
CYLAVAIL	numeric	4	
DEVICE	character	7	
MAXCYLS	numeric	4	
MAXTRKS	numeric	4	
MODULID	numeric	4	
NRALTRKS	numeric	4	
NRDSCB0	numeric	4	
NRDSCBS	numeric	4	
NRUNEXTS	numeric	4	
SMFTIME	numeric	8	DATETIME19.2
SYSTEM	character	4	
TRKAVAIL	numeric	4	
UCBTYP	numeric	4	HEX8.
UNITADR	numeric	4	HEX3.
VOLOWNER	character	10	
VOLSER	character	6	
VTOCADDR	numeric	4	HEX10.
VTOCIND	numeric	4	

```
**********MEMBER=TYPE19**********************************;
DATA TYPE19
              (KEEP=CYLAVAIL DEVICE MAXCYLS MAXTRKS MODULID
                    NRALTRKS NRDSCB0 NRDSCBS NRUNEXTS SMFTIME
                    SYSTEM TRKAVAIL UCBTYP UNITADR VOLOWNER
                    VOLSER VTOCADDR VTOCIND);
LENGTH DEFAULT=4 SMFTIME 8 ;
FORMAT SMFTIME DATETIME19.2 VTOCADDR HEX10. UNITADR HEX3.
       UCBTYP HEX8.;
  INFILE SMF STOPOVER LENGTH=LENGTH COL=COL RECFM=VBS LRECL=32756;
  INPUT @2 ID PIB1. @3 SMFTIME SMFSTAMP8. @11 SYSTEM $4. @;
  IF ID=19;
  GOTO TYPE19;
TYPE19:
  INPUT @17 VOLSER $6. @23 VOLOWNER $10. @33 UCBTYP PIB4.
        @35 DEVCLASS PIB1. @36 DEVTYPE PIB1. @37 VTOCADDR PIB5.
        @42 VTOCIND PIB1. @43 NRDSCBS PIB2. @45 NRDSCB0 PIB2.
        @47 NRALTRKS PIB2. @49 CYLAVAIL PIB2. @51 TRKAVAIL PIB2.
        @53 MAXCYLS PIB2. @55 MAXTRKS PIB2. @57 NRUNEXTS PIB2.
        @61 UNITADR PIB2. @63 MODULID PIB2. @;
  LINK UCBTYP;
  OUTPUT TYPE19;
  RETURN;
_DEVICE
```

The TYPE20 Data Set: JOB/TSO Initiation

The TYPE20 data set contains one observation for each type 20 SMF record. A type 20 SMF record is written at job initiation or TSO LOGON, and contains the initiation time of the job/session and accounting information. TYPE20 is normally not very important, since most of its information is repeated in TYPE535, written at job/session termination. However, for jobs or sessions that were active when the system crashed, TYPE20 is the only source of accounting information.

Contents

ACCOUNT1-
ACCOUNT9   Nine account fields (see NRFLDS and LEN1-LEN9).

JOB   Job name (batch), user ID (TSO).

LEN1-LEN9   Lengths of the nine account fields (see NRFLDS).

LOCLINFO   Locally defined field, filled in by an installation-written SMF exit routine.

NRFLDS   Number of account fields (see ACCOUNT1-ACCOUNT9).

PGMRNAME   Programmer name field from JOB statement.

RACFGRUP   RACF group identification (zero if RACF is not active).

RACFTERM   RACF Terminal Name used by this session (TSO).

RACFUSER   RACF user identification.

READTIME   Job read-in (TSO LOGON) time stamp.

SMFTIME   Initiation time stamp.

SYSTEM   Identification of the system on which the job or session initiated.

variable	type	length	format
ACCOUNT1- ACCOUNT9	character	40	
JOB	character	8	
LEN1-LEN9	numeric	4	
LOCLINFO	character	8	
NRFLDS	numeric	4	
PGMRNAME	character	20	
RACFGRUP	character	8	
RACFTERM	character	8	
RACFUSER	character	8	
READTIME	numeric	8	DATETIME19.2
SMFTIME	numeric	8	DATETIME19.2
SYSTEM	character	4	

```
*********MEMBER=TYPE20*********************************;
DATA TYPE20
            (KEEP=ACCOUNT1-ACCOUNT9 JOB LEN1-LEN9 LOCLINFO
                 NRFLDS PGMRNAME RACFGRUP RACFTERM RACFUSER
                 READTIME SMFTIME SYSTEM);
LENGTH DEFAULT=4 READTIME SMFTIME 8;
FORMAT SMFTIME READTIME DATETIME19.2;
  INFILE SMF STOPOVER LENGTH=LENGTH COL=COL RECFM=VBS LRECL=32756;
  INPUT @2 ID PIB1.@;
 IF ID=20;
  GOTO TYPE20;
TYPE20:
  INPUT @3 SMFTIME SMFSTAMP8. @11 SYSTEM $4.
        @15 JOB $8. @23 READTIME SMFSTAMP8. @;
_JOBCK
  INPUT @31 LOCLINFO $8. @41 PGMRNAME $20. @61 NRFLDS PIB1. @;
  LINK ACCTGET;
 IF NRFLDS=0 THEN LOC=LOC+7;
 IF LENGTH>=LOC+25 THEN
  INPUT @LOC+2 RACFGRUP $8. RACFUSER $8. RACFTERM $8.;
  OUTPUT TYPE20;
  RETURN;
_ACCTGET
```

The TYPE21 Data Set:
Tape Error Statistics by Volume (ESV)

The TYPE21 data set contains one observation for each type 21 SMF record. A type 21 SMF record is written for every dismount of a tape volume (actually, every dismount following a successful mount; if an incorrect volume is mounted and rejected by the system, there is no corresponding type 21 record).

TYPE21 contains statistics on the tape errors and I/O counts for each volume. Unfortunately, the name of the job that used the tape is not contained in the record, making job analysis quite complex. However, the TYPE21 analysis is of considerable value in tracking and identifying bad tape volumes and drives. See chapter 7.

Contents

BLKSIZE   Blocksize. Zero if record format is unblocked, record length is variable, or access method is EXCP.

CLEAN   Number of cleaner actions during read.

DENSITY   Tape density: 200, 556, 800, 1600, or 6250.

ERASE   Number of erase actions during write.

ERRORS   Total errors.

NOISE   Number of noise blocks detected—**always** a hardware error.

PERMREAD   Number of permanent read errors.

PERMWRIT   Number of permanent write errors.

SIOCOUNT   Number of I/O actions attempted (SIOs issued).

SMFTIME   Dismount time stamp.

SYSTEM   Identification of system on which tape was dismounted.

TEMPREAD   Number of temporary read errors.

TEMPWRIT   Number of temporary write errors.

UNITADR   Unit address.

VOLSER   Volume serial number of dismounted tape. Blank for non-labeled tape and for tapes that failed volume verification (i.e., wrong tape mounted by operator).

variable	type	length	format
BLKSIZE	numeric	4	
CLEAN	numeric	4	
DENSITY	character	4	
ERASE	numeric	4	
ERRORS	numeric	4	
NOISE	numeric	4	
PERMREAD	numeric	4	
PERMWRIT	numeric	4	
SIOCOUNT	numeric	4	
SMFTIME	numeric	8	DATETIME19.2
SYSTEM	character	4	
TEMPREAD	numeric	4	
TEMPWRIT	numeric	4	
UNITADR	numeric	4	HEX3.
VOLSER	character	6	

```
**********MEMBER=TYPE21**********************************;
DATA TYPE21
            (KEEP=BLKSIZE CLEAN DENSITY ERASE ERRORS NOISE
                PERMREAD PERMWRIT SIOCOUNT SMFTIME SYSTEM
                TEMPREAD TEMPWRIT UNITADR VOLSER);
LENGTH DEFAULT=4 SMFTIME 8;
FORMAT SMFTIME DATETIME19.2 UNITADR HEX3.;
  INFILE SMF STOPOVER LENGTH=LENGTH COL=COL RECFM=VBS LRECL=32756;
  INPUT @2 ID PIB1. @;
 IF ID=21;
  GOTO TYPE21;
TYPE21:
  INPUT @3 SMFTIME SMFSTAMP8. @11 SYSTEM $4. @17 VOLSER $6.
        @23 UNITADR PIB2. @29 TEMPREAD PIB1.  @30 TEMPWRIT PIB1.
        @31 SIOCOUNT PIB2. @33 PERMREAD PIB1.  @34 PERMWRIT PIB1.
        @35 NOISE PIB1. @36 ERASE PIB2. @38 CLEAN PIB2.
        @40 DENS PIB1. @41 BLKSIZE PIB2. @;
 IF DENS=3   THEN DENSITY=' 200';
 IF DENS=67  THEN DENSITY=' 556';
 IF DENS=131 THEN DENSITY=' 800';
 IF DENS=195 THEN DENSITY='1600';
 IF DENS=211 THEN DENSITY='6250';
  ERRORS=PERMREAD+PERMWRIT+NOISE+ERASE+MAX(CLEAN,TEMPREAD);
  OUTPUT TYPE21;
  RETURN;
```

The TYPE22 Data Set: Configuration

The TYPE22 data set contains several observations for each type 22 SMF record. A type 22 record is written after every IPL and after every VARY CPU, VARY CH (channel) VARY STOR (real memory), or VARY ONLINE, S (mass storage) operator command. TYPE22 contains one observation per CPU, channel storage, or MSS contained in a type 22 record, so that changes in CPU, channels, memory, or MSS can be tracked. (Note that the MSS segment is not decoded, but the first 4 bytes of the MSS segment are given.)

Contents

CHAN   Channel section only. Channel number.

CHANMODL   Channel section only. Channel model number.

CHANTYPE   Channel section only. Channel type: BYTE MUX, BLOCK MUX, or SELECTOR.

CPU   CPU or channel section only. CPU number: 0 for UP, 0 or 1 for MP.

CPUTYPE   CPU section only. CPU model number (168, 3033, etc).

LOWADDR   Storage section only. Address of lowest page in real contiguous storage.

MSSBITS   MSS section only. First four bytes of the forty-byte MSS pattern. See SMF manual *(OS/VS2 MVS System Programming Library: System Management Facilities, GC28-0706-1)* for decode.

NRPAGES   Storage section only. Number of pages in real contiguous storage. (Page=4K=4096 bytes).

REASON   Record creation reason: IPL; VARY ONLINE; VARY OFFLINE; MSS AT IPL; VARY ONLINE,S; or VARY OFFLINE,S.

SMFTIME   Event time stamp.

SUBSYS   Subsystem identification of device.

SYSTEM   Identification of system on which event occurred.

variable	type	length	format
CHAN	numeric	4	HEX2.
CHANMODL	numeric	4	
CHANTYPE	character	9	
CPU	numeric	4	
CPUTYPE	numeric	4	HEX4.
LOWADDR	numeric	4	
MSSBITS	character	4	$HEX8.
NRPAGES	numeric	4	
REASON	character	14	
SMFTIME	numeric	8	DATETIME19.2
SUBSYS	character	3	
SYSTEM	character	4	

```
**********MEMBER=TYPE22**********************************;
DATA TYPE22
              (KEEP=CHAN CHANMODL CHANTYPE CPU CPUTYPE LOWADDR
                    MSSBITS NRPAGES REASON SMFTIME SUBSYS SYSTEM);
LENGTH DEFAULT=4 SMFTIME 8;
FORMAT MSSBITS $HEX8. SMFTIME DATETIME19.2 CHAN HEX2.
       CPUTYPE HEX4.;
  INFILE SMF STOPOVER LENGTH=LENGTH COL=COL RECFM=VBS LRECL=32756;
  INPUT @2 ID PIB1. @3 SMFTIME SMFSTAMP8. @11 SYSTEM $4. @;
 IF ID=22;
  GOTO TYPE22;
TYPE22:
  INPUT  @3 SMFTIME SMFSTAMP8. @11 SYSTEM $4.
         @15 RECIND PIB2. @17 NRSECT PIB2. @;
 IF RECIND=1 THEN REASON='IPL            ';
 IF RECIND=2 THEN REASON='VARY ONLINE    ';
 IF RECIND=3 THEN REASON='VARY OFFLINE   ';
 IF RECIND=4 THEN REASON='MSS AT IPL     ';
 IF RECIND=5 THEN REASON='VARY ONLINE,S  ';
 IF RECIND=6 THEN REASON='VARY OFFLINE,S';
LOOP22: IF NRSECT<=0 THEN RETURN;
   CPU=.;
   CPUTYPE=.;
   CHANTYPE='
   CHAN=.;
   LOWADR=.;
   NRPAGES=.;
  INPUT +1 SECID PIB1. @;
 IF SECID=1 THEN LINK CPU22;
 IF SECID=2 THEN LINK CHAN22;
 IF SECID=3 THEN LINK STOR22;
 IF SECID=4 THEN LINK MSS22;
 IF SECID=5 THEN LINK ONLINE;
 IF SECID=6 THEN LINK OFFLINE;
   NRSECT=NRSECT-1;
  GOTO LOOP22;
```

```
OUT22:
  OUTPUT TYPE22;
  RETURN;
CPU22:
  INPUT CPUTYPE PIB2. +1 CPU PIB1. @;
  LINK OUT22;
  RETURN;
CHAN22:
  INPUT TYPECH1 PIB1. CHANMODL PIB1. CHAN PIB1. CPU PIB1. @;
 IF TYPECH1=0 THEN CHANTYPE='SELECTOR ';
 IF TYPECH1=16 THEN CHANTYPE='BYTE MUX';
 IF TYPECH1=32 THEN CHANTYPE='BLOCK MUX';
  LINK OUT22;
  RETURN;
STOR22:
  INPUT LOWADDR PIB2. NRPAGES PIB2. @;
  LINK OUT22;
  RETURN;
MSS22:
  INPUT MSSBITS $4. @;
  LINK OUT22;
  RETURN;
ONLINE:
  INPUT +1 SUBSYS $3. @;
  LINK OUT22;
  RETURN;
OFFLINE:
  INPUT +1 SUBSYS $3. @;
  LINK OUT22;
  RETURN;
```

The TYPE23 Data Set: SMF Statistics
(MVS/SE2 only)

This appendix describes the variables in the new type 23 record, written in MVS/SE2 systems.

An SMF type 23 record is written at user-specified intervals, and contains statistics on the usage of SMF during the last interval. TYPE23 contains one observation per type 23 record.

Contents

INTERVAL   Interval (HHMMSS) at which records will be written.

MAXBUFF   Maximum number of full buffers during the interval.

NBUFWRIT   Number of buffers actually written to MAN data set during the interval.

NRECWRIT   Number of SMF records (logical) written during the interval.

NRSUSPND   Number of times SMF recording was suspended due to insufficient buffers during the interval.

PRODUCT   'SMF'.

RELEASE   Operating system release number.

SMFTIME   Time this record was written to SMF.

SUBTYPE   Sub type id=0.

SYSTEM   Identification of this system.

VERSION   RMF version='04'.

variable	type	length	format
INTERVAL	numeric	4	TIME12.2
MAXBUFF	numeric	4	
NBUFWRIT	numeric	4	
NRECWRIT	numeric	4	
NRSUSPND	character	8	
PRODUCT	character	8	
RELEASE	character	4	
SMFTIME	numeric	8	DATETIME19.2
SUBTYPE	numeric	4	
SYSTEM	character	4	
VERSION	character	2	

```
*********MEMBER=TYPE23***********************************;
DATA TYPE23
          (KEEP=INTERVAL MAXBUFF NBUFWRIT NRECWRIT NRSUSPND
               PRODUCT RELEASE SMFTIME SUBTYPE SYSTEM VERSION);
LENGTH DEFAULT=4 SMFTIME 8 ;
FORMAT INTERVAL TIME12.2  SMFTIME DATETIME19.2 ;
  INFILE SMF STOPOVER LENGTH=LENGTH COL=COL RECFM=VBS LRECL=32756;
  INPUT @2 ID PIB1. @;
 IF ID=23;
GOTO TYPE23;
TYPE23:
  INPUT @2 ID PIB1. @3 SMFTIME SMFSTAMP8. @11 SYSTEM $4.
        @17 OFFPROD PIB4. @21 LENPROD PIB2. @23 NRPROD PIB2.
        @25 OFFSYST PIB4. @29 LENSYST PIB2. @31 NRSYST PIB2.
        @33 OFFSMF  PIB4. @37 LENSMF  PIB2. @39 NRSMF  PIB2. @;
   IF OFFPROD NE Ø AND NRPROD NE Ø THEN LINK PRODUCT;
   IF OFFSYST NE Ø AND NRSYST NE Ø THEN LINK SYSTEM;
   IF OFFSMF  NE Ø AND NRSMF  NE Ø THEN LINK SMF;
    OUTPUT TYPE23;
    RETURN;
PRODUCT:
   OFFPROD=OFFPROD-3;
  INPUT @OFFPROD SUBTYPE PIB2. VERSION $2. PRODUCT $8. @;
    RETURN;
SYSTEM:
   OFFSYST=OFFSYST-3;
  INPUT @OFFSYST HH 2. MM 2. SS 2. RELEASE $4. @;
    INTERVAL=HMS(HH,MM,SS);
    RETURN;
SMF:
   OFFSMF=OFFSMF-3;
  INPUT @OFFSMF NBUFWRIT PIB4. MAXBUFF PIB4. NRSUSPND PIB4.
      NRECWRIT PIB4. @;
    RETURN;
```

The TYPE25 Data Set: JES3 Device Allocation

The TYPE25 data set contains one observations for each type 25 SMF record. One type 25 record per job is written by JES3 for all device allocations that result from DD statements; additional type 25 records are written for each group of JES3 allocations for private catalogs, and a type 25 record is written for each dynamic allocation request.

TYPE25 contains the count of volumes fetched and mounted by JES3, and time stamps of fetch processing, manual start setup, first volume mount time, and device verification. It is very useful for tracking usage of JES3 devices and analysis of fetch/setup queue delays.

Contents

ALLOCATN   Source of device allocation:

value	meaning
AUTO	automatic allocation by JES3
CATLG	catalog allocation by JES3
DYNAM	dynamic allocation
MANL	manual allocation by operator
NOCAT	non-cataloged allocation by JES3
USER	allocation by user DD statement

DISKMNTS   Number of disk volumes mounted for the job.

DSKFETCH   Number of disk volumes fetched for the job.

FETCTIME   Fetch-processing-start time stamp.

JOB   Job name (batch) user ID (TSO).

LOCLINFO   Locally defined field, filled in by an installation written SMF exit routine.

MNTTIME   First-volume-mount-message time stamp. (If no mounts were required, MNTTIME will contain the time of JES3 allocation).

MSSALOCS   Number of mass storage volume requests allocated.

READTIME   Job read-in (TSO LOGON) time stamp.

SMFTIME   Event time stamp.

STRTTIME   START SETUP time stamp (missing if automatic allocation).

SYSTEM   Identification of system on which record was written.

TAPEMNTS   Number of tape volumes mounted.

TAPFETCH   Number of tape volumes fetched.

VERFTIME   Device verification time stamp.

variable	type	length	format
ALLOCATN	character	5	
DISKMNTS	numeric	4	
DSKFETCH	numeric	4	
FETCTIME	numeric	8	DATETIME19.2
JOB	character	8	
LOCLINFO	character	8	
MNTTIME	numeric	8	DATETIME19.2
MSSALOCS	numeric	4	
READTIME	numeric	4	
SMFTIME	numeric	8	DATETIME19.2
STRTTIME	numeric	8	DATETIME19.2
SYSTEM	character	4	
TAPEMNTS	numeric	4	
TAPFETCH	numeric	4	
VERFTIME	numeric	8	DATETIME19.2

```
*********MEMBER=TYPE25*************************************;
DATA TYPE25
     (KEEP=ALLOCATN DISKMNTS DSKFETCH FETCTIME JOB LOCLINFO
           MNTTIME MSSALOCS READTIME SMFTIME STRTTIME SYSTEM
           TAPEMNTS TAPFETCH VERFTIME);
LENGTH DEFAULT=4 FETCTIME MNTTIME SMFTIME STRTTIME VERFTIME 8;
FORMAT FETCTIME MNTTIME SMFTIME STRTTIME VERFTIME DATETIME19.2;
  INFILE SMF STOPOVER LENGTH=LENGTH COL=COL RECFM=VBS LRECL=32756;
  INPUT @2 ID PIB1. @;
 IF ID=25;
GOTO TYPE25;
TYPE25:
  INPUT @3 SMFTIME SMFSTAMP8. @11 SYSTEM $4.
        @15 JOB $8. @23 READTIME SMFSTAMP8. @;
_JOBCK
  INPUT @31 LOCLINFO $8. @39 ALOCIND1 PIB1. @41 TAPFETCH PIB4.
        @45 DSKFETCH PIB4. @49 FETCTIME SMFSTAMP8.
        @57 STRTTIME SMFSTAMP8. @65 TAPEMNTS PIB4.
        @69 DISKMNTS PIB4. @73 MNTTIME SMFSTAMP8.
        @81 VERFTIME SMFSTAMP8. @89 MSSALOCS PIB4. @;
 IF ALOCIND1          >127 THEN ALLOCATN='USER ';
 IF ALOCIND1          <128 THEN ALLOCATN='DYNAM';
 IF MOD(ALOCIND1,128)>=64 THEN ALLOCATN='CATLG';
 IF MOD(ALOCIND1,128)< 64 THEN ALLOCATN='NOCAT';
 IF MOD(ALOCIND1,64)>=32 THEN ALLOCATN='MANL';
 IF MOD(ALOCIND1,64) < 32 THEN ALLOCATN='AUTO';
 OUTPUT TYPE25;
 RETURN;
```

The TYPE26J2 Data Set: JES2 Purge Record

The TYPE26J2 data set contains one observation for each type 26 record, written by JES2 for each job or session at purge time when all SYSOUT, including held SYSOUT, has been processed.

TYPE26J2 contains time stamps of the time on and off each JES2 processor (reader, converter, execution, and output), as well as the system identification of each processor. It is the only source of I/O counts processed to the spool on behalf of the job or session.

TYPE26J2 is very important for analysis of job scheduling. See chapter 4.

Contents

ACCT   Programmer accounting number.

CANCELED Job was canceled by the operator.

CONVRTTM Duration the job was in converter.

CVTRPROC Procedure name used for JCL conversion.

DEVNAME   NJE only. Job transmitter device name.

ENDPRTY   Output selection priority when the output was selected.

ESTELPTM Estimated elapsed time.

ESTPRINT Estimated output lines.

ESTPUNCH Estimated output cards.

EXECNODE NJE only. Execution node name.

INDEVICE Input device name:
              value   meaning
              INTRDR   job read in through internal reader
                          (includes TSO submissions)
              TSOINRDR TSO session

| | R101.RD3 | e.g., job read in through device RD3 at remote 101 |
| | READER1 | e.g., job read in through local device READER1 |

INPRTY   Job selection priority at read-in time.

INROUTE   Input remote number. Zero for local or TSO submission or TSO session.

INTRDR   Job read in through an internal reader; blank or Y.

JCNVTIME   Converter-start time stamp. Can be missing if job was canceled before converter started.

JENDTIME   Execution-processor-end time stamp. Time of last execution end. Will be missing if system crashed while job was executing, or if job was FORCED from system.

JESNR   JES-assigned JOB/TSO/STC number. Three unique counters are maintained for JOB, TSO, and system tasks by JES.

JFINTIME   Output-processor-stop time stamp. All output is now available to the print queue.

JOB   Job name (batch), user ID (TSO).

JOB__TSO   Job or TSO flag:

value	meaning
blank	system task
J	batch job
T	TSO session

JOBCLASS   Job class. For TSO, this will print as a blank, but contains X'E0'.

JOBID   Job identification: JOB, TSO or STC (system task), followed by four-digit JES2-assigned job number. See JESNR.

JPRNTIME   Output-processor-start time stamp. Beginning of print queue time. Actual printing does not necessarily start at this time.

JPURTIME   Job purge time stamp. All printing/punching for the job session has been completed.

JRDRTIME   Completion of read-in time stamp.

JSTRTIME   Execution-processor-start time stamp. Will be missing if job had a syntax error in the converter, or if job was canceled before execution.

LASTNODE   NJE only. Last node name.

LINPERPG   Lines per page.

LOCLINFO   Locally defined field, filled in by an installation-written SMF exit routins.

MSGCLASS   Output message class for SYSMSG, from JOB statement or default.

NETACCT   NJE only. Network accounting number.

NEXTNODE   NJE only. Next node name.

NPASSWRD   JES2 Release 4.0 only. New password (RACF) if this job changed password. See OPASSWRD.

ONPRTY   Selection priority at JSTRTIME.

OPASSWRD   JES2 release 4.0 only. Old password. See NPASSWORD.

OPTEXBAT   Execution batching option: blank or Y.

OPTJBLOG   No job log option: blank or Y (i.e., no job log).

OPTJOURN   No journal option: blank or Y (i.e., no journaling).

OPTOUTPT   No output option: blank or Y (i.e., no output).

ORIGJBID   NJE only. Original job identification (see JOBID).

ORIGNODE   NJE only. Original node name.

OUTFORM   Output form number.

PGMRNAME   Programmer name field from JOB statement.

PRNTCOPY   Print copies.

PRPRTY   Selection priority when the output was selected for printing/punching.

PRROUTE   Remote number to which SYSMSG printing is routed.

PRTYCARD   Priority statement present or PRTY parameter specified on JOB statement: blank or Y.

PUROUTE   Remote number to which punching is to be routed.

READTIME   Job read-in (TSO LOGON) time stamp.

RERUN   Job was re-run by JES: blank or Y.

RESTART   RESTART=Y was specified: blank or Y.

ROOM   Programmer room number.

SETUP   SETUP card(s) were present: blank or Y.

SPOOLCRD   Number of input lines (JCL and SYSIN) put on the spool by JES reader.

SPOOLINE   Number of lines of output put on the spool. The actual printing of these lines will be counted in TYPE6 records. Multiple copy printing is spooled, and hence counted here, only once.

SPOOLPUN   Number of punched cards put on the spool. See SPOOLINE.

SUBSYS   JES2.

SYSCVRT   ID of system that converted this job.

SYSEXEC   ID of system that executed this job.

SYSOUTP   ID of system that processed output for job (i.e., JPRNTIME to JFINTIME). Not necessarily related to system on which printing occurred; see TYPE6 for that system ID.

SYSREAD   ID of system that read in this job.

SYSTEM   ID of system that purged this job.

SYSTRANS   NJE only. Job transmitter system ID.

TRANBEGN NJE only. Job began (start) transmission time stamp.

TRANEND NJE only. Job end (stop) transmission time stamp.

TYPETASK Type of task:

value	meaning
BATCH	batch job
TSO	TSO session
SYS_TASK	system task

TYPRUN Type of run. Value of TYPRUN parameter: blank, COPY, HOLD or SCAN.

variable	type	length	format
ACCT	character	4	
CANCELED	character	1	
CONVRTTM	numeric	4	TIME12.2
CVTRPROC	character	8	
DEVNAME	character	8	
ENDPRTY	numeric	8	
ESTELPTM	numeric	4	TIME12.2
ESTPRINT	numeric	4	
ESTPUNCH	numeric	4	
EXECNODE	character	8	
INDEVICE	character	8	
INPRTY	numeric	4	
INROUTE	numeric	4	
INTRDR	character	1	
JCNVTIME	numeric	8	DATETIME19.2
JENDTIME	numeric	8	DATETIME19.2
JESNR	numeric	4	
JFINTIME	numeric	8	DATETIME19.2
JOB	character	8	
JOB_TSO	character	1	
JOBCLASS	character	1	
JOBID	character	8	
JPRNTIME	numeric	8	DATETIME19.2
JPURTIME	numeric	8	DATETIME19.2
JRDRTIME	numeric	8	DATETIME19.2
JSTRTIME	numeric	8	DATETIME19.2
LASTNODE	character	8	
LINPERPG	numeric	4	
LOCLINFO	character	8	
MSGCLASS	character	1	
NETACCT	character	8	
NEXTNODE	character	8	
NPASSWRD	character	8	
ONPRTY	numeric	4	
OPASSWRD	character	8	
OPTEXBAT	character	1	
OPTJBLOG	character	1	
OPTJOURN	character	1	

OPTOUTPT	character	1	
ORIGJBID	character	8	
ORIGNODE	character	8	
OUTFORM	character	4	
PGMRNAME	character	20	
PRNTCOPY	numeric	4	
PRPRTY	numeric	4	
PRROUTE	numeric	4	
PRTYCARD	character	1	
PUROUTE	numeric	4	
READTIME	numeric	8	DATETIME19.2
RERUN	character	1	
RESTART	character	1	
ROOM	character	4	
SETUP	character	1	
SPOOLCRD	numeric	4	
SPOOLINE	numeric	4	
SPOOLPUN	numeric	4	
SUBSYS	character	4	
SYSCVRT	character	4	
SYSEXEC	character	4	
SYSOUTP	character	4	
SYSREAD	character	4	
SYSTEM	character	4	
SYSTRANS	character	4	
TRANBEGN	numeric	8	DATETIME19.2
TRANEND	numeric	8	DATETIME19.2
TYPETASK	character	8	
TYPRUN	character	4	

```
**********MEMBER=TYPE26J2**************************************;
DATA TYPE26J2
            (KEEP=ACCT CANCELED CONVRTTM CVTRPROC DEVNAME ENDPRTY
             ESTELPTM ESTPRINT ESTPUNCH EXECNODE INDEVICE
             INPRTY INROUTE INTRDR JCNVTIME JENDTIME JESNR
             JFINTIME JOB JOB_TSO JOBCLASS JOBID JPRNTIME
             JPURTIME JRDRTIME JSTRTIME LASTNODE LINPERPG
             LOCLINFO MSGCLASS NETACCT NEXTNODE NPASSWRD
             ONPRTY OPASSWRD OPTEXBAT OPTJBLOG OPTJOURN
             OPTOUTPT ORIGJBID ORIGNODE OUTFORM PGMRNAME
             PRNTCOPY PRPRTY PRROUTE PRTYCARD PUROUTE
             READTIME RERUN RESTART ROOM SETUP SPOOLCRD
             SPOOLINE SPOOLPUN SUBSYS SYSCVRT SYSEXEC
             SYSOUTP SYSREAD SYSTEM SYSTRANS TRANBEGN
             TRANEND TYPETASK TYPRUN );
LENGTH DEFAULT=4 JPURTIME READTIME JRDRTIME JCNVTIME JSTRTIME
             JENDTIME JPRNTIME JFINTIME TRANBEGN TRANEND 8;
FORMAT JPURTIME READTIME JRDRTIME JCNVTIME JSTRTIME JENDTIME
       JPRNTIME JFINTIME TRANBEGN TRANEND DATETIME19.2
       ESTELPTM CONVRTTM TIME12.2;
  INFILE SMF STOPOVER LENGTH=LENGTH COL=COL RECFM=VBS LRECL=32756;
  INPUT @2 ID PIB1. @;
 IF ID=26;
  GOTO TYPE26J2;
TYPE26J2:
  INPUT @3 JPURTIME SMFSTAMP8. @11 SYSTEM $4.
        @15 JOB $8. @23 READTIME SMFSTAMP8. @;
```

```
_JOBCK
  INPUT @31 LOCLINFO $8. @43 SUBS PIB2. @45 NETFLAG PIB1. @;
  IF SUBS=2;
     SUBSYS='JES2';
     INPUT @51 JOBINFO1 PIB1. JOBINFO2 PIB1. @53 JESNR 4. @57 JOBID $8.
           @65 PGMRNAME $20. @85 MSGCLASS $1. @86 JOBCLASS $1.
           @87 INPRTY PIB1. @88 ONPRTY PIB1. @89 PRPRTY PIB1.
           @90 ENDPRTY PIB1. @91 INROUTE PIB2. @93 INDEVICE $8.
           @101 ACCT $4. @105 ROOM $4. @109 ESTELPTM PIB4.
           @113 ESTPRINT PIB4. @117 ESTPUNCH PIB4. @121 OUTFORM $4.
           @125 PRNTCOPY PIB2. @127 LINPERPG PIB2. @129 PRROUTE PIB2.
           @131 PUROUTE PIB2. @;
  IF JOBINFO1>128           THEN TYPETASK='BATCH    ';
  IF MOD(JOBINFO1,128)>=64 THEN TYPETASK='TSO';
  IF MOD(JOBINFO1,64) >=32 THEN TYPETASK='SYS_TASK';
  IF MOD(JOBINFO1,32) >=16 THEN OPTJOURN='Y';
  IF MOD(JOBINFO1,16) >= 8 THEN OPTOUTPT='Y';
  IF MOD(JOBINFO1,8)  >= 4 THEN TYPRUN='SCAN';
  IF MOD(JOBINFO1,4)  >= 2 THEN TYPRUN='COPY';
  IF MOD(JOBINFO1,2)  >= 1 THEN RESTART='Y';
  IF JOBINFO2>128           THEN PRTYCARD='Y';
  IF MOD(JOBINFO2,128)>=64 THEN SETUP='Y';
  IF MOD(JOBINFO2,64) >=32 THEN TYPRUN='HOLD';
  IF MOD(JOBINFO2,32) >=16 THEN OPTJBLOG='Y';
  IF MOD(JOBINFO2,16) >= 8 THEN OPTEXBAT='Y';
  IF MOD(JOBINFO2,8)  >= 4 THEN INTRDR='Y';
  IF MOD(JOBINFO2,4)  >= 2 THEN RERUN='Y';
  IF MOD(JOBINFO2,2)  >= 1 THEN CANCELED='Y';
     INPRTY=FLOOR(INPRTY/16);
     ONPRTY=FLOOR(ONPRTY/16);
     PRPRTY=FLOOR(PRPRTY/16);
     ENDPRTY=FLOOR(ENDPRTY/16);
  IF INROUTE>=256 THEN INROUTE=INROUTE-256;
  IF PRROUTE>=256 THEN PRROUTE=PRROUTE-256;
  IF PUROUTE>=256 THEN PUROUTE=PUROUTE-256;
  IF LENGTH=248 OR LENGTH=328 THEN GOTO JES240;
  IF LENGTH=232 OR LENGTH=312 THEN GOTO JES241;
  PUT '**** INVALID LENGTH TYPE26 RECORD ' LENGTH= _ALL_;
  LIST;ABORT;
JES240:
  INPUT @133 CVTRPROC $8. @141 OPASSWRD $8. @149 NPASSWRD $8.
        @161 JRDRTIME SMFSTAMP8. @169 JCNVTIME SMFSTAMP8.
        @177 JCNETIME SMFSTAMP8. @185 JSTRTIME SMFSTAMP8.
        @193 JENDTIME SMFSTAMP8. @201 JPRNTIME SMFSTAMP8.
        @209 JFINTIME SMFSTAMP8. @221 SPOOLCRD PIB4.
        @225 SPOOLINE PIB4. @229 SPOOLPUN PIB4. @233 SYSREAD $4.
        @237 SYSCVRT $4. @241 SYSEXEC $4. @245 SYSOUTP $4. @;
GOTO REST26J2;
JES241:
  INPUT @133 CVTRPROC $8.
        @145 JRDRTIME SMFSTAMP8. @153 JCNVTIME SMFSTAMP8.
        @161 JCNETIME SMFSTAMP8. @169 JSTRTIME SMFSTAMP8.
        @177 JENDTIME SMFSTAMP8. @185 JPRNTIME SMFSTAMP8.
        @193 JFINTIME SMFSTAMP8. @205 SPOOLCRD PIB4.
        @209 SPOOLINE PIB4. @213 SPOOLPUN PIB4. @217 SYSREAD $4.
        @221 SYSCVRT $4. @225 SYSEXEC $4. @229 SYSOUTP $4. @;
REST26J2:
     CONVRTTM=JCNETIME-JCNVTIME;
  IF 'JOB'<=JOBID<='JOB9' THEN JOB_TSO='J';
  IF 'TSU'<=JOBID<='TSU9' THEN JOB_TSO='T';
  IF MOD(NETFLAG,32)<16 THEN GOTO OUT262;
     INPUT +4 SYSTRANS $4. TRANBEGN SMFSTAMP8. TRANEND SMFSTAMP8.
              NETACCT $8. ORIGJBID $8. DEVNAME $8. ORIGNODE $8.
              EXECNODE $8. NEXTNODE $8. LASTNODE $8. @;
  OUT262:
    OUTPUT TYPE26J2;
    RETURN;
```

The TYPE26J3 Data Set: JES3 Purge Record

The TYPE26J3 data set contains one observation for each type 26 record, written by JES3 for each job or session when all SYSOUT, including held SYSOUT, has been processed (i.e., at purge time).

TYPE26J3 contains time stamps of the time on and off each JES3 processor (reader, converter, execution, and output), as well as the system identification of each processor. It is the only source of I/O counts processed to the spool on behalf of the job or session.

TYPE26J3 is very important for analysis of job scheduling. See chapter 4.

Contents

ACCOUNT1-
ACCOUNT9   First nine account fields (see NRFLDS and LEN1-LEN9).

CANCELED   Job was canceled by the operator: Y if canceled, otherwise blank

CLASS   Job class, taken from CLASS= on a MAIN statement or the default JES3 job class (JS3BATCH). See JOBCLASS.

CONVRTTM   Duration the job was in the converter.

CVRTPROC   Converter procedure name (DDname) used for JCL conversion. Taken from PROC= parameter on a MAIN statement, or the default.

DEADLINE   Deadline scheduling time stamp, taken from DEADLINE parameter on MAIN statement.

DEADLMET   Deadline job met deadline scheduling time: Y if met, blank otherwise.

DEADLREQ   Deadline scheduling requested (i.e., DEADLINE specified): blank or Y if yes.

DEADLTYP   Deadline schedule type, if DEADLINE specified on MAIN statement. (Valid types are A through Z and 0 through 9).

ENTERDJ   Job entered system via DJ (dump job) processing: blank or Y if yes.

ENTERNJP   Job entered system via NJP (network job processing): blank or Y is yes.

ESTELPTM   Estimated elapsed duration.

ESTPRINT   Estimated output lines, taken from LINES= on MAIN statement or 1000*JOBLINES default in TVT.

ESTPUNCH   Estimated punched cards output, taken from CARDS= on MAIN statement or 100*JOBCARDS default in TVT.

INDEVICE   Input device name:

Source of job	contains
JES3 device	JES3 logical input device name
NJP	line name
TSO	user identification

INPRTY   JES3 job selection priority when job was initially read in. Taken from PRTY= on JOB statement, class default priority from main processor job class priority table, or default priority from TVT.

INTRDR   Job was entered via the internal reader: blank or Y if yes.

JCNVTIME   Converter-processor-start time stamp.

JENDTIME   Execution-processor-end time stamp.

JESNR   JES3-assigned job number.

JFINTIME   Output-processor-stop time stamp. Filled in when an RQ is removed from the writer queue, when all output OSEs are deleted/released, or when a request from the SYSOUT interface is processed. It does not correspond to the completion of printing for the job.

JOB   Job name (batch), user ID (TSO).

JOBCLASS   Job class, taken from CLASS= on JOB statement. Will be blank if class was taken from default or if CLASS= was specified on MAIN statement. If blank, actual class will be in the variable CLASS, above.

JOBID Job identification. Format is ttt−nnnn where ttt is type (JOB=job, STC=started task, TSU=TSO session) and nnnn is the same as JESNR.

JPRNTIME Output-processor-start time stamp. Filled in when output service starts to process the job's data sets for later printing.

JPURTIME Job purge time stamp. All SYSOUT processing has been completed and the job/session is purged.

JRDRTIME Job reader-stop time stamp. (READTIME is the start time stamp).

JSTRTIME Execution-processor-start time stamp.

LEFTDJ Job left this system via DJ (dump job) processing: blank or Y if yes.

LEFTNJP Job left this system via NJP (network job processing): blank or Y if yes.

LEN1-LEN9 Lengths of the nine accounting fields. (See NRFLDS).

LNJPTERM Name of local NJP terminal supplied by the JES3 initilization deck.

LOCLINFO Locally defined field, filled in by an installation-written SMF exit routine.

MSGCLASS Message class (taken from MSGCLASS= on JOB card).

NETCARD Dependent job (i.e., NET statement was processed): blank or Y if yes.

NETNAME Name of the dependent job net to which this job belongs (taken from NET statement).

ONPRTY JES3 job selection priority when this job was selected for the execution processor.

PGMRNAME Programmer name field from JOB statement.

PROCESS   Process job (i.e., PROCESS statement processed): blank or Y is yes.

PRTYCARD   Job scheduling priority was specified via PRTY= on JOB statement: blank or Y if yes.

READTIME   Job read-in (TSO LOGON) time stamp.

RERUN   Job was re-run on an ASP or JES3 reader: blank or Y if yes.

SETUP   Job was processed by pre-execution setup: blank or Y if yes.

SPOOLCRD   Number of input lines placed on JES3 spool; includes JCL and SYSIN lines.

SPOOLINE   Number of output lines placed on JES3 spool.

SPOOLPUN   Number of punched cards placed on JES3 spool.

SUBSYS   Subsystem, always JES3.

SYSCVRT   System identification of conversion processor.

SYSEXEC   System identification of execution processor.

SYSOUTP   System identification of output processor.

SYSREAD   System identification of input processor.

SYSTEM   System identification of the purging system.

TONJPSYS   Name of system to which job is sent via NJP.

TYPRUN   Type of run. TYPRUN=HOLD specified on JOB statement: blank or HOLD if yes.

variable	type	length	format
ACCOUNT1-ACCOUNT9	character	40	
CANCELED	character	1	
CLASS	character	8	
CONVRTTM	numeric	4	TIME12.2
CVTRPROC	character	8	
DEADLINE	numeric	8	DATETIME19.2
DEADLMET	character	1	
DEADLREQ	character	1	
DEADLTYP	character	1	
ENTERDJ	character	1	
ENTERNJP	character	1	
ESTELPTM	numeric	4	TIME12.2
ESTPRINT	numeric	4	
ESTPUNCH	numeric	4	
INDEVICE	character	8	
INPRTY	numeric	4	
INTRDR	character	1	
JCNVTIME	numeric	8	DATETIME19.2
JENDTIME	numeric	8	DATETIME19.2
JESNR	numeric	4	
JFINTIME	numeric	8	DATETIME19.2
JOB	character	8	
JOBCLASS	character	1	
JOBID	character	8	
JPRNTIME	numeric	8	DATETIME19.2
JPURTIME	numeric	8	DATETIME19.2
JRDRTIME	numeric	8	DATETIME19.2
JSTRTIME	numeric	8	DATETIME19.2
LEFTDJ	character	1	
LEFTNJP	character	1	
LEN1-LEN9	numeric	4	
LNJPTERM	character	8	
LOCLINFO	character	8	
MSGCLASS	character	1	
NETCARD	character	1	
NETNAME	character	8	
ONPRTY	numeric	4	
PGMRNAME	character	20	
PROCESS	character	1	
PRTYCARD	character	1	
READTIME	numeric	8	DATETIME19.2
RERUN	character	1	
SETUP	character	1	
SPOOLCRD	numeric	4	
SPOOLINE	numeric	4	
SPOOLPUN	numeric	4	
SUBSYS	character	4	
SYSCVRT	character	4	
SYSEXEC	character	4	
SYSOUTP	character	4	
SYSREAD	character	4	
SYSTEM	character	4	
TONJPSYS	character	8	
TYPRUN	character	4	

```
**********MEMBER=TYPE26J3**********************************;
DATA TYPE26J3
        (KEEP=ACCOUNT1-ACCOUNT9 CANCELED CLASS CONVRTTM CVTRPROC
             DEADLINE DEADLMET DEADLREQ DEADLTYP ENTERDJ ENTERNJP
             ESTELPTM ESTPRINT ESTPUNCH INDEVICE INPRTY INTRDR
             JCNVTIME JENDTIME JESNR JFINTIME JOB JOBCLASS
             JOBID JPRNTIME JPURTIME JRDRTIME JSTRTIME
             LEFTDJ LEFTNJP LEN1-LEN9 LNJPTERM LOCLINFO
             MSGCLASS NETCARD NETNAME ONPRTY PGMRNAME PROCESS
             PRTYCARD READTIME RERUN SETUP SPOOLCRD SPOOLINE
             SPOOLPUN SUBSYS SYSCVRT SYSEXEC SYSREAD SYSOUTP
             SYSTEM TONJPSYS TYPRUN);
LENGTH DEFAULT=4 DEADLINE JPURTIME READTIME JRDRTIME JCNVTIME
                 JSTRTIME JENDTIME JPRNTIME JFINTIME 8;
FORMAT DEADLINE READTIME JRDRTIME JCNVTIME
       JSTRTIME JENDTIME JPRNTIME JFINTIME DATETIME19.2
       ESTELPTM CONVRTTM TIME12.2;
  INFILE SMF STOPOVER LENGTH=LENGTH COL=COL RECFM=VBS LRECL=32756;
  INPUT @2 ID PIB1. @;
 IF ID=26;
  GOTO TYPE26J3;
TYPE26J3:
  INPUT @3 JPURTIME SMFSTAMP8. @11 SYSTEM $4.
        @15 JOB $8. @23 READTIME SMFSTAMP8. @;
_JOBCK
  INPUT @31 LOCLINFO $8. @43 SUBS PIB2. @;
 IF SUBS=5;
   SUBSYS='JES3';
  INPUT @51 JOBINFO1 PIB1. JOBINFO2 PIB1. @53 JESNR 4. @57 JOBID $8.
        @65 PGMRNAME $20. @85 MSGCLASS $1. @86 JOBCLASS $1.
        @87 INPRTY PIB1. @88 ONPRTY PIB1. @93 INDEVICE $8.
        @109 ESTELPTM PIB4. @113 ESTPRINT PIB4. @117 ESTPUNCH PIB4.
        @121 DEADLTYP $1. @125 DEVGROUP $8. @;
  IF JOBINFO1>128           THEN NETCARD ='Y';
  IF MOD(JOBINFO1,128)>=64 THEN DEADLREQ='Y';
  IF MOD(JOBINFO1,64) >=32 THEN DEADLMET='Y';
  IF MOD(JOBINFO1,32) >=16 THEN PROCESS ='Y';
  IF MOD(JOBINFO1,16) >= 8 THEN LEFTNJP ='Y';
  IF MOD(JOBINFO1,8)  >= 4 THEN ENTERNJP='Y';
  IF MOD(JOBINFO1,4)  >= 2 THEN LEFTDJ  ='Y';
  IF MOD(JOBINFO1,2)  >= 1 THEN ENTERDJ ='Y';
  IF JOBINFO2>128           THEN PRTYCARD='Y';
  IF MOD(JOBINFO2,128)>=64 THEN SETUP='Y';
  IF MOD(JOBINFO2,64) >=32 THEN TYPRUN='HOLD';
  IF MOD(JOBINFO2,8)  >= 4 THEN INTRDR='Y';
  IF MOD(JOBINFO2,4)  >= 2 THEN RERUN='Y';
  IF MOD(JOBINFO2,2)  >= 1 THEN CANCELED='Y';
    INPRTY=FLOOR(INPRTY/16);
    ONPRTY=FLOOR(ONPRTY/16);
  INPUT @133 CVTRPROC $8. @141 TONJPSYS $8. @149 LNJPTERM $8.
        @157 NETNAME $8. @165 DEADLINE SMFSTAMP8. @173 CLASS $8.
        @185 JRDRTIME SMFSTAMP8. @193 JCNVTIME SMFSTAMP8.
        @201 JCNENDTM SMFSTAMP8. @209 JSTRTIME SMFSTAMP8.
        @217 JENDTIME SMFSTAMP8. @225 JPRNTIME SMFSTAMP8.
        @233 JFINTIME SMFSTAMP8. @245 SPOOLCRD PIB4.
        @249 SPOOLINE PIB4. @253 SPOOLPUN PIB4. @257 SYSREAD $4.
        @261 SYSCVRT $4. @265 SYSEXEC $4. @269 SYSOUTP $4.
        @273 NRFLDS PIB1. @;
  LINK ACCTGET;
    CONVRTTM=JCNENDTM-JCNVTIME;
  IF 'JOB'<=JOBID<='JOB9' THEN JOB_TSO='J';
  IF 'TSU'<=JOBID<='TSU9' THEN JOB_TSO='T';
  OUTPUT TYPE26J3;
  RETURN;
ACCTGET
```

The TYPE30 Data Set:
Work Termination and Interval Reporting
(MVS/SE 2.0 only)

This appendix describes the variables in the new type 30 record, written in MVS/SE2 systems.

An SMF type 30 record is written at the initiation, and at the normal or abnormal termination of a batch job step, a batch job, a TSO session, or a started task. A type 30 record is also written at the expiration of an accounting interval for any of the preceding classes of work.

Contents

ABEND Step completion indicator.

value	meaning
blank	normal completion
CANCEXIT	step was cancelled by an SMF exit; see CONDCODE
CRSH	step was active when operating system crashed.
FLUSH	step was flushed (previous step had failed)
OTHER	step ABENDed for unknown reason; see CONDCODE
RESTART	step was restarted; subsequent restart will have program name of IEFRSTRT
RETURN	step completed with non-zero condition code; see CONDCODE
SYSTEM	step completed with system ABEND; see CONDCODE
USER	step completed with user ABEND; see CONDCODE

ACCOUNT1- Nine account fields on the JOB statement.
ACCOUNT9 See LEN1-LEN9 and NRFLDS.

ACTIVETM Step active time. Duration that the SRM viewed the task as active.

ALOCTIME Allocation time stamp.

AVGWKSET   Average working set size, in pages (i.e., 4096-byte).

BLKSTRAN   Total blocks of unit record data transferred.

COMPAGIN   Common area page-ins.

COMRECLM   Common area page-reclaims.

CONDCODE   Condition code. See ABEND.

ABEND value	contents of CONDCODE	
	value	cancelled by
CANCEXIT	16	IEFUSI (step initiation)
	32	IEFUJI (job initiation)
	64	IEFUJV (job validation)
	8	IEFACTRT (account/time validation)
OTHER	completion code value	
RETURN	return code value	
SYSTEM	system ABEND code	
USER	user ABEND code	

CPISRBTM   Initiator CPU time under the SRB.

CPITCBTM   Initiator CPU time under the TCB.

CPUSRBTM   Duration that processor was executing instructions under all SRBs (service request blocks) for this task.

CPUTCBTM   Duration that processor was executing instructions under all TCBs (task control blocks) for this task.

CPUUNITS   The TCB CPU service units received.

DASNMNTS   Number of non-specific DASD mounts.

DASSMNTS   Number of specific volume DASD mounts.

DPRTY   Dispatching priority.

D2314DRV   The number of different 2314 disk drives that were allocated to this step.

D3330DRV   The number of different 3330 "mountable" disk drives that were allocated to this step, where "mountable" is defined by an explicit list of unit addresses in the __EXCPGET macro.

ELAPSTM   Duration that the job was initiated for this execution.

EXCP2305   EXCPs to 2305 devices.

EXCP2314   EXCPs to 2314 devices.

EXCP3330   EXCPs to 3330 devices.

EXCP3340   EXCPs to 3340 devices.

EXCP3350   EXCPs to 3350 devices.

EXCPCNT   Total number of EXCPs during the RJE session.

EXCPCOMM   EXCPs to communications devices.

EXCPDASD   Sum of EXCPs to 2305, 2314, 3330, 3340, and 3350 devices.

EXCPGRAF   EXCPs to graphics devices.

EXCPMSS   EXCPs to mass storage volume.

EXCPTAPE   EXCPs to tape volumes.

EXCPTOT   Total step EXCPs.

EXCPUREC   EXCPs to unit record devices that were allocated directly to the step. This does not include EXCPs to the JES spool devices.

EXCPVIO   EXCPs to virtual I/O.

INITTIME   Initiation time stamp.

INPRTY   Job selection priority at read-in time.

IOUNITS   MVS/SE only. I/O service units used by this step.

JESNR   JES-assigned JOB/TSO/STC number. Three unique counters are maintained for JOB, TSO, and system tasks by JES.

JOB   Job name (batch); user ID (TSO).

JOBCLASS   Job class.

LEN1-LEN9   Lengths of the nine account fields on the JOB statement. See NRFLDS and ACCOUNT1-ACCOUNT9.

LOADTIME   Load (problem program start) time stamp.

LOCLINFO   Locally defined field, filled in by an installation-written SMF exit routine.

LPAGINS   Link pack area page-ins.

LPARECLM   Link pack area reclaims.

MSOUNITS   Memory service units received.

MSSNMNTS   Number of non-specific MSS mounts.

MSSSMNTS   Number of specific volume MSS mounts.

NDASDDD   Number of DD statement that allocated DASD devices.

NRFLDS   Number of accounting fields on the step EXEC statement (normally zero, since most installations do accounting at the job rather than step level).

NRTRANS   Number of transactions as counted by the SRM.

NTAPEDD   Number of DD statements that allocated TAPE devices.

NUMDD   Total number of DD statements in this step. Note that
NUMDD–(NDASDD + NTAPEDD)
equals the number of DDs for JES, VIO, MSS, COMM, UREC, and graphics allocations.

PAGEINS   Number of page-ins.

PAGEOUTS   Number of page-outs.

PAGESECS   Page-seconds used by this step. Divide this variable by CPUTCBTM seconds to get the AVGWKSET value.

PERFGRP   Performance group in which this step executed.

PGMRNAME   Programmer name field from JOB statement

PKEY   Storage-protect key.

PRODUCT   Product name: 'SMF'

PROGRAM   Program name (PGM=) from EXEC statement. If backward reference was used, the PROGRAM value is '*.DD'. If the current step is a restarted step, its PROGRAM value and that of all subsequent steps will be 'IEFRSTRT'.

PVTAREA   If VIRTREAL='V' (virtual storage), the PVTAREA value is the size of the private area in 1024 (1K) bytes, which is constant and is the maximum region size (address space) that can be requested. If VIRTREAL='R' (real storage), the PVTAREA value is the REGION requested in K.

PVTBOT   If VIRTREAL='V' (virtual storage), the PVTBOT value is the address space used (in K) from the bottom of the private area—subpools 0-127, 251, and 252. If VIRTREAL='R', the PVTBOT value is the amount of contiguous real storage used, in K.

PVTTOP   If VIRTREAL='V' (virtual storage), the PVTTOP value is the address space used, in K, from the top of the private area—subpools 229, 239, 236-237, 253-255, and also including LSQA and SWA. If VIRTREAL='R', the PVTTOP value is the amount of storage used that was not from the contiguous storage reserved for the program.

RACFGRUP   RACF group identification (zero if RACF is not active).

RACFTERM   RACF terminal name used by this session (TSO).

RACFUSER   RACF user identification.

RDRDEVCL   Reader device class.

RDRDEVT   Reader device type.

RDRTM   Duration the MVS reader was active while reading this job.

READTIME   Job read-in (TSO logon) time stamp.

RECLAIMS   Pages reclaimed.

RESIDTM   Duration that the step was resident in real storage.

SERVUNIT   Total step service units received.

SKIPFLAG	'Y' if previous interval was skipped.
SMFTIME	Time stamp when record was written.
SRBUNITS	The CPU (SRB only) service units received.
STEPNAME	The step name that appeared on the EXEC PGM= statement. Note that this is **not** the stepname that is used on an EXEC statement for a procedure.
STEPNR	The step number. This number is reset to 1 when a job is cancelled and restarted, so that it is possible for the same job to have steps with duplicate values. Additionally, this field starts back at 1 after the 256th step. This value is thus of limited usefulness.
SUBSYS	Subsystem name (JOB/TSO/STC).
SWAPS	Number of times this step was swapped out.
SWPAGIN	Number of pages swapped in.
SWPAGOUT	Number of pages swapped out.
SYSINCNT	Number of card-image records in DD DATA and DD * data sets read by the reader for this step.
SYSTEM	Identification of the system on which the step executed.
TAPEDRVS	The number of different tape drives that were allocated to this step.
TAPNMNTS	Number of non-specific tape mounts.
TAPSMNTS	Number of specific volume tape mounts.
TGETS	TSO only. The number of terminals GETS satisfied—the number of times that the TSO user pushed the ENTER key.
TPUTS	TSO only. The number of terminal PUTS issued—the number of times that one or more lines were sent to the terminal.

TYPE   Event type which caused this record

value	meaning
JOBINIT	Record written at job/session/task initiation
INTERVAL	An interval record for job/session/task—contains "delta" resources
STEP DELTA	An interval record written at step termination for the time since the last interval until termination—contains "delta" resources
STEP TERM	Step/session/task termination record—contains step total resources
JOB TERM	Job/session/task termination record—contains job total resources

VERSION   Version number: 01.

VIOPAGIN Virtual I/O page-ins.

VIOPAGOU Virtual I/O page-outs.

VIORECLM Virtual I/O page reclaims.

VIRTREAL Type of address space requested.

value	requested
R	real storage (ADDRSPC=R specified)
V	virtual storage

variable	type	length	format
ABEND	character	8	
ACCOUNT1-ACCOUNT9	numeric	4	HEX4.
ACTIVETM	numeric	4	TIME12.2
ALOCTIME	numeric	8	DATETIME19.2
AVGWKSET	numeric	4	5.
BLKSTRAN	numeric	4	
COMPAGIN	numeric	4	
COMRECLM	numeric	4	
CONDCODE	numeric	3	HEX4.
CPISRBTM	numeric	4	
CPITCBTM	numeric	4	
CPUSRBTM	numeric	4	TIME12.2
CPUTCBTM	numeric	4	TIME12.2
CPUUNITS	numeric	4	
DASNMNTS	numeric	4	
DASSMNTS	numeric	4	
DPRTY	numeric	4	
D2314DRV	numeric	4	
D3330DRV	numeric	4	
ELAPSTM	numeric	4	TIME12.2

EXCP2305	numeric	4	
EXCP2314	numeric	4	
EXCP3330	numeric	4	
EXCP3340	numeric	4	
EXCP3350	numeric	4	
EXCPCNT	numeric	4	
EXCPCOMM	numeric	4	
EXCPDASD	numeric	4	
EXCPGRAF	numeric	4	
EXCPMSS	numeric	4	
EXCPTAPE	numeric	4	
EXCPTOT	numeric	4	
EXCPUREC	numeric	4	
EXCPVIO	numeric	4	
INITTIME	numeric	8	DATETIME19.2
INPRTY	numeric	4	
IOUNITS	numeric	4	
JESNR	numeric	4	
JOB	character	8	
JOBCLASS	character	1	
LEN1-LEN9	numeric	4	
LOADTIME	numeric	8	DATETIME19.2
LOCLINFO	character	8	
LPAGINS	numeric	4	
LPARECLM	numeric	4	
MSOUNITS	numeric	4	
MSSNMNTS	numeric	4	
MSSSMNTS	numeric	4	
NDASDDD	numeric	4	
NRFLDS	numeric	4	
NRTRANS	numeric	4	
NTAPEDD	numeric	4	
NUMDD	numeric	4	
PAGEINS	numeric	4	
PAGEOUTS	numeric	4	
PAGESECS	numeric	4	
PAGESTOL	numeric	4	
PERFGRP	numeric	2	
PGMRNAME	character	20	
PKEY	numeric	2	HEX2.
PRODUCT	character	8	
PROGRAM	character	8	
PVTAREA	numeric	4	
PVTBOT	numeric	4	
PVTTOP	numeric	4	
RACFGRUP	character	8	
RACFTERM	character	8	
RACFUSER	character	8	
RDRDEVCL	numeric	4	
RDRDEVT	numeric	4	
RDRTM	numeric	4	TIME12.2
READTIME	numeric	8	DATETIME19.2
RECLAIMS	numeric	8	
RESIDTM	numeric	4	TIME12.2
SERVUNIT	numeric	4	
SKIPFLAG	character	1	
SMFTIME	numeric	8	DATETIME19.2

SRBUNITS	numeric	4
STEPNAME	character	8
STEPNR	numeric	4
SUBSYS	character	4
SWAPS	numeric	4
SWPAGIN	numeric	4
SWPAGOUT	numeric	4
SYSINCNT	numeric	4
SYSTEM	character	4
TAPEDRVS	numeric	4
TAPNMNTS	numeric	4
TAPSMNTS	numeric	4
TGETS	numeric	4
TPUTS	numeric	4
TYPE	character	10
VERSION	character	2
VIOPAGIN	numeric	4
VIOPAGOU	numeric	4
VIORECLM	numeric	4
VIRTREAL	character	1

```
**********MEMBER=TYPE30*************************************;
DATA TYPE30
     (KEEP= ABEND ACCOUNT1-ACCOUNT9 ACTIVETM ALOCTIME AVGWKSET
            BLKSTRAN COMPAGIN COMRECLM CONDCODE CPISRBTM
            CPITCBTM CPUSRBTM CPUTCBTM CPUUNITS DASNMNTS
            DASSMNTS DPRTY D2314DRV D3330DRV ELAPSTM EXCP2305
            EXCP2314 EXCP3330 EXCP3340 EXCP3350 EXCPCNT EXCPCOMM
            EXCPDASD EXCPGRAF EXCPMSS EXCPTAPE EXCPTOT EXCPUREC
            EXCPVIO INITTIME INPRTY IOUNITS JESNR JOB JOBCLASS
            LEN1-LEN9 LOADTIME LPAGINS LPARECLM MSOUNITS MSSNMNTS
            MSSSMNTS NDASDD NRFLDS NRTRANS NTAPEDD NUMDD PAGEINS
            PAGEOUTS PAGESECS PAGESTOL PERFGRP PGMRNAME
            PKEY PRODUCT PROGRAM PVTAREA PVTBOT PVTTOP RACFGRP
            RACFTERM RACFUSER RDRDEVCL RDRDEVT RDRTM READTIME
            RECLAIMS RESIDTM SERVUNIT SKIPFLAG SMFTIME SRBUNITS
            STEPNAME STEPNR SUBSYS SWAPS SWPAGINS SWPAGOUT
            SYSINCNT SYSTEM TAPEDRVS TAPNMNTS TAPSMNTS TGETS
            TPUTS TYPE LOCLINFO VERSION VIOPAGIN VIOPAGOU
            VIORECLM VIRTREAL);
LENGTH DEFAULT=4 SMFTIME READTIME REND INITTIME ALOCTIME INITTIME
                  LOADTIME 8;
FORMAT ALOCTIME INITTIME LOADTIME READTIME REND SMFTIME DATETIME19.2
       ACTIVETM ELAPSTM CPUTCBTM CPUSRBTM
                          CPITCBTM CPISRBTM RESIDTM      TIME12.2
       AVGWKSET                                          5.
       PKEY                                              HEX2.
       CONDCODE                                          HEX3.;
   INFILE SMF STOPOVER LENGTH=LENGTH COL=COL RECFM=VBS LRECL=32756;
   INPUT @2 ID PIB1. @;
  IF ID=30;
GOTO TYPE30;
TYPE30:
   INPUT @2 ID PIB1. @3 SMFTIME SMFSTAMP8. @11 SYSTEM $4.
         @15 SUBSYS $4.
         @21 OFFPROD  PIB4. @25 LENPROD PIB2. @27 NRPROD PIB2.
         @29 OFFID    PIB4. @33 LENID   PIB2. @35 NRID   PIB2.
         @37 OFFUREC  PIB4. @41 LENUREC PIB2. @43 NRUREC PIB2.
```

```
            @45 OFFCOMP  PIB4. @49 LENCOMP PIB2. @51 NRCOMP PIB2.
            @53 OFFCPU   PIB4. @57 LENCPU  PIB2. @59 NRCPU  PIB2.
            @61 OFFACCT  PIB4. @65 LENACCT PIB2. @67 NRACCT PIB2.
            @69 OFFSTOR  PIB4. @73 LENSTOR PIB2. @75 NRSTOR PIB2.
            @77 OFFPERF  PIB4. @81 LENPERF PIB2. @83 NRPERF PIB2.
            @85 OFFOPER  PIB4. @89 LENOPER PIB2. @91 NROPER PIB2.
            @93 OFFEXCP  PIB4. @97 LENEXCP PIB2. @99 NUMDD PIB2.@;
IF OFFPROD NE 0 AND NRPROD NE 0 THEN LINK PRODUCT;
IF OFFID   NE 0 AND NRID   NE 0 THEN LINK ID;
_JOBCK
IF OFFUREC NE 0 AND NRUREC NE 0 THEN LINK UREC;
IF OFFCOMP NE 0 AND NRCOMP NE 0 THEN LINK COMP;
IF OFFCPU  NE 0 AND NRCPU  NE 0 THEN LINK CPU;
IF OFFACCT NE 0 AND NRACCT NE 0 THEN LINK ACCT;
IF OFFSTOR NE 0 AND NRSTOR NE 0 THEN LINK STOR;
IF OFFPERF NE 0 AND NRPERF NE 0 THEN LINK PERF;
IF OFFOPER NE 0 AND NROPER NE 0 THEN LINK OPER;
IF OFFEXCP NE 0 AND NUMDD  NE 0 THEN LINK EXCP;
IF CPUTCBTM>0 THEN AVGWKSET=PAGESECS/CPUTCBTM;
   OUTPUT TYPE30;
   RETURN;
PRODUCT:
   OFFPROD=OFFPROD-3;
   INPUT @OFFPROD SUBTYPE PIB2. +2 VERSION $2. PRODUCT $8. @;
IF SUBTYPE=1 THEN TYPE='JOBINIT   ';
IF SUBTYPE=2 THEN TYPE='INTERVAL  ';
IF SUBTYPE=3 THEN TYPE='STEP DELTA';
IF SUBTYPE=4 THEN TYPE='STEP TERM ';
IF SUBTYPE=5 THEN TYPE='JOB  TERM ';
   RETURN;
ID:
   OFFID=OFFID-3;
   INPUT @OFFID  JOB $8. PROGRAM $8. STEPNAME $8. LOCLINFO $8.
       JESNR $8. STEPNR PIB2. JOBCLASS $1. +1 PERFGRP PIB2.
       INPRTY PIB2. ALOCTIME PIB4.2 LOADTIME PIB4.2
       INITTIME SMFSTAMP8. READTIME SMFSTAMP8. REND SMFSTAMP8.
       PGMRNAME $20. RACFGRP $8. RACFUSER $8. RACFTERM $8. @;
   ALOCTIME=DHMS(DATEPART(INITTIME),0,0,ALOCTIME);
   LOADTIME=DHMS(DATEPART(INITTIME),0,0,LOADTIME);
   RDRTM=REND-READTIME;
   RETURN;
UREC:
   OFFUREC=OFFUREC-3;
   INPUT @OFFUREC SYSINCNT PIB4. BLKSTRAN PIB4. TPUTS PIB4.
       TGETS PIB4. RDRDEVCL PIB1. RDRDEVT PIB1. +2 @;
   RETURN;
COMP:
   OFFCOMP=OFFCOMP-3;
   INPUT @OFFCOMP COMPCODE PIB2. TERMIND1 PIB1. TERMIND2 PIB1. @;
* TERMINATION INDICATOR DECODES;
* BIT MEANS (TERMIND1)              BIT  MEANS (TERMIND2)             ;
* 0   SYSTEM ABEND                  0    EXCP COUNT MAY BE WRONG      ;
* 1   CANCEL IEFUJV                 1    PREVIOUS INTERVAL SKIPPED    ;
* 2   CANCEL IEFUJI                                                   ;
* 3   CANCEL IEFUSI                                                   ;
* 4   CANCEL IFACTRT                                                  ;
* 5   STEP IS TO BE RESTARTED                                         ;
* 6   STEP ABENDED                                                    ;
* 7   STEP FLUSHED                                                    ;
 IF MOD(TERMIND2,128)>=64 THEN SKIPFLAG='Y';
 IF MOD(TERMIND1,4)>=2 THEN AB=1;
 IF MOD(TERMIND1,8)>=4 THEN RE=1;
   EX=FLOOR(MOD(TERMIND1,128)/8);
 IF MOD(TERMIND1,2)=1 THEN FL=1;
 IF AB=1 AND COMPCODE>=32768 THEN ABEND='USER    ';
 IF AB=1 AND COMPCODE<16384 THEN ABEND='SYSTEM';
```

```
IF AB=1 AND ABEND=' ' THEN ABEND='OTHER ';
IF ABEND='OTHER' THEN CONDCODE=COMPCODE;
IF AB NE 1 AND COMPCODE >= 16384 THEN COMPCODE=COMPCODE-16384;
IF ABEND='USER' THEN CONDCODE=COMPCODE-32768;
IF ABEND NE 'USER' THEN CONDCODE=COMPCODE;
IF ABEND = ' ' AND CONDCODE NE 0 THEN ABEND='RETURN';
IF EX>=1 THEN ABEND='CANCEXIT';
IF RE=1 THEN ABEND='RESTART';
IF EX LT 1 AND FL =1 THEN ABEND='FLUSH';
IF EX >0 THEN CONDCODE=EX;
IF TERMIND1>=128 THEN ABEND='CRASH';
IF ABEND NE 'USER' AND ABEND NE 'RETURN' THEN RETURN;
  DGT1=FLOOR(CONDCODE/1000);CONDCODE=CONDCODE-1000*DGT1;
  DGT2=FLOOR(CONDCODE/100);CONDCODE=CONDCODE-100*DGT2;
  DGT3=FLOOR(CONDCODE/10);DGT4=CONDCODE-10*DGT3;
  CONDCODE=DGT4+16*DGT3+256*DGT2+4096*DGT1;
  RETURN;
CPU:
  OFFCPU=OFFCPU-3;
  INPUT @OFFCPU DPRTY PIB2. +2 CPUTCBTM PIB4.2 CPUSRBTM PIB4.2
    CPITCBTM PIB4.2 CPISRBTM PIB4.2 @;
  RETURN;
ACCT:
  NRFLDS=NRACCT;
  BEGIN=OFFACCT-3;
  INPUT @BEGIN @;
  LINK ACCTGET;
  RETURN;
STOR:
  OFFSTOR=OFFSTOR-3;
  INPUT @OFFSTOR PVTAREA PIB2. STORFLG PIB1. PKEY PIB1.
    PVTBOT PIB2. PVTTOP PIB2. PAGEINS PIB4. PAGEOUTS PIB4.
    RECLAIMS PIB4. SWAPS PIB4. SWPAGINS PIB4. SWPAGOUT PIB4.
    VIOPAGIN PIB4. VIOPAGOU PIB4. VIORECLM PIB4. COMPAGIN PIB4.
    COMRECLM PIB4. LPAGINS PIB4. LPARECLM PIB4.
    PAGESTOL PIB4. PAGESECS PIB8.3 @;
    VIRTREAL='V';
  IF STORFLG>=128 THEN VIRTREAL='R';
  RETURN;
PERF:
  OFFPERF=OFFPERF-3;
  INPUT @OFFPERF SERVUNIT PIB4. CPUUNITS PIB4. SRBUNITS PIB4.
    IOUNITS PIB4. MSOUNITS PIB4. ACTIVETM PIB4.2 ELAPSTM PIB4.2
    RESIDTM PIB4.2 NRTRANS PIB4. @;
   ACTIVETM=HMS(ACTIVETM*1.024/3.6E4,0,0);
   RESIDTM=HMS(RESIDTM*1.024/3.6E4,0,0);
   ELAPSTM=HMS(ELAPSTM*1.024/3.6E4,0,0);
  RETURN;
OPER:
  OFFOPER=OFFOPER-3;
  INPUT @OFFOPER DASNMNTS PIB4. DASSMNTS PIB4. TAPNMNTS PIB4
    TAPSMNTS PIB4. MSSNMNTS PIB4. MSSSMNTS PIB4. @;
  RETURN;
EXCP:
  BEGIN=OFFEXCP-3;
  LINK EXCPGET;
  RETURN;
_ACCTGET _EXCPGET
```

The TYPE31 Data Set: TSO Initialization

The TYPE31 data set contains one observation for each type 31 SMF record, written each time TSO is started. TYPE31 contains several TSO option values that are important to TSO performance.

TYPE31 can be used to estimate TSO availability. See chapter 9.

Contents

BUFFSIZE   Size of timesharing buffer.

LWAITHI   Maximum number of input buffers allowed per terminal before LWAIT—locking of the terminal's keyboard.

LWAITLO   RESTART threshold. The number of input buffers that must be freed in order for a user to be freed from LWAIT.

MINBUFF   Number of buffers reserved on the free queue. If fewer than this number of buffers are available, the system LWAITs.

NRBUFFER   Number of timesharing buffers.

OWAITHI   Maximum number of output buffers allowed per terminal before OWAIT—locking of the terminal's keyboard.

OWAITLO   OWAIT threshold. The number of output buffers that must be freed in order for a user to be freed from OWAIT.

SMFTIME   MODIFY TCAM command event time stamp.

SYSTEM   Identification of system on which TSO was started.

TSBSIZE   Size of timesharing buffers, in bytes.

variable	type	length	format
BUFFSIZE	numeric	4	
LWAITHI	numeric	4	
LWAITLO	numeric	4	
MINBUFF	numeric	4	
NRBUFFER	numeric	4	
OWAITHI	numeric	4	
OWAITLO	numeric	4	
SMFTIME	numeric	8	DATETIME19.2
SYSTEM	character	4	
TSBSIZE	numeric	4	

```
*********MEMBER=TYPE31***********************************;
DATA TYPE31
                (KEEP=BUFFSIZE LWAITHI LWAITLO MINBUFF NRBUFFER
                   OWAITHI OWAITLO SMFTIME SYSTEM
                   TSBSIZE);
LENGTH DEFAULT=4 SMFTIME 8;
FORMAT SMFTIME DATETIME19.2;
  INFILE SMF STOPOVER LENGTH=LENGTH COL=COL RECFM=VBS LRECL=32756;
  INPUT @2 ID PIB1. @;
 IF ID=31;
  GOTO TYPE31;
TYPE31:
  INPUT @3 SMFTIME SMFSTAMP8. @11 SYSTEM $4.
        @15 NRBUFFER PIB2. @17 BUFFSIZE PIB2. +2
        @21 OWAITHI PIB2. @23 LWAITHI PIB2.
        @25 OWAITLO PIB2. @27 LWAITLO PIB2.
        @29 MINBUFF PIB2. +2 @33 TSBSIZE PIB1. ;
  OUTPUT TYPE31;
  RETURN;
```

The TYPE32 Data Set: TSO Command Record

The appendix describes the variables in the new TYPE32 record, written in MVS/SE2 systems.

An SMF type 32 record is written at the normal or abnormal termination of a TSO session, and at the expiration of an accounting interval for a TSO session. There is one observation for each command executed in each interval or session in TYPE32.

Contents

ALOCTIME	Allocation time stamp.
COMMAND	Name of command executed.
CMDCOUNT	Count of TSO commands issued.
CPUSRBTM	Duration that processor was executing instructions under all SRBs (service request blocks) for this command.
CPUTCBTM	Duration that processor was executing instructions under all TCBs (task control blocks) for this command.
EXCPS	EXCPs for this command.
INITTIME	Initiation time stamp for this session.
INPRTY	Job selection priority at logon time.
JESNR	JES-assigned TSO number.
JOB	TSO user ID.
JOBCLASS	Job class.
LOADTIME	Load (problem program start) time stamp.
LOCLINFO	Locally defined field, filled in by an installation-written SMF exit routine.

PERFGRP   Performance group in which this command executed.

PGMRNAME   Programmer name field.

PRODUCT   Product name: 'TSO'.

PROGRAM   Program name (PGM=) from EXEC statement. If backward reference was used, the PROGRAM value is '*.DD'. If the current step is a restarted step, its PROGRAM value and that of all subsequent step will be 'IEFRSTRT'.

RACFGRUP   RACF group identification (zero if RACF is not active).

RACFTERM   RACF terminal name used by this session (TSO).

RACFUSER   RACF user identification.

READTIME   TSO logon time stamp.

SMFTIME   Time this record was written to SMF.

STEPNAME   The step name that appeared on the EXEC PGM= statement. Note that this is **not** the stepname that is used on an EXEC statement for a procedure.

STEPNR   The step number. For TSO, STEPNR should always be 1.

SUBSYS   Subsystem name: TSO.

SYSTEM   Identification of the system on which the step executed.

TGETS   The number of terminals GETS satisfied—the number of times that the TSO user pushed the ENTER key.

TPUTS   The number of terminal PUTS issued—the number of times that one or more lines were sent to the terminal.

TRANS   Transactions for this command.

TYPE   Type of command record:

value	meaning
INTERVAL	interval record, no detail statistics
SESSION	total session record, no detail statistics
DETAIL INT	interval record with detailed statistics
DETAIL SES	total session record with detailed statistics

VERSION   Version number: 01

variable	type	length	format
ALOCTIME	numeric	8	DATETIME19.2
COMMAND	numeric	8	
CMOCOUNT	numeric	4	
CPUSRBTM	numeric	4	TIME12.2
CPUTCBTM	numeric	4	TIME12.2
EXCPS	numeric	4	
INITTIME	numeric	8	DATETIME19.2
INPRTY	numeric	4	
JESNR	numeric	4	
JOB	character	8	
JOBCLASS	character	1	
LOADTIME	numeric	8	
LOCLINFO	character	8	
PERFGRP	numeric	2	
PGMRNAME	character	20	
PRODUCT	character	8	
PROGRAM	character	8	
RACFGRUP	character	8	
RACFTERM	character	8	
RACFUSER	character	8	
READTIME	numeric	8	DATETIME19.2
SMFTIME	numeric	8	DATETIME19.2
STEPNAME	character	8	
STEPNR	numeric	4	
SUBSYS	character	4	
SYSTEM	character	4	
TGETS	numeric	4	
TPUTS	numeric	4	
TRANS	numeric	4	
TYPE	character	10	
VERSION	character	2	

```
**********MEMBER=TYPE32**********************************;
DATA TYPE32
    (KEEP= ALOCTIME COMMAND CMDCOUNT CPUSRBTM CPUTCBTM EXCPS
          INITTIME INPRTY JESNR JOB JOBCLASS LOADTIME PERFGRP
          PGMRNAME PRODUCT PROGRAM RACFGRP RACFTERM RACFUSER
          READTIME SMFTIME STEPNAME STEPNR SUBSYS SYSTEM TGETS
          TPUTS TRANS TYPE LOCLINFO VERSION);
LENGTH DEFAULT=4 SMFTIME 8 ;
FORMAT CPUSRBTM CPUTCBTM                           TIME12.2
      ALOCTIME INITTIME LOADTIME READTIME SMFTIME DATETIME19.2 ;
  INFILE SMF STOPOVER LENGTH=LENGTH COL=COL RECFM=VBS LRECL=32756;
  INPUT @2 ID PIB1. @;
 IF ID=32;
GOTO TYPE32;
TYPE32:
  INPUT @2 ID PIB1. @3 SMFTIME SMFSTAMP8. @11 SYSTEM $4.
        @15 SUBSYS $4.
        @21 OFFPROD  PIB4. @25 LENPROD PIB2. @27 NRPROD PIB2.
```

```
          @29 OFFID     PIB4. @33 LENID   PIB2. @35 NRID    PIB2.
          @37 OFFTSO    PIB4. @41 LENTSO  PIB2. @43 NRTSO  PIB2. @;
     IF OFFPROD  NE 0 AND NRPROD  NE 0 THEN LINK PRODUCT;
     IF OFFID    NE 0 AND NRID    NE 0 THEN LINK ID;
     IF OFFTSO   NE 0 AND NRTSO   NE 0 THEN LINK TSO;
       OUTPUT TYPE32;
       RETURN;
   PRODUCT:
        OFFPROD=OFFPROD-3;
     INPUT @OFFPROD SUBTYPE PIB2. VERSION $2. PRODUCT $8.@;
     IF SUBTYPE=1 THEN TYPE='INTERVAL    ';
     IF SUBTYPE=2 THEN TYPE='SESSION     ';
     IF SUBTYPE=3 THEN TYPE='DETAIL INT';
     IF SUBTYPE=4 THEN TYPE='DETAIL SES';
       RETURN;
   ID:
        OFFID=OFFID-3;
     INPUT @OFFID   JOB $8. PROGRAM $8. STEPNAME $8. LOCLINFO $8.
          JESNR $8. STEPNR PIB2. JOBCLASS $1. +1 PERFGRP PIB2.
          INPRTY PIB2. ALOCTIME PIB4.2 LOADTIME PIB4.2 @;
   INPUT INITTIME PIB4.2 INITDATE PD3. +1 @;
   INITTIME=DHMS(DATEJUL(INITDATE),0,0,INITTIME);
   INPUT                   READTIME SMFSTAMP8. REND SMFSTAMP8.
          PGMRNAME $20. RACFGRP $8. RACFUSER $8. RACFTERM $8. @;
     ALOCTIME=DHMS(DATEPART(INITTIME),0,0,ALOCTIME);
     LOADTIME=DHMS(DATEPART(INITTIME),0,0,LOADTIME);
     RDRTM=REND-READTIME;
       RETURN;
   TSO:
        OFFTSO=OFFTSO-3;
     INPUT @OFFTSO @;
   LOOP32TS:
    IF NRTSO<=0 THEN RETURN;
     INPUT COMMAND $8. CMDCOUNT PIB4. CPUTCBTM PIB4.2 CPUSRBTM PIB4.2
          TGETS PIB4. TPUTS PIB4. TRANS PIB4. EXCPS PIB4. @;
      OUTPUT TYPE32;
      NRTSO=NRTSO-1;
      GOTO LOOP32TS;
   RUN;PAGE;
```

The TYPE40 Data Set: Dynamic Allocation

The TYPE40 data set contains one observation for each type 40 SMF record, written for each dynamic allocation that is freed (unallocated), concatenated, or deconcatenated. TYPE40 contains observations for jobs as well as for TSO sessions, since both tasks can issue dynamic allocation.

TYPE40 is necessary to account for all EXCPs, especially for TSO sessions. When a dynamic allocation is freed, the EXCPs to that allocation are contained in TYPE40. When any dynamic allocation is deconcatenated, all EXCPs thus far are written out in the type 40 record and the TIOT (from which the type 4/34 is written) EXCP counters are zeroed. Thus it is necessary to sum the EXCPs in TYPE40 with the EXCPs in TYPE434 to get total EXCPs for a task.

Contents

DYNAM   Type of event.

value	meaning
CONCAT	concatenation
DECAT	deconcatenation
UNALOC	unallocation

D2314DRV   Number of different 2314 disk drives that were allocated in this dynamic allocation.

D3330DRV   Number of different 3330 disk drives that were allocated in this dynamic allocation.

ERROR   Possible error in EXCP count: blank or EXCPCNT WRONG.

EXCP2305   EXCPs to 2305 devices.

EXCP2314   EXCPs to 2314 devices.

EXCP3330   EXCPs to 3330 devices.

EXCP3340   EXCPs to 3340 devices.

EXCP3350   EXCPs to 3350 devices.

EXCPCOMM   EXCPs to communications devices.

EXCPDASD   Sum of EXCPs to 2305, 2314, 3330, 3340 and 3350 devices.

EXCPGRAF   EXCPs to graphics devices.

EXCPMSS   EXCPs to mass storage volumes.

EXCPTAPE   EXCPs to tape devices.

EXCPTOT   Total EXCPs in this allocation.

EXCPUREC   EXCPs to unit record devices that were directly allocated to the tasks that issued this dynamic allocation (i.e., does not include EXCPs to JES devices, since they are not dynamically allocated.).

EXCPVIO   EXCPs to virtual I/O.

JOB   Job name (batch) or user ID (TSO).

NDASDDD   Number of DASD devices allocated in this dynamic allocation.

NTAPEDD   Number of tape devices allocated in this dynamic allocation.

NUMDD   Total number of devices allocated in this dynamic allocation.

READTIME   Job read-in (TSO LOGON) time stamp.

SMFTIME   Event time stamp.

STEPNR   Step number. This number is reset to 1 when a job is canceled and restarted, so it is possible for the same job to have steps with duplicate values. Addditionally, this field starts back at 1 after the 256th step. It is thus of limited usefulness.

SYSTEM   Identification of the system on which the dynamic allocation occurred.

TAPEDRVS   Number of different tape drives that were allocated in this dynamic allocation.

228 *TYPE40*

variable	type	length	format
DYNAM	character	6	
D2314DRV	numeric	4	
D3330DRV	numeric	4	
ERROR	character	13	
EXCP2305	numeric	4	
EXCP2314	numeric	4	
EXCP3330	numeric	4	
EXCP3340	numeric	4	
EXCP3350	numeric	4	
EXCPCOMM	numeric	4	
EXCPDASD	numeric	4	
EXCPGRAF	numeric	4	
EXCPMSS	numeric	4	
EXCPTAPE	numeric	4	
EXCPTOT	numeric	4	
EXCPUREC	numeric	4	
EXCPVIO	numeric	4	
JOB	character	8	
NDASDDD	numeric	4	
NTAPEDD	numeric	4	
NUMDD	numeric	4	
READTIME	numeric	8	DATETIME19.2
SMFTIME	numeric	8	DATETIME19.2
STEPNR	numeric	4	
SYSTEM	character	4	
TAPEDRVS	numeric	4	

```
*********MEMBER=TYPE40********************************;
DATA TYPE40
            (KEEP=DYNAM D2314DRV D3330DRV ERROR EXCP2305
                  EXCP2314 EXCP3330 EXCP3340 EXCP3350 EXCPCOMM
                  EXCPDASD EXCPGRAF EXCPMSS EXCPTAPE EXCPTOT
                  EXCPUREC EXCPVIO JOB NDASDDD NTAPEDD
                  NUMDD READTIME SMFTIME STEPNR SYSTEM TAPEDRVS);
LENGTH DEFAULT=4 SMFTIME READTIME 8;
FORMAT SMFTIME READTIME DATETIME19.2 ;
  INFILE SMF STOPOVER LENGTH=LENGTH COL=COL RECFM=VBS LRECL=32756;
  INPUT @2 ID PIB1. @;
 IF ID=40;
  GOTO TYPE40;
TYPE40:
  INPUT @3 SMFTIME SMFSTAMP8. @11 SYSTEM $4.
        @15 JOB $8. @23 READTIME SMFSTAMP8. @;
_JOBCK
  INPUT @39 STEPNR PIB1. @40 FUNCIND PIB1. @41 RECIND PIB1.
        @61 NUMDD PIB2. @;
 IF FUNCIND=2 THEN DYNAM='UNALOC';
 IF FUNCIND=3 THEN DYNAM='CONCAT';
 IF FUNCIND=4 THEN DYNAM='DECAT';
 IF RECIND NE 0 THEN ERROR='EXCPCNT WRONG';
   BEGIN=63;
  LINK EXCPGET;
  OUTPUT TYPE40;
  RETURN;
_EXCPGET
```

The TYPE4345 Data Set: JES Start/Stop

The TYPE4345 data set contains one observation for each type 43 or 45 record written by JES2 or JES3. Other subsystems, such as VSPC, write type 43 and 45 records but have a different subsystem identification (SUBSYS) and are included in other appendices. JES type 45 records are written when the JES is stopped, type 43 when JES is started.

TYPE4345 contains options and descriptions as to the reason for the start/stop and is thus useful in tracking subsystem availability. See chapter 9.

Contents

AUTOINIT   JES2 start only. Request automatic initiator: blank or Y.

COLDSTRT   Cold start: blank or Y.

COMMAND   Command that caused this record to be written.

JES2 value	meaning
S JES2	start JES2
$P JES2	stop JES2
$E JES2	reclaim job processing; see RECLMSYS
JES ABEND	JES2 abnormally terminated; see CONDCODE

JES3 value	meaning
S JES3	start JES3
P JES3	stop JES3
SYST INTRCHG	Dynamic system interchange was invoked by the operator to convert a local to a global processor
JES3 ABEND	JES3 abnormally terminated; see CONDCODE

CONDCODE   JES2 completion code when JES abnormally terminated; see COMMAND.

FORMAT   JES2 start only. Format the spool: blank or Y.

HOTSTRT   JES3 start only. Hot start: blank or Y.

INITDECK   JES3 start only. Initialization deck origin type (taken from operator's response to WTOR). See MEMBER.

value	meaning
N	JCL in JES3 procedure
M	data set in JES3 procedure
U	unit at specified address

LISTCARD   JES2 start only. List replacement card option: blank or Y.

MEMBER   JES3 start only. Member name of initialization deck if INITDECK=N or M; unit address of initialization decks if INITDECK=U.

PROCESOR   JES3 only. Processor:

value	meaning
JES3 GLOBAL	this is the JES3 global processor
JES3 LOCAL	this is a JES3 local processor
LOCAL RESET	this local processor is being reset to global

PROCNAME   JES3 start only. Procedure name.

QUEUEANL   JES3 start only. Start is with JES3 queue analysis: blank or Y.

RECLMSYS   JES2 only. Identification of system whose job processing is to be reclaimed. (i.e., COMMAND was $E SYS).

SMFTIME   Event time stamp.

SUBSYS   Subsystem: JES2 or JES3.

SYSTCODE   JES3 ABEND only. System completion code.

SYSTEM   System identification of this processor.

USERCODE   JES3 ABEND only. User completion code.

WRMSTRT   JES3 start only. Warm start: blank or Y.

variable	type	length	format
AUTOINIT	character	1	
COLDSTRT	character	1	
COMMAND	character	14	
CONDCODE	numeric	4	HEX4.
FORMAT	character	1	
HOTSTRT	character	1	
INITDECK	character	1	
LISTCARD	character	1	
MEMBER	character	8	
PROCESOR	character	11	
PROCNAME	character	8	
QUEUEANL	character	1	
RECLMSYS	character	4	
SMFTIME	numeric	8	DATETIME19.2
SUBSYS	character	4	
SYSTCODE	numeric	4	HEX3.
SYSTEM	character	4	
USERCODE	numeric	4	HEX3.
WRMSTRT	character	1	

```
**********MEMBER=TYPE4345********************************;
DATA TYPE4345
                (KEEP=AUTOINIT COLDSTRT COMMAND CONDCODE FORMAT
                 HOTSTRT INITDECK LISTCARD MEMBER PROCESOR
                 PROCNAME QUEUEANL RECLMSYS SMFTIME SUBSYS
                 SYSTCODE SYSTEM USERCODE WRMSTRT);
LENGTH DEFAULT=4 SMFTIME 8;
FORMAT CONDCODE HEX4. SMFTIME DATETIME19.2 SYSTCODE USERCODE HEX3.;
  INFILE SMF STOPOVER LENGTH=LENGTH COL=COL RECFM=VBS LRECL=32756;
  INPUT @2 ID PIB1. @;
 IF ID=43 OR ID=45;
  GOTO TYPE4345;
TYPE4345:
  INPUT @3 SMFTIME SMFSTAMP8. @11 SYSTEM $4. @15 SUBS PIB2. @;
 IF SUBS=2 THEN GOTO JES2;
 IF SUBS=5 THEN GOTO JES3;
* THE RETURN IS NEEDED BECAUSE THIS MAY BE A VSPC TYPE 43-45 RECORD;
*  AND IN THE MACRO VERSION, THE LABEL TYPE4345 IS LINKED TO;
  RETURN;
JES2:
  SUBSYS='JES2';
 IF ID=45 THEN GOTO PJES;
  INPUT @23 STARTIND PIB1. @;
 IF STARTIND>=128 THEN GOTO RECLAIM;
  COMMAND='S JES2        ';
  INPUT @24 STARTOPT PIB1. ;
 IF STARTOPT>128          THEN FORMAT='Y';
 IF MOD(STARTOPT,128)>=64 THEN COLDSTRT='Y';
 IF MOD(STARTOPT,64) >=32 THEN AUTOINIT='Y';
 IF MOD(STARTOPT,32) >=16 THEN LISTCARD='Y';
  OUTPUT TYPE4345;
  RETURN;
RECLAIM:
  COMMAND='$E SYS';
  INPUT @25 RECLMSYS $4. ;
```

```
  OUTPUT TYPE4345;
  RETURN;
PJES:
  COMMAND='$P JES2';
  INPUT @21 TERMIND PIB1. @;
 IF TERMIND>=128 THEN GOTO JESABEND;
  OUTPUT TYPE4345;
  RETURN;
JESABEND:
  INPUT @23 CONDCODE PIB2. ;
   COMMAND='JES ABEND';
  OUTPUT TYPE4345;
  RETURN;
JES3:
  SUBSYS='JES3';
 IF ID=45 THEN GOTO PJES3;
  INPUT @23 STARTIND PIB1. @26 INITDECK $1. @27 MEMBER $8.
        @35 PROCNAME $8. @;
  COMMAND='S JES3';
 IF STARTIND>128 THEN COLDSTRT='Y';
 IF MOD(STARTIND,128)>=64 THEN WRMSTRT='Y';
 IF MOD(STARTIND,64)>=32 THEN HOTSTRT='Y';
 IF MOD(STARTIND,32)>=16 THEN QUEUEANL='Y';
 IF MOD(STARTIND,16)>=8 THEN PROCESOR='JES3 GLOBAL';
 IF MOD(STARTIND,8)>=4 THEN PROCESOR='JES3 LOCAL';
 IF MOD(STARTIND,2)>=1 THEN PROCESOR='LOCAL RESET';
  OUTPUT TYPE4345;
  RETURN;
PJES3:
  COMMAND='P JES3';
  INPUT @21 TERMIND PIB1. @;
 IF TERMIND>128 THEN GOTO JES3ABND;
 IF TERMIND>127 THEN COMMAND='SYST INTERCHG';
  GOTO CONDCODE;
JES3ABND:
  COMMAND='JES3 ABEND';
CONDCODE:
  INPUT @22 COMPL1 PIB2. @23 COMPL2 PIB2. @;
   SYSTCODE=FLOOR(COMPL1/16);
   USERCODE=MOD(COMPL2,4096);
  OUTPUT TYPE4345;
  RETURN;
```

The TYPE43PC Data Set:
VSPC Startup/Modify/Termination

The TYPE43PC data set contains one observation for each type 43 record written by the VSPC subsystem. A type 43 record is written whenever VSPC is started, modified, or terminated. Note that other sub-systems also write records 43; VSPC records are recognized by the subsystem identification field in the record. These records are useful in tracking availability of VSPC.

Contents

EVENT   Event for which record was written: STARTUP, MODIFY, TERMINATION.

HALTUSER   User identification of the user issuing HALT.

NRLOGDON   Number of users logged on at start of termination.

OPTIONS   VSPC options at start or modify. See VSPC source module ASUIOP to decode.

PROCNAME   VSPC startup procedure nam

SMFTIME   Time that this event occurred.

SYSTEM   Identification of the system on which VSPC executed.

TERMREAS   Reason VSPC terminated: HALTED, HALT/NOSAVE, STOPPED, ABNORMAL.

variable	type	length	format
EVENT	character	4	
HALTUSER	numeric	4	
NRLOGDON	numeric	4	
OPTIONS	character	73	
PROCNAME	character	8	
SMFTIME	numeric	8	DATETIME19.2
SYSTEM	character	4	
TERMREAS	character	11	

```
*********MEMBER=TYPE43PC********************************;
DATA TYPE43PC
   (KEEP= EVENT HALTUSER NRLOGDON OPTIONS PROCNAME
                       SMFTIME SYSTEM TERMREAS);
LENGTH DEFAULT=4 SMFTIME 8;
FORMAT SMFTIME DATETIME19.2;
   INFILE SMF STOPOVER LENGTH=LENGTH COL=COL RECFM=VBS LRECL=32756;
   INPUT @2 ID PIB1. @;
 IF ID=43 OR ID=44 OR ID=45;
   GOTO TYPE43PC;

  TYPE43PC:
   INPUT @3 SMFTIME SMFSTAMP8. @11 SYSTEM $4. @15 SUBS PIB2. @;
* THE FOLLOWING TEST FOR SUBS SELECTS TYPE 43,44 OR 45 RECORDS;
*  FOR THE VSPC SUB-SYSTEM (I.E., NOT JES TYPE 43 OR 45 RECORDS);
  IF SUBS NE 6 THEN RETURN;
  IF ID=43 OR ID=44 THEN
   INPUT @21 PROCNAME $8. @29 OPTIONS S73. @;
  IF ID=45  THEN
   INPUT @21 PROCNAME $8. @29 TERMFLG PIB1. @30 HALTUSER PIB3.
          @33 NRLOGDON PIB2. @;
  IF ID=43 THEN EVENT='STARTUP    ';
  IF ID=44 THEN EVENT='MODIFY     ';
  IF ID=45 THEN EVENT='TERMINATION';
  IF ID NE 45 THEN GOTO OUTPC;
  IF TERMFLG >= 128 THEN GOTO HALTPC;
  IF TERMFLG >= 64 THEN GOTO STOPPC;
  IF TERMFLG >= 32 THEN GOTO PCABTERM;
  GOTO OUTPC;
HALTPC:
  TERMREAS='HALTED      ';
  TERMFLG=TERMFLG=128;
  IF TERMFLG>=16 THEN TERMREAS='HALT/NOSAVE';
  GOTO OUTPC;
  RETURN;
STOPPC:
  TERMREAS='STOPPED';
  GOTO OUTPC;
PCABTERM:
  TERMREAS='ABNORMAL';
OUTPC:
 OUTPUT TYPE43PC;
  RETURN;
```

The TYPE4789 Data Set: Remote Job Entry Session

The TYPE4789 data set contains one observation for each type 47, 48 or 49 SMF record. Type 47 SMF records are written when a remote line is started or when a remote user signs on. Type 48 SMF records are written when a remote line is stopped or a remote user signs off. Type 49 SMF records are written when a remote user attempts to sign on with an invalid password.

The TYPE4789 data set contains the line name and statistics on EXCPs and error conditions. By matching up sign-on and sign-off, the connect time of RJE/RJP users can be determined and an analysis of line usage can be made. See chapter 9.

Contents

EVENT   Event description:

JES2 or 3 value	meaning
SIGNON	remote user signed on
SIGNOFF	remote user signed off
S LNE	line was started
P LNE	line was stopped
INVALID PASSWORD	user attempted sign-on with invalid password

JES3 only value	meaning
TERMINAL NOT DEFINED	terminal is not defined
LINE ALREADY ON	line was already on
TERM ALREADY ON	terminal was already on

EXCPCNT   Signoff only. Total number of EXCPs during the RJE session.

LINENR   Line number.

LINERRS   JES3 signoff/P LNE only. Number of line errors.

NRBUSCKS   JES3 signoff/P LNE only. Number of bus-out checks.

NRCMDREJ	JES3 signoff/P LNE only. Number of command rejects.
NRDATACK	Signoff/P LNE only. Number of data checks.
NREQUPCK	JES3 signoff/P LNE only. Number of equipment checks.
NRINTVRQ	JES3 signoff/P LNE only. Number of interventions required.
NRLOSTDT	JES3 signoff/P LNE only. Number of lost data events.
NRNEGAK	Signoff/P LNE only. Number of negative acknowledgments to write text.
NROTHR	JES2 signoff/P LNE only. Number of other errors.
NROVERUN	JES3 signoff/P LNE only. Number of data overruns.
NRTIMEOT	Signoff/P LNE only. Number of time-outs to read text.
PASSWORD	Password. (If event is INVALID PASSWORD, this variable contains the invalid password.)
RMOTID	Remote ID number.
SIGNON	Message text (columns 35-70) of the SIGNON line.
SMFTIME	Event time stamp.
SUBSYS	Subsystem: JES2 or JES3
SYSTEM	System identification on which this event occurred.
UCBNAME	Signoff/P LNE only. Line adapter address.

variable	type	length	format
EVENT	character	18	
EXCPCNT	numeric	4	
LINENR	numeric	4	
LINERRS	numeric	4	
NRBUSCKS	numeric	4	
NRCMDREJ	numeric	4	
NRDATACK	numeric	4	
NREQUPCK	numeric	4	
NRINTVRQ	numeric	4	
NRLOSTDT	numeric	4	
NRNEGAK	numeric	4	
NROTHR	numeric	4	
NROVERUN	numeric	4	
NRTIMEOT	numeric	4	
PASSWORD	character	8	
RMOTID	numeric	4	
SIGNON	character	36	
SMFTIME	numeric	8	DATETIME19.2
SUBSYS	character	4	
SYSTEM	character	4	
UCBNAME	character	3	

```
*********MEMBER=TYPE4789********************************;
DATA TYPE4789
             (KEEP=EVENT EXCPCNT LINENR LINERRS NRBUSCKS NRCMDREJ
              NRDATACK NREQUPCK NRINTVRQ NRLOSTDT NRNEGAK
              NROTHR NROVERUN NRTIMEOT PASSWORD RMOTID
              SIGNON SMFTIME SUBSYS SYSTEM UCBNAME);
LENGTH DEFAULT=4 SMFTIME 8;
FORMAT SMFTIME DATETIME19.2;
  INFILE SMF STOPOVER LENGTH=LENGTH COL=COL RECFM=VBS LRECL=32756;
  INPUT @2 ID PIB1. @;
 IF ID=47 OR ID=48 OR ID=49;
  GOTO TYPE4789;
TYPE4789:
  INPUT @3 SMFTIME SMFSTAMP8. @11 SYSTEM $4. @15 SUBS PIB2.
        @21 IND PIB2.  @41 PASSWORD $8. @;
 IF SUBS=2 THEN SUBSYS='JES2';
 IF SUBS=5 THEN SUBSYS='JES3';
  IF SUBSYS='JES2' OR SUBSYS='JES3';
*    TEST FOR BLANK TO SEE HOW LONG REMOTE NUMBER IS AND GET IT;
  INPUT @25 RMT $3. @;
 IF RMT NE 'RMT' THEN GOTO LINE;
  INPUT @28 RMOTID 3. @;
LINE:
  INPUT @37 LINENR 3. @;
 IF ID=47 THEN GOTO ON;
 IF ID=48 THEN GOTO OFF;
 IF ID=49 THEN GOTO INVALID;
ON:
 IF IND=1 THEN EVENT='SIGNON                   ';
 IF IND=2 THEN EVENT='S LNE';
 IF IND=1 THEN INPUT @51 SIGNON  $36. @;
  OUTPUT TYPE4789;
  RETURN;
OFF:
 IF IND=1 THEN EVENT='SIGNOFF';
 IF IND=2 THEN EVENT='P LNE';
 IF SUBSYS='JES2' THEN
  INPUT @49 EXCPCNT PIB4. @53 NRNEGAK PIB4. @57 NRDATACK PIB4.
        @61 NRTIMEOT PIB4. @65 NROTHR PIB4. @69 UCBNAME $3. @;
 IF SUBSYS='JES3' THEN
      INPUT @49 EXCPCNT PIB4. @53 LINERRS PIB4.
            @57 NRTIMEOT PIB2. @59 NRNEGAK PIB2. @61 NRCMDREJ PIB1.
            @62 NRINTVRQ PIB1. @63 NRBUSCKS PIB1. @64 NREQUPCK PIB1.
            @65 NRDATACK PIB1. @66 NROVERUN PIB1. @67 NRLOSTDT PIB1.
            @77 UCBNAME $3. ;
  OUTPUT TYPE4789;
  RETURN;
INVALID:
 IF SUBSYS='JES2' THEN GOTO JES2IN;
 IF IND>128 THEN EVENT='TERMINAL NOT DEFINED';
 IF MOD(IND,128)>=64 THEN EVENT='INVALID PASSWORD';
 IF MOD(IND,64)>=32 THEN EVENT='LINE ALREADY ON';
 IF MOD(IND,32)>=16 THEN EVENT='TERM ALREADY ON';
  GOTO I49;
JES2IN:
  EVENT='INVALID PASSWORD';
I49:
 IF LENGTH>=86 THEN INPUT @51 SIGNON  $36. @;
  OUTPUT TYPE4789;
  RETURN;
```

The TYPE47PC Data Set: VSPC User LOGON

The TYPE47PC data set contains one observation for each type 47 record written by the VSPC subsystem. A type 47 record is written whenever a VSPC user successfully logs on, or when the VSPC Service Program AC-COUNT control statement is executed. The data is needed to determine the duration of VSPC sessions by matching with TYPE48PC.

Contents

JOBENTID   Job entry ID code.

LANGATTR   Language attribute assigned.

LIBRPROJ   Project library identification number.

LIBRTYPE   Library type code.

LOGOFF   Status of previous logoff:

NOT OFF	Service Program ACCOUNT: not logged off from last session
LOCKED	Service Program ACCOUNT: user locked
ACCT REC	Service Program ACCOUNT: this is a record from ACCOUNT
CONTINUE	workspace was saved at last normal logoff

PLIBYTES   Bytes of DASD space in the project/public libraries.

PRIVCLAS   Privileged class indicators.

SMFTIME   Time of LOGON.

SYSTEM   Identification of system on which VSPC executed.

ULIBYTES   Bytes of DASD space in this user's library.

VSPCUSER   User identification number.

variable	type	length	format
JOBENTID	character	6	
LANGATTR	numeric	4	
LIBRPROJ	numeric	4	
LIBRTYPE	numeric	4	
LOGOFF	character	8	
PLIBYTES	numeric	4	
PRIVCLAS	numeric	4	
SMFTIME	numeric	8	DATETIME19.2
SYSTEM	character	4	
ULIBYTES	numeric	4	
VSPCUSER	numeric	4	

```
**********MEMBER=TYPE47PC********************************;
DATA TYPE47PC
    (KEEP= JOBENTID LANGATTR LIBRPROJ LIBRTYPE LOGOFF PLIBYTES
           PRIVCLAS SMFTIME SYSTEM ULIBYTES VSPCUSER);
LENGTH DEFAULT=4 SMFTIME 8;
FORMAT SMFTIME DATETIME19.2;
    INFILE SMF STOPOVER LENGTH=LENGTH COL=COL RECFM=VBS LRECL=32756;
    INPUT @2 ID PIB1. @;
  IF ID=47;
   GOTO TYPE47PC;
TYPE47PC:
   INPUT @3 SMFTIME SMFSTAMP8. @11 SYSTEM $4. @15 SUBS PIB2. @;
  IF SUBS NE 6 THEN RETURN;
   INPUT @21 LOGFLG PIB1. @22 VSPCUSER PIB3. @25 LIBRTYPE PIB1.
         @26 LIBRPROJ PIB3. @29 JOBENTID $6. @35 LANGATTR PIB1.
         @36 PRIVCLAS PIB1. @37 ULIBYTES PIB4. @41 PLIBYTES PIB4. @;
  IF MOD(LOGFLG,8)>=4 THEN GOTO SPACTREC;
  IF MOD(LOGFLG,64)>=32 THEN LOGOFF='CONTINUE';
     GOTO OUT47PC;
SPACTREC:
  IF LOGFLG>=128 THEN LOGOFF='NOT OFF';
  IF MOD(LOGFLG,2)=1 THEN LOGOFF='LOCKED';
  IF LOGOFF=' ' THEN LOGOFF='ACCT REC';
OUT47PC:
   OUTPUT TYPE47PC;
    RETURN;
```

The TYPE48PC Data Set: VSPC User LOGOFF

The TYPE48PC data set contains one observation for every type 48 record written by the VSPC subsystem. A type 48 record from VSPC (recognizable by the subsystem identification field) is written whenever:
- a user issues the OFF command.
- an interpreter foreground processor issues a TOFF
- a CANCEL command is issued for a user
- a user is disconnected by line drop or telephone hang-up
- a STOP is issued by the system console operator against VSPC
- a VSPC HALT command is issued
- at LOGON, VSPC recognizes that the previous session was incomplete
- the VSPC Service Program ACCOUNT command is issued

TYPE48PC is the accounting record for VSPC users, and contains resource consumption data describing this session as well as the total resources used by this user since creation.

Contents

AVGWKSET   Average working set size for this session, in pages (4096 bytes).

CPUTCBTM   CPU time recorded for this session.

EXCPCOMM   EXCP counts to teleprocessing (communications) device during this session.

EXCPDASD   EXCP counts to DASD devices during this session.

LOGFLG   Logoff flags.

LOGOFF   Logoff indicator:

INCOMPLETE	record for a previously incomplete session
CANCEL	CANCEL issued
CONT/SAVE	CONTINUE, workspace saved in this logoff
CONT/PURG	CONTINUE purged in this logoff
HALT/STOP	HALT or STOP issued
LOCKED	user locked

PAGESECS   Memory space-time usage (K byte-seconds).

PLIBYTES   Bytes of DASD space in the project/public libraries.

PRNTPAGE   Number of pages sent to hardcopy device during this session.

SELAPSTM   Connect time (elapsed session time) for this session.

SMFTIME   Time of LOGOFF event.

SYSTEM   Identification of system on which VSPC executed.

TOTCPUTM   Total CPU time to date for this user.

TOTEXCPC   Total communications (teleprocessing) EXCPs to date for this user.

TOTEXCPD   Total DASD EXCPs to date for this user.

TOTPAGSC   Total memory space-time usage (page seconds) to date for this user.

TOTPRNT   Total hardcopy pages to date for this user.

TOTSELTM   Total connect time to date for this user.

ULIBYTES   Bytes of DASD space in this user's library.

VSPCUSER   User identification number.

variable	type	length	format
AVGWKSET	numeric	4	
CPUTCBTM	numeric	4	TIME12.2
EXCPCOMM	numeric	4	
EXCPDASD	numeric	4	
LOGFLG	numeric	2	HEX2.
LOGOFF	character	10	
PAGESECS	numeric	4	
PLIBYTES	numeric	4	
PRNTPAGE	numeric	4	
SELAPSTM	numeric	4	TIME12.2
SMFTIME	numeric	8	DATETIME19.2
SYSTEM	character	4	
TOTCPUTM	numeric	4	TIME12.2
TOTSELTM	numeric	4	TIME12.2
TOTPRNT	numeric	4	
TOTPAGSC	numeric	4	
TOTEXCPC	numeric	4	
TOTEXCPD	numeric	4	
ULIBYTES	numeric	4	
VSPCUSER	numeric	4	

```
**********MEMBER=TYPE48PC*********************************;
DATA TYPE48PC
     (KEEP=AVGWKSET CPUTCBTM EXCPCOMM EXCPDASD LOGFLG LOGOFF PAGESECS
           PLIBYTES PRNTPAGE SELAPSTM SMFTIME SYSTEM TOTCPUTM TOTSELTM
           TOTPRNT TOTPAGSC TOTEXCPC TOTEXCPD ULIBYTES VSPCUSER);
LENGTH DEFAULT=4 SMFTIME 8 LOGFLG 2;
FORMAT SMFTIME DATETIME19.2 LOGFLG HEX2.
          CPUTCBTM SELAPSTM TOTCPUTM TOTSELTM TIME12.2;
  INFILE SMF STOPOVER LENGTH=LENGTH COL=COL RECFM=VBS LRECL=32756;
  INPUT @2 ID PIB1. @;
 IF ID=48;
  GOTO TYPE48PC;
TYPE48PC:
  INPUT @3 SMFTIME SMFSTAMP8. @11 SYSTEM $4. @15 SUBS PIB2. @;
 IF SUBS NE 6 THEN RETURN;
  INPUT @21 LOGFLG PIB1. @22 VSPCUSER PIB3. @25 CPUTCBTM PIB4.2
        @29 SELAPSTM PIB4. @33 PRNTPAGE PIB4. @37 PAGESECS PIB4.
        @41 EXCPDASD PIB4. @45 EXCPCOMM PIB4. @49 ULIBYTES PIB4.
        @53 PLIBYTES PIB4. @57 TOTCPUTM PIB4.2 @61 TOTSELTM PIB4.
        @65 TOTPRNT PIB4. @69 TOTPAGSC PIB4. @73 TOTEXCPD PIB4.
        @77 TOTEXCPC PIB4. @;
  IF CPUTCBTM>0 THEN AVGWKSET=PAGESECS/CPUTCBTM;
 IF MOD(LOGFLG,8)>=4 THEN GOTO SPACTREC;
 IF LOGFLG>=128  THEN LOGOFF='INCOMPLETE';
    GOTO OUT48PC;
SPACTREC:
 IF MOD(LOGFLG,128)>=64 THEN LOGOFF='CANCEL';
 IF MOD(LOGFLG,64)>=32  THEN LOGOFF='CONT/SAVE';
 IF MOD(LOGFLG,32)>=16  THEN LOGOFF='CONT/PURGE';
 IF MOD(LOGFLG,16)>=8   THEN LOGOFF='HALT/STOP';
 IF MOD(LOGFLG,2)>=1    THEN LOGOFF='LOCKED';
OUT48PC:
   OUTPUT TYPE48PC;
   RETURN;
```

The TYPE49PC Data Set: VSPC Security

The TYPE49PC data set contains one observation written by the VSPC sub-system. A type 49 record is written whenever a VSPC user incorrectly specifies a password at LOGON or at access to a VSPC file.

Contents

FILENAME   Name of the file for which access was attempted (blank if LOGON event).

FILOWNER   VSPC user identification number of the owner of the file.

LIBRNUM   Library number of the accessed file.

SMFTIME   Time of this event.

SYSTEM   Identification of the system on which VSPC executed.

VSPCUSER   User identification of violator.

variable	type	length	format
FILENAME	numeric	11	
FILOWNER	numeric	4	
LIBRNUM	numeric	4	
SMFTIME	numeric	8	DATETIME19.2
SYSTEM	character	4	
VSPCUSER	numeric	4	

```
*********MEMBER=TYPE49PC********************************;
DATA TYPE49PC
     (KEEP=LIBRNUM FILENAME FILEOWNR SMFTIME SYSTEM VSPCUSER);
LENGTH DEFAULT=4 SMFTIME 8;
FORMAT SMFTIME DATETIME19.2;
  INFILE SMF STOPOVER LENGTH=LENGTH COL=COL RECFM=VBS LRECL=32756;
  INPUT @2 ID PIB1. @;
  IF ID=49;
  GOTO TYPE49PC;
TYPE49PC:
  INPUT @3 SMFTIME SMFSTAMP8. @11 SYSTEM $4. @15 SUBS PIB2. @;
  IF SUBS NE 6 THEN RETURN;
  INPUT @21 VSPCUSER PIB3. @;
  IF LENGTH LT 43 THEN GOTO OUT49PC;
  INPUT @24 LIBRNUM PIB3. @29 FILENAME $11. @41 FILEOWNR PIB3. @;
OUT49PC:
  OUTPUT TYPE49PC;
    RETURN;
```

The TYPE5568 Data Set: Network Job Entry Accounting

The TYPE5568 data set contains one observation for each type 55, 56, or 58 SMF record. Type 55 SMF records are written at each node in a network when a start-networking command is executed. The initial sign-on is recorded at the node to which the sign-on was sent, and the response sign-on is recorded at the node that originated the initial sign-on. Type 58 records are similarly written at each node when a networking session is terminated. Type 56 SMF records are written whenever an attempt to sign on contains an invalid password. (Note that there are additional entries in TYPE26J2 if NJE is defined.)

TYPE5568 is thus important for accounting the passage of jobs through an NJE network.

Contents

EVENT   Event type.

value	meaning
INITIAL SIGNON	initial sign-on event
SIGNON RESPONSE	response sign-on
INVALID SIGNON	invalid password on initial sign-on
INVALID RESPONSE	invalid password on response sign-on
SIGNOFF	signoff

LINENAME   Line name.

LINEPWRD   Line password.

MEMBERNR   Member number.

NODENAME   Node number.

NODEPWRD   Node password (will contain the invalid password if EVENT is INVALID SIGNON or INVALID RESPONSE.

SMFTIME   Event time stamp on this system.

SUBSYS   Subsystem: JES2.

SYSTEM   Identification of this system.

variable	type	length	format
EVENT	character	15	
LINENAME	character	8	
LINEPWRD	character	8	
MEMBERNR	numeric	4	
NODENAME	character	8	
NODEPWRD	character	8	
SMFTIME	numeric	8	DATETIME19.2
SUBSYS	character	4	
SYSTEM	character	4	

```
*********MEMBER=TYPE5568*********************************;
DATA TYPE5568
             (KEEP=EVENT LINENAME LINEPWRD MEMBERNR NODENAME
                  NODEPWRD SMFTIME SUBSYS SYSTEM);
LENGTH DEFAULT=4 SMFTIME 8;
FORMAT SMFTIME DATETIME19.2;
  INFILE SMF STOPOVER LENGTH=LENGTH COL=COL RECFM=VBS LRECL=32756;
  INPUT @2 ID PIB1. @;
 IF ID=55 OR ID=56 OR ID=58;
  GOTO TYPE5568;
TYPE5568:
  INPUT @3 SMFTIME SMFSTAMP8. @11 SYSTEM $4.
        @15 SUBS PIB2. @21 NODENAME $8. @29 MEMBERNR PIB1.@;
 IF SUBS=2 THEN SUBSYS='JES2';
 IF SUBSYS='JES2';
 IF ID=55 OR ID=56 THEN INPUT
        @30 STATFLG PIB1. @31 LINEPWRD $8. @39 NODEPWRD $8.
        @47 LINENAME $8. @;
 IF ID=58 THEN INPUT @31 LINENAME $8.@;
 IF ID=55 AND STATFLG > 127 THEN EVENT='SIGNON RESPONSE';
 IF ID=55 AND STATFLG < 128 THEN EVENT='INITIAL SIGNON';
 IF ID=56 AND STATFLG > 127 THEN EVENT='INVALID RESPONSE';
 IF ID=56 AND STATFLG < 128 THEN EVENT='INVALID SIGNON';
 IF ID=58 THEN EVENT='SIGNOFF';
  OUTPUT TYPE5568;
  RETURN;
```

The TYPE57 Data Set: NJE SYSOUT Transmission

The TYPE57 data set contains one observation for each type 57 SMF record, which are written in an NJE environment for each SYSOUT transmission through the network.

TYPE57 contains start and stop times, as well as a count of records transmitted, and is thus useful in tracking NJE performance as well as accounting for NJE.

Contents

CURRJBID   Current job identification. (See TYPE26J2 data set, JOBID variable description.)

DEVNAME   SYSOUT transmitter device name.

EXECNODE   Execution node name.

NETACCT   Network account number.

NEXTNODE   Next node name

ORIGJBID   Original job identification. (See TYPE26J2 data set JOBID variable description.)

ORIGNODE   Original node name.

RECOUNT   Count of logical TP records.

SMFTIME   Event time stamp.

SUBSYS   Subsystem: JES2.

SYSOUTP   SYSOUT transmitter system identification.

SYSTEM   Identification of this system.

TRANBEGN   SYSOUT transmitter-begin (start) time stamp.

TRANEND   SYSOUT transmitter-end (stop) time stamp.

variable	type	length	format
CURRJBID	character	8	
DEVNAME	character	8	
EXECNODE	character	8	
NETACCT	character	8	
NEXTNODE	character	8	
ORIGJBID	character	8	
ORIGNODE	character	8	
RECOUNT	numeric	4	
SMFTIME	numeric	8	DATETIME19.2
SUBSYS	character	4	
SYSOUTP	character	4	
SYSTEM	character	4	
TRANBEGN	numeric	8	DATETIME19.2
TRANEND	numeric	8	DATETIME19.2

```
**********MEMBER=TYPE57************************************;
DATA TYPE57
      (KEEP=CURRJBID DEVNAME EXECNODE NETACCT NEXTNODE
            ORIGJBID ORIGNODE RECOUNT SMFTIME SUBSYS SYSOUTP
            SYSTEM TRANBEGN TRANEND);
LENGTH DEFAULT=4 SMFTIME TRANBEGN TRANEND 8;
FORMAT SMFTIME TRANBEGN TRANEND DATETIME19.2;
  INFILE SMF STOPOVER LENGTH=LENGTH COL=COL RECFM=VBS LRECL=32756;
  INPUT @2 ID PIB1. @;
 IF ID=57;
  GOTO TYPE57;
TYPE57:
  INPUT @3 SMFTIME SMFSTAMP8. @11 SYSTEM $4.
        @15 SUBS PIB2. @21 ORIGJBID $8. @29 CURRJBID $8.
        @37 ORIGNODE $8. @45 EXECNODE $8. @53 NEXTNODE $8.
        @61 DEVNAME $8. @69 TRANBEGN SMFSTAMP8.
        @77 TRANEND SMFSTAMP8. @85 NETACCT $8.
        @93 SYSOUTP $4. @97 RECOUNT PIB4. @;
 IF SUBS=2 THEN SUBSYS='JES2';
 IF SUBSYS='JES2';
  OUTPUT TYPE57;
  RETURN;
```

The TYPE62 Data Set: VSAM Component/Cluster Opened

The TYPE62 data set contains one observation for each type 62 SMF record, written when a VSAM component or cluster is opened, whether or not the open is successful.

TYPE62 contains information about the job/session that opened the component/cluster and about the volumes involved. It is thus useful in tracking VSAM usage, since it gives the time when the open was issued. By matching with TYPE64, the duration that VSAM data sets are open can be determined.

Contents

CATNAME   Name of the catalog in which the component or cluster is defined.

CATVOL   Volume serial number of the volume containing the catalog.

DEVICE   Device type of the volume containing the component or cluster (e.g., 3330, 3350, etc).

ENTRNAME   Name of the component or cluster being opened.

JOB   Job name (batch) or user ID (TSO) that opened the cluster/component.

LOCLINFO   Locally defined field filled in by an installation-written SMF exit routine.

NRVOLS   Number of on-line volumes containing the component or cluster. Also, TYPE62 will contain this number of observations for each multi-volume type 62 SMF record.

READTIME   Job read-in (TSO LOGON) time stamp.

SMFTIME   Open time stamp.

STATUS	Open status:	

value	meaning
SUCCESSFUL	component/cluster was opened successfully
FAILED	security violation (invalid password)

SYSTEM   System identification on which open was issued.

UCBTYPE   UCB type control block for this VOLSER.

VOLSEQNR   Sequence number of this VOLSER.

VOLSER   Volume serial number of the volume containing the component or cluster.

variable	type	length	format
CATNAME	character	44	
CATVOL	character	6	
DEVICE	character	7	
ENTRNAME	character	44	
JOB	character	8	
LOCLINFO	character	8	
NRVOLS	numeric	4	
READTIME	numeric	8	DATETIME19.2
SMFTIME	numeric	8	DATETIME19.2
STATUS	character	10	
SYSTEM	character	4	
UCBTYPE	numeric	4	HEX8.
VOLSEQNR	numeric	4	
VOLSER	character	6	

```
*********MEMBER=TYPE62********************************;
DATA TYPE62
           (KEEP=CATNAME CATVOL DEVICE ENTRNAME JOB LOCLINFO
                 NRVOLS READTIME SMFTIME STATUS SYSTEM UCBTYPE
                 VOLSEQNR VOLSER);
LENGTH DEFAULT=4 SMFTIME READTIME 8;
FORMAT UCBTYPE HEX8. SMFTIME READTIME DATETIME19.2;
INFILE SMF STOPOVER LENGTH=LENGTH COL=COL RECFM=VBS LRECL=32756;
  INPUT @2 ID PIB1. @;
 IF ID=62;
  GOTO TYPE62;
TYPE62:
  INPUT @3 SMFTIME SMFSTAMP8. @11 SYSTEM $4.
        @15 JOB $8. @23 READTIME SMFSTAMP8. @;
_JOBCK
  INPUT @31 LOCLINFO $8. @39 OSI PIB1. @43 CATNAME $44.
        @87 CATVOL $6. @93 ENTRNAME $44. @137 NRVOLS PIB2. @;
 IF OSI>=128 THEN STATUS='SUCCESSFUL';
 IF 64 <= OSI < 128 THEN STATUS='FAILED';
```

```
   M2=-2;
    VOLSEQNR=.;
    LOOPCNT=NRVOLS;
LOOP62:
    VOLSEQNR+1;
 IF LOOPCNT<=0 THEN RETURN;
  INPUT VOLSER $6. UCBTYPE PIB4. +M2 DEVCLASS PIB1. DEVTYPE PIB1.@;
  LINK UCBTYP;
  OUTPUT TYPE62;
  LOOPCNT=LOOPCNT-1;
  GOTO LOOP62;
   UNITADR=.;
  _DEVICE
```

The TYPE6367 Data Set: VSAM Entry Defined/Deleted

The TYPE6367 data set contains one observation for each type 63 or type 67 SMF record. A type 63 SMF record is written when a VSAM catalog entry (i.e., a component, cluster, catalog, alternate index, path, or non-VSAM data set) is defined or altered. A type 67 SMF record is written when a VSAM catalog entry is deleted. TYPE6367 observations describe the job causing the action and the affected VSAM entry, as well as providing the old catalog record for deletions and alterations and the new catalog record for definitions and alterations. The catalog record (new for type 63 and old for type 67) is decoded by the VSAMCAT macro, and many variables in TYPE6367 come from the catalog record portion of these SMF records. The variable TYPE describes the event that caused the observation to be created.

TYPE6367 is useful in tracking usage of VSAM data sets, especially for audit trails of creation and deletion.

The catalog record is documented separately by IBM in publication SYS26-3826-3.

Contents

BUFSIZE Data/index only. Buffer size.

CATENTRY Entry name in the catalog record. Same as ENTRNAME.

CATNAME Name of catalog in which entry is defined.

CATRECSZ Size of the (new) catalog record.

CINUM Control internal number of this catalog record.

CLUST Cluster only. Type of cluster.

value	meaning
blank	N/A
PAGESPACE	the cluster describes a page space
SWAPSPACE	the cluster describes a swap space

COMP   Data/index only.

value	meaning
blank	N/A
NOT USEABLE	the component is not usable

COMPONENT Type of component being processed.

value	meaning
CLUSTER	VSAM cluster
DATA COMP	VSAM data component
INDX COMP	VSAM index component
CATLG	VSAM catalog
NON VSAM	non-VSAM data set
GEN GDG	generation data group
ALIAS	alias

CRADEVT   CRA device type (zeros if catalog is not recoverable or if there is no associated CRA volume).

CRADTIME   Data/index only. Creation time stamp.

CRAIDNO   CRA control internal number (zeros if catalog is not recoverable or if there is no associated CRA volume).

CRATIME   Cluster only. CRA creation time.

CRAVOL   CRA volume serial (zeros if catalog is not recoverable or if there is no associated CRA volume).

DSCRDT   Cluster/data set creation date (YYDDD).

DSET   Data/index only: blank, or INTERNAL if this is an internal system data set.

DSEXTD   Cluster/data set expiration date (YYDDD).

ENTRNAME   Entry name.

ERASE   Data/index only. Data set attribute: blank, or Y if data set or index is to be overwritten with binary zeros when deleted.

GDGDELET   Generation data group deletion action to be taken when GDGLIMIT is exceeded:

value	meaning
A	delete all generations from catalog
O	delete only the oldest generation from catalog

GDGSCRAT   Generation data group scratch action to be taken when GDGLIMIT is exceeded.

value	meaning
D	don't scratch DSCB-1 of deleted data sets
S	scratch DSCB-1 of deleted data sets

GDGLIMIT   Maximum number of GDG levels.

GENLVLS   Generation level difference string.

HARBADS   Data/index only. High-allocated RBA of the data set or index.

HURBADS   Data/index only. High-used RBA of the data set or index.

INHIBIT   Data/index only. Data set attribute: Y if update of data set or index is inhibited.

JOB   Job name (batch), user ID (TSO).

LOCLINFO   Locally defined field, filled in by an installation-written SMF exit routine.

LRECL   Data only. Logical record size of the data set.

OLDRECSZ   Size of old catalog record before alteration.

OPENIND   Data/index only. Open indicator flag: X'80' if the data set is open for output.

OWNERID   Owner of the data set (specified when data set was defined).

PRIMSPACE   Data/index only. Primary space allocation for the data set or index (specified when data set or index was defined). See SPACOPTN.

READTIME   Job read-in (TSO LOGON) time stamp.

RECOVRBL   Data/index only. Data set attribute: Y if this catalog is recoverable.

RELIND   VSAM Release indicator:

value	meaning
0	non-enhanced VSAM
1	enhanced VSAM

REUSABLE   Data/index only. Data set attribute: Y if the cluster associated with this component is reusable.

SCONSPAC   Data/index only. Secondary space allocation for the data set or index (specified when data set or index was defined). See SPACOPTN.

SECFLAGS   Security flags. X'80' if record is RACF-protected.

SHARING   Data/index only. Data set sharing attributes:

value	meaning
READ OR	data set can be shared by READ users **or** it can be used by one UPDATE/OUTPUT user
READ AND	data set can be shared by READ users **and** one UPDATE/OUTPUT user
FULLY	data set can be fully shared
FULLY WITH	data set can be fully shared, with assistance supplied by VSAM

SMFTIME   Event time stamp.

SPACE   Data/index only. Space options:

value	meaning
CYL	space request specified in cylinders
TRK	space request specified in tracks

SPEED   Data/index only. Data set attribute: Y if the DASD device for the data set or index is not to be preformatted before records are written.

SYSTEM   ID of system that purged this job.

TEMPXPOR   Data/index only. Data set attribute: Y if this is temporary export (i.e., the original copy of this data set or index is not to be deleted, even though another copy of it exists somewhere else).

TRKOVFLO   Data/index only. Data set attribute: Y if track overflow (can be set only in a data catalog record that describes a pagespace).

TYPE   Type of event:

value	meaning
NEW DEFN	new definition
ALT DEFN	altered definition

PATH ALT	path defined or altered	
ALT INDX	alternate index defined or altered	
UNCATLG	uncataloged	
SCRATCH	scratched	
PATHDEL	path deleted	
ALTINDX	alternate index deleted	
UNCATSCR	uncataloged and scratched	

UNIQUE Data/index only. Data set attribute: Y if unique (data set or index must reside in a data space all its own).

XSYSSHR Data/index only. Data set sharing across systems:

value	meaning
FULLY	the data set can be fully shared
FULLY WITH	the data set can be fully shared with assistance supplied by VSAM

variable	type	length	format
BUFSIZE	numeric	4	
CATENTRY	character	44	
CATNAME	character	44	
CATRECSZ	numeric	4	
CINUM	numeric	4	
CLUST	character	9	
COMP	character	11	
COMPONT	character	9	
CRADEVT	numeric	4	HEX8.
CRADTIME	numeric	8	DATETIME19.2
CRAIDNO	numeric	4	
CRATIME	numeric	4	HHMM8.2
CRAVOL	character	6	
DSCRDT	numeric	4	
DSET	character	8	
DSEXTD	numeric	4	
ENTRNAME	character	44	
ERASED	character	1	
GDGDELET	character	1	
GDGLIMIT	numeric	4	
GDGSCRAT	character	1	
GENLVLS	numeric	4	
HARBADS	numeric	4	
HURBADS	numeric	4	
INHIBIT	character	1	
JOB	character	8	
LOCLINFO	character	8	
LRECL	numeric	4	
OLDRECSZ	numeric	4	
OPENIND	numeric	4	HEX2.
OWNERID	character	8	
PRIMSPACE	numeric	4	
READTIME	numeric	8	DATETIME19.2

RECOVRBL	character	1	
RELIND	numeric	4	
REUSABLE	character	1	
SCONSPAC	numeric	4	
SECFLAGS	numeric	4	HEX2.
SHARING	character	11	
SMFTIME	numeric	8	DATETIME19.2
SPACE	character	3	
SPEED	character	1	
SYSTEM	character	4	
TEMPXPOR	character	1	
TRKOVFLO	character	1	
TYPE	character	8	
UNIQUE	character	1	
XSYSSHR	character	11	

```
**********MEMBER=TYPE6367*********************************;
DATA TYPE6367
        (KEEP=  BUFSIZE CATENTRY CATNAME CATRECSZ CINUM CLUST
                COMP COMPONT CRADEVT CRADTIME CRAIDNO CRATIME
                CRAVOL DSCRDT DSET DSEXTD ENTRNAME ERASED GDGDELET
                GDGLIMIT GDGSCRAT GENLVLS HARBADS HURBADS INHIBIT
                JOB LOCLINFO LRECL OLDRECSZ OPENIND OWNERID
                PRIMSPAC READTIME RECOVRBL RELIND REUSABLE
                SCONSPAC SECFLAGS SHARING SMFTIME SPACE SPEED
                SYSTEM TEMPXPOR TRKOVFLO TYPE UNIQUE XSYSSHR );
LENGTH DEFAULT=4 SMFTIME READTIME 8;
FORMAT ENTYPE1 ENTYPE2 HEX2. SMFTIME READTIME DATETIME19.2;
  INFILE SMF STOPOVER LENGTH=LENGTH COL=COL RECFM=VBS LRECL=32756;
  INPUT @2 ID PIB1. @;
 IF ID=63 OR ID=67;
  GOTO TYPE6367;
TYPE6367:
  INPUT @3 SMFTIME SMFSTAMP8. @11 SYSTEM $4.
        @15 JOB $8. @23 READTIME SMFSTAMP8. @;
_JOBCK
  INPUT @31 LOCLINFO $8. @39 ENTYPE1 PIB1. @40 ENTYPE2 PIB1. @;
  IF ID=63 THEN INPUT  @41 CATRECSZ PIB2. @43 OLDRECSZ PIB2.
        @45 CATNAME $44. @85 ENTRNAME $44. +4 @;
  IF ID=67 THEN INPUT @41 CATNAME $44. @85 ENTRNAME $44.
        @129 CATRECSZ PIB2. @;
_VSAMCAT
-IF ID=67 THEN GOTO TYP67;
  IF ENTYPE1          >127 THEN TYPE='NEW DEFN';
  IF MOD(ENTYPE1,128)>=64 THEN TYPE='ALT DEFN';
  IF MOD(ENTYPE1,4)  >= 2 THEN TYPE='PATH ALT';
  IF MOD(ENTYPE1,2)  >= 1 THEN TYPE='ALT INDX';
GOTO TYP;
TYP67:
  IF ENTYPE1          >127 THEN TYPE='UNCATLG';
  IF MOD(ENTYPE1,128)>=64 THEN TYPE='SCRATCH';
  IF MOD(ENTYPE1,128)>=64 AND ENTYPE1>127 THEN TYPE='UNCATSCR';
  IF MOD(ENTYPE1,4)  >= 2 THEN TYPE='PATHDEL';
  IF MOD(ENTYPE1,2)  >= 1 THEN TYPE='ALTINDX';
TYP:
  IF ENTYPE2          >127 THEN COMPONT='CLUSTER   ';
  IF MOD(ENTYPE2,128)>=64 THEN COMPONT='DATA COMP';
  IF MOD(ENTYPE2,64) >=32 THEN COMPONT='INDX COMP';
  IF MOD(ENTYPE2,32) >=16 THEN COMPONT='CATLG';
  IF MOD(ENTYPE2,16) >= 8 THEN COMPONT='NON VSAM';
  IF MOD(ENTYPE2,8)  >= 4 THEN COMPONT='GEN GDG';
  IF MOD(ENTYPE2,4)  >= 2 THEN COMPONT='ALIAS';
  OUTPUT TYPE6367;
   RETURN;
```

The TYPE64 Data Set: VSAM Component or Cluster Status

The TYPE64 data set contains one observation for each type 64 SMF record, written when a VSAM component or cluster is closed, is switched to another volume, or when no more space is available. When a cluster is closed, a separate type 64 record is written for each component in the cluster.

TYPE64 contains description of the VSAM component/cluster and accounting statistics such as number of records, deletes, EXCPs, and so on. The statistics are presented as the totals since creation, and the change in the total due to this job's use of the VSAM component/cluster.

Contents

ACCASPLT   Accumulated number of control areas that were split in the component from creation to this open.

ACCDELET   Accumulated number of records that were deleted from the component from creation to this open.

ACCEXCPS   Accumulated number of EXCPs from creation to this open.

ACCINSRT   Accumulated number of records that were inserted in the components from creation to this open.

ACCISPLT   Accumulated number of control intervals that were split in the components from creation to this open.

ACCLEVEL   Accumulated number of levels in the index from creation to this open.

ACCNEXTS   Accumulated number of extents from creation to this open.

ACCNRECS   Accumulated number of records in the component from creation to this open.

ACCRETRV   Number of records that were retrieved from the component from creation to this open.

ACCUNUCI   Number of unused control intervals in the components from creation to this open.

ACCUPDAT   Number of records that were updated in the component from creation to this open.

BEGCCHH1-   Beginning cylinder and tracks (where CC is the cylinder
BEGCCHH3   number and HH, for head, is the track number) of the first three extents.

BLKSIZE   Physical blocksize.

CATNAME   Name of the catalog in which the component is defined.

CHGASPLT   Change in number of control areas that were split from this open until EOV/CLOSE.

CHGDELET   Change in number of records that were deleted from this open until EOV/CLOSE

CHGEXCPS   Change in number of EXCPs from this open until EOV/CLOSE.

CHGINSRT   Change in number of records that were inserted in the component from this open until EOV/CLOSE.

CHGISPLT   Change in number of control intervals that were split in the component from this open until EOV/CLOSE.

CHGLEVEL   Change in the number of levels in the index from this open until EOV/CLOSE.

CHGNEXTS   Change in the number of extents from this open until EOV/CLOSE.

CHGNRECS   Change in number of records in the component from this open until CLOSE/EOV.

CHGRETRV   Change in number of records that were retrieved from this open until CLOSE/EOV.

CHGUNUCI   Change in number of unused control intervals from this open until CLOSE/EOV.

CHGUPDAT   Change in number of records that were updated from this open until CLOSE/EOV.

CISIZE   Control interval size.

COMPONT   Component being processed: DATA or INDEX.

DDNAME   DDname. (Zeroes for catalog or catalog recovery area; blank if concatenated).

DEVICE1-   Device type for first three extents (e.g., 3330, 3350, etc.).
DEVICE3   From __DEVICE macro.

ENDCCHH1-   Ending cylinder and track of first three extents. See
ENDCCHH3   BEGCCHH1-BEGCCHH3.

ENTRNAME   Name of the component being processed.

HIGHRBA   Highest used relative byte address (RBA) of the component.

JOB   Jobname (batch), user ID (TSO).

KEYLEN   Key length.

LOCLINFO   Locally defined field, filled in by an installation-written SMF exit routine.

MAXLRECL   Maximum logical record size.

NREXTENT   Number of extents in this record.

READTIME   Job read-in (TSO LOGON) time stamp.

SITUATN   Situation description (reason record was written).

value	meaning
COMPONENT CLOSED	component closed
VOL SWITCHED	volume switched
NO SPACE AVAIL	no space available

SMFTIME   Event time stamp.

SPINDLE1-   Spindle identification(s) of first three extents.
SPINDLE3

SYSTEM   System identification.

TRKNOTAL   Number of tracks that were requested but could not be allocated.

UCBTYPE1- UCB type(s) of first three extents.
UCBTYPE3

UNITADR1- Unit address(es) of first three extents.
UNITADR3

VOL1-VOL3 Volume serial number(s) of first three extents.

variable	type	length	format
ACCASPLT	numeric	4	
ACCDELET	numeric	4	
ACCEXCPS	numeric	4	
ACCINSRT	numeric	4	
ACCISPLT	numeric	4	
ACCLEVEL	numeric	4	
ACCNEXTS	numeric	4	
ACCNRECS	numeric	4	
ACCRETRV	numeric	4	
ACCUNUCI	numeric	4	
ACCUPDAT	numeric	4	
BEGCCHH1	numeric	4	HEX8.
BEGCCHH2	numeric	4	HEX8.
BEGCCHH3	numeric	4	HEX8.
BLKSIZE	numeric	4	
CATNAME	character	44	
CHGASPLT	numeric	4	
CHGDELET	numeric	4	
CHGEXCPS	numeric	4	
CHGINSRT	numeric	4	
CHGISPLT	numeric	4	
CHGLEVEL	numeric	4	
CHGNEXTS	numeric	4	
CHGNRECS	numeric	4	
CHGRETRV	numeric	4	
CHGUNUCI	numeric	4	
CHGUPDAT	numeric	4	
CISIZE	numeric	4	
COMPONT	character	5	
DDNAME	character	8	
DEVICE1	character	7	
DEVICE2	character	7	
DEVICE3	character	7	
ENDCCHH1	numeric	4	HEX8.
ENDCCHH2	numeric	4	HEX8.
ENDCCHH3	numeric	4	HEX8.
ENTRNAME	character	44	
HIGHRBA	numeric	4	
JOB	character	8	
KEYLEN	numeric	4	
LOCLINFO	character	8	
MAXLRECL	numeric	4	
NREXTENT	numeric	4	
READTIME	numeric	8	DATETIME19.2

SITUATN	character	16	
SMFTIME	numeric	8	DATETIME19.2
SPINDLE1	numeric	4	HEX4.
SPINDLE2	numeric	4	HEX4.
SPINDLE3	numeric	4	HEX4.
SYSTEM	character	4	
TRKNOTAL	numeric	4	
UCBTYPE1	numeric	4	HEX8.
UCBTYPE2	numeric	4	HEX8.
UCBTYPE3	numeric	4	HEX8.
UNITADR1	numeric	4	HEX3.
UNITADR2	numeric	4	HEX3.
UNITADR3	numeric	4	HEX3.
VOL1	character	6	
VOL2	character	6	
VOL3	character	6	

```
**********MEMBER=TYPE64********************************;
DATA TYPE64
            (KEEP=ACCASPLT ACCDELET ACCEXCPS ACCINSRT ACCISPLT
                  ACCLEVEL ACCNEXTS ACCNRECS ACCRETRV ACCUNUCI
                  ACCUPDAT BEGCCHH1-BEGCCHH3 BLKSIZE  CATNAME
                  CHGASPLT CHGDELET CHGEXCPS CHGINSRT CHGISPLT
                  CHGLEVEL CHGNEXTS CHGNRECS CHGRETRV CHGUNUCI
                  CHGUPDAT CISIZE COMPONT DDNAME DEVICE1-DEVICE3
                  ENDCCHH1-ENDCCHH3 ENTRNAME HIGHRBA JOB KEYLEN
                  LOCLINFO MAXLRECL NREXTENT READTIME SITUATN SMFTIME
                  SPINDLE1-SPINDLE3 SYSTEM TRKNOTAL UCBTYPE1-UCBTYPE3
                  UNITADR1-UNITADR3 VOL1-VOL3);
LENGTH DEFAULT=4 SMFTIME READTIME 8;
FORMAT SMFTIME READTIME DATETIME19.2 UNITADR1-UNITADR3 HEX3.
       BEGCCHH1-BEGCCHH3 ENDCCHH1-ENDCCHH3 UCBTYPE1-UCBTYPE3 HEX8.
       SPINDLE1-SPINDLE3 HEX4.;
  INFILE SMF STOPOVER LENGTH=LENGTH COL=COL RECFM=VBS LRECL=32756;
  INPUT @2 ID PIB1. @;
 IF ID=64;
  GOTO TYPE64;
TYPE64:
  INPUT @3 SMFTIME SMFSTAMP8. @11 SYSTEM $4.
        @15 JOB $8. @23 READTIME SMFSTAMP8. @;
_JOBCK
  INPUT @31 LOCLINFO $8. @39 SITUIND PIB1. @40 COMPIND PIB1.
        @41 CATNAME $44. @85 ENTRNAME $44. @129 TRKNOTAL PIB2.
        @131 HIGHRBA PIB4. @135 LENEXT PIB2. @;
 IF SITUIND>=128          THEN SITUATN='COMPONENT CLOSED';
 IF MOD(SITUIND,128)>=64 THEN SITUATN='VOL SWITCHED';
 IF MOD(SITUIND,64) >=32 THEN SITUATN='NO SPACE AVAIL';
 IF COMPIND>=128          THEN COMPONT='DATA ';
 IF MOD(COMPIND,128)>=64 THEN COMPONT='INDEX';
   NREXTENT=LENEXT/26;
   M2=-2;
   DEVICE='        ';
 IF NREXTENT<=Ø THEN GOTO STATS;
  INPUT BEGCCHH1 PIB4. ENDCCHH1 PIB4. VOL1 $6. UNITADR PIB2.
        SPINDLE1 PIB2. UCBTYPE1 PIB4. +M2 DEVCLASS PIB1.
        DEVTYPE PIB1. +4 @;
  LINK UCBTYP;
   DEVICE1=DEVICE;
   UNITADR1=UNITADR;
```

```
 IF NREXTENT=1 THEN GOTO STATS;
   INPUT BEGCCHH2 PIB4. ENDCCHH2 PIB4. VOL2 $6. UNITADR PIB2.
         SPINDLE2 PIB2. UCBTYPE2 PIB4. +M2 DEVCLASS PIB1.
         DEVTYPE PIB1. +4 @;
   LINK UCBTYP;
    DEVICE2=DEVICE;
    UNITADR2=UNITADR;
 IF NREXTENT=2 THEN GOTO STATS;
   INPUT BEGCCHH3 PIB4. ENDCCHH3 PIB4. VOL3 $6. UNITADR PIB2.
         SPINDLE3 PIB2. UCBTYPE3 PIB4. +M2 DEVCLASS PIB1.
         DEVTYPE PIB1. +4 @;
   LINK UCBTYP;
    DEVICE3=DEVICE;
    UNITADR3=UNITADR;
 IF NREXTENT>=3 THEN GOTO STATS;
STATS:
   LOC=137+LENEXT+4;
   INPUT @LOC
         ACCLEVEL PIB4. ACCNEXTS PIB4. ACCNRECS PIB4. ACCDELET PIB4.
         ACCINSRT PIB4. ACCUPDAT PIB4. ACCRETRV PIB4. ACCUNUCI PIB4.
         ACCISPLT PIB4. ACCASPLT PIB4. ACCEXCPS PIB4. CHGLEVEL PIB4.
         CHGNEXTS PIB4. CHGNRECS PIB4. CHGDELET PIB4. CHGINSRT PIB4.
         CHGUPDAT PIB4. CHGRETRV PIB4. CHGUNUCI  IB4. CHGISPLT PIB4.
         CHGASPLT PIB4. CHGEXCPS PIB4. BLKSIZE PIB4. CISIZE   PIB4.
         MAXLRECL PIB4. KEYLEN   PIB2. DDNAME $8. ;
   OUTPUT TYPE64;
   RETURN;
_DEVICE
```

The TYPE68 Data Set: VSAM Entry Renamed

The TYPE68 data set contains one observation for every type 68 SMF record, written whenever a VSAM catalog entry (component, cluster, catalog, alternate index, path, or non-VSAM data set) is renamed.

The TYPE68 observation identifies the job that renamed the entry and describes the entry, including the old and new names. TYPE68 is important in constructing an audit trail of VSAM usage.

Contents

CATNAME   Name of the catalog in which the entry is defined.

JOB   Job name (batch) or user ID (TSO).

LOCLINFO   Locally defined field, filled in by an installation-written SMF exit routine.

NEWENTRY   New name of the entry.

OLDENTRY   Old name of the entry.

READTIME   Job read-in (TSO LOGON) time stamp.

SMFTIME   Rename event time stamp.

SYSTEM   Identification of system on which rename occurred.

variable	type	length	format
CATNAME	character	44	
JOB	character	8	
LOCLINFO	character	8	
NEWENTRY	character	44	
OLDENTRY	character	44	
READTIME	numeric	8	DATETIME19.2
SMFTIME	numeric	8	DATETIME19.2
SYSTEM	character	4	

```
*********MEMBER=TYPE68******************************************;
DATA TYPE68
              (KEEP=CATNAME JOB LOCLINFO NEWENTRY OLDENTRY READTIME
              SMFTIME SYSTEM);
LENGTH DEFAULT=4 SMFTIME READTIME 8;
FORMAT READTIME SMFTIME DATETIME19.2;
  INFILE SMF STOPOVER LENGTH=LENGTH COL=COL RECFM=VBS LRECL=32756;
  INPUT @2 ID PIB1. @;
 IF ID=68;
  GOTO TYPE68;
TYPE68:
  INPUT @3 SMFTIME SMFSTAMP8. @11 SYSTEM $4.
        @15 JOB $8. @23 READTIME SMFSTAMP8. @;
_JOBCK
  INPUT @31 LOCLINFO $8. @39 CATNAME $44. @83 OLDENTRY $44.
        @127 NEWENTRY $44. @;
  OUTPUT TYPE68;
  RETURN;
```

The TYPE69 Data Set: VSAM Data Space Defined, Extended, or Deleted

The TYPE69 data set contains one observation for every type 69 SMF record, written whenever a VSAM data space is defined, extended, or deleted. (A type 69 is not written when an entire VSAM catalog or a unique VSAM data set is defined or deleted; see TYPE6367.)

The TYPE69 observation contains a description of the job causing this event, and a description of the volume on which the data space was (or is) allocated. Unfortunately, TYPE69 contains no information to identify the event as a definition, extension, or deletion. The amount of free space after the event is given and it may be possible to infer which event occurred from those statistics, but to do so will require an understanding of the installation's VSAM policies.

Contents

CATNAME   Name of catalog in which the data space is defined.

JOB   Job name (batch) or user ID (TSO).

LOCLINFO   Locally defined field, filled in by an installation-written SMF exit routine.

NRCYL   Number of cylinders in the largest contiguous unallocated area in any data space on the volume.

NRFREEXT   Number of free data space extents on the affected volume after this event.

NRTRK   Number of tracks (in addition to the number of cylinders) in the largest contiguous unallocated area in any data space on the volume.

NRUNCYL   Number of unallocated cylinders in all the data spaces on the volume.

NRUNTRK   Number of unallocated tracks (in addition to the number of unallocated cylinders) in all the data spaces on the volume.

READTIME   Job read-in (TSO LOGON) time stamp.

SMFTIME   Event time stamp.

SPINDLE   Spindle identification.

SYSTEM   Identification of system on which event occurred.

UNITADR   Unit address of this volume.

VOLSER   Volume serial number.

variable	type	length	format
CATNAME	character	44	
JOB	character	8	
LOCLINFO	character	8	
NRCYL	numeric	4	
NRFREEXT	numeric	4	
NRTRK	numeric	4	
NRUNCYL	numeric	4	
NRUNTRK	numeric	4	
READTIME	numeric	8	DATETIME19.2
SMFTIME	numeric	8	DATETIME19.2
SPINDLE	numeric	4	HEX4.
SYSTEM	character	4	
UNITADR	numeric	4	HEX3.
VOLSER	character	6	

```
*********MEMBER=TYPE69*********************************;
DATA TYPE69
            (KEEP=CATNAME JOB LOCLINFO NRCYL NRFREEXT
                NRTRK NRUNCYL NRUNTRK READTIME SMFTIME
                SPINDLE SYSTEM UNITADR VOLSER);
LENGTH DEFAULT=4 SMFTIME READTIME 8;
FORMAT READTIME SMFTIME DATETIME19.2 SPINDLE HEX4. UNITADR HEX3.;
  INFILE SMF STOPOVER LENGTH=LENGTH COL=COL RECFM=VBS LRECL=32756;
  INPUT @2 ID PIB1. @;
IF ID=69;
  GOTO TYPE69;
TYPE69:
  INPUT @3 SMFTIME SMFSTAMP8. @11 SYSTEM $4.
        @15 JOB $8.   @23 READTIME SMFSTAMP8. @;
_JOBCK
  INPUT @31 LOCLINFO $8. @39 UNITADR PIB2.
        @41 SPINDLE PIB2. @43 NRFREEXT PIB2. @45 NRUNCYL PIB2.
        @47 NRUNTRK PIB2. @49 NRCYL PIB2. @51 NRTRK PIB2.
        @53 CATNAME $44. @97 VOLSER $6. ;
  OUTPUT TYPE69;
  RETURN;
```

RMF Records

Resource Measurement Facility (RMF) is an IBM Program Product that has replaced MF/1 in MVS. RMF writes records to the SMF data set and these records are described in the following sections.

Some of the data in the RMF records is sampled, while other data is accumulated. The installation defines the interval at which RMF records are written, as well as the cycle at which samples are taken. For long-term monitoring, an interval of 60 minutes and a cycle of 1000 milliseconds are recommended, as this combination seems to produce excellent information at little overhead. RMF records are thus produced hourly (but not on the hour), with 3600 samples per hour. The actual duration of the interval (which can vary slightly due to enqueues) is given in the following SAS data sets as the DURATM variable. RMF is documented by IBM in a separate manual, *OS/VS2 MVS Resource Measurement Facility (RMF): Version 2 Reference and User's Guide*, SC28-0922-0.

RMF records are numbered in the 70's.

The TYPE70 Data Set: CPU Activity and Address Space Statistics

The TYPE70 data set contains one observation for each type 70 SMF record. Type 70 records are written at each RMF interval and contain the accumulated CPU wait time (for each CPU in the case of an MP) and statistics on the number of address spaces that were in various states (i.e. READY, IN, OUT, WAIT, etc.) and statistics on the type of address spaces (i.e. batch, TSO, started tasks). TYPE70 also contains a bit mapping (SUPATERN) that describes all Selectable Units that are installed, and additionally contains the actual CPU type and hardware serial number of the system.

TYPE70 is essential in the analysis of the utilization of the processor since it provides the only source of data describing the total CPU usage. See chapter 11, "Recovery of Batch CPU Time."

Contents

BATCH0-
BATCH36   Percent of samples when the number of batch users was 0, 1-2, 3-4, 5-6, 7-8, 9-10, 11-15, 16-20, 21-25, 26-30, 31-35, 36 or more.

BATCHAVG   Average number of batch users over the RMF interval.

BATCHMAX   Maximum number of batch users over the RMF interval.

BATCHMIN   Minimum number of batch users over the RMF interval.

CAI0-
CAI1   Configuration activity indicator for CPU(s).

value	meaning
2	CPU was varied on- or off-line during the measurement interval
1	CPU is currently on-line at end of interval

CPUSER0-
CPUSER1   Serial number of CPU(s).

CPUTYPE   CPU model numbers: 158, 168, 3033, etc.

CPUWAITM Total processor wait time during this interval, i.e., time that the CPU was not executing instrutions.

CPUWAIT0 Processor 0 wait time (minutes). For a uni-processor, this will equal CPUWAIT.

CPUWAIT1 Only for multi-processor. Processor 1 wait time (minutes).

CYCLE Sample cycle length (in milliseconds). At each CYCLE, a sampling observation is made.

DURATM Duration of this RMF interval. At the end of each DURAT, all data gathered and sampled is written to SMF.

**IN0-
IN36** Percent of samples when the number of IN users was **0**, **1-2**, **3-4**, **5-6**, **7-8**, **9-10**, **11-15**, **16-20**, **21-25**, **26-30**, **31-35**, **36** or more.

INAVG Average number of IN users over the RMF interval.

INMAX Maximum number of IN users over the RMF interval.

INMIN Minimum number of IN users over the RMF interval.

**LRDY0-
LRDY36** MVS/SE only. Percent of samples when the number of LOGICAL READY users was **0**, **1-2**, **3-4**, etc.

LRDYAVG Average number of LOGICAL READY users over the RMF interval.

LRDYMAX Maximum number of LOGICAL READY users over the RMF interval.

LRDYMIN Minimum number of LOGICAL READY users over the RMF interval.

**LWAIT0-
LWAIT36** MVS/SE only. Percent of samples when the number of LOGICAL WAITING users was **0**, **1-2**, **3-4**, etc.

LWAITAVG Average number of LOGICAL WAITING users over the RMF interval.

LWAITMAX Maximum number of LOGICAL WAITING users over the RMF interval.

LWAITMIN Minimum number of LOGICAL WAITING users over the RMF interval.

NRCPUS Number of CPUs online at the end of the interval that had no VARY activity during the interval. Normally, 1 for UP and 2 for MP.

NRSAMPLE Number of samples in this RMF interval (Samples are taken at CYCLE intervals.)

OUT0-
OUT36 Percent of samples when the number of OUT users was **0**, **1**-2, **3**-4, **5**-6, **7**-8, **9**-10, **11**-15, **16**-20, **21**-25, **26**-30, **31**-35, or **36** or more.

OUTAVG Average number of OUT users over the RMF interval.

OUTMAX Maximum number of OUT users over the RMF interval.

OUTMIN Minimum number of OUT users over the RMF interval.

PCTCPBY0 Percent of DURATM in which CPU number 0 was executing instructions (i.e., CPU busy).

PCTCPBY1 Percent of DURATM in which CPU number 1 was executing instructions.

PCTCPUBY Percent of CPU busy. For UP, this is PCTCPBY0. For MP, this is the sum of CPU active for both processors divided by twice DURATM.

READY0-
READY15 Percent of samples when the number of READY users was 0, 1, 2, . . . 14, 15 or greater.

READYAVG Average number of READY users over the RMF interval.

READYMAX Maximum number of READY users over the RMF interval.

READYMIN Minimum number of READY users over the RMF interval.

RELEASE Operating system release number and level. (e.g., 0370 for Release 3 Level 7, or 3.7)

SMFTIME Approximate ending time stamp of the RMF interval (actually, this is when the record was moved to the buffer).

STARTIME Beginning of RMF interval time stamp.

STC0-
STC36 Percent of samples when the number of STARTED tasks was 0, **1**-2, **3**-4, **5**-6, **7**-8, **9**-10, **11**-15, **16**-20, **21**-25, **26**-30, **31**-35, or **36** or more.

STCAVG Average number of STARTED tasks during the RMF interval.

STCMAX Maximum number of STARTED tasks during the RMF interval.

STCMIN Minimum number of STARTED tasks during the RMF interval.

SUPATERN Bit pattern for installed Selectable Units. High order bit is SU0 (Initial System).

SYSTEM Identification of this system.

TSO0- Percent of samples when the number of TSO users was **0**,
TSO36 1-2, **3**-4, **5**-6, **7**-8, **9**-10, **11**-15, **16**-20, **21**-25, **26**-30, **31**-35, or **36** or more.

TSOAVG Average number of TSO users during the RMF interval.

TSOMAX Maximum number of TSO users during the RMF interval.

TSOMIN Minimum number of TSO users during the RMF interval.

VERSION RMF version number.

value	meaning
01	MF/1
02	RMF Version 1
03	RMF Version 2
04	RMF Version 2 Release 2 (SE)
05	RMF Version 2 Release 2 Feature (SE 2)

WAIT0- Percent of samples when the number of WAITING users was
WAIT36 0, **1**-2, **3**-4, **5**-6, **7**-8, **9**-10, **11**-15, **16**-20, **21**-25, **26**-30, **31**-35, or **36** or more.

WAITAVG Average number of WAITING users during the RMF interval.

WAITMAX Maximum number of WAITING users during the RMF interval.

WAITMIN Minimum number of WAITING users during the RMF interval.

variable	type	length	format
BATCH0	numeric	4	5.1
BATCH1	numeric	4	5.1
BATCH3	numeric	4	5.1
BATCH5	numeric	4	5.1
BATCH7	numeric	4	5.1
BATCH9	numeric	4	5.1
BATCH11	numeric	4	5.1
BATCH16	numeric	4	5.1
BATCH21	numeric	4	5.1
BATCH26	numeric	4	5.1
BATCH31	numeric	4	5.1
BATCH36	numeric	4	5.1
BATCHAVG	numeric	4	
BATCHMAX	numeric	4	
BATCHMIN	numeric	4	
CAI0	numeric	4	
CAI1	numeric	4	
CPUSER0	numeric	3	HEX6.
CPUSER1	numeric	3	HEX6.
CPUTYPE	numeric	4	HEX4.
CPUWAIT0	numeric	4	TIME12.2
CPUWAIT1	numeric	4	TIME12.2
CPUWAITM	numeric	4	TIME12.2
CYCLE	numeric	4	HEX8.
DURATM	numeric	4	TIME12.2
IN0	character	4	5.1
IN1	character	4	5.1
IN3	character	4	5.1
IN5	character	4	5.1
IN7	character	4	5.1
IN9	character	4	5.1
IN11	character	4	5.1
IN16	character	4	5.1
IN21	character	4	5.1
IN26	character	4	5.1
IN31	character	4	5.1
IN36	character	4	5.1
INAVG	numeric	4	5.1
INMAX	numeric	4	
INMIN	numeric	4	
LRDY0	numeric	4	5.1
LRDY1	numeric	4	5.1
LRDY3	numeric	4	5.1
LRDY5	numeric	4	5.1
LRDY7	numeric	4	5.1
LRDY9	numeric	4	5.1
LRDY11	numeric	4	5.1
LRDY16	numeric	4	5.1
LRDY21	numeric	4	5.1
LRDY26	numeric	4	5.1
LRDY31	numeric	4	5.1
LRDY36	numeric	4	5.1
LRDYAVG	numeric	4	5.1
LRDYMAX	numeric	4	
LRDYMIN	numeric	4	

LWAIT0	numeric	4	5.1
LWAIT1	numeric	4	5.1
LWAIT3	numeric	4	5.1
LWAIT5	numeric	4	5.1
LWAIT7	numeric	4	5.1
LWAIT9	numeric	4	5.1
LWAIT11	numeric	4	5.1
LWAIT16	numeric	4	5.1
LWAIT21	numeric	4	5.1
LWAIT26	numeric	4	5.1
LWAIT31	numeric	4	5.1
LWAIT36	numeric	4	5.1
LWAITAVG	numeric	4	5.1
LWAITMAX	numeric	4	
LWAITMIN	numeric	4	
NRCPUS	numeric	4	
NRSAMPLE	numeric	4	
OUT0	numeric	4	5.1
OUT1	numeric	4	5.1
OUT3	numeric	4	5.1
OUT5	numeric	4	5.1
OUT7	numeric	4	5.1
OUT9	numeric	4	5.1
OUT11	numeric	4	5.1
OUT16	numeric	4	5.1
OUT21	numeric	4	5.1
OUT26	numeric	4	5.1
OUT31	numeric	4	5.1
OUT36	numeric	4	5.1
OUTAVG	numeric	4	5.1
OUTMAX	numeric	4	
OUTMIN	numeric	4	
PCTCPBY0	numeric	4	5.1
PCTCPBY1	numeric	4	5.1
PCTCPUBY	numeric	4	5.1
READY0-15	numeric	4	5.1
READYAVG	numeric	4	5.1
READYMAX	numeric	4	
READYMIN	numeric	4	
RELEASE	character	4	
SMFTIME	numeric	8	DATETIME19.2
STARTIME	numeric	8	DATETIME19.2
STC0	numeric	4	5.1
STC1	numeric	4	5.1
STC3	numeric	4	5.1
STC5	numeric	4	5.1
STC7	numeric	4	5.1
STC9	numeric	4	5.1
STC11	numeric	4	5.1
STC16	numeric	4	5.1
STC21	numeric	4	5.1
STC26	numeric	4	5.1
STC31	numeric	4	5.1
STC36	numeric	4	5.1
STCAVG	numeric	4	5.1
STCMAX	numeric	4	
STCMIN	numeric	4	
SUPATERN	character	14	HEX28.

SYSTEM	character	4	
TSO0	numeric	4	5.1
TSO1	numeric	4	5.1
TSO3	numeric	4	5.1
TSO5	numeric	4	5.1
TSO7	numeric	4	5.1
TSO9	numeric	4	5.1
TSO11	numeric	4	5.1
TSO16	numeric	4	5.1
TSO21	numeric	4	5.1
TSO26	numeric	4	5.1
TSO31	numeric	4	5.1
TSO36	numeric	4	5.1
TSOAVG	numeric	4	5.1
TSOMAX	numeric	4	
TSOMIN	numeric	4	
VERSION	character	2	
WAIT0	numeric	4	5.1
WAIT1	numeric	4	5.1
WAIT3	numeric	4	5.1
WAIT5	numeric	4	5.1
WAIT7	numeric	4	5.1
WAIT9	numeric	4	5.1
WAIT11	numeric	4	5.1
WAIT16	numeric	4	5.1
WAIT21	numeric	4	5.1
WAIT26	numeric	4	5.1
WAIT31	numeric	4	5.1
WAIT36	numeric	4	5.1
WAITAVG	numeric	4	5.1
WAITMAX	numeric	4	
WAITMIN	numeric	4	

```
**********MEMBER=TYPE7072*********************************;
DATA TYPE70
           (KEEP=BATCH0 BATCH1 BATCH3 BATCH5 BATCH7 BATCH9
                 BATCH11 BATCH16 BATCH21 BATCH26 BATCH31
                 BATCH36 BATCHAVG BATCHMAX BATCHMIN
                 CAI0-CAI1 CPUSER0-CPUSER1 CPUTYPE
                 CPUWAIT0-CPUWAIT1 CPUWAITM CYCLE DURATM
                 IN0 IN1 IN3 IN5 IN7 IN9
                 IN11 IN16 IN21 IN26 IN31
                 IN36 INAVG INMAX INMIN
                 LRDY0 LRDY1 LRDY3 LRDY5 LRDY7 LRDY9
                 LRDY11 LRDY16 LRDY21 LRDY26 LRDY31
                 LRDY36 LRDYAVG LRDYMAX LRDYMIN
                 LWAIT0 LWAIT1 LWAIT3 LWAIT5 LWAIT7 LWAIT9
                 LWAIT11 LWAIT16 LWAIT21 LWAIT26 LWAIT31
                 LWAIT36 LWAITAVG LWAITMAX LWAITMIN
                 NRCPUS NRSAMPLE
                 OUT0 OUT1 OUT3 OUT5 OUT7 OUT9
                 OUT11 OUT16 OUT21 OUT26 OUT31
                 OUT36 OUTAVG OUTMAX OUTMIN
                 PCTCPBY0-PCTCPBY1 PCTCPUBY
                 READY0-READY15 READYAVG READYMAX READYMIN
                 RELEASE SMFTIME STARTIME
                 STC0 STC1 STC3 STC5 STC7 STC9
```

```
                    STC11 STC16 STC21 STC26 STC31
                    STC36 STCAVG STCMAX STCMIN
                    SUPATERN SYSTEM
                    TSO0 TSO1 TSO3 TSO5 TSO7 TSO9
                    TSO11 TSO16 TSO21 TSO26 TSO31
                    TSO36 TSOAVG TSOMAX TSOMIN
                    VERSION
                    WAIT0 WAIT1 WAIT3 WAIT5 WAIT7 WAIT9
                    WAIT11 WAIT16 WAIT21 WAIT26 WAIT31
                    WAIT36 WAITAVG WAITMAX WAITMIN)
        TYPE72
                 (KEEP=ACTIVETM CPUCOEFF CPURFC CPUSRBTM CPUTCBTM CPUTM
                    CPUTYPE CPUUNITS CYCLE DOMAIN DURATM ELAPSTM ERV
                    FLAGS72 HIGHPG IOCCOEFF IOCRFC IOUNITS IPSNAME
                    MSOCOEFF MSOUNITS OBJCTIVE PERFGRP
                    PERIOD RELEASE RESIDTM SERVICE SMFTIME
                    SRBCOEFF SRBUNITS SSQELAP STARTIME SU_SEC
                    SWAPSEQ SYSTEM TRANS TSLGROUP VERSION WKLOAD);
  LENGTH DEFAULT=4 SMFTIME STARTIME 8;
  FORMAT SMFTIME STARTIME                        DATETIME19.2
        ACTIVETM CPUTCBTM CPUSRBTM CPUTM CPUWAITM DURATM
        CPUWAIT0-CPUWAIT1 DURATM ELAPSTM RESIDTM      TIME12.2
        FLAGS72                                  HEX2.
        CPUTYPE                                  HEX4.
        CPUSER0-CPUSER1                          $HEX6.
        SUPATERN                                 $HEX28.
        BATCH0 BATCH1 BATCH3 BATCH5 BATCH7 BATCH9 BATCH11
        BATCH16 BATCH21 BATCH26 BATCH31 BATCH36 BATCHAVG
        IN0 IN1 IN3 IN5 IN7 IN9 IN11
        IN16 IN21 IN26 IN31 IN36 INAVG
        LRDY0 LRDY1 LRDY3 LRDY5 LRDY7 LRDY9 LRDY11
        LRDY16 LRDY21 LRDY26 LRDY31 LRDY36 LRDYAVG
        LWAIT0 LWAIT1 LWAIT3 LWAIT5 LWAIT7 LWAIT9 LWAIT11
        LWAIT16 LWAIT21 LWAIT26 LWAIT31 LWAIT36 LWAITAVG
        OUT0 OUT1 OUT3 OUT5 OUT7 OUT9 OUT11
        OUT16 OUT21 OUT26 OUT31 OUT36 OUTAVG
        PCTCPBY0-PCTCPBY1 PCTCPUBY READY0-READY15 READYAVG
        STC0 STC1 STC3 STC5 STC7 STC9 STC11
        STC16 STC21 STC26 STC31 STC36 STCAVG
        TSO0 TSO1 TSO3 TSO5 TSO7 TSO9 TSO11
        TSO16 TSO21 TSO26 TSO31 TSO36 TSOAVG
        WAIT0 WAIT1 WAIT3 WAIT5 WAIT7 WAIT9 WAIT11
        WAIT16 WAIT21 WAIT26 WAIT31 WAIT36 WAITAVG WKLOAD 5.1;
   INFILE SMF STOPOVER LENGTH=LENGTH COL=COL RECFM=VBS LRECL=32756;
   INPUT @2 ID PIB1. @;
  IF ID=70 OR ID=72 THEN GOTO TYPE7072;
    DELETE;
  TYPE7072:
    IF ID=72 THEN GOTO TYPE72;
    INPUT @3 SMFTIME SMFSTAMP8. @11 SYSTEM $4.
          @17 STARTIME PDTIME4. @21 STARDATE PD4. @25 DURATM PD4.
          @29 CPUTYPE PIB2. @33 NRSAMPLE PIB4. @37 VERSION $2.
          @41 RELEASE $4. @45 CYCLE PD4. @;
  * FOLLOWING CODE DEFINES THE VARIABLE SU_SEC, WHICH IS RETAINED;
  * FROM THE TYPE 70 AND USED IN THE TYPE 72 CODE TO CONVERT;
  * CPUUNITS TO CPU TIME;
  * SET SU_SEC FROM CPUTYPE FOR CONVERSION OF CPU SERVICE TO SAS TIMES;
  * THERE ARE SEVERAL DIFFERENT SOURCES OF DATA FOR CONVERSION;
  * PROCESSOR (VALUE)   SU_SEC   SRM SEC/REAL SEC   CPU DEPENDENT VALUE;
  *   3033    12339    261.3     6.250               160            ;
  *   3032    12338    166.0     3.968               252            ;
  *   3031    12337     64.2     1.529               654            ;
  *   168      360     151.0     3.597               278            ;
  *   165      357     125.0     2.976               336            ;
```

```
*  158          344        51.2        1.220                   820              ;
*  155-2        341        42.0        1.000                  1000              ;
*  148          328        29.0*        .690*                 1542*             ;
*  145          325        24.0         .571                  1750              ;
*         * THE 148 VALUES ARE BASED ON INTERPOLATION;
 IF CPUTYPE=12339 THEN SU_SEC=261.3;
 IF CPUTYPE=12338 THEN SU_SEC=166.0;
 IF CPUTYPE=12337 THEN SU_SEC=64.2;
 IF CPUTYPE=360   THEN SU_SEC=151;
 IF CPUTYPE=357   THEN SU_SEC=125;
 IF CPUTYPE=344   THEN SU_SEC=51.2;
 IF CPUTYPE=341   THEN SU_SEC=42.0;
 IF CPUTYPE=328   THEN SU_SEC=29;
 IF CPUTYPE=325   THEN SU_SEC=24;
   RETAIN CPUTYPE SU_SEC;
    STARTIME=DHMS(DATEJUL(STARDATE),0,0,STARTIME);
    DURATM=60*FLOOR(DURATM/100000)+MOD(DURATM,100000)/1000;
  INPUT @51 NRCPUS PIB2. @57 SUPATERN $14. +2 @;
    NRCPU=NRCPUS;
CPULOOP:
  INPUT CPUWAITM PIB8. CPUID PIB2. +1 CAI PIB1. +1 CPUSER $3. @;
*      EIGHT BYTES DIVIDED BY 4096 FOR BIT 51 =1 MICROSECONDS;
*      AND DIVIDED BY 1E6 TO CONVERT TO SECONDS (SAS TIME ALSO);
    CPUWAITM=CPUWAITM/(4096*1E6);
    PCTCPUBY=100*(DURATM-CPUWAITM)/DURATM;
  IF CPUID=1 THEN GOTO CPU1;
    CPUWAIT0=CPUWAITM;
    PCTCPBY0=PCTCPUBY;
    CAI0=CAI;
    CPUSER0=CPUSER;
  GOTO CPUCK;
CPU1:
    CPUWAIT1=CPUWAITM;
    PCTCPBY1=PCTCPUBY;
    CAI1=CAI;
    CPUSER1=CPUSER;
CPUCK:
   NRCPU=NRCPU-1;
  IF NRCPU>0 THEN GOTO CPULOOP;
    CPUWAITM=SUM(CPUWAIT0,CPUWAIT1);
    PCTCPUBY=(100*(NRCPUS*DURATM-CPUWAITM))/(NRCPUS*DURATM);
  INPUT READYMIN PIB2. READYMAX PIB2. READYAVG PIB4.
        (READY0-READY15) (PIB4.)
        INMIN PIB2. INMAX PIB2. INAVG PIB4.
        (IN0 IN1 IN3 IN5 IN7 IN9 IN11
        IN16 IN21 IN26 IN31 IN36) (PIB4.)
        OUTMIN PIB2. OUTMAX PIB2. OUTAVG PIB4.
        (OUT0 OUT1 OUT3 OUT5 OUT7 OUT9 OUT11
        OUT16 OUT21 OUT26 OUT31 OUT36) (PIB4.)
        WAITMIN PIB2. WAITMAX PIB2. WAITAVG PIB4.
        (WAIT0 WAIT1 WAIT3 WAIT5 WAIT7 WAIT9 WAIT11
        WAIT16 WAIT21 WAIT26 WAIT31 WAIT36) (PIB4.)
        BATCHMIN PIB2. BATCHMAX PIB2. BATCHAVG PIB4.
        (BATCH0 BATCH1 BATCH3 BATCH5 BATCH7 BATCH9 BATCH11
        BATCH16 BATCH21 BATCH26 BATCH31 BATCH36) (PIB4.)
        STCMIN PIB2. STCMAX PIB2. STCAVG PIB4.
        (STC0 STC1 STC3 STC5 STC7 STC9 STC11
        STC16 STC21 STC26 STC31 STC36) (PIB4.)
        TSOMIN PIB2. TSOMAX PIB2. TSOAVG PIB4.
        (TSO0 TSO1 TSO3 TSO5 TSO7 TSO9 TSO11
        TSO16 TSO21 TSO26 TSO31 TSO36) (PIB4.)@;
* TEST FOR MVS/SE ADDITIONS;
  IF LENGTH >= COL +111 THEN INPUT
        LRDYMIN PIB2. LRDYMAX PIB2. LRDYAVG PIB4.
```

```
        (LRDYØ LRDY1 LRDY3 LRDY5 LRDY7 LRDY9 LRDY11
         LRDY16 LRDY21 LRDY26 LRDY31 LRDY36) (PIB4.)
         LWAITMIN PIB2. LWAITMAX PIB2. LWAITAVG PIB4.
         (LWAITØ LWAIT1 LWAIT3 LWAIT5 LWAIT7 LWAIT9 LWAIT11
         LWAIT16 LWAIT21 LWAIT26 LWAIT31 LWAIT36) (PIB4.)@;
INVSAMP=100/NRSAMPLE;
READYAVG=READYAVG/NRSAMPLE;
READYØ=READYØ*INVSAMP;
READY1=READY1*INVSAMP;
READY2=READY2*INVSAMP;
READY3=READY3*INVSAMP;
READY4=READY4*INVSAMP;
READY5=READY5*INVSAMP;
READY6=READY6*INVSAMP;
READY7=READY7*INVSAMP;
READY8=READY8*INVSAMP;
READY9=READY9*INVSAMP;
READY10=READY10*INVSAMP;
READY11=READY11*INVSAMP;
READY12=READY12*INVSAMP;
READY13=READY13*INVSAMP;
READY14=READY14*INVSAMP;
READY15=READY15*INVSAMP;
INAVG=INAVG/NRSAMPLE;
INØ=INØ*INVSAMP;
IN1=IN1*INVSAMP;
IN3=IN3*INVSAMP;
IN5=IN5*INVSAMP;
IN7=IN7*INVSAMP;
IN9=IN9*INVSAMP;
IN11=IN11*INVSAMP;
IN16=IN16*INVSAMP;
IN21=IN21*INVSAMP;
IN26=IN26*INVSAMP;
IN31=IN31*INVSAMP;
IN36=IN36*INVSAMP;
OUTAVG=OUTAVG/NRSAMPLE;
OUTØ=OUTØ*INVSAMP;
OUT1=OUT1*INVSAMP;
OUT3=OUT3*INVSAMP;
OUT5=OUT5*INVSAMP;
OUT7=OUT7*INVSAMP;
OUT9=OUT9*INVSAMP;
OUT11=OUT11*INVSAMP;
OUT16=OUT16*INVSAMP;
OUT21=OUT21*INVSAMP;
OUT26=OUT26*INVSAMP;
OUT31=OUT31*INVSAMP;
OUT36=OUT36*INVSAMP;
WAITAVG=WAITAVG/NRSAMPLE;
WAITØ=WAITØ*INVSAMP;
WAIT1=WAIT1*INVSAMP;
WAIT3=WAIT3*INVSAMP;
WAIT5=WAIT5*INVSAMP;
WAIT7=WAIT7*INVSAMP;
WAIT9=WAIT9*INVSAMP;
WAIT11=WAIT11*INVSAMP;
WAIT16=WAIT16*INVSAMP;
WAIT21=WAIT21*INVSAMP;
WAIT26=WAIT26*INVSAMP;
WAIT31=WAIT31*INVSAMP;
WAIT36=WAIT36*INVSAMP;
BATCHAVG=BATCHAVG/NRSAMPLE;
BATCHØ=BATCHØ*INVSAMP;
BATCH1=BATCH1*INVSAMP;
```

```
        BATCH3=BATCH3*INVSAMP;
        BATCH5=BATCH5*INVSAMP;
        BATCH7=BATCH7*INVSAMP;
        BATCH9=BATCH9*INVSAMP;
        BATCH11=BATCH11*INVSAMP;
        BATCH16=BATCH16*INVSAMP;
        BATCH21=BATCH21*INVSAMP;
        BATCH26=BATCH26*INVSAMP;
        BATCH31=BATCH31*INVSAMP;
        BATCH36=BATCH36*INVSAMP;
        STCAVG=STCAVG/NRSAMPLE;
        STC0=STC0*INVSAMP;
        STC1=STC1*INVSAMP;
        STC3=STC3*INVSAMP;
        STC5=STC5*INVSAMP;
        STC7=STC7*INVSAMP;
        STC9=STC9*INVSAMP;
        STC11=STC11*INVSAMP;
        STC16=STC16*INVSAMP;
        STC21=STC21*INVSAMP;
        STC26=STC26*INVSAMP;
        STC31=STC31*INVSAMP;
        STC36=STC36*INVSAMP;
        TSOAVG=TSOAVG/NRSAMPLE;
        TSO0=TSO0*INVSAMP;
        TSO1=TSO1*INVSAMP;
        TSO3=TSO3*INVSAMP;
        TSO5=TSO5*INVSAMP;
        TSO7=TSO7*INVSAMP;
        TSO9=TSO9*INVSAMP;
        TSO11=TSO11*INVSAMP;
        TSO16=TSO16*INVSAMP;
        TSO21=TSO21*INVSAMP;
        TSO26=TSO26*INVSAMP;
        TSO31=TSO31*INVSAMP;
        TSO36=TSO36*INVSAMP;
IF  LRDYAVG=. THEN GOTO OUT70;
        LRDYAVG=LRDYAVG/NRSAMPLE;
        LRDY0=LRDY0*INVSAMP;
        LRDY1=LRDY1*INVSAMP;
        LRDY3=LRDY3*INVSAMP;
        LRDY5=LRDY5*INVSAMP;
        LRDY7=LRDY7*INVSAMP;
        LRDY9=LRDY9*INVSAMP;
        LRDY11=LRDY11*INVSAMP;
        LRDY16=LRDY16*INVSAMP;
        LRDY21=LRDY21*INVSAMP;
        LRDY26=LRDY26*INVSAMP;
        LRDY31=LRDY31*INVSAMP;
        LRDY36=LRDY36*INVSAMP;
        LWAITAVG=LWAITAVG/NRSAMPLE;
        LWAIT0=LWAIT0*INVSAMP;
        LWAIT1=LWAIT1*INVSAMP;
        LWAIT3=LWAIT3*INVSAMP;
        LWAIT5=LWAIT5*INVSAMP;
        LWAIT7=LWAIT7*INVSAMP;
        LWAIT9=LWAIT9*INVSAMP;
        LWAIT11=LWAIT11*INVSAMP;
        LWAIT16=LWAIT16*INVSAMP;
        LWAIT21=LWAIT21*INVSAMP;
        LWAIT26=LWAIT26*INVSAMP;
        LWAIT31=LWAIT31*INVSAMP;
        LWAIT36=LWAIT36*INVSAMP;
OUT70:
    OUTPUT TYPE70;
    RETURN;
```

```
TYPE72:
   INPUT @3 SMFTIME SMFSTAMP8. @11 SYSTEM $4.
         @17 STARTIME PDTIME4. @21 STARDATE PD4. @25 DURATM PD4.
         @45 CYCLE PD4. @;
      STARTIME=DHMS(DATEJUL(STARDATE),0,0,STARTIME);
      DURATM=60*FLOOR(DURATM/100000)+MOD(DURATM,100000)/1000;
   INPUT @30 FLAGS72 PIB1. @31 PERFGRP PIB2. @37 VERSION $2.
         @41 RELEASE $4. @51 NRPERIOD PIB2. @55 HIGHPG PIB2.
         @57 IPSNAME $8. @65 IOCRFC 3. @68 CPURFC 3.
         @71 ERV 6. @77 IOCCOEFF 4. @81 CPUCOEFF 4. @85 MSOCOEFF 4. @;
      PERIOD=1;
  IF VERSION<='03' THEN GOTO LOOP72;
   INPUT @89 SRBCOEFF 4. @;
  IF VERSION<='04' THEN GOTO LOOP72;
   INPUT @93 OPTNAME $8. @101 ICSNAME $8. @109 SUBSYSTM $4.
         @113 CLASS72 $10. @123 USER72 $10. @133 TRANNAME $10. @;
LOOP72:
  IF NRPERIOD=0 THEN RETURN;
   INPUT TRANS PIB4. ACTIVETM PIB4. SERVICE PIB4. ELAPSTM PIB4.
         WKLOAD PIB4. MSOUNITS PIB4. IOUNITS PIB4. CPUUNITS PIB4.
         RESIDTM PIB4. SWAPSEQ PIB4. DOMAIN PIB2. OBJCTIVE PIB1.
         TSLGROUP PIB1. @;
      WKLOAD=WKLOAD/256;
* CONVERT ACTIVE, ELAPSED,  AND RESIDENT INTO SAS TIMES (SECONDS);
      ACTIVETM=ACTIVETM*1024/(1E6);
      ELAPSTM=ELAPSTM*1024/(1E6);
      RESIDTM=RESIDTM*1024/(1E6);
      CPUTCBTM=CPUUNITS/(CPUCOEFF*SU_SEC);
  IF VERSION <='03' THEN GOTO OUT72;
   INPUT SRBUNITS PIB4. SSQELAP PIB8. @;
      CPUSRBTM=SRBUNITS/(SRBCOEFF*SU_SEC);
OUT72:
   CPUTM=SUM(CPUTCBTM,CPUSRBTM);
  IF SERVICE NE 0 THEN OUTPUT TYPE72;
    NRPERIOD=NRPERIOD-1;
    PERIOD=PERIOD+1;
   GOTO LOOP72;
```

Note: With MVS SE2, SP1 and later, report performance groups, when defined, will create TYPE72 records for each of the RPGNS. To SMF, there is no difference between a control performance group and a report performance group. Thus, it is not correct to take the sum of the TYPE72 data as the cpu time in the PERFGRPS. It is, rather, necessary to exclude the report performance groups from any cpu analysis (because the cpu time in the RPGN's is already included in the control PGN's TYPE72 record).

The TYPE71 Data Set: Paging and Swapping Activity

The TYPE71 data set contains one observation for every type 71 SMF record, written at each RMF interval. The type 71 records contain statistics on paging activity. Paging statistics that are more meaningful as rates are converted in TYPE71 to units per second. Additional statistics are provided (usually the minimum, maximum and average values) about the paging resources available, such as fixed frames, slots, etc. TYPE71 also describes the swap rate for the various types of swaps that can occur.

TYPE71 is important in resource analysis, since it can identify whether or not real memory is limiting performance and whether the IPS is properly specified by analysis of swap types and rates.

Contents

ASMNVSC Number of local page data set slots allocated to non-VIO private area pages.

ASMSLOTS Total number of local page data set slots.

ASMSLOTX Number of local page data set slots that have not been allocated.

ASMVSC Number of local page data set slots allocated to VIO private area pages.

CSAFXAV MVS/SE only. Average number of CSA fixed frames. (See LPCSFXAV.)

CSAFXMN MVS/SE only. Minimum number of CSA fixed frames. (See LPDCFXMN.)

CSAFXMX MVS/SE only. Maximum number of CSA fixed frames. (See LPCSFXMX.)

CSAPGAV MVS/SE only. Average number of CSA pagable frames. (See LPCSPGAV.)

CSAPGMN MVS/SE only. Minimum number of CSA pagable frames. (See LPCSPGMN.)

CSAPGMX   MVS/SE only. Maximum number of CSA pagable frames. (See LPCSPGMX.)

CYCLE   Sample cycle length (in milliseconds). At each CYCLE, a sampling observation is made.

DURATM   Duration of this RMF interval. At the end of each DURAT, all data gathered and sampled is written to SMF.

FIXEDAV   Average number of private area fixed frames.

FIXEDMN   Minimum number of private area fixed frames.

FIXEDMX   Maximum number of private area fixed frames.

LPAFXAV   MVS/SE only. Average number of LPA fixed frames.

LPAFXMN   MVS/SE only. Minimum number of LPA fixed frames.

LPAFXMX   MVS/SE only. Maximum number of LPA fixed frames.

LPAGINS   MVS/SE only. Non-VIO, non-swap page-in rate (per second) in the LPA.

LPAPGAV   MVS/SE only. Average number of LPA pagable frames.

LPAPGMN   MVS/SE only. Minimum number of LPA pagable frames.

LPAPGMX   MVS/SE only. Maximum number of LPA pagable frames.

LPARECLM   MVS/SE only. Non-VIO, non-swap reclaim rate (per second) in the LPA.

LPCSFXAV   MVS(non-SE). Average number of CSA+LPA fixed frames. MVS/SE: sum of LPAFXAV and CSAFXAV.

LPCSFXMN   MVS(non-SE). Minimum number of CSA+LPA fixed frames. MVS/SE: sum of LPAFXMN and CSAFXMN.

LPCSFXMX   MVS(non-SE). Maximum number of CSA+LPA fixed frames. MVS/SE: sum of LPAFXMX and CSAFXMX.

LPSWRCLM   MVS/SE only. Non-VIO swap reclaim rate (per second) in the LPA.

LSQAFXAV   MVS/SE only. Average number of LSQA fixed frames.

LSQAFXMN   MVS/SE only. Minimum number of LSQA fixed frames.

LSQAFXMX   MVS/SE only. Maximum number of LSQA fixed frames.

LSWBEG   MVS/SE only. Number of logical swap-outs at the beginning of the interval.

LSWEND   MVS/SE only. Number of logical swap-outs at the end of the interval.

NRSAMPLE   Number of samples taken in this RMF interval. (Samples are taken at CYCLE intervals.)

PAGBLAV   Average number of private area pagable frames.

PAGBLMN   Minimum number of private area pagable frames.

PAGBLMX   Maximum number of private area pagable frames.

PAGING   Total paging rate (per second) (Non-VIO non-swap page-ins + pageouts).

PFRATE   Total page fault rate (per second). (Non-VIO non-swap page-ins + reclaims).

PRVFXAV   Average number of private area fixed frames.

PRVFXMN   Minimum number of private area fixed frames.

PRVFXMX   Maximum number of private area fixed frames.

PRVPGAV   Average number of private area pagable frames.

PRVPGMN   Minimum number of private area pagable frames.

PRVPGMX   Maximum number of private area pagable frames.

PVTAFC   Number of available page frames in real storage at the end of the interval.

PVTAFCAV   Average number of unused page frames.

PVTAFCMN   Minimum number of unused page frames.

PVTAFCMX   Maximum number of unused page frames.

PVTCAIN   Non-VIO page-in rate (per second) in CSA.

PVTCAOUT   Non-VIO page-out rate (per second) in CSA.

PVTCAREC   Non-VIO reclaim rate (per second) in CSA.

PVTFPFN   Number of page frames in nucleus.

PVTNPIN   Total non-VIO non-swap page-in rate (per second). This includes page-ins required through page faults, specific page requests, and page fixes. It excludes page reclaims, VIO, and swaps.

PVTNPOUT   Total non-VIO non-swap page-out rate (per second).

PVTNPREC   Total non-VIO page reclaim rate (per second).

PVTPOOL   Number of page frames defined in real storage. (This does not include frames occupied by the nucleus (see PVTFPFN), nor frames marked as bad or offline.

PVTSPIN   Total swap-in page rate (per second) including LSQA, fixed pages, and active pages when swapped in. Excludes reclaims.

PVTSPOUT   Total swap-out page rate (per second).

PVTVAMI   VIO page-in rate (per second).

PVTVAMO   VIO page-out rate (per second).

PVTVAMR   VIO reclaim rate (per second).

RELEASE   Operating system release number and level (e.g., 0370 for Release 3 level 7, or 3.7)

SLOTLOMN   Minimum total number of local page data set slots.

SLOTLOMX   Maximum total number of local page data set slots.

SLOTNGAV   Average number of unusable local page data set slots.

SLOTNGMN   Minimum number of unusable local page data set slots.

SLOTNGMX   Maximum number of unusable local page data set slots.

SLOTNVAV   Average number of local page data set slots allocated to non-VIO private area pages.

SLOTNVMN   Minimum number of local page data set slots allocated to non-VIO private area pages.

SLOTNVMX   Maximum number of local page data set slots allocated to non-VIO private area pages.

SLOTUNAV   Average number of local page data set slots that are not allocated.

SLOTUNMN   Minimum number of local page data set slots that are not allocated.

SLOTUNMX   Maximum number of local page data set slots that are not allocated.

SLOTVIAV   Average number of local page data set slots that are allocated to VIO.

SLOTVIMN   Minimum number of local page data set slots that are allocated to VIO.

SLOTVIMX   Maximum number of local page data set slots that are allocated to VIO.

SMFTIME   Approximate interval end time stamp (actually, the time the record was moved to the buffer).

SQAFXAV   Average number of SQA fixed frames.

SQAFXMN   Minimum number of SQA fixed frames.

SQAFXMX   Maximum number of SQA fixed frames.

STARTIME   Beginning of RMF interval time stamp.

SWAPAS   Number of swap-outs because 70% of all local page slots are allocated (i.e., auxiliary storage shortage).

SWAPDW   Number of swap-outs because of detected wait (i.e., address space waited too long in a wait state without issuing the WAIT, LONG=YES macro).

SWAPEX   Number of exchange swaps (one user in a domain is swapped out to allow another user in the same domain with higher workload level to be swapped in).

SWAPLGPY   MVS/SE only. Number of logically swapped-out address spaces that had to be physically swapped out before they were ready to execute again.

SWAPNQ   Number of swap-outs required to swap in a user that is enqueued upon a needed system resource.

SWAPNS   MVS/SE only. Numbers of swap-outs because an address space has been made non-swappable.

SWAPRS   Number of swap-outs due to a shortage of real pagable frames.

SWAPS   Total swap rate (per second).

SWAPSHRT   MVS/SE only. Number of logical swap-out candidates because of a short input terminal wait time.

SWAPTI   MVS. Number of swap-outs due to a terminal waiting for input.
                MVS/SE. Number of logical swap-out candidates due to a terminal waiting for input.

SWAPTO   MVS: Number of swap-outs due to a terminal waiting for output buffers.
                MVS/SE: Number of logical swap-out candidates due to a terminal waiting for output buffers.

SWAPUS   Number of unilateral swaps (i.e., swap because the actual multiprogramming level for a domain exceeded the target multiprogramming level.)

SWAPVR   Number of swap-outs because V=R or non-swappable was specified in the Program Properties Table.

SWAPWT   Number of swap-outs caused by user request wait states.

SYSTEM   Identification of this system.

VERSION   RMF version number.

value	meaning
01	MF/1
02	RMF Version 1
03	RMF Version 2
04	RMF Version 2 Release 2 (SE)
05	RMF Version 2 Release 2 Feature (SE2)

variable	type	length	format
ASMNVSC	numeric	4	
ASMSLOTS	numeric	4	
ASMSLOTX	numeric	4	
ASMVSC	numeric	4	
CSAFXAV	numeric	4	
CSAFXMN	numeric	4	
CSAFXMX	numeric	4	
CSAPGAV	numeric	4	
CSAPGMN	numeric	4	
CSAPGMX	numeric	4	
CYCLE	numeric	4	
DURATM	numeric	4	TIME12.2
FIXEDAV	numeric	4	
FIXEDMN	numeric	4	
FIXEDMX	numeric	4	
LWAITAVG	numeric	4	
LPAFXAV	numeric	4	
LPAFXMN	numeric	4	
LPAFXMN	numeric	4	
LPAGINS	numeric	4	5.1
LPAPGAV	numeric	4	
LPAPGMN	numeric	4	
LPAPGMX	numeric	4	
LPARECLM	numeric	4	5.1
LPCSFXAV	numeric	4	
LPCSFXMN	numeric	4	
LPCSFXMX	numeric	4	
LPSWRCLM	numeric	4	5.1
LSQAFXAV	numeric	4	
LSQAFXMN	numeric	4	
LSQAFXMX	numeric	4	
LSWBEG	numeric	4	
LSWEND	numeric	4	
NRSAMPLE	numeric	4	
PAGBLAV	numeric	4	
PAGBLMN	numeric	4	
PAGBLMX	numeric	4	
PAGING	numeric	4	5.1
PFRATE	numeric	4	5.1
PRVFXAV	numeric	4	
PRVFXMN	numeric	4	
PRVFXMX	numeric	4	
PRVPGAV	numeric	4	

PRVPGMN	numeric	4	
PRVPGMX	numeric	4	
PVTAFC	numeric	4	
PVTAFCAV	numeric	4	
PVTAFCMN	numeric	4	
PVTAFCMX	numeric	4	
PVTCAIN	numeric	4	5.1
PVTCAOUT	numeric	4	5.1
PVTCAREC	numeric	4	5.1
PVTFPFN	numeric	4	
PVTNPIN	numeric	4	5.1
PVTNPOUT	numeric	4	5.1
PVTNPREC	numeric	4	5.1
PVTPOOL	numeric	4	
PVTSPIN	numeric	4	5.1
PVTSPOUT	numeric	4	5.1
PVTAMI	numeric	4	5.1
PVTVAMO	numeric	4	5.1
PVTVAMR	numeric	4	5.1
RELEASE	numeric	4	
SLOTLOMN	numeric	4	
SLOTLOMX	numeric	4	
SLOTNGAV	numeric	4	
SLOTNGMN	numeric	4	
SLOTMGMX	numeric	4	
SLOTNVAV	numeric	4	
SLOTNVMN	numeric	4	
SLOTNVMX	numeric	4	
SLOTUNAV	numeric	4	
SLOTUNMN	numeric	4	
SLOTUNMX	numeric	4	
SLOTVIAV	numeric	4	
SLOTVIMN	numeric	4	
SLOTVIMX	numeric	4	
SMFTIME	numeric	8	DATETIME19.2
SQAFXAV	numeric	4	
SQAFXMN	numeric	4	
SQAFXMX	numeric	4	
STARTIME	numeric	8	DATETIME19.2
SWAPAS	numeric	4	
SWAPDW	numeric	4	
SWAPEX	numeric	4	
SWAPLGPY	numeric	4	
SWAPNQ	numeric	4	
SWAPNS	numeric	4	
SWAPRS	numeric	4	
SWAPS	numeric	4	5.1
SWAPSHRT	numeric	4	
SWAPTI	numeric	4	
SWAPTO	numeric	4	
SWAPUS	numeric	4	
SWAPVR	numeric	4	
SWAPWT	numeric	4	
SYSTEM	character	4	
VERSION	character	2	

```
**********MEMBER=TYPE71********************************;
DATA TYPE71
                (KEEP=ASMNVSC ASMSLOTS ASMSLOTX ASMVSC CSAFXAV
                      CSAFXMN CSAFXMX CSAPGAV CSAPGMN CSAPGMX
                      CYCLE DURATM FIXEDAV FIXEDMN FIXEDMX
                      LPAFXAV LPAFXMN LPAFXMX LPAGINS LPAPGAV
                      LPAPGMN LPAPGMX LPARECLM LPCSFXAV LPCSFXMN
                      LPCSFXMX LPSWRCLM LSQAFXAV LSQAFXMN LSQAFXMX
                      LSWBEG LSWEND NRSAMPLE PAGBLAV PAGBLMN
                      PAGBLMX PAGING PFRATE PRVFXAV PRVFXMN
                      PRVFXMX PRVPGAV PRVPGMN PRVPGMX PVTAFC
                      PVTAFCAV PVTAECMN PVTAFCMX PVTCAIN PVTCAOUT
                      PVTCAREC PVTFPFN PVTNPIN PVTNPOUT PVTNPREC
                      PVTPOOL PVTSPIN PVTSPOUT PVTVAMI
                      PVTVAMO PVTVAMR RELEASE SLOTLOMN
                      SLOTLOMX SLOTNGAV SLOTNGMN SLOTNGMX SLOTNVAV
                      SLOTNVMN SLOTNVMX SLOTUNAV SLOTUNMN SLOTUNMX
                      SLOTVIAV SLOTVIMN SLOTVIMX SMFTIME SQAFXAV
                      SQAFXMN SQAFXMX STARTIME SWAPAS SWAPDW SWAPEX
                      SWAPLGPY SWAPNQ SWAPNS SWAPRS SWAPS SWAPSHRT
                      SWAPTI SWAPTO SWAPUS SWAPVR SWAPWT SYSTEM VERSION)
LENGTH DEFAULT=4 SMFTIME STARTIME 8;
FORMAT SMFTIME STARTIME                               DATETIME19.2
       DURATM                                         TIME12.2
       PAGING PFRATE PVTNPIN PVTNPOUT PVTNPREC SWAPS
       PVTSPIN PVTSPOUT PVTVAMI PVTVAMO PVTVAMR PVTCAIN
       PVTCAOUT PVTCAREC LPAGINS LPARECLM LPSWRCLM          5.1;
  INFILE SMF STOPOVER LENGTH=LENGTH COL=COL RECFM=VBS LRECL=32756;
  INPUT @2 ID PIB1. @;
 IF ID=71;
  GOTO TYPE71;
TYPE71:
   INPUT @3 SMFTIME SMFSTAMP8. @11 SYSTEM $4.
        @17 STARTIME PDTIME4. @21 STARDATE PD4. @25 DURATM PD4.
        @33 NRSAMPLE PIB4. @37 VERSION $2. @41 RELEASE $4.
        @45 CYCLE PD4. @;
    STARTIME=DHMS(DATEJUL(STARDATE),0,0,STARTIME);
    DURATM=60*FLOOR(DURATM/100000)+MOD(DURATM,100000)/1000;
   INPUT   @53 PVTNPIN  PIB4.  @57 PVTNPOUT PIB4.
        @61 PVTNPREC PIB4. @65 SWAPS    PIB4. @69 PVTSPIN   PIB4.
        @73 PVTSPOUT PIB4. @77 PVTVAMI  PIB4. @81 PVTVAMO   PIB4.
        @85 PVTVAMR  PIB4. @89 PVTCAIN  PIB4. @93 PVTCAOUT  PIB4.
        @97 PVTCAREC PIB4. @;
  IF VERSION>='04' THEN INPUT @101 LPAGINS PIB4. @105 LPARECLM PIB4.
           @109 LPSWRCLM PIB4. @;
       INPUT @113 PVTAFC  PIB4. @117 PVTPOOL  PIB4.
        @121 ASMSLOTS PIB4. @125 ASMVSC  PIB4. @129 ASMNVSC  PIB4.
        @133 ASMSLOTX PIB4. @137 PVTFPFN  PIB4. @141 PVTAFCMN PIB4.
        @145 PVTAFCMX PIB4. @149 PVTAFCAV PIB4. @153 CSAPGMN  PIB4.
        @157 CSAPGMX  PIB4. @161 CSAPGAV  PIB4. @165 PRVPGMN  PIB4.
        @169 PRVPGMX  PIB4. @173 PRVPGAV  PIB4. @177 PAGBLMN  PIB4.
        @181 PAGBLMX  PIB4. @185 PAGBLAV  PIB4. @189 SQAFXMN  PIB4.
        @193 SQAFXMX  PIB4. @197 SQAFXAV  PIB4. @201 CSAFXMN  PIB4.
        @205 CSAFXMX  PIB4. @209 CSAFXAV  PIB4. @213 PRVFXMN  PIB4.
        @217 PRVFXMX  PIB4. @221 PRVFXAV  PIB4. @225 FIXEDMN  PIB4.
        @229 FIXEDMX  PIB4. @233 FIXEDAV  PIB4. @237 SLOTUNMN PIB4.
        @241 SLOTUNMX PIB4. @245 SLOTUNAV PIB4. @249 SLOTVIMN PIB4.
        @253 SLOTVIMX PIB4. @257 SLOTVIAV PIB4. @261 SLOTNVMN PIB4.
        @265 SLOTNVMX PIB4. @269 SLOTNVAV PIB4. @273 SLOTNGMN PIB4.
        @277 SLOTNGMX PIB4. @281 SLOTNGAV PIB4. @285 SLOTLOMN PIB4.
        @289 SLOTLOMX PIB4. +4 @297 SWAPTI   PIB4.
        @301 SWAPWT   PIB4. @305 SWAPDW   PIB4. @309 SWAPUS   PIB4.
        @313 SWAPVR   PIB4. @317 SWAPAS   PIB4. @321 SWAPRS   PIB4.
        @325 SWAPEX   PIB4. @329 SWAPNQ   PIB4. @333 SWAPTO   PIB4.@;
   INVTIME=1/DURATM;
```

```
   PVTNPIN =PVTNPIN *INVTIME;
   PVTNPOUT=PVTNPOUT*INVTIME;
   PVTNPREC=PVTNPREC*INVTIME;
   SWAPS=   SWAPS   *INVTIME;
   PVTSPIN =PVTSPIN *INVTIME;
   PVTSPOUT=PVTSPOUT*INVTIME;
   PVTVAMI =PVTVAMI *INVTIME;
   PVTVAMO =PVTVAMO *INVTIME;
   PVTVAMR =PVTVAMR *INVTIME;
   PVTCAIN =PVTCAIN *INVTIME;
   PVTCAOUT=PVTCAOUT*INVTIME;
   PVTCAREC=PVTCAREC*INVTIME;
   PAGING=PVTNPIN+PVTNPOUT;
   PFRATE=PVTNPIN+PVTNPREC;
 IF VERSION>='04' THEN GOTO TYPE71SE;
   LPCSPGMN=CSAPGMN;
   LPCSPGMX=CSAPGMX;
   LPCSPGAV=CSAPGAV;
   LPCSFXMN=CSAFXMN;
   LPCSFXMX=CSAFXMX;
   LPCSFXAV=CSAFXAV;
   CSAPGMN=.;
   CSAPGMX=.;
   CSAPGAV=.;
   CSAFXMN=.;
   CSAFXMX=.;
   CSAFXAV=.;
  GOTO OUT71;
TYPE71SE:
  INPUT  @337 SWAPNS   PIB4. @341 SWAPSHRT PIB4. @345 SWAPLGPY PIB4.
         @349 LSWBEG   PIB4. @353 LSWEND   PIB4. @357 LPAPGMN  PIB4.
         @361 LPAPGMX  PIB4. @365 LPAPGAV  PIB4. @369 LPAFXMN  PIB4.
         @373 LPAFXMX  PIB4. @377 LPAFXAV  PIB4. @381 LSQAFXMN PIB4.
         @385 LSQAFXMX PIB4. @389 LSQAFXAV PIB4. @;
   LPCSPGMN=LPAPGMN+CSAPGMN;
   LPCSPGMX=LPAPGMX+CSAPGMX;
   LPCSPGAV=LPAPGAV+CSAPGAV;
   LPCSFXMN=LPAFXMN+CSAFXMN;
   LPCSFXMX=LPAFXMX+CSAFXMX;
   LPCSFXAV=LPAFXAV+CSAFXAV;
   LPAGINS =LPAGINS *INVTIME;
   LPARECLM=LPARECLM*INVTIME;
   LPSWRCLM=LPSWRCLM*INVTIME;
OUT71:
  OUTPUT TYPE71;
  RETURN;
```

The TYPE72 Data Set: Workload Activity

The TYPE72 data set contains multiple observations for each type 72 SMF record, written at each RMF interval. The type 72 record contains multiple segments, one segment for each period of each performance group defined in the IPS. The TYPE72 data set contains one observation for each period of each performance group that received any service during the interval. Each observation contains the TCBCPU units (in MVS/SE, the SRBCPU units are also given) and the I/O and MSO units, along with the sum of the active resident times in this interval, and the sum of the elapsed times of tasks that ended transactions in this interval.

By retaining the CPU type from the previous type 70 record, it is possible to convert CPU service units to units of time, and thus TYPE72 provides complete data on usage of the CPU by each performance group. Thus the total utilization of the processor can be identified to elements of the installation's workload. See chapter 11, "Recovery of Batch CPU Time."

Contents

ACTIVETM   Transaction-active duration. This includes the total time that each transaction was in real storage plus any swapped-out time that the transaction was not in a long wait state. It does not include time between job steps for batch transactions.

CPUCOEFF   CPU TCB service definition coefficient (from Installation Performance Specification, IPS).

CPURFC   CPU resource factor coefficient (from IPS).

CPUSRBTM   CPU SRB duration used by this performance group (PER-FGRP) in this period (PERIOD) during this RMF interval.

CPUTCBTM   CPU TCB duration used by this performance group (PER-FGRP) in this period (PERIOD) during this RMF interval.

CPUTM   Sum of CPUTCBTM and CPUSRBTM.

CPUTYPE   CPU model number (e.g. 158, 168, 3033, etc.). Note that this is kept from the immediately preceding type 70 record since the CPUTYPE is not contained in the type 72 record. CPUTYPE is necessary to convert CPU service units to units of CPU time.

CPUUNITS CPU TCB service units delivered to this performance group in this period during this interval.

CYCLE Sample cycle length (in milliseconds). At each cycle, a sampling observation is made.

DOMAIN Domain number.

DURATM Duration of this RMF interval. At the end of each DURAT, all data gathered and sampled is written to SMF.

ELAPSTM Sum of elapsed duration of all transactions that ended in this performance group period.

ERV ERV resource manager coefficient (from IPS).

FLAGS72 MVS/SE only. Undocumented flag field.

HIGHPG Highest performance group number defined in IPS.

IOCCOEFF IOC service definition coefficient (from IPS).

IOCRFC IOC resource factor coefficient (from IPS).

IOUNITS I/O service units delivered to this performance group in this period during this interval.

IPSNAME Name of IPS member in SYS1.PARMLIB.

MSOCOEFF Main storage service definition coefficient.

MSOUNITS Main storage service units delivered to this performance group in this period during this interval.

NRSAMPLE Number of samples taken in this RMF interval (Samples are taken at CYCLE intervals.)

OBJECTIVE Performance objective number for this PERFGRP and PERIOD.

PERFGRP Performance group number.

PERIOD   Performance group (PG) period number.

RELEASE   Operating system release number and level (e.g., 0370 for Release 3 level 7, or 3.7)

RESIDTM   Transaction residency duration.

SERVICE   Total service units delivered to this performance group in this period during this interval.

SMFTIME   Approximate ending time stamp of interval (actually, the time the record is moved to SMF)

SRBCOEFF   MVS/SE only. SRB service definition coefficient (from IPS).

SRBUNITS   MVS/SE only. SRB service units delivered to this performance group in this PG period during this interval.

SSQELAP   MVS/SE only. Sum of the square of the elapsed times of all ended transactions in this PG period. Used to calculate standard deviation in RMF reports.

STARTIME   Beginning of RMF interval time stamp.

SU__SEC   Conversion coefficient set from CPUTYPE to convert CPU and SRB service units to CPU minutes.

SWAPSEQ   Number of swap seqences for this performance group in this period during this interval.

SYSTEM   System identification of this system.

TRANS   Number of transactions in the performance group period that ended in this interval.

TSLGROUP   MVS/SE only. Time slice group number.

VERSION   RMF version number.

value	meaning
01	MF/1
02	RMF Version 1
03	RMF Version 2
04	RMF Version 2 Release 2 (SE)
05	RMF Version 2 Release 2 Feature (SE2)

WKLOAD   Workload level of all transactions.

variable	type	length	format
ACTIVE	numeric	4	TIME12.2
COUCOEFF	numeric	4	
CPURFC	numeric	4	
CPUSRBTM	numeric	4	TIME12.2
CPUTCBTM	numeric	4	TIME12.2
CPUTM	numeric	4	TIME12.2
CPUTYPE	numeric	4	HEX4.
CPUUNITS	numeric	4	
CYCLE	numeric	4	
DOMAIN	numeric	4	
DURATM	numeric	4	TIME12.2
ELAPSTM	numeric	4	TIME12.2
ERV	numeric	4	
FLAGS72	numeric	4	HEX2.
HIGHPG	numeric	4	
IOCCOEFF	numeric	4	
IOCRFC	numeric	4	
IOUNITS	numeric	4	
IPSNAME	character	8	
MSOCOEFF	numeric	4	
MSOUNITS	numeric	4	
NRSAMPLE	numeric	4	
OBJECTIVE	numeric	4	
PERFGRP	numeric	4	
PERIOD	numeric	4	
RELEASE	character	4	
RESIDTM	numeric	4	TIME12.2
SERVICE	numeric	4	
SMFTIME	numeric	8	DATETIME19.2
SRBCOEFF	numeric	4	
SRBUNITS	numeric	4	
SSQELAP	numeric	4	
STARTIME	numeric	8	DATETIME19.2
SU_SEC	numeric	4	
SWAPSEQ	numeric	4	
SYSTEM	character	4	
TRANS	numeric	4	
TSLGROUP	numeric	4	
VERSION	character	2	
WKLOAD	numeric	4	

The TYPE72 data set is created concurrently with the TYPE70 data set; the SAS code is found in the TYPE70 appendix.

The TYPE73L Data Set:
Logical Channel Activity

The TYPE73L data set contains multiple observations for each type 73 SMF record. Type 73 SMF records are written at each RMF interval and contain multiple segments for each logical channel. There is one observation in TYPE73L for each logical channel segment in each type 73 SMF record. TYPE73L contains the total number of I/O requests started or queued (SIOCOUNT) and the percentage that were deferred (PCTDEFER) as well as the percentage of samples when the queue length for each logical channel was 0, 1, 2, 3, or 4 and over. Thus TYPE73L is the most valuable source of data on the overall I/O environment, since not only are I/O counts given, but delays due to non-availability of paths can also be seen.

Contents

AVGENQUE   Average number of requests enqueued for this logical channel.

CHANMAP   MVS only. Bit pattern of physical channels that are included in this logical channel. High-order bit is physical channel 0.

CHANMAP0   MVS/SE only. Bit pattern of physical channels that are included in this logical channel from CPU 0. High-order bit is physical channel 0.

CHANMAP1   MVS/SE only. Same as CHANMAP0 for CPU1.

CPUMAP   MVS only. Bit pattern of processors connected to this logical channel. High-order bit is CPU 0.

CYCLE   Sample cycle length (in milliseconds). At each CYCLE, a sampling observation is made.

C0ANYCH   Percent of samples when any physical channel was busy on CPU0.

C0BYWT   Percent of samples when any physical channel was busy on CPU0 and CPU0 was in a wait state.

C1ANYCH   Percent of samples when any physical channel was busy on CPU1.

C1BYWT　　Percent of samples when any physical channel was busy on CPU1 and CPU1 was in a wait state.

DEFCUBY　　MVS/SE only. Number of requests deferred because control unit busy.

DEFDEVBY　　MVS/SE only. Number of requests deferred because device busy.

DEFERED　　Total deferred requests for this logical channel in this RMF interval.

DEFLCHBY　　Number of requests deferred because of logical channel busy.

DEFPHYBY　　Number of requests deferred because of physical channel busy.

DURATM　　Duration of this RMF interval. At end of each DURAT, all data gathered and sampled is written to SMF.

FQCUBY　　MVS/SE only. Frequency counter for control unit busy deferred I/O requests.

FQDEVBY　　MVS/SE only. Frequency counter for device busy deferred I/O requests.

FQLCHRQ　　Frequency counter for logical channel busy deferred I/O requests.

FQPHYRQ　　Frequency counter for physical channel busy deferred I/O requests.

LCHAN　　Logical channel number.

LCI　　MVS/SE only. Logical channel configuration changed during the interval: blank or Y.

LPCHANBY　　MVS only. Percentage of samples when physical channel busy occurred.

LPPARTBY　　MVS only. Percentage of samples when physical channel partial busy occurred.

NRENQUES　　Total number of enqueued requests observed for the interval (at each sample, the current number of enqueued requests are added to this value).

NRSAMPLE   Number of samples taken in this RMF interval (samples are taken at LCYCLE intervals).

PCTDEFCU   MVS/SE only. Percent of total SIO count deferred due to control unit busy.

PCTDEFDV   MVS/SE only. Percent of total SIO count deferred due to device busy.

PCTDEFER   Percent of total SIO count deferred for any reason.

PCTDEFLC   Percent of total SIO count deferred for logical channel busy.

PCTDEFPY   Percent of total SIO count deferred for physical channel busy.

QUEUE0   Percent of samples when there were no requests queued for this logical channel.

QUEUE1-
QUEUE4   Percent of samples when there were [1, 2, 3, 4 or more] requests queued for this logical channel.

RELEASE   Operating system release number and level (e.g., 0370 for Release 3 Level 7, or 3.7).

SIOCOUNT   Total number of successful start I/Os.

SMFTIME   Approximate ending time stamp of RMF interval. (Actually, the time the record is moved to SMF.)

STARTIME   Beginning-of-RMF-interval time stamp.

SYSTEM   Identification of this system.

VERSION   RMF version number.

value	meaning
01	MF/1
02	RMF Version 1
03	RMF Version 2
04	RMF Version 2 Release 2 (SE)
05	RMF Version 2 Release 2 Feature (SE2)

variable	type	length	format
AVGENQUE	numeric	4	5.3
CHANMAP	character	4	HEX4.
CHANMAP0	numeric	4	HEX4.
CHANMAP1	numeric	4	HEX4.
CPUMAP	numeric	4	HEX4.
CYCLE	numeric	4	
C0ANYCH	numeric	4	5.1
C0BYWT	numeric	4	5.1
C1ANYCH	numeric	4	5.1
C1BYWT	numeric	1	5.1
DEFCUBY	numeric	4	
DEFDEVBY	numeric	4	
DEFERED	numeric	4	
DEFLCHBY	numeric	4	
DEFPHYBY	numeric	4	
DURATM	numeric	4	TIME12.2
FQCUBY	numeric	4	
FQDEVBY	numeric	4	
FQLCHRQ	numeric	4	
FQPHYRQ	numeric	4	
LCHAN	numeric	4	
LCI	character	1	
LPCHANBY	numeric	4	5.1
LPPARTBY	numeric	4	5.1
NRENQUES	numeric	4	
NRSAMPLE	numeric	4	
PCTDEFCU	numeric	4	5.1
PCTDEFDV	numeric	4	5.1
PCTDEFER	numeric	4	5.1
PCTDEFLC	numeric	4	5.1
PCTDEFPY	numeric	4	5.1
QUEUE0	numeric	4	5.1
QUEUE1	numeric	4	5.1
QUEUE2	numeric	4	5.1
QUEUE3	numeric	4	5.1
QUEUE4	numeric	4	5.1
RELEASE	character	4	
SIOCOUNT	numeric	4	
SMFTIME	numeric	8	DATETIME19.2
STARTIME	numeric	8	DATETIME19.2
SYSTEM	character	4	
VERSION	character	2	

```
**********MEMBER=TYPE73*********************************;
DATA TYPE73P
                (KEEP=CHAN CHANTYPE CPUID CYCLE COANYCH COBYWT
                      C1ANYCH C1BYWT DURATM IDWRONG NRSAMPLE ONLINE
                      PCHANBY PCHANWT RELEASE SIOCOUNT SMFTIME
                      STARTIME SYSTEM VARIED VERSION)
      TYPE73L
                (KEEP=AVGENQUE CHANMAP CHANMAP0 CHANMAP1 CPUMAP
                      CYCLE COANYCH COBYWT C1ANYCH C1BYWT
                      DEFCUBY DEFDEVBY DEFERED DEFLCHBY DEFPHYBY
                      DURATM FQCUBY FQDEVBY FQLCHRQ FQPHYRQ
                      LCHAN LCI LPCHANBY LPPARTBY NRENQUES NRSAMPLE
                      PCTDEFCU PCTDEFDV PCTDEFER PCTDEFLC PCTDEFPY
                      QUEUE0-QUEUE4 RELEASE SIOCOUNT
                      SMFTIME STARTIME SYSTEM VERSION);
LENGTH DEFAULT=4 SMFTIME STARTIME 8;
FORMAT SMFTIME STARTIME                                    DATETIME19.2
       DURATM                                             TIME12.2
       CHANMAP CHANMAP0 CHANMAP1 CPUMAP                     HEX4.
       COANYCH C1ANYCH COBYWT C1BYWT PCHANBY PCHANWT
       LPCHANBY LPPARTBY QUEUE0-QUEUE4 PCTDEFLC PCTDEFPY
       PCTDEFER PCTDEFCU PCTDEFDV                           5.1
       AVGENQUE                                             5.3;
  INFILE SMF STOPOVER LENGTH=LENGTH COL=COL RECFM=VBS LRECL=32756;
  INPUT @2 ID PIB1. @;
 IF ID=73;
  GOTO TYPE73;
TYPE73:
   INPUT @3 SMFTIME SMFSTAMP8. @11 SYSTEM $4.
         @17 STARTIME PDTIME4. @21 STARDATE PD4. @25 DURATM PD4.
         @33 NRSAMPLE PIB4. @37 VERSION $2. @41 RELEASE $4.
         @45 CYCLE PD4. @;
   STARTIME=DHMS(DATEJUL(STARDATE),0,0,STARTIME);
   DURATM=60*FLOOR(DURATM/100000)+MOD(DURATM,100000)/1000;
   INPUT  @51 NRPCHANS PIB2. @55 NRLCHANS PIB2.
          @61 COANYCH PIB4. @65 C1ANYCH PIB4. @69 COBYWT PIB4.
          @73 C1BYWT PIB4. @;
   COANYCH=100*COANYCH/NRSAMPLE;
   C1ANYCH=100*C1ANYCH/NRSAMPLE;
   COBYWT =100*COBYWT/NRSAMPLE;
   C1BYWT =100*C1BYWT/NRSAMPLE;
PCHAN:
  IF NRPCHANS=0 THEN GOTO LCHAN;
   INPUT CPUID PIB2. CHAN PIB1. CHANIND PIB1. SIOCOUNT PIB4.
         PCHANBY PIB4. PCHANWT PIB4. @;
  IF MOD(CHANIND,64)>=32 THEN CHANTYPE='BLOCK MUX';
  IF MOD(CHANIND,32)>=16 THEN CHANTYPE='BYTE MUX';
  IF CHANTYPE=' ' THEN CHANTYPE='SELECTOR';
  IF MOD(CHANIND,8)>=4 THEN IDWRONG='Y';
  IF MOD(CHANIND,4)>=2 THEN VARIED='Y';
  IF MOD(CHANIND,2)=1 THEN ONLINE='Y';
   PCHANBY=100*PCHANBY/NRSAMPLE;
   PCHANWT=100*PCHANWT/NRSAMPLE;
   OUTPUT TYPE73P;
   NRPCHANS=NRPCHANS-1;
   GOTO PCHAN;
LCHAN:
  IF NRLCHANS=0 THEN RETURN;
  IF VERSION <= '03' THEN INPUT
           LCHAN PIB2. +2 CHANMAP PIB2. CPUMAP PIB2.
           LPCHANBY PIB4. LPPARTBY PIB4. @;
  IF VERSION >= '04' THEN INPUT
           LCHAN PIB2. CHANMAP1 PIB2. CHANMAP0 PIB2. +10 @;
   INPUT SIOCOUNT PIB4. (QUEUE0-QUEUE4) (PIB4.) NRENQUES PIB4.
         DEFPHYBY PIB4. DEFLCHBY PIB4. FQPHYRQ PIB4. FQLCHRQ PIB4. @;
```

```
  IF VERSION<='Ø3' THEN GOTO NONSE;
    INPUT DEFCUBY PIB4. DEFDEVBY PIB4. FQCUBY PIB4. FQDEVBY PIB4.
          LC PIB2. +2 @;
  IF LC=1 THEN LCI='Y';
    GOTO QUEUE;
NONSE:
    LPCHANBY=100*LPCHANBY/NRSAMPLE;
    LPPARTBY=100*LPPARTBY/NRSAMPLE;
QUEUE:
    QUEUEØ=100*QUEUEØ/NRSAMPLE;
    QUEUE1=100*QUEUE1/NRSAMPLE;
    QUEUE2=100*QUEUE2/NRSAMPLE;
    QUEUE3=100*QUEUE3/NRSAMPLE;
    QUEUE4=100*QUEUE4/NRSAMPLE;
    AVGENQUE=NRENQUES/NRSAMPLE;
    DEFERED=SUM(DEFCUBY,DEFDEVBY,DEFLCHBY,DEFPHYBY);
  IF SIOCOUNT<=Ø THEN GOTO OUT73L;
    PCTDEFLC=100*DEFLCHBY/SIOCOUNT;
    PCTDEFPY=100*DEFPHYBY/SIOCOUNT;
    PCTDEFER=100*DEFERED/SIOCOUNT;
  IF VERSION<='Ø3' THEN GOTO OUT73L;
    PCTDEFCU=100*DEFCUBY/SIOCOUNT;
    PCTDEFDV=100*DEFDEVBY/SIOCOUNT;
OUT73L:
    OUTPUT TYPE73L;
    NRLCHANS=NRLCHANS-1;
    GOTO LCHAN;
```

The TYPE73P Data Set: Physical Channel Activity

The TYPE73P data set contains multiple observations for each type 73 SMF record. Type 73 SMF records are written at each RMF interval and contain multiple segments for each physical channel. There is one observation in TYPE73P for each physical channel section in each type 73 SMF record. TYPE73P contains the number of start I/0s (SIO count) issued for each channel, and the percent of samples when the channel was busy (PCHANBY).

TYPE73P is very important in attempting to balance the utilization of the physical channels.

Note that TYPE73P and TYPE73L are built concurrently from type 73 records, although they contain different information.

Contents

CHAN   Physical channel number.

CHANTYPE   Channel type:
                BYTE MUX, BLOCK MUX, or SELECTOR

CPUID   CPU to which this channel is connected and for which this data applies.

CYCLE   Sample cycle length (in milliseconds). At each CYCLE, a sampling observation is made.

C0ANYCH   Percent of samples when any physical channel was busy on CPU0.

C0BYNT   Percent of samples when any physical channel was busy on CPU0 and PUC0 was in a wait state.

C1ANYCH   Percent of samples when any physical channel was busy on CPU1.

C1BYWT   Percent of samples when any physical channel was busy on CPU1 and CPU1 was in a wait state.

DURATM   Duration of this RMF interval. At end of each DURAT, all data gathered and sampled is written to SMF.

IDWRONG   Invalid channel identification (Y or blanks). An error occurred when RMF constructed this record. CHAN is in error and CHANTYPE will be SELECTOR.

NRSAMPLE   Number of samples taken in this RMF interval. (Samples are taken at CYCLE intervals.)

ONLINE   Channel is currently online at end of RMF interval: blank or Y.

PCHANBY   Percent of samples when channel was busy. This number will always be zero for byte multiplexor channels, even though the channel was busy.

PCHANWT   Percent of samples in which this channel was busy and the CPU (CPUID) was in the wait state. Also zero for byte multiplexor channels.

RELEASE   Operating system release number and level (e.g., 0370 for Release 3 Level 7, or 3.7).

SIOCOUNT   Number of successful start I/Os issued to this channel by this CPU during this RMF interval. This includes redundant successful start I/O Fast Release instructions, but not "sense" start I/Os.

SMFTIME   Approximate ending time stamp of RMF interval. (Actually, the time the record is moved to SMF.)

STARTIME   Beginning-of-RMF-interval time stamp.

SYSTEM   Identification of this system.

VARIED   Channel was varied during this interval, data is invalid: blank or Y.

VERSION   RMF version number.

value	meaning
01	MF/1
02	RMF Version 1
03	RMF Version 2
04	RMF Version 2 Release 2 (SE)
05	RMF Version 2 Release 2 Feature (SE2)

variable	type	length	format
CHAN	numeric	4	
CHANTYPE	character	9	
CPUID	numeric	4	
CYCLE	numeric	4	
C0ANYCH	numeric	4	5.1
C0BYWT	numeric	4	5.1
C1ANYCH	numeric	4	5.1
C1BYWT	numeric	4	5.1
DURATM	numeric	4	TIME12.2
IDWRONG	character	1	
NRSAMPLE	numeric	4	
ONLINE	character	1	
PCHANBY	numeric	4	5.1
PCHANWT	numeric	4	5.1
RELEASE	character	4	
SIOCOUNT	numeric	4	
SMFTIME	numeric	8	DATETIME19.2
STARTIME	numeric	8	DATETIME19.2
SYSTEM	character	4	
VARIED	character	1	
VERSION	character	2	

The TYPE73P data set is built concurrently with the TYPE73L data set; the SAS code is found in the TYPE73L appendix

The TYPE74 Data Set: Device Activity

The TYPE74 data set contains multiple observations for each type 74 SMF record. Type 74 SMF records are written at each RMF interval and contain multiple segments, one for each device in the system. There is one observation in TYPE74 for each device in each type 74 SMF record that had either a non-zero start I/O count, samples in which the device was busy, an average queue length greater than zero, or was allocated during the RMF interval. Thus TYPE74 contains one observation for every device that was active during the RMF interval.

TYPE74 contains statistics on the start I/O counts, percent of requests deferred, and percent of samples when there were 0, 1, 2, 3, or more than 4 requests queued for each device.

TYPE74 is important because it provides the only source of information on device activity. Data from TYPE73L and TYPE73P data sets can identify channels that are out of balance. TYPE74 will identify the heavily used devices on those channels and is thus used to identify devices which should be relocated to different channels and control units. In MVS/SE, statistics on control unit busy are also provided in TYPE74 permitting an additional degree of I/O balancing.

Contents

AVDSOPEN   Average number of data sets open on the device.

AVGENQUE   Average number of requests enqueued for this device.

BASE   If non-blank, this is the base exposure of a multiple-exposure device: blank or Y.

CUBUSY   Percent of samples when the control unit was busy. For MVS, this value is generally in error, as there are errors in setting this counter. For MVS/SE, the value is generally accurate.

CYCLE   Sample cycle length (in milliseconds). At each CYCLE, a sampling observation is made.

DEFERED   Number of requests deferred (queued) because device was busy and control unit was not busy.

DEVBUSY   Percent of samples in which the device was busy and the control unit was not busy.

DEVICE   Device type (e.g., 3330, 3350, etc.) From __DEVICE macro.

DURATM   Duration of the RMF interval. At end of each DURATM, all data gathered and sampled is written to SMF.

LCHAN   Logical channel number to which this device is associated.

MOUNT   Percent of samples (time) during which a mount was pending for this device.

NOTREADY   Percent of samples (time) during which this device was not ready.

NRBASEBY   Percent of samples (time) during which the base exposure of a multiple exposure device was busy while the control unit was not busy.

NRSAMPLE   Number of samples taken in this RMF interval. (Samples are taken at CYCLE intervals).

ONLINE   Device is on-line at end of interval flag: blank or Y.

PCTALOC   Percent of samples (time) during which this device was allocated.

PCTDEFER   Percent of total SIO count to this device deferred because device was busy and control unit was not.

PCTDELAY   Percent of samples when this device was delayed because another CPU had reserved this device or was delayed because head of string was not available.

PCTQUEDV   MVS/SE only. Percent of samples when requests were queued while the device was busy.

PCTQUEPA   MVS/SE only. Percent of samples when requests were queued while the path was busy.

PCTRESVD   Percent of samples when this CPU had reserved the device (i.e., potential delay to the other CPU in a shared DASD environment).

QUEUE0   Percent of samples when there were no requests queued for this device.

QUEUE1-   Percent of samples when there were [1, 2, 3, 4, or more] requests queued for this device.
QUEUE4

RELEASE   Operating system release number and level. (e.g., 0370 for Release 3 Level 7, or 3.7).

SIOCOUNT   Total number of successful start I/Os for this device.

SMFTIME   Approximate ending time stamp of RMF interval. (Actually, the time the record is moved to SMF.)

STARTIME   Beginning-of-RMF-interval time stamp.

SYSTEM   Identification of this system.

UCBTYPE   UCB unit type bytes 1-4. (See DEVICE.)

UNITADR   Unit address of this device.

VARY   Flag that data is invalid because device was varied during this interval: blank or Y.

VERSION   RMF version number.

value	meaning
01	MF/1
02	RMF Version 1
03	RMF Version 2
04	RMF Version 2 Release 2 (SE)
05	RMF Version 2 Release 2 Feature (SE2)

VOLSER   Volume serial number on this device at the end of the interval.

variable	type	length	format
AVDSOPEN	numeric	4	5.1
AVGENQUE	numeric	4	5.3
BASE	character	1	
CUBUSY	numeric	4	5.1
CYCLE	numeric	4	
DEFERED	numeric	4	
DEVBUSY	numeric	4	5.1
DEVICE	character	7	

DURATM	numeric	4	TIME12.2
LCHAN	numeric	4	
MOUNT	numeric	4	
NOTREADY	numeric	4	
NRBASEBY	numeric	4	
NRSAMPLE	numeric	4	
ONLINE	character	1	
PCTALOC	numeric	4	5.1
PCTDEFER	numeric	4	5.1
PCTDELAY	numeric	4	5.1
PCTQUEDV	numeric	4	5.1
PCTQUEPA	numeric	4	5.1
PCTRESVD	numeric	4	5.1
QUEUE0	numeric	4	5.1
QUEUE1	numeric	4	5.1
QUEUE2	numeric	4	5.1
QUEUE3	numeric	4	5.1
QUEUE4	numeric	4	5.1
RELEASE	character	4	
SIOCOUNT	numeric	4	
SMFTIME	numeric	8	DATETIME19.2
STARTIME	numeric	8	DATETIME19.2
SYSTEM	character	4	
UCBTYPE	numeric	4	HEX8.
UNITADR	numeric	4	HEX3.
VARY	character	1	
VERSION	character	2	
VOLSER	character	6	

```
**********MEMBER=TYPE74**********************************;
DATA TYPE74
                (KEEP=AVDSOPEN AVGENQUE BASE CUBUSY CYCLE DEFERED
                      DEVBUSY DEVICE DURATM LCHAN MOUNT NOTREADY
                      NRBASEBY NRSAMPLE ONLINE PCTALOC PCTDEFER
                      PCTDELAY PCTQUEDV PCTQUEPA PCTRESVD
                      QUEUE0-QUEUE4 RELEASE SIOCOUNT
                      SMFTIME STARTIME SYSTEM UCBTYPE
                      UNITADR VARY VERSION VOLSER);
 LENGTH DEFAULT=4 SMFTIME STARTIME 8;
 FORMAT SMFTIME STARTIME                                 DATETIME19.2
        DURATM                                           TIME12.2
        PCTQUEDV PCTQUEPA PCTDEFER PCTDELAY PCTRESVD
        AVDSOPEN CUBUSY DEVBUSY PCTALOC QUEUE0-QUEUE4     5.1
        UNITADR                                          HEX3.
        UCBTYPE                                          HEX8.
        AVGENQUE                                          5.3 ;
   INFILE SMF STOPOVER LENGTH=LENGTH COL=COL RECFM=VBS LRECL=32756;
   INPUT @2 ID PIB1. @;
  IF ID=74;
  GOTO TYPE74;
 TYPE74:
   INPUT @3 SMFTIME SMFSTAMP8. @11 SYSTEM $4.
         @17 STARTIME PDTIME4. @21 STARDATE PD4. @25 DURATM PD4.
         @33 NRSAMPLE PIB4. @37 VERSION $2. @41 RELEASE $4.
         @45 CYCLE PD4. @;
    STARTIME=DHMS(DATEJUL(STARDATE),0,0,STARTIME);
    DURATM=60*FLOOR(DURATM/100000)+MOD(DURATM,100000)/1000;
```

```
    M2=-2;
   INPUT @31 UCBTY3 PIB2. @51 NRDEV PIB2. @61 @;
LOOP74:
  IF NRDEV=0 THEN RETURN;
   INPUT UNITADR PIB2. +1 DEVIND PIB1. UCBTYPE PIB4.
          +M2 DEVCLASS PIB1. DEVTYPE PIB1. VOLSER $6.
          LCHAN PIB2. SIOCOUNT PIB4. DEVBUSY PIB4. NRREQENQ PIB4.
          NRBASEBY PIB4. NOTREADY PIB4. PCTALOC PIB4. CUBUSY PIB4.
          DEFERED PIB4. AVDSOPEN PIB4. (QUEUE0-QUEUE4) (PIB4.)
          PCTRESVD PIB4. MOUNT PIB4. PCTDELAY PIB4. @;
  IF VERSION<='03' THEN GOTO REST74;
   INPUT PCTQUEDV PIB4. PCTQUEPA PIB4. @;
    PCTQUEDV=100*PCTQUEDV/NRSAMPLE;
    PCTQUEPA=100*PCTQUEPA/NRSAMPLE;
REST74:
    UNITADR=FLOOR(UNITADR/16);
   LINK UCBTYP;
  IF MOD(DEVIND,8)>=4 THEN BASE='Y';
  IF MOD(DEVIND,4)>=2 THEN VARY='Y';
  IF MOD(DEVIND,2)>=1 THEN ONLINE='Y';
    QUEUE0=100*QUEUE0/NRSAMPLE;
    QUEUE1=100*QUEUE1/NRSAMPLE;
    QUEUE2=100*QUEUE2/NRSAMPLE;
    QUEUE3=100*QUEUE3/NRSAMPLE;
    QUEUE4=100*QUEUE4/NRSAMPLE;
    DEVBUSY=100*DEVBUSY/NRSAMPLE;
    AVGENQUE=NRREQENQ/NRSAMPLE;
    NRBASEBY=100*NRBASEBY/NRSAMPLE;
   MOUNT=100*MOUNT/NRSAMPLE;
   NOTREADY=100*NOTREADY/NRSAMPLE;
    PCTALOC=100*PCTALOC/NRSAMPLE;
    CUBUSY=100*CUBUSY/NRSAMPLE;
    AVDSOPEN=AVDSOPEN/NRSAMPLE;
    PCTRESVD=100*PCTRESVD/NRSAMPLE;
    PCTDELAY=100*PCTDELAY/NRSAMPLE;
  IF SIOCOUNT NE 0 THEN PCTDEFER=100*DEFERED/SIOCOUNT;
  IF SIOCOUNT NE 0 OR DEVBUSY NE 0 OR AVGENQUE NE 0
     OR PCTALOC NE 0 THEN OUTPUT TYPE74;
    NRDEV=NRDEV-1;
   GOTO LOOP74;
 _DEVICE
```

The TYPE75 Data Set: Page/Swap Data Set Activity

The TYPE75 data set contains one observation for every type 75 SMF record. Type 75 SMF records are written for each RMF interval, and one TYPE75 record is written for each page and for each swap data set that is monitored during each interval.

TYPE75 contains statistics on the utilization of the page and swap data sets. TYPE75 is important because it provides the percent data set busy (DSBUSY) as seen by the auxiliary storage manager (ASM). Additionally, under MVS/SE the number of pages transferred to or from the page data set is contained in TYPE75. TYPE75 is thus very important in conjunction with TYPE71 to determine whether paging rate is excessive and whether sufficient page and swap data sets exist in the system.

Contents

AVGUSED   Average number of slots/swap sets used.

CYCLE   Sample cycle length (in milliseconds). At each CYCLE, a sampling observation is made.

DEVICE   Device type (e.g., 3330, 3350, etc.) From _DEVICE macro.

DSBUSY   Percent of samples (time) during which this data set was being used by ASM.

DURATM   Duration of the RMF interval. At the end of each DURATM, all data gathered and sampled is written to SMF.

MAXUSED   Maximum number of slots/swap sets used.

MINUSED   Minimum number of slots/swap sets used.

NRPAGTRF   MVS/SE only. Number of pages transferred to or from the data set during the interval.

NRSAMPLE   Number of samples taken in this RMF interval. (Samples are taken at CYCLE intervals).

NRSAMREQ   Number of requests for the data set observed during RMF sampling.

PAGEDSN   Name of page/swap data set.

PAGETYPE   Type of paging data set: PLPA, COMMON, DUPLEX, LOCAL, SWAP.

RELEASE   Operating system release number and level. (e.g., 0370 for Release 3 Level 7, or 3.7)

SIOCOUNT   MVS/SE only. Number of I/O requests for this data set.

SLOTS   Total number of slots/swap sets in this data set.

SMFTIME   Approximate ending time stamp of RMF interval. (Actually, the time the record is moved to SMF.)

STARTIME   Beginning-of-RMF-interval time stamp.

SYSTEM   Identification of this system.

UCBTYPE   UCB unit type bytes 1-4. (See DEVICE).

UNITADR   Unit address of this device.

UNUSABLE   Flag if this data set is unusable: blank or Y.

UNUSLOTS   Number of unusable slots/swap sets.

VARY   Flag that data is invalid because device was varied during this interval: blank or Y.

VERSION   RMF version number.

value	meaning
01	MF/1
02	RMF Version 1
03	RMF Version 2
04	RMF Version 2 Release 2 (SE)
05	RMF Version 2 Release 2 Feature (SE2)

VOLSER   Volume serial number of device containing this data set.

variable	type	length	format
AVGUSED	numeric	4	
CYCLE	numeric	4	
DEVICE	character	7	
DSBUSY	numeric	4	5.1
DURATM	numeric	4	TIME12.2
MAXUSED	numeric	4	
MINUSED	numeric	4	
NRPAGTRF	numeric	4	
NRSAMPLE	numeric	4	
NRSAMREQ	numeric	4	
PAGEDSN	character	44	
PAGETYPE	character	4	
RELEASE	character	4	
SIOCOUNT	numeric	4	
SLOTS	numeric	4	
SMFTIME	numeric	8	DATETIME19.2
STARTIME	numeric	8	DATETIME19.2
SYSTEM	character	4	
UCBTYPE	numeric	4	HEX8.
UNITADR	numeric	4	
UNUSABLE	character	1	
UNUSLOTS	numeric	4	
VARY	character	1	
VERSION	character	2	
VOLSER	character	6	

```
**********MEMBER=TYPE75**********************************;
DATA TYPE75
              (KEEP=AVGUSED CYCLE DEVICE DSBUSY DURATM MAXUSED
                    MINUSED NRPAGTRF NRSAMPLE NRSAMREQ
                    PAGEDSN PAGETYPE RELEASE SIOCOUNT SLOTS
                    SMFTIME STARTIME SYSTEM UCBTYPE UNITADR
                    UNUSABLE UNUSLOTS VARY VERSION VOLSER);
LENGTH DEFAULT=4 SMFTIME STARTIME 8;
FORMAT SMFTIME STARTIME                        DATETIME19.2
       DSBUSY                                  5.1
       UCBTYPE                                 HEX8.
       DURATM                                  TIME12.2;
  INFILE SMF STOPOVER LENGTH=LENGTH COL=COL RECFM=VBS LRECL=32756;
  INPUT @2 ID PIB1. @;
 IF ID=75;
  GOTO TYPE75;
TYPE75:
  INPUT @3 SMFTIME SMFSTAMP8. @11 SYSTEM $4.
        @17 STARTIME PDTIME4. @21 STARDATE PD4. @25 DURATM PD4.
        @33 NRSAMPLE PIB4. @37 VERSION $2. @41 RELEASE $4.
        @45 CYCLE PD4. @;
   STARTIME=DHMS(DATEJUL(STARDATE),0,0,STARTIME);
   DURATM=60*FLOOR(DURATM/100000)+MOD(DURATM,100000)/1000;
  INPUT @53 PAGEDSN $44. @97 PAGETY PIB1.
        @100 UCBTYPE PIB4. @102 DEVCLASS PIB1. @103 DEVTYPE PIB1.
        @104 UNITADR PIB2. @106 VOLSER $6. @117 SLOTS PIB4.
        @121 MAXUSED PIB4. @125 MINUSED PIB4. @129 AVGUSED PIB4.
        @133 UNUSLOTS PIB4. @137 DSBUSY PIB4.
        @141 NRSAMREQ PIB4. @;
```

```
IF PAGETY>=128          THEN  PAGETYPE='PLPA  ';
IF MOD(PAGETY,128)>=64  THEN PAGETYPE='COMMON';
IF MOD(PAGETY,64)>=32   THEN PAGETYPE='DUPLEX';
IF MOD(PAGETY,32)>=16   THEN PAGETYPE='LOCAL';
IF MOD(PAGETY,16)>=8    THEN PAGETYPE='SWAP';
IF MOD(PAGETY,8)>=4     THEN UNUSABLE='Y';
IF MOD(PAGETY,4)>=2     THEN VARY='Y';
IF VERSION >='Ø4' THEN
 INPUT SIOCOUNT PIB4. NRPAGTRF PIB4. @;
  DSBUSY=1ØØ*DSBUSY/NRSAMPLE;
  UNITADR=FLOOR(UNITADR/16);
 LINK UCBTYP;
 OUTPUT TYPE75;
 RETURN;
_DEVICE
```

The TYPE76 Data Set: Trace Record

The TYPE76 data set contains multiple observations for every type 76 SMF record. TYPE76 SMF records are written at the end of each RMF interval when tracing of specific SRM fields was requested, and are very useful for tracking specific information in the MVS SRM. For each field that is traced, each type 76 SMF record contain multiple segments containing the values of the traced field. The TYPE76 data set contains one observation for each sample value of each field in each type76 SMF record.

TYPE76 thus is primarily used to analyze trace data when the RMF trace option is used. See the discussion of the trace option in the RMF manual.

Contents

CYCLE   Sample cycle length (in milliseconds). At each CYCLE, a sampling observation is made.

DURATM   Duration of the RMF interval. At the end of each DURAT, all data gathered and sampled is written to SMF.

END   Ending value of traced field in each sample set (i.e., each time of the trace).

FIELDNME   Name of RMF field which this record reports.

INTRVEND   Value of traced field at the end of the RMF interval.

INTRVMAX   Maximum value of traced field during the RMF interval.

INTRVMIN   Minimum value of traced field during the RMF interval.

INTRVSSQ   Sum of the squared values of traced field during the RMF interval.

INTRVSUM   Sum of the values of traced field during the RMF interval.

MAX   Maximum value of traced field in each sample set (i.e., each line of the trace).

MIN   Minimum value of traced field in each sample set (i.e., each line of the trace).

NRSAMPLE   Number of samples taken in the RMF interval.

NRSETS   Number of sample sets (i.e., lines of data) in the trace.

OPTIONS   Options specified for this field name.
                     bit   **meaning when one**
                     1   minimum value requested
                     2   maximum value requested
                     3   sum value requested
                     4   sum of squared values requested
                     5   end value requested
                     6   all options requested
                     7   domain tracing terminated
                     8   this entry is a domain field

RELEASE   Operating system release number and level. (e.g., 0370 for Release 3 Level 7, or 3.7)

SAMP_LST   Number of samples in the last sample set being built when the RMF interval ended.

SAMP_SET   Number of samples in each sample set.

SMFTIME   Approximate ending time stamp of RMF interval. (Actually, the time the record is moved to SMF.)

SSQ   Sum of squared values of the traced field in each sample set (i.e., each line of the trace).

STARTIME   Beginning-of-RMF-interval time stamp.

SUM   Sum of values of the traced field in each sample set (i.e., end line of the trace).

SYSTEM   Identification of this system.

VERSION   RMF version number.
                     value   **meaning**
                     01   MF/1
                     02   RMF Version 1
                     03   RMF Version 2
                     04   RMF Version 2 Release 2 (SE)
                     05   RMF Version 2 Release 2 Feature (SE2)

variable	type	length	format
CYCLE	numeric	4	
DURATM	numeric	4	TIME12.2
END	numeric	4	
FIELDNME	numeric	4	
INTRVEND	numeric	4	
INTRVMAX	numeric	4	
INTRVMIN	numeric	4	
INTRVSSQ	numeric	4	
INTRVSUM	numeric	4	
MAX	numeric	4	
MIN	numeric	4	
NRSAMPLE	numeric	4	
NRSETS	numeric	4	
OPTIONS	numeric	4	
RELEASE	character	4	
SAMP_LST	numeric	4	
SAMP_SET	numeric	4	
SMFTIME	numeric	8	DATETIME19.2
SSQ	numeric	4	
STARTIME	numeric	8	DATETIME19.2
SUM	numeric	4	
SYSTEM	character	4	
VERSION	character	2	

```
**********MEMBER=TYPE76**********************************;
DATA TYPE76
                  (KEEP=CYCLE DURATM END FIELDNME INTRVEND INTRVMIN
                    INTRVMAX INTRVSSQ INTRVSUM MIN MAX NRSAMPLE
                    NRSETS OPTIONS RELEASE SAMP_LST SAMP_SET
                    SMFTIME STARTIME SSQ SUM SYSTEM VERSION);
LENGTH DEFAULT=4 SMFTIME STARTIME 8;
FORMAT SMFTIME STARTIME                              DATETIME19.2
        DURATM                                       TIME12.2  ;
  INFILE SMF STOPOVER LENGTH=LENGTH COL=COL RECFM=VBS LRECL=32756;
  INPUT @2 ID PIB1. @;
 IF ID=76;
  GOTO TYPE76;
TYPE76:
  INPUT @3 SMFTIME SMFSTAMP8. @11 SYSTEM $4.
        @17 STARTIME PDTIME4. @21 STARDATE PD4. @25 DURATM PD4.
        @33 NRSAMPLE PIB4. @37 VERSION $2. @41 RELEASE $4.
        @45 CYCLE PD4. @;
   STARTIME=DHMS(DATEJUL(STARDATE),0,0,STARTIME);
   DURATM=60*FLOOR(DURATM/100000)+MOD(DURATM,100000)/1000;
   INPUT @53 NRSETS PIB2. @57 FIELDNME $8.
        @65 OPTIONS PIB1. @66 LENSETS PIB1. @67 LENFLD PIB1.
        @69 SAMP_SET PIB2. @71 SAMP_LST PIB2. @73 INTRVMIN PIB4.
        @77 INTRVMAX PIB4. @81 INTRVSUM PIB8. @89 D0 PIB4.
        @93 INTRVSSQ PIB8. @101 INTRVEND PIB4. @;
 IF OPTIONS>127          -      THEN OMIN=1;
 IF MOD(OPTIONS,128)>=64 THEN OMAX=1;
 IF MOD(OPTIONS, 64)>=32 THEN OSUM=1;
 IF MOD(OPTIONS, 32)>=16 THEN OSSQ=1;
 IF MOD(OPTIONS, 16)>= 8 THEN OEND=1;
 IF MOD(OPTIONS,  8)>= 4 THEN OALL=1;
   INTRVSSQ=INTRVSSQ+D0*16**9;
 IF LENFLD<=2 THEN GOTO HALFWORD; IF LENFLD<=4 THEN GOTO FULLWORD;
  PUT '*** ERROR, LENFLD NE 2 OR 4 ***' _ALL_ ;STOP;
HALFWORD:
   LOOPCNT=NRSETS;
HALFLOOP:
 IF LOOPCNT <=0 THEN RETURN;
 IF OMIN OR OALL THEN INPUT MIN PIB2. @;
 IF OSUM OR OALL THEN INPUT SUM PIB6. @;
 IF OMAX OR OALL THEN INPUT MAX PIB2. @;
 IF OSSQ OR OALL THEN INPUT SSQ PIB8. @;
 IF OEND OR OALL THEN INPUT END PIB2. @;
  OUTPUT TYPE76;
   LOOPCNT=LOOPCNT-1;
  GOTO HALFLOOP;
FULLWORD:
   LOOPCNT=NRSETS;
FULLLOOP:
 IF LOOPCNT <=0 THEN RETURN;
 IF OMIN OR OALL THEN INPUT MIN PIB4. @;
 IF OSUM OR OALL THEN INPUT SUM PIB8. @;
 IF OMAX OR OALL THEN INPUT MAX PIB4. @;
 IF OSSQ OR OALL THEN DO;INPUT D0 PIB4. SSQ PIB8. @;
                        SSQ=D0*16**9+SSQ;
                    END;
 IF OEND OR OALL THEN INPUT END PIB4. @;
  OUTPUT TYPE76;
   LOOPCNT=LOOPCNT-1;
  GOTO FULLLOOP;
```

The TYPE77 Data Set: Enqueue Records

The TYPE77 data set contains multiple observations for every type 77 SMF record, written at the end of each RMF interval. The type 77 record contains multiple segments for each resource that was enqueued upon during the interval.

The TYPE77 data set contains one observation for every resource that was enqueued upon during the interval. TYPE77 provides statistics on the duration of the enqueue conflict and the current owner and awaiting owners for each of the enqueue events. It is especially valuable in determining those resources for which conflicts are occuring at the enqueue level. By looking at the resource names in TYPE77, unexpected QNAMEs will often be discovered that are causing performance degradation.

Contents

CURROWN   Number of current owners using the enqueued resource.

CURRWAIT   Number of current tasks waiting for the resource.

DURATM   Duration of the RMF interval.

EVENTS   Total number of contention events that occurred in the interval.

JOBOWN1-2 Task name of current owner (#1, #2).

JOBWANT1-2 Task name of waiting owner (#1, #2).

MAXEXC   Maximum number of exclusive requests.

MAXTM   Maximum duration of contention time.

MAXSHR   Maximum number of shared requests.

MINEXC   Minimum number of exclusive requests.

MINORQCB   Minor name length status.

MINTM	Minimum duration of contention time.
MINSHR	Minimum number of shared requests.
QNAME	Major name (QNAME in ENQ macro) of resource for which contention occurred.
QUEUE1-4	Number of events during which there were [1, 2, 3, 4 or more] requests waiting on this resource.
RELEASE	Operating system release and level. (e.g., 0370 for Release 3 Level 7, or 3.7).

RESIND   Resource indicator flag.

bit	value	meaning
1	1	resource still in contention
2	1	scope of systems
2	0	scope of system
3	1	owner has exclusive control
3	0	owner shares the resource
4	1	JOBWAIT1 wants exclusive use
4	0	JOBWAIT1 wants shared use
5	1	JOBWAIT2 wants exclusive use
5	0	JOBWAIT2 wants shared use

RNAME	Minor name (RNAME in ENQ macro) of resource for which contention occurred.
SMFTIME	Approximate ending time stamp of RMF interval. (Actually, the time the record is moved to SMF.)
STARTIME	Beginning-of-RMF-interval time stamp.

STATIND   Enqueue status indicator

bit	value	meaning
1	1	enqueue summary table is full
2	1	specified resource had no contention
3	1	enqueue had bad CPU clock
4	1	enqueue processing event ABENDed
5	1	detailed data requested
	0	summary data requested

SYSTEM	Identification of this system.

TOTLTM   Total resource contention duration (seconds).

VERSION   RMF version.

value	meaning
01	MF/1
02	RMF Version 1
03	RMF Version 2
04	RMF Version 2 Release 2 (SE)
05	RMF Version 2 Release 2 Feature (SE2)

WAITS   Total number of waiting requests during the interval.

variable	type	length	format
CURROWN	numeric	4	
CURRWAIT	numeric	4	
DURATM	numeric	4	TIME12.2
EVENTS	numeric	4	
JOBOWN1	character	8	
JOBOWN2	character	8	
JOBWANT1	character	8	
JOBWANT2	character	8	
MAXEXC	numeric	4	
MAXSHR	numeric	4	
MAXTM	numeric	4	TIME12.2
MINEXC	numeric	4	
MINORQCB	numeric	4	
MINSHR	numeric	4	
MINTM	numeric	4	TIME12.2
QNAME	character	8	
QUEUE1	numeric	4	
QUEUE2	numeric	4	
QUEUE3	numeric	4	
QUEUE4	numeric	4	
RELEASE	character	4	
RESIND	numeric	4	
RNAME	character	44	
SMFTIME	numeric	8	DATETIME19.2
STARTIME	numeric	8	DATETIME19.2
STATIND	numeric	4	
SYSTEM	character	4	
TOTLTM	numeric	4	TIME12.2
VERSION	character	2	
WAITS	numeric	4	

```
**********MEMBER=TYPE77*****************************;
DATA TYPE77
                (KEEP=CURROWN CURRWAIT DURATM EVENTS
                      JOBOWN1-JOBOWN2 JOBWANT1-JOBWANT2
                      MAXEXC MAXSHR MAXTM MINEXC MINORQCB
                      MINSHR MINTM QNAME QUEUE1-QUEUE4
                      RELEASE RESIND RNAME SMFTIME STARTIME
                      STATIND SYSTEM TOTLTM VERSION WAITS);
LENGTH DEFAULT=4 SMFTIME STARTIME 8;
FORMAT SMFTIME STARTIME                          DATETIME19.2
       DURATM MAXTM MINTM TOTLTM                 TIME12.2 ;
  INFILE SMF STOPOVER LENGTH=LENGTH COL=COL RECFM=VBS LRECL=32756;
  INPUT @2 ID PIB1. @;
 IF ID=77;
  GOTO TYPE77;
TYPE77:
  INPUT @3 SMFTIME SMFSTAMP8. @11 SYSTEM $4.
        @17 STARTIME PDTIME4. @21 STARDATE PD4. @25 DURATM PD4.
        @37 VERSION $2. @41 RELEASE $4. @;
   STARTIME=DHMS(DATEJUL(STARDATE),0,0,STARTIME);
   DURATM=60*FLOOR(DURATM/100000)+MOD(DURATM,100000)/1000;
  INPUT @51 NRSECT PIB2. @55 STATIND PIB1. +1 @;
LOOP77:
 IF NRSECT=0 THEN RETURN;
  INPUT QNAME $8. RNAME $44. MINTM PIB4. MAXTM PIB4. TOTLTM PIB4.
    +2 (QUEUE1-QUEUE4) (PIB2.) WAITS PIB2. MINEXC PIB2. MAXEXC PIB2.
    MINSHR PIB2. MAXSHR PIB2. EVENTS PIB2. MINORQCB PIB1.
    RESIND PIB1. CURROWN PIB2. CURRWAIT PIB2.
    (JOBOWN1-JOBOWN2) ($8.) (JOBWANT1-JOBWANT2) ($8.) @;
    MINTM=MINTM*1024E-6;
    MAXTM=MAXTM*1024E-6;
    TOTLTM=TOTLTM*1024E-6;
  OUTPUT TYPE77;
    NRSECT=NRSECT-1;
  GOTO LOOP77;
```

The TYPE90 Data Set: Operator Commands Record

This appendix describes the variables in the new type 90 record, written in MVS/SE2 systems.

An SMF type 90 record is written whenever any of the commands listed below opposite the COMMAND variable is issued by an operator. There is one observation in TYPE90 for every type 90 SMF record.

Contents

ACTIVE   Name of the current active MAN data set.

BITS   A bit map (hex) that describes which SMF records (0-255) will be written for each SUBSYS.

CHANGE   Domain values that were changed by the SET DMN command (see appropriate NEWxxx variable): MIN, MAX, WEIGHT, AOBJ, DOPJ, FWKLD.

COMMAND   Name of command issued by operator. Possible values:

SET TIME	SET DATE	SET DMN	SET IPS
SET SMF	SWITCH SMF	HALT EOD	IPL PROMPT
IPL SMF	IPL SRM	SET OPT	SET ICS

DOMAIN   Domain that was changed.

DOWNTIME   Value of the time of system crash (IPL PROMPT) (entered by operator).

EVENTIME   Time of this command.

EXIT1-
EXIT15   Name of each exit that will be taken for each SUBSYS.

ICSNAME   Name of the (new) Installation Control Specification (ICS).

INTRVAL   Interval duration.

IPLREASN   Reason for this IPL (entered by operator).

IPSNAME	Name of the (new) Installation Performance Specification (IPS).
JWT	Job wait time parameter.
LISTDSN	LISTDSN option: Y or N.
MAXBUFF	Maximum SMF buffers permitted.
MINBUFF	Minimum SMF buffers permitted.
NEWAOBJ	New AOBJ value.
NEWDOBJ	New DOBJ value.
NEWDSN	Name of new SMF data set to which SMF will now record.
NEWEIGHT	New WEIGHT value.
NEWFWKLD	New FWKLD value.
NEWMAX	New MAX value.
NEWMIN	New MIN value.
NEWNAME	New OPT or ICS name.
NEWTIME	Time after SET TIME/SET DATE issued.
OLDDSN	Old SMF data set name.
OLDNAME	Old OPT or ICS name.
OLDTIME	Time before SET TIME/SET DATE issued.
OPERATOR	Operator's name (IPL PROMPT).
OPTNAME	Name of OPT member.
PRODUCT	Product name (SMF, SRM, SUP, etc.)
PROMPT	IPL PROMPT desired: IPLR, NONE, LIST.
REC	Temporary data set records: PERM or ALL.
RELEASE	Release number.

SMFTIME   Time this record was written to SMF.

STATUS   Status in HHMMSS.

SUBSYS   Detail flag: X'80'.

SYSTEM   Identification of this system.

VERSION   Version number: '01'.

variable	type	length	format
ACTIVE	character	10	
BITS	character	32	
CHANGE	character	6	
COMMAND	character	11	
DOMAIN	numeric	4	
DOWNTIME	numeric	8	DATETIME19.2
EVENTIME	numeric	8	DATETIME19.2
EXIT1-EXIT15	character	8	
ICSNAME	character	8	
INTERVAL	character	8	
IPLREASN	character	65	
IPSNAME	character	8	
JWT	character	4	
LISTDSN	character	1	
MAXBUFF	numeric	4	
MAXDORM	character	4	
MINBUFF	numeric	4	
NEWAOBJ	numeric	4	
NEWDOBJ	numeric	4	
NEWDSN	character	10	
NEWEIGHT	numeric	4	
NEWFWKLD	numeric	4	
NEWMAX	numeric	4	
NEWMIN	numeric	4	
NEWNAME	character	8	
NEWTIME	numeric	8	DATETIME19.2
OLDDSN	character	10	
OLDNAME	character	8	
OLDTIME	numeric	8	DATETIME19.2
OPERATOR	character	20	
OPTNAME	character	8	
PRODUCT	character	8	
PROMPT	character	4	
REC	character	4	
RELEASE	character	4	
SMFTIME	numeric	8	DATETIME19.2
STATUS	character	6	
SUBFLAG	character	1	
SUBSYS	character	4	
SYSTEM	character	4	
VERSION	numeric	4	

```
**********MEMBER=TYPE90************************************;
DATA TYPE90
     (KEEP=ACTIVE BITS CHANGE COMMAND DOMAIN DOWNTIME EVENTIME
      EXIT1-EXIT15 ICSNAME INTERVAL IPLREASN IPSNAME JWT LISTDSN
      MAXBUFF MAXDORM MINBUFF NEWAOBJ NEWDOBJ NEWDSN NEWEIGHT
      NEWFWKLD NEWMAX NEWMIN NEWNAME NEWTIME OLDDSN OLDNAME
      OLDTIME OPERATOR OPTNAME PRODUCT PROMPT REC RELEASE
      SMFTIME STATUS SUBFLAG SUBSYS SYSTEM VERSION);
LENGTH DEFAULT=4 SMFTIME OLDTIME NEWTIME EVENTIME DOWNTIME 8 ;
FORMAT SMFTIME OLDTIME NEWTIME EVENTIME DOWNTIME DATETIME19.2;
  INFILE SMF STOPOVER LENGTH=LENGTH COL=COL RECFM=VBS LRECL=32756;
  INPUT @2 ID PIB1. @;
  IF ID=90;
GOTO TYPE90;
TYPE90:
   INPUT @2 ID PIB1. @3 SMFTIME SMFSTAMP8. @11 SYSTEM $4.
        @17 OFFPROD PIB4. @21 LENPROD PIB2. @23 NRPROD PIB2.
        @25 OFFDATA PIB4. @29 LENDATA PIB2. @31 NRDATA PIB2.
        @;
  IF OFFPROD NE 0 AND NRPROD NE 0 THEN GOTO PRODUCT;
  RETURN;
PRODUCT:
     OFFPROD=OFFPROD-3;
  INPUT @OFFPROD SUBTYPE PIB2. VERSION 2. PRODUCT $8. @;
     OFFDATA=OFFDATA-3;
  IF SUBTYPE=1 OR SUBTYPE=2 THEN GOTO SETTIME;
  IF SUBTYPE=3 THEN GOTO SETDMN;
  IF SUBTYPE=4 THEN GOTO SETIPS;
  IF SUBTYPE=5 OR SUBTYPE=9 THEN GOTO SETSMF;
  IF SUBTYPE=6 OR SUBTYPE=7 THEN GOTO SWITCHSM;
  IF SUBTYPE=8 THEN GOTO IPLPROMP;
  IF SUBTYPE=10 THEN GOTO IPLSRM;
  IF SUBTYPE=11 THEN GOTO SETOPT;
  IF SUBTYPE=12 THEN GOTO SETICS;
  RETURN;
SETTIME:          * SUBTYPE 1 OR 2 ;
  INPUT @OFFDATA OLDTIME SMFSTAMP8. NEWTIME SMFSTAMP8.@;
  IF SUBTYPE=1 THEN COMMAND='SET TIME   ';
  IF SUBTYPE=2 THEN COMMAND='SET DATE   ';
  OUTPUT TYPE90;
  RETURN;
SETDMN:           * SUBTYPE 3;
  INPUT @OFFDATA TOD PIB8. DOMAIN PIB1. DOMFLAG PIB1.
     NEWMIN PIB1. NEWMAX PIB1. NEWEIGHT PIB1. NEWAOBJ PIB1.
     NEWDOBJ PIB1. NEWFWKLD PIB1. @;
_TOD
  IF DOMFLAG='10000000'B THEN CHANGE='MIN   ';
  IF DOMFLAG='01000000'B THEN CHANGE='MAX   ';
  IF DOMFLAG='00100000'B THEN CHANGE='WEIGHT';
  IF DOMFLAG='00010000'B THEN CHANGE='AOBJ';
  IF DOMFLAG='00001000'B THEN CHANGE='DOBJ';
  IF DOMFLAG='00000100'B THEN CHANGE='FWKLD';
     COMMAND='SET DMN';
  OUTPUT TYPE90;
  RETURN;
SETIPS:           * SUBTYPE 4;
  INPUT @OFFDATA TOD PIB8. OLDNAME $8. NEWNAME $8. @;
_TOD
     COMMAND='SET IPS';
  OUTPUT TYPE90;
  RETURN;
SETSMF:           * SUBTYPE 5 OR 9 ;
  INPUT @OFFDATA OFFSMF PIB4. LENSMF PIB2. NRSMF PIB2.
        OFFDATAX PIB4. LENDATAX PIB2. NRDATAX PIB2.
        OFFSUBS  PIB4. LENSUBS  PIB2. NRSUBS  PIB2. @;
    OFFSMF=OFFSMF-3;
```

```
INPUT @OFFSMF MAXDORM $4. STATUS $6. JWT $4. SYSTEM $4.
       MINBUFF PIB1. MAXBUFF PIB1. SWITCHES PIB1. +3
       RELEASE $4. EVENTIME SMFSTAMP8. @;
IF SWITCHES>=128 THEN PROMPT='ALL ';
IF MOD(SWITCHES,128)>=64 THEN PROMPT='LIST';
IF MOD(SWITCHES,64) >=32 THEN PROMPT='IPLR';
IF MOD(SWITCHES,32) >=16 THEN PROMPT='NONE';
IF MOD(SWITCHES,16) >= 8 THEN REC='PERM';
IF MOD(SWITCHES,8)  >= 4 THEN REC='ALL';
IF MOD(SWITCHES,4)  >= 2 THEN LISTDSN='Y';
IF MOD(SWITCHES,2)  =  1 THEN LISTDSN='N';
IF SUBTYPE=5 THEN COMMAND='SET SMF';
IF SUBTYPE=9 THEN COMMAND='IPL SMF';
* THE FOLLOWING INPUT PICKS UP ONLY THE ACTIVE MAN DATA SET;
*  THERE ARE AS MANY DATA SEGMENTS AS THERE ARE DEFINED MAN DATA SETS;
*  THIS CODE COULD BE EXPANDED TO GIVE ALL DEFINED MAN DATA SETS.;
   OFFDATAX=OFFDATAX-3;
   OFFSUBS=OFFSUBS-3;
 INPUT @OFFDATAX ACTIVE $10. @OFFSUBS @;
LOOP90SM:
  IF NRSUBS<=0 THEN RETURN;
  INPUT SUBSYS $4. SUBFLAG $1. +3 INTERVAL $8. BITS $32.
  (EXIT1-EXIT15) ($8.) @;
  OUTPUT TYPE90;
  NRSUBS=NRSUBS-1;
  GOTO LOOP90SM;
SWITCHSM:        * SUBTYPE 6;
  INPUT @OFFDATA OLDDSN $10. NEWDSN $10. EVENTIME SMFSTAMP8. @;
    COMMAND='SWITCH SMF';
  IF SUBTYPE=7 THEN COMMAND='HALT EOD';
  OUTPUT TYPE90;
  RETURN;
IPLPROMP:    * SUBTYPE 8;
  INPUT @OFFDATA DTIME $CHAR8. IPLREASN $65. OPERATOR $20.
     EVENTIME SMFSTAMP8. @;
    DOWNTIME=INPUT(DTIME,TIME8.);
    COMMAND='IPL PROMPT';
  OUTPUT TYPE90;
  RETURN;
IPLSRM:          * SUBTYPE 10;
  INPUT @OFFDATA TOD PIB8. IPSNAME $8. OPTNAME $8.
    ICSNAME $8. @;
  _TOD
    COMMAND='IPL SRM';
  OUTPUT TYPE90;
  RETURN;
SETOPT:          * SUBTYPE 11;
  INPUT @OFFDATA TOD PIB8. OLDNAME $8. NEWNAME $8. @;
  _TOD
    COMMAND='SET OPT';
  OUTPUT TYPE90;
  RETURN;
SETICS:          * SUBTYPE 12;
  INPUT @OFFDATA TOD PIB8. OLDNAME $8. NEWNAME $8. @;
  _TOD
    COMMAND='SET ICS';
  OUTPUT TYPE90;
  RETURN;
```

ADDENDUM

Part One. Documentation of variables added by changes through change 54.

The code distributed with this book changes as IBM adds information to the SMF and RMF records. The descriptions in each of the TYPE appendices have not been updated to document each of these new variables, but the following documentation provides for these new SAS variables.

DATA SET: TYPE434

EXCP3375	numeric	4	EXCPs to 3375 devices
EXCP3380	numeric	4	EXCPs to 3380 devices
EXCPDASD	numeric	4	includes EXCPs to 3375 and 3380 devices

DATA SET: TYPE6

NODE	numeric	4	node number at which printing occurred

DATA SET: TYPE26J3

NJEACCT	character	8	networking account number
NJEBLDG	character	8	programmer's building number
NJEDEPT	character	8	programmer's department number
NJEJOBNM	character	8	job name
NJEJOBNO	character	8	original JES3 assigned job number
NJEPRGMR	character	20	programmer's name
NJEROOM	character	8	programmer's room number
NJEUSRID	character	8	tso user identification
NJEXEQNM	character	8	execution node name
NJEXEQU	character	8	execution user identification

DATA SET: TYPE30

EXCP3375	numeric	4	EXCPs to 3375 devices
EXCP3380	numeric	4	EXCPs to 3380 devices
EXCPDASD	numeric	4	includes EXCPs to 3375 and 3380 devices
STOLPAG	numeric	4	number of pages stolen from this address space

DATA SET: TYPE40

EXCP3375	numeric	4	EXCPs to 3375 devices
EXCP3380	numeric	4	EXCPs to 3380 devices
EXCPDASD	numeric	4	includes EXCPs to 3375 and 3380 devices

DATA SET: TYPE50

CONTROLR	character	8	intelligent controller name
INPIOS	numeric	4	number of inbound PIUs
NCPSLOWS	numeric	4	number of times NCP entered slowdown
NRATTNS	numeric	4	total number of attentions received
NREADATN	numeric	4	attentions on ending status of read channel PGMs
NRREADS	numeric	4	count of read channel PGMs
NRWRITES	numeric	4	count of write channel PGMs

OUTPIOS	numeric	4	number of outbound PIUs
RDBUFUSE	numeric	4	total number of read buffers used.
SMFTIME	numeric	8	datetime record was written
SYSTEM	character	4	system ID on which record was written
TCBCOUNT	numeric	4	maximum dump–load–restart requests

DATA SET: TYPE71

PVTMVCLC	numeric	4	number of pages moved between the V5R area and the reconfigurable area.
PVTMVDWN	numeric	4	number of pages moved to a location below 16MB. Non–zero value indicates at least one user is using an improper sequence to obtain storage and fix pages, and thereby degrading system performance. (The correct sequence, which eliminates these unnecessary moves, is to obtain storage, fix it, and then finally to reference it).
PVTMVUP0	numeric	4	number of pages moved up to a frame above the 16MB line that are not likely to be moved at a later time to a frame below the 16MB line
PVTMVUP1	numeric	4	number of pages moved up to a frame above the 16MB line that are likely to be moved at a later time to a frame below the 16MB line.
RECLEVEL			0=R record contains data for pageable frames 1=R record contains data for total frames

DATA SET: TYPE72

CLASS72	character	8	name of class associated with this PERFGRP
ICSNAME	character	8	name of IEAICSXX member
OPTNAME	character	8	name of IEAOPTXX member
PERFRPGN	numeric	4	report performance group number. If this observation is for a report performance group, this will be nonmissing and will contain the report performance group number (RPGN). Remember that resources tracked to a RPGN will always be included in the TYPE 72 observation for the control performance group (PERFGRP), and can also be included in other RPGN as well. Therefore, CPU utilization studies which merge TYPE 72s and TYPE 70s (such as member usage) must exclude observations from all RPGNs TYPE 72 observations so as to calculate MVS overhead correctly.
SUBSYSTM	character	8	name of subsystem associated with this PERFGRP class
TRANNAME	character	8	name of transaction associated with this PERFGRP
USER72	character	8	user identification associated with this PERFGRP

DATA SET: TYPE73P

AVGENQUE	numeric	4	average number of requests enqueued for this physical channel
AVGREQST	numeric	4	average number of requests outstanding for physical channel
QUEUE0	numeric	4	percent of samples when no requests were queued for this physical channel
QUEUE1=4	numeric	4	percent of samples when 1,2,3 or more than 4 requests were queued for this physical channel

DATA SET: TYPE74

DEFERCUB	numeric	4	number of requests deferred because control unit was busy
DEFERSVD	numeric	R	number of requests deferred because the device was reserved by another CPU
NREXPOSR	numeric	4	number of exposures if this is a multiple exposure device
PCTDEFCU	numeric	4	percent of SIOs deferred because control unit busy
PCTDEFRS	numeric	4	percent of SIOs deferred because of reserves

DATA SET: TYPE75

VIOALOWD	character	1	'Y' if VIO paging is allowed to this data set

DATA SET: TYPE76

OPTNS76	numeric	4	rename of original variable options

DATA SET: TYPE77

SYSOWN1–2	character	4	system ID on which JOBOWN1 and JOBOWN2 are executing
SYSWANT1–2	character	4	system ID on which JOBWANT1 and JOBWANT2 are executing

DATA SET: TYPE90

INTRVL90	character	8	rename of original variable interval
MAXDORM	character	4	current maxdorm time value
RECPARM	character	4	rename of original variable rec
SUBFLAG	numeric	4	if 5 '1.'B, detail recording is on for this subsystem
VERSN90	numeric	4	rename of original variable version

Part Two. Occurrences of the same variable name with different lengths.

Sometimes a character variable with the same name but with different lengths appears in several data sets. This causes a problem when data sets with the common variable are merged with MERGE or SET statements. In that case, the length of the variable is set by the first data set name encountered in the SET or MERGE statement. In building multiple TYPE data sets with the MACROs, the __CDE MACRO defines the length of the variables in its TYPE data set, so that simple reordering of the position of the __CDE MACRO to place the longest length first avoids the problem. Alternatively, the use of the INFORMAT statement before the first __CDE MACRO guarantees the desired length. The following list identifies the data sets in which this potential problem exists:

VARIABLE	LENGTH	DATA SETS
ABEND	$8.	TYPE434,TYPE30
ABEND	$6.	TYPE535
COMMAND	$8.	TYPE32
COMMAND	$14.	TYPE4345
COMMAND	$11.	TYPE90
COMPONT	$9.	TYPE6367
COMPONT	$5.	TYPE64
EVENT	$11.	TYPE43PC
EVENT	$18.	TYPE4789,5234
EVENT	$15.	TYPE5568
LOGOFF	$8.	TYPE47PC
LOGOFF	$10.	TYPE48PC
NEWNAME	$44.	TYPE1718
NEWNAME	$8.	TYPE90
REASON	$7.	TYPE8911
REASON	$14.	TYPE22
STATUS	$14.	TYPE6
STATUS	$10.	TYPE62
SUBSYS	$3.	TYPE22
SUBSYS	$4.	TYPE6,26J2,26J3,30,32,4345,4789,5234,57,90
TYPE	$5.	TYPE6,1415
TYPE	$10.	TYPE30,32
TYPE	$8.	TYPE6367

VARIABLE	LENGTH	DATA SETS
ABEND	$8.	TYPE434,TYPE30
ABEND	$6.	TYPE535
COMMAND	$8.	TYPE32
COMMAND	$14.	TYPE4345
COMMAND	$11.	TYPE90
COMPONT	$9.	TYPE6367
COMPONT	$5.	TYPE64
EVENT	$11.	TYPE43PC
EVENT	$18.	TYPE4789,5234
EVENT	$15.	TYPE5568
LOGOFF	$8.	TYPE47PC
LOGOFF	$10.	TYPE48PC
NEWNAME	$44.	TYPE1718
NEWNAME	$8.	TYPE90
REASON	$7.	TYPE8911
REASON	$14.	TYPE22
STATUS	$14.	TYPE6
STATUS	$10.	TYPE62
SUBSYS	$3.	TYPE22
SUBSYS	$4.	TYPE6,26J2,26J3,30,32,4345,4789,5234,57,90
TYPE	$5.	TYPE6,1415
TYPE	$10.	TYPE30,32
TYPE	$8.	TYPE6367

Index